**Marianna Charountaki** is a lecturer in Kurdish Politics and International Relations in the School of History, Politics and International Relations at the University of Leicester. She is also the Director of the Kurdistan International Studies Unit. Her research interests range from foreign policy analysis to the international relations of the broader Middle East. She is author of *The Kurds and US Foreign Policy: International Relations in the Middle East since 1945* (2010) as well as articles in *Harvard International Review*, *Journal of American Foreign Policy Interests*, *Third World Quarterly*, *Perceptions: Journal of International Affairs* and *Journal of Arabian Studies*.

'With analytical richness, strong insights and excellent data, this book is an original contribution to our understanding of Iran–Turkey relations.'

Anoush Ehteshami, Professor of International Relations in the School of Government and International Affairs, Durham University

'This book pursues an in-depth analysis of the most important determinants to influence Iranian and Turkish foreign policies. Based on outstanding empirical research, which will be of interest to scholars of International Relations, it attempts to bring a holistic approach to the politics of the Middle Eastern region.'

Sayyed Ataollah Mohajerani, novelist, historian and former Minister of Culture of Iran (1996–2000)

'This volume takes a much needed holistic approach to relations between Turkey and Iran and the region they are part of. It cuts across the usual geographical and theoretical boundaries to offer a multi-level analysis of the situation and would be of interest to scholars of any, or all, parts of the area encompassed by the Caucasus and the Middle East.'

Natalie Martin, Lecturer in International Relations, Nottingham Trent University

# IRAN AND TURKEY

## International and Regional Engagement in the Middle East

MARIANNA CHAROUNTAKI

## I.B. TAURIS

LONDON • NEW YORK • OXFORD • NEW DELHI • SYDNEY

I.B. TAURIS
Bloomsbury Publishing Plc
50 Bedford Square, London, WC1B 3DP, UK
1385 Broadway, New York, NY 10018, USA

BLOOMSBURY, I.B. TAURIS and the I.B. Tauris logo
are trademarks of Bloomsbury Publishing Plc

First published in Great Britain 2018
Paperback edition published 2020

A catalogue record for this book is available from the British Library.

A catalog record for this book is available from the Library of Congress.

ISBN: HB: 978-1-7883-1180-9
PB: 978-1-8386-0471-4
ePDF: 978-1-7867-3380-1
eBook: 978-1-7867-2380-2

Series: Library of International Relations 87

Typeset by OKS Prepress Services, Chennai, India

To find out more about our authors and books visit
www.bloomsbury.com and sign up for our newsletters.

# Contents

| | | |
|---|---|---|
| *List of Illustrations* | | ix |
| *Preface* | | x |
| *Acknowledgements* | | xii |
| *List of Abbreviations* | | xiii |

**1. Introduction** — 1

Introduction — 1

Literature Review: A Critique — 5

Determinants of Turkish–Iranian Relations: A Justification — 9

*Driving forces of Turkish–Iranian foreign policies* — 10

*Principles influencing foreign policy* — 15

*Factors shaping foreign policy practice* — 16

Methodology: An Interdisciplinary and Comparative Examination from a Multi-actor Perspective — 26

Conclusion — 28

**2. Determinants of Iranian–Turkish Relations: A Historical Review** — 31

Introduction — 31

*Sunni Ottoman Empire versus Shiite Persian Safavids: Structural parameters* — 34

The Role of the Elites: Army and *Ulama* versus Army and Ayatollahs — 37

Turkish versus Iranian Republicanism: International
Interference as an External Force                                        39
The Influence of the Cold War on Turkish–Iranian
Politics                                                                 44
*Iran and Turkey in the 1950s and 1970s*                                 44
Islamist Turkey versus Islamic Iran: The Impact of
Foreign Policy Principles                                                48
*The National Interest: A generator of stability*                        49
*Laicism versus Islamism*                                                51
*Hegemony versus dominance*                                              52
Conclusion                                                               52

3.  **Turkey–Iran Relations during the Cold War**                        55
Introduction                                                             55
The Iranian Revolution and its Impact on the Cold War                    60
Non-state Actors as Facilitator of State Foreign Policy                  74
*The role of Hizbullah and the PKK factor*                               74
*The Kurds of Iraq: A key determinant*                                   76
Iraq as Factor under the Prism of Gulf War I                             80
External Interference: The US Role versus Soviet
Influence                                                                84
Economics of War: Iranian–Turkish Economic and
Political Alliances                                                      88
*The shifting balance of power*                                          88
Conclusion                                                               90

4.  **Turkish–Iranian Relations in the 1990s: The Impact of
Gulf War II and the Consolidation of the Kurdish Status**               95
Introduction                                                             95
The Impact of Gulf War II on Turkish–Iranian Relations                  100
*The role of the leadership as reflected in foreign policy
discourse and practice*                                                 100
*The role of Iraq: External mediation and direct use of force*          103
*Dimensions of political economy*                                       111
*KRG and PKK: Determinants of foreign policy*                           113
Gulf War II and its Aftermath: The Role of the Kurds                    120
Conclusion                                                              124

5.  **The Iraq War and the Rise of Non-state Actors**
    **(2001–2010)**                                             128
    Introduction                                                128
    The Role of Iraq in the Formulation of Turkish–Iranian
        Relations: Political and Economic Considerations        133
    Non-state Actors in Iranian and Turkish Foreign
        Policies: The Kurds as a Force for Change               141
    The Iranian versus the Turkish Model                        148
    *Energy politics*                                           148
    *Foreign policy and security*                               151
    Iranian–Turkish Rapprochement: International and
        Regional Structures                                     158
    Epilogue: Towards a Conceptual Analysis                     159
    Conclusion                                                  164

6.  **Turkish–Iranian Relations under the Lens of the**
    **Syrian Crisis: A New Era for Middle Eastern Politics**    167
    Introduction                                                167
    The Syrian Factor                                           174
    *The role of external interference in the Syrian crisis*    179
    *The Army: A continuous institutional power*                190
    Kurdistan between Iran and Turkey: Implications of
        the War on Islamic State                                192
    *Energy politics: The Kurds – a bridge between Iran
        and Turkey*                                             201
    *The Kurdish role in the Iranian and Turkish responses
        to the Syrian crisis*                                   204
    Conclusion                                                  207

7.  **Conclusions and Conceptualisations**                      213
    Introduction                                                213
    Empirical and Conceptual Implications                       217
    A New Pattern of Alliances: The International
        Dimension                                               225
    *The Kurds: A determinant in regional restructuring*        225
    *A changing balance of power: Instruments of
        transformation*                                         229
    *Sunni–Shia conflict: A clash of interests*                 231

| | |
|---|---|
| *Economic parameters* | 233 |
| Theoretical Framework: A Model of Multi-dimensional Interrelations | 234 |
| Conclusion | 239 |
| *Appendix   KCK Structure* | 244 |
| *Notes* | 247 |
| *Bibliography* | 307 |
| *Index* | 339 |

# List of Illustrations

FIGURES

Figure 6.1 A model for multi-dimensional interactions in international relations.                                    195

Figure 7.1  Polygonal interrelations.                                    239


MAPS

Map 1 General regional map illustrating the area and current borders between Turkey and Iran.                      xvi

Map 2 Indicative contemporary map depicting the Ottoman and Safavid Empires.                                       xvii

Map 3 Original map indicating Kurdish territorial claims in Iran and Turkey as well as potential Kurdish access to the Mediterranean Sea.                                   xviii

# Preface

\

This book examines the dynamic role played by interactions between Iran and Turkey and analyses the primary factors directing their foreign policies, while also exploring their influence on regional and global politics. The book traces the evolution of these determinants in Turkish–Iranian relations and their subsequent impact on regional events and policies from 1979, pursuing an interdisciplinary, holistic and critical analysis that offers extensive primary source-based empirical research. The research also highlights the important part played by non-state actors on the stage of Middle Eastern politics as a worthy subject for analysis in its own right.

Conceptually, the book presents a fresh and alternative outlook by offering an original theoretical map supported by new and thought-provoking research material concerning the effects of material and ideational (external or internal) factors along with the interaction between actors of state and non-state status on the formulation of Turkish and Iranian policies. This places the study and its subject matter in a theoretical framework for the first time, and thereby makes a valuable contribution in filling a gap in the current literature as well as within the IR discipline.

Turkish and Iranian policies increasingly seem to dictate the Middle Eastern course of events, and therefore the book is very timely, while its scope is wide-ranging, covering the role of most central states in the Middle East (Iran, Iraq, Turkey, Syria), along with international powers (US, Russia), international institutions (EU) and non-state actors (the Kurds). Addressing topical political and IR matters alongside carefully considered conceptual insights make this study a valuable contribution to subject areas such as foreign policy-making, international relations, Middle Eastern politics and Kurdish studies, while the book's original intensively researched approach will undoubtedly make a significant contribution to the academic canon and stimulate future research in this field.

# Acknowledgements

This book is an extension of research carried out for my post-doctoral research at the University of Reading a project that could not have been written without the participation and support of my interviewees, and, in particular, the KRG leadership. I would also like to express my appreciation to the PKK leadership and Turkish MPs in Ankara whose valuable input added an extra dimension to the book as well as my Iranian interviewees (one of whom chose to remain anonymous for security reasons) that helped me to present an accurate assessment of the Iranian viewpoint.

I would also like to sincerely thank Professor Alex Cudsi (Panteion University in Athens) for the encouragement to engage with this particular subject-matter and who gave generous support during the initial stages of this enterprise. The substantial contribution of Emeritus Professor Ewan Anderson and Dr Younis Al Lahwej (University of Reading) through feedback and advice in the final stages of the completion of my post-doctoral research has also been crucial and is greatly appreciated.

This book is dedicated to all those scholars who work to increase knowledge by their contributions to the field of political science in the hope of enlightening political elites, and the politicians who strive for peaceful relations in the broader region of the Middle East. Most of all, I dedicate these pages to those currently suffering in lands that have known war and devastation, particularly the people of Syria.

# List of Abbreviations

| | |
|---|---|
| AIPAC | American Israel Public Affairs Committee |
| AK Parti/AKP | Adalet ve Kalkınma Partisi – Justice and Development Party |
| AP | *Adalet Partisi* – Justice Party |
| Basij | سازمان بسیج مستضعفین), The Organization for Mobilization of the Oppressed) |
| BTC | Baku–Tbilisi–Ceyhan pipeline |
| BTE | Baku–Tbilisi–Erzurum Pipeline (also known as South Caucasus Pipeline / Shah Deniz Pipeline) |
| CDS | The Council of Democratic Syria |
| CENTO | Central Treaty Organization |
| CHP | Cumhuriyet Halk Partisi, Republican People's Party |
| CIA | Central Intelligence Agency |
| D-8 | Developing–8 |
| DBP | Democratic Regions Party, Partiya Herêman a Demokratîk |
| DECA | Defense and Economic Cooperation Agreement |
| DP | *Demokrat Parti* – Democratic Party |
| DTP | Democratic Society Party |
| ECO | Economic Cooperation Organization |
| EU | European Union |
| FMI | The Freedom Movement of Iran |

| | |
|---|---|
| FP | Fazilet Partisi, Islamist Virtue Party |
| FSA | Free Syrian Army |
| GAP | Güneydoğu Anadolu Projesi, Southeastern Anatolia Project |
| GCC | Gulf Cooperation Council |
| HDP | Halkların Demokratik Partisi, People's Democratic Party |
| IAEA | International Atomic Energy Agency |
| ILSA | Iran–Libya Sanctions Act |
| INC | Iraqi National Congress |
| IR | International Relations |
| IRGC | Iran Revolutionary Guard Corps, The Army of the Guardians of Islamic Revolution |
| ISIL/IS | Islamic State of Iraq and the Levant/ Islamic State |
| ISNA | Iranian Students' News Agency |
| KCK | Democratic Confederation of Kurdistan |
| KDP | Kurdistan Democratic Party, پارتی دیموکراتی کوردستان |
| KDPI | Democratic Party of Iranian Kurdistan Partî Dêmokiratî Kurdistanî Êran |
| KDSP | Kurdistan Democratic Solution Party |
| KGK | People's Congress of Kurdistan or Kongra-Gel |
| KKK | Koma Komalen Kurdistan |
| KNA | Kurdistan National Assembly |
| KRG | Kurdistan Regional Government |
| KRI | Kurdistan Region of Iraq |
| MENA | Middle East and North Africa |
| MHP | Nationalist Movement Party |
| MNP | Millî Nizam Partisi, National Order Party |
| NATO | North Atlantic Treaty Organization |
| NCC | National Coordination Committee |
| NOC | North Oil Company |
| NPF | Communists into the National Progressive Front |
| NSP | Millî Selâmet Partisi, National Salvation Party |
| OIC | Organization of Islamic Cooperation |
| PIN | Party of the Iranian Nation |
| PMU | Popular Mobilisation Units |
| PKK | Partiya Karkerên Kurdîstan, Kurdistan Workers' Party |

| | |
|---|---|
| PLO | Palestine Liberation Organization |
| PNAC | Project for a New American Century |
| PUK | Patriotic Union of Kurdistan |
| PYD | Partiya Yekîtiya Demokrat, The Democratic Union Party |
| RCD | Regional Cooperation for Development |
| RFE/RL | Radio Free Europe/Radio Liberty |
| RP | Refah Partisi, Welfare Party (WP) |
| SALT II | Strategic Arms Limitation Talks II |
| SAVAK | Organization of Intelligence and National Security |
| SCIRI | Shi'a Supreme Council for Islamic Revolution in Iraq |
| SDF | Syrian Democratic Forces |
| SHP | Sosyaldemokrat Halkçı Parti, Social Democrat Populist Party |
| TAG-BF | Turkish–Azerbaijani–Georgian Business Forum |
| TANAP | Trans-Anatolian Natural Gas Pipeline |
| TEV DEM | Tevgera Civaka Demokratîk, The Movement for a Democratic Society |
| UN | United Nations |
| UNSC | United Nations Security Council |
| YPG | Yekîneyên Parastina Gel, People's Protection (or Defence) Units |

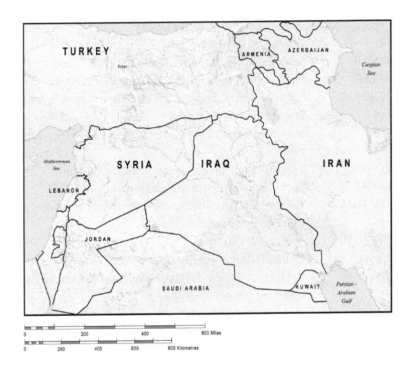

MAP 1  General regional map illustrating the area and current borders between Turkey and Iran.

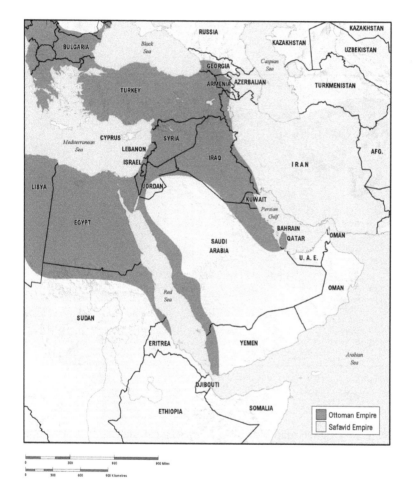

MAP 2   Indicative contemporary map depicting the Ottoman and
Safavid Empires.

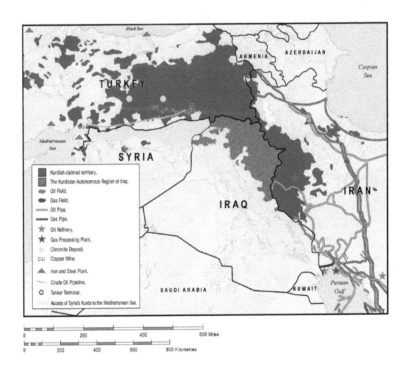

MAP 3   Original map indicating Kurdish territorial claims in Iran and
Turkey as well as potential Kurdish access to the Mediterranean Sea.

# CHAPTER 1

# Introduction

*Minor differences between Iran and Turkey would not affect long-standing relations between the two countries.*[1]

Reza Qelichkhan

## INTRODUCTION

International relations in the Middle Eastern region have been changing at an unprecedented rate following landmark events such as the two Gulf Wars,[2] the so-called Arab Spring[3] and the rise of the Islamic State, formerly known as the Islamic State of Iraq, and the Levant (داعش, IS, formed in June, 2014). However, the study of the impact of such changes has been given insufficient prominence by the current literature, mainly because researchers have continued to emphasise the role of inter-state relations as the driving force behind the international relations system, although this is no longer the case. Recent events have strengthened the role of regional powers such as Turkey and Iran and increasingly shown that major international powers can no longer be regarded as the only dominant actors when it comes to determining the agenda in the international arena.

The main focus of this book is (1) to address the major factors that have influenced the process of formulating Iranian and Turkish foreign policies since their genesis (2) to trace their evolution chronologically (3) to examine their effect on the contemporary state of affairs in the Middle East vis-à-vis the regime changes that have drawn a sharp line between different systems of governance in Iran and Turkey, mainly from 1979 onwards and (4) to demonstrate how these determinants can be conceptualised within the frame of International Relations discipline.

Therefore, the aims of the book are: firstly, to explore these factors and assess their impact at the domestic, regional and international level, a topic largely overlooked by the current published literature;[4] and secondly, to evaluate these findings within the framework of current IR theories. This research is especially important as the Middle Eastern region today, as so often in its history, has become a political crucible with regional and international repercussions on global affairs.

The period under examination is of particular significance as it sets the foundation for a season of great yet gradual change in the relations between Iran and Turkey starting with the rise of Iran as an Islamic State versus Turkey's secularism from 1979 until recently.

Likewise, the emergence of various forms of non-state entities, such as the Kurdistan Regional Government in 1992 (KRG), Hizbullah in 1985 (حزب الله, Hizbu-llāh – Party of God) in Lebanon, Syria's Autonomous Cantons (November, 2013, Rojavayê Kurdistan, Western Kurdistan) or even the KCK in 2007 (Koma Civakên Kurdistan, Group of Communities in Kurdistan founded by the PKK – Partiya Karkerên Kurdîstan, Kurdistan Workers' Party) in Turkey all indicate that we can no longer regard state powers as the sole key influences within the region and the broader international relations system and that such non-state actors have also played a part in setting the direction of events and policies.

Any thorough assessment of regional and global political developments must, of necessity, involve the consideration of multiple actors, examining their stake in the region and its conflicts, vis-à-vis the fading significance of power parity, by careful analysis of the possible paths through which they potentially contribute to either peace-building or conflict on both a regional and global scale. However, that is not to discount the historically important powers which, evidently, continue to play a significant role. During his visit to Turkey in August, 2012, the Iranian former Foreign Minister, Ali Akbar Salehi declared that 'only if Turkey and Iran work together can they resolve the conflicts in the region, particularly the conflict in Syria, since without any of those great players the creation or the advent of peace and stability in the region, particularly in countries like Syria, will be very difficult'.[5]

Yet, the Middle Eastern political scenery has completely changed since the outbreak of the Arab Uprisings in December, 2010 which has had a knock-on effect on the previous main players, a situation exacerbated by the continuation of sectarian conflict in Iraq, Syria and Yemen. Sectarianism in Syria and Turkey's Syrian policy undermined further the former Turkish Premier Ahmet Davutoğlu's 'Strategic Depth' doctrine founded on his 'zero problems with neighbours' principle, and as a consequence, has undoubtedly had a negative impact on Ankara's foreign policy.

Reza Altun referred to Turkish–Iranian relations as 'the centre, the primary region, where the conflicts and wars are being conducted [with ultimate purpose] of reshaping the Middle Eastern region in accordance with the paradigm of capitalist modernity. These conflicts are not local but target the change of the current status quo.'[6] Therefore, the objective of this book is not just to review, explain Turko-Iranian relations as a relation per se and analyse it as such, or to rehash its involvement in the context of war or peace – considering that the last major war fought was nearly 500 years ago at Chaldiran as a result of religious differences[7] – but to look at the way Turkey and Iran's foreign policies have had to change and adapt as political and economic alliances within the region shift and change.

Conversely, the analysis of Middle Eastern politics necessarily reflects the nature of regional politics, and thus brings in the role of non-state actors in addition to state powers. The interactions between Turkey and Iran, two states that have shared a 499 km border since the 17th century, provide a crucial lens for observing the intrinsic nature of the politics of the region. In this sense, any discussion about Turkey and Iran reflects the broader concerns of Middle Eastern politics since both actors have been engaged in every single development of significance.

A similar perspective is represented in Altun's argument, 'the present state of conflicts in the Middle East goes beyond Turkey and Iran but it is being conducted through them as main (f)actors in the emergence of these new political forms in the region'.[8] This idea has even greater force when the situations of non-Arab states like Iran, Turkey and Israel are compared to the overall weakening of the Arab states. This seems to be the result perhaps of a greater desire for survival as the non-Arab states continue to move towards stronger engagement with other powers at the regional and international level; interestingly, a contradiction to the views expressed in many scholarly arguments.[9] In addition, the impact of non-Arab states on regional politics is an under-explored dynamic in the field of IR and, as such, has not been analysed in a comprehensive way. Through examination of the surrounding events we can therefore understand that this is not merely an inter-state or a bilateral issue but one that has affected the whole region, especially over recent years, reaching its climax with the Syrian crisis (March 2011) where the religious-sectarian dimension along with foreign policy interests came prominently into play.[10] More importantly still, it acted as the catalyst for Turkish and Iranian re-entry into regional and international politics as major powers whereas the Iraq War and its aftermath following US withdrawal from Iraq (December 2011) was significant, drawing Iran and Turkey closer together in regional politics, and giving them a more central role in determining regional and international developments.

Overall, the book's objective – built on my previous work which conducted an examination of IR theories together with in-depth critiques of them – is to pave the way for the introduction of a new theoretical approach, originally presented in my earlier book.[11] In this book, I plan to develop this process still further to examine international politics from a multi-actor perspective on both regional and global levels, and, in particular, shift the focus from predominantly concentrating on major international powers to the roles played by regional powers and non-state groups in order to reveal the significance of their interactions.[12] Specifically, the book aims to fill a gap within the International Relations discipline by placing the respective case study within a theoretical framework for the first time, an essential course of action given the heavy involvement of other non-state entities, powerful states and international organisations. This is of critical value as an interdisciplinary and comparative approach that has not been employed holistically in other works thus far.

## LITERATURE REVIEW: A CRITIQUE

Robert Olson elects not to use IR theories 'as there is no IR theory that addresses adequately'[13] the theme under examination and thus is able to cover these polygonal interrelations. He therefore resorts to the 'omni-balancing theory' to explain Turkish and Iranian foreign policies[14] but refers to the role of the Kurds without highlighting its importance as a factor in regional politics in its own right.[15] Instead, Olson attempts to explain the Kurdish issue via the relations between the two respective states rather than as an independent influential factor[16] that impacts on states' foreign policies, but rather considering 'each Kurdish organisation [as a mere] proxy of its neighbour'.[17]

In fact Kurdish movements regularly implement the policy that best suits their own interests in regional politics,[18] while, contrary to Olson who claims that 'the trans-state Kurdish question and intra-state Kurdish problems have not affected larger geostrategic interests of either states', we can definitely argue on the basis of the contemporary literature that the Kurdish issue has indeed significantly affected the policies of states such as Iran and Turkey and also the US.[19]

The 'omni-balancing theory' that the author adopts, also some-what confusingly referred to by him as the 'omnibalancing model', focuses on the balance between internal and external threats which favours state leadership and the interests of elites and regimes at the expense of the state's centrality and even of non-state elites' or leaderships' impact on the decision making process, which seems rather an 'either/or' explanation. Therefore, this theory fails to give sufficient consideration to the role of the Kurds or even their leadership's ability to influence and bring about change, even though Olson himself had highlighted such factors as important in relation to the Kurds earlier. This contradiction is even more evident when the author aims to employ 'the model with the exception that in the case of Turkey and Iran the states rather than the leaders should be the focus' as opposed to his sub-theory's claims.[20] The model is also

unable to adequately explain Ankara's 2012 new foreign policy
dogma of 'external threats' where Turkish Armed Forces focus on the
threats coming from outside rather than on internal ones as they did
previously.[21]

On the contrary, the study undertaken in this book takes a different
approach, and aims to diverge from the static state-centric and threat
perceptions view dominant in the current literature where analysis is
routinely pursued from the perspective of state relations and any role
played by other factors is not given proper consideration. This is often
the case with an analysis that has a focus on threat perception which
can be an ideational reality as is the case in Olson's view which
perceives Kurdish policies and actions as posing a threat to the
respective regimes. Such an outlook weakens the analytical scope,
especially when the role of the state, as a traditionally powerful and
central actor of the international relations system that has been
repeatedly proven in research carried out in a historical context, is
already apparent. In addition, such a stance can distort the findings
on how different factors of state, non-state or ideational and
structural status impact, interact and influence those states'
foreign policies whose *stimuli*, already known, are perceived to
originate only from them, rather than being produced in response to
other sources.

The case of the Kurdish movements is important when considered
in this light and their role as mediators or, more indirectly, providing
a connection through their relations with the host states is also
recognised by Olson. However, in contrast to Olson, who focuses
only in quite general terms on Turkish–Iranian policies toward the
Kurdish issue,[22] this book demonstrates the impact of Iranian foreign
policy on Turkish policies and *vice versa* through the factors that
influence these policies rather than merely making observations on
the resultant episodes produced by these factors per se.

Suleyman Elik's book (published around the same time as Elliot
Hentov's *Asymmetry of Interest: Turkish-Iranian Relations since 1979*)
places state actors and the context in which they operate at the centre
of the analysis. Elik presents a series of themes concerning Turkish–
Iranian relations and divides them into chapters in the form of
independent papers.

In contrast, this book moves away from the temptation to indulge in a detailed cataloguing of the events that have taken place between Iran and Turkey or be prompted by the respective factors influencing their relationship. Instead it aims to carry out a systematic chronological thematic division, which, while different from that of Elik or Hentov, is consistent with those dynamics that have shaped mutual foreign policies on the basis of the most significant historical episodes. Domestic and external determinants that need to be considered will be discussed as they arise.

Elik mainly concentrates on a revision of the 'middle powers relations theory', examining the diplomatic crises between the two states as well as the need for 'securitisation of domestic politics to maintain regime survival'.[23] Elaborating on Olson's writings, he also perceives 'religion and ideology as internal threats'.[24] On the other hand, this research project does take a more in-depth approach by pursuing a political analysis of the most important determinants to influence Turkish and Iranian relations as well as their impact upon Middle Eastern politics. Taking into consideration the way that today's scholars in the political sciences, particularly in the field of International Relations (IR), continually strive to move one step further in their arguments to effectively conceptualise the impact of the emergence of external and internal, regional, international, and global powers, and how they affect international relations, the theoretical objective of this book is thus to fill the gap between theory and practice as no previous research on the topic in question has been done up to this point. In doing this, the analysis aims to go beyond the traditional security and sociological approaches representing a kind of 'micro level analysis on middle power states'[25] and is determined to avoid any generalisations represented in a predilection for broad statements such as: 'middle powers have sufficient force ... to maintain themselves without help from others' and the like.[26]

Pursuing the path of middle power theory, as in this case, is less helpful for three reasons. Although the study does make a valuable contribution through its incorporation of internal and non-measured factors of power and their effect on the extent and limits of those states' foreign policy behaviour regarding regional issues in tandem with the examining of outcomes of cooperation and conflict, such an approach still offers a very narrow and limited scope. Another weakness is that once again the focus is on interstate relations rather than how these factors can be theoretically explained. Furthermore, the dual nature of power is complex and consists of multiple dimensions which may derive from a diversity of factors. On the one hand the nature of power can range from economic or military strength to the power of ideas, cultures and ideologies that shape the identities of the actors, while, on the other, this duality is expressed through the power's allocation and diffusion to multiple actors rather than just states, revealing thus the co-existence of multiple centres of power.

This then strongly denotes that the 'middle power' study approach examining the position of states within a hierarchy of power by which a state's behaviour in international and regional politics is determined by its level of power compared to others can no longer be judged by a single method of comparison.[27] Last, but not least, the relation between power and influence, including the well-known 'middle power diplomacy', is disproportionate, and thus can bear no real connection to their ranking, quantification or measurement. Therefore, this book differs from earlier studies as it does not limit itself to explaining 'the relationship between Iran and Turkey as two middle power states through history' as Elik attempted to do in his 'modified version of middle power state theory'.[28]

Instead, I pursue a holistic view, looking at triggering events as factors of influence on the two major states' policies. Most crucially, in its observations on the rise of non-state entities, this work covers contemporary politics and recent phenomena such as the Arab uprisings which have provided the momentum for the transformation of the Middle Eastern region, a development that is totally absent from Elik's book, published in January 2011,[29] or from a limited number of other short articles on the subject matter.[30]

The similar work done by Elliot Hentov is informative, but largely pursues a critical historical overview without particular reference to specific factors and is also weakened by its lack of primary sources such as interviews with high profile officials and other political figures. Instead, it relies on news disseminated in the press, and his analysis is placed against a theoretical framework based around the domestic politics adopted by both states.[31]

The lack of references to current events in his overview can be seen vividly when reflecting on the Syrian crisis which has been of great significance for international politics and had a tremendous impact on current affairs in the Middle East within the context of the Arab Uprisings. However, Hentov's prime argument is limited to the 'asymmetry of interest', according to which 'Turkey [until the November 2002 elections] viewed Iran as an important neighbour and formidable power at the centre of its foreign policy discourse, whereas Tehran saw Ankara as a marginal player ... neglecting Turkish relevance or dismissing it as a US client regime', a statement which rather oversimplifies this interrelation.[32]

This position was rarely the case even in the past, and is certainly no longer so, not only because of the fact that there was no direct 'parity of interest between Turkish and Iranian leaders'[33] which was exacerbated during the Syrian crisis, but also owing to complications arising from this 'either/or' approach and the realities of historical regional interrelations vis-à-vis Gulf War I.[34] The argument also falls down if the Iranian viewpoint is taken into account. Dr. Ata'ollah Mohajerani, a key Iranian political figure, argues that 'Turkey is different from Iran ... [as] a player with a global role. Turkey has an absolutely different foreign policy, good relations with the US, and alliances with powers such as Israel'[35] despite occasional ups and downs in their relations.

However, as the information provided is based around accurate and well-considered historical accounts, Elik and Hentov's books are useful as a basis to pursue a deeper analysis of the factors that have influenced Turkey and Iran's foreign policies. On these grounds, the authors act as informative guides to historical incidents that the two powers have had a share in and their significance.

## DETERMINANTS OF TURKISH–IRANIAN RELATIONS: A JUSTIFICATION

Considering the two states' previous relations, particular factors that have influenced their mutual policies will be raised and explained in a brief historical review. Therefore, this research project will focus on a critical political analysis to explore the primary factors responsible for directing Iranian and Turkish foreign policies chronologically, whether in a substantive or provisional sense. Specifically, I aim to examine the role played by interactions between Turkey and Iran, and also bring non-state actors onto the stage of Middle Eastern politics as a worthy subject for analysis in their own right, rather than merely an add-on to state powers. Based on this empirical case study, I also outline a theoretical map which opens up exciting possibilities for new research to examine the effects of interaction between actors of state and non-state status on regional and global politics in more depth, thus building on and advancing my previous work.[36]

### Driving forces of Turkish–Iranian foreign policies

From my viewpoint, foreign policy seems to be an interactive process undertaken by an individual or a number of individuals who differ according to the institution they represent. Final decisions are mainly articulated by the most dominant figure in the hierarchy, namely, the leadership, and this can be influenced by many different structural and ideational factors (internal or external), the context according to which decisions are taken and by which actors operate, and the agendas of the actors involved, whether state or non-state decision-makers. As the end product of this process, these decisions constitute responses to the activities of other actors in the international system and may stem from states or non-state entities.[37]

When it comes to the factors that contribute to the formulation of foreign policy, I focus on the fundamentals or constituents that contribute to the maximisation of the agent's control, power and influence, given that foreign policy decisions are partly reflections of the external on the domestic and *vice versa*. At this point it is crucial to make a distinction between the process and its end results as opposed to the contributing factor(s).

Thus, we find the Turkish and the Iranian non-Arab models, other than Israel, taking up positions that reflect their different outlooks. In that sense both models are unique in their own right. Yet the fact that I explain the Iranian model as occupying a completely contrary position to the Turkish model is per se a clear indication of its difference and complexity in comparison to the rest of the Middle Eastern entities. Thus, the Iranian model is not only different from that of Turkey but also the rest of the Middle Eastern entities, reflecting its complex nature among its neighbouring states.

Iran is certainly a special case in terms of religion, structure and foreign policy orientation. Since the 16th century it has represented the Shi'a Jaafari School of Islamic thought of the Twelver Shiite as opposed to the prevalent Sunni Hanafi school of Islam in Turkey. It is operated on a dual socio-political structure with an autonomous predominantly clerical establishment. This is largely responsible for the foreign policy outlook and consists of the Leadership (*Velayat-e-faqih*, the Rule of the Jurisprudent) under the protection of the Islamic Revolutionary Guard Corps versus the Presidential power which, in sharp contradiction to the Turkish paradigm, lacks the ability to directly influence the foreign policy orientation to the extent that the Turkish Presidency in Ankara now does since Erdoğan came to power, a trend that has continued up at least until the present day.

In 2008 Recep Tayyip Erdoğan would claim that 'Turkey has achieved a balance between Islam, democracy, secularism and modernity. [Our government] demonstrates that a religious person can protect the idea of secularism. In the West the AK Parti [AKP, The Justice and Development Party, *Adalet ve Kalkınma Partisi*, 2001] is always portrayed as being "rooted in religion". This is not true. The AK Parti is not a party just for religiously observant people – we are the party of the average Turk. We are absolutely against ethnic nationalism, regional nationalism and religious chauvinism. Turkey, with its democracy, is a source of inspiration to the rest of the Islamic world.'[38] In contrast, the revolutionary characteristics of Iranian foreign policy can be clearly traced through four key events in the last century; the Constitutional Revolution (1905–1907), the Petroleum Revolution as Iranians identify the 1953 Iranian coup d'état (1953), the Iranian Revolution (1979) and finally the Green Movement, a political movement that emerged in the aftermath of the 2009 Presidential elections in Iran, fuelling demands for the removal of Mahmoud Ahmadinejad (2005–2013). This revolutionary dimension has also manifested itself in Tehran's support of Hizbullah in the 2006

Lebanon War, and of Hamas (*Harakat al-Muqawamah al-Islamiyyah,* the Islamic Resistance Movement) in 2009 and 2014.

It is from this perspective of Iran as 'revolutionary' that US President Barack Obama feared that a nuclear-armed Iran could become a potential 'game changer'.[39] And it is this same perspective that has crystallised the Iranian view of a persistent hostile US perception toward its goals and policies. Indeed, Iranian foreign policy does aim at changing the traditional regional rule or order as its Middle Eastern vision views stability in the region as only possible through change. This is a completely different interpretation from Turkey's viewpoint which is in alliance with NATO and the US or, until recently, Israel. The most typical expression of this Iranian perspective's uniqueness as reflected in the Iranian foreign policy discourse and practice is represented in Saeb Tabrizi's (1601–1672) text of the Iranian poem:

دشمن دوست نما را نتوان کرد علاج

How should we deal with an enemy who has the face of a friend?

شاخه را مرغ چه داند که قفس خواهد شد؟

How can a bird understand that what was once a branch will be his cage?

Iran's approach is more complex and is based on four pillars. The security of the regime is the primary concern of the Supreme Leader who approves all the political, foreign policy and security decisions within the framework of the Council of National Security as indicated in Article 176 of the Constitutional Law which unites all different political segments within Iranian politics. The second characteristic of the clerical outlook is identified by nationalistic and ideological ambitions based on an Iranian worldview informed by an imperial past which seeks for the restoration of Iran's rightful place. This sense of superiority is derived from its historical heritage as Persia, one of the world's most ancient nations, and is coupled with the ideological worldview of the Shi'a clergy which perceives its leaders as bearing responsibility for the entire Muslim community (*Vali-e-amr-e-Muslemin*). These factors help to explain Iran's perception of itself as a superior power destined 'to be strong in global affairs … Ahmadinejad was saying we like to play a role in the world. Iran wants to be a big player in the region. That is why it supported Hizbullah in Lebanon 30 years ago. After 2003, the important card in Iran's hands has also been Iraq where its influence has become greater. Hamilton Baker's Report mentioned that behind every stone and every tree in Iraq you find the Iranian influence.'[40]

However, at the same time, Iranians see themselves as a minority surrounded by Arab and Sunni regimes and this sectarian dimension is currently prevalent in regional politics, while the roots of the ideological or foreign policy that constantly provokes political differences with Turkey can be also traced to this element. It is this outlook that is responsible for Iran's acts and behaviour, seeing itself as victimised (*mazoloom*) unit.

Iran's third pillar is strategic opportunism demonstrated by the regime's attempts to identify gaps that it can exploit, even within its own borders. This is linked to Iran's fourth and final pillar – the ideological notion of resistance – shown in its policy to support any group, national liberation movement or other radicalised force against what it perceives as imperialist forces, especially in Iraq in the aftermath of Saddam Hussein's overthrow (March 2003). An extension of this policy is its support to Hizbullah to help Lebanese Shi'a fight off the Israeli occupation of Southern Lebanon in 1982 which was carried out as a resistance act against the Zionist enemy. It has increasingly taken this stance from the Khomeini Revolution onwards, leading to Western policy's denial of the legitimacy of the regime in Iran which is increasingly viewed as standing in opposition to the democratic values promoted by the West. As a consequence, Iran feels that it is facing an existential threat from the West as the latter is not prepared to recognise the clerical regime currently in power.

It thus seems that Iran's strategic pragmatism complements the Iranian geopolitical approach, i.e., the ideological notion of resistance, and employs it where needed as in the case of Irangate (1986) under Ronald Reagan's Presidency during his second term of office. This is true of Iran's compromising relations with the Taliban in Afghanistan (since 2001) and also its role in the Syrian crisis and support of the Palestinian Sunni Hamas, advantageous moves that have enabled Iran to increase its regional influence on the one hand, and, on the other, force Israel into making concessions.

In its traditional role as a moderate, secular, and primarily pro-Western power, Turkey has sought regional stability, not through change but through preservation of the existing order. Therefore, it primarily supports the status quo with the exception of revisionist tensions in cases that, traditionally, Ankara considers obstacles to the expansion of its influence and geostrategic power. The Syrian crisis is a case in point, where Turkey's meddling in the crisis has involved the government in claims that it supports extremist groups.[41] This ad hoc behaviour directly contrasts with the inherently revolutionary and resistance model represented by Iran which favours revisionist, radical forces and factional warfare. Accordingly, any sort of instability or change in the regional status quo immediately puts Tehran into a winning position.

Consequently, current developments in the Middle East are advancing Iran's geopolitical interests, while Ankara is striving to reposition itself in a more favourable light, especially since the outbreak of the Syrian crisis and the need to improve its relations with the Arab states. In more recent times, this has been increasingly important as Tehran's foreign policy forms the basis of the Axis of Resistance and draws strength from its goal of becoming a catalyst in the region as a dynamic force for change.

The rise of the AK Parti to power on 3 November 2002 undeniably changed the trajectory of Turkish politics to such an extent that the ongoing competition between Iran and Turkey (which can be traced back historically to the Ottoman and Safavid power struggles as the next chapter will explore) is now being explicitly played out on the political level. The vying for pole position as the two governments, one Islamic and the other one Islamist, compete in the region for the same goal of domination is watched with interest in politics worldwide. According to a highly placed Iranian political figure, 'Turkey uses the Muslim Brotherhood [الإخوان المسلمون] in Tunisia, Egypt and Syria for its big plans to re-establish the Ottoman Empire.'[42]

Turkey's former Prime Minister, Ahmet Davutoğlu, claims that: 'Turkey seeks to play the role of a global actor'[43] which has a strikingly similar ring to the Iranian position that: 'Iran wants to be a big player in the region and strong in global affairs.'[44] The Syrian crisis has thus become the pretext for each actor to take steps to get the upper hand.

The ultimate goal of both states is the maximisation of their influence and power, yet they differ widely in the means and rhetoric they pursue to achieve that goal. Scholars often debate about how this relation between Tehran and Ankara can best be described. Even though it might seem a minor contribution to the current literature, I would still call such a dynamic interrelation one of necessity, or of competing necessity for survival and dominance, as although it may be founded on and built around their competition for survival, it does not change the fact that they both need each other. Although each has its own allies, they share the same regional rivals.[45]

## *Principles influencing foreign policy*

It is a common belief that the course of events directly after the Arab Uprisings, a landmark in political science for the way it has impacted on the foreign policies of international powers, has created a new environment of sectarianism in the sense that the existing Sunni–Shia divide in the region, triggered by the onset of the Iraq War (March 2003), has widened. Important events like US President Barack Obama's rapprochement with Iran under Hassan Rouhani after the former's move to initiate the first direct and official communication since 1979, and historically the beginning of the Iranian Revolution itself, have been crucial signposts heralding the changes ushering in a new political climate in the Middle East.

The impact of surprising events of both internal and external kinds such as 9/11 and the terrorist acts in 2001 pose the interesting theory that material structures, internal or external, can play a key role in shaping state foreign policies just as much as internal or external ideational structures. The latter are related to the identity of the decision-makers, whether individuals, state or non-state actors, their interests, intentions and ideas, including others' fixed perceptions of them, irrespective of these actors' actual practices and actions which will also inevitably be scrutinised as they come under the spotlight. For instance, charges originally levelled at the Turkish government that they had exaggerated the Iranian threat appear somewhat rash today in view of the agitating role of Tehran in fomenting regional sectarian divisions for its own benefit, especially considering the repercussions caused by the rise of IS on the regional balance of power which in turn has seen the increasing empowerment of Tehran at the expense of Turkey and other Sunni segments of Middle Eastern society.

In principle, interrelations between these structures and the agents involved, whether of state or non-state status, have had an impact on both the formulation of foreign policies and the regional political theatre.[46] In that sense, an overview of the interplay between ideational factors (i.e. such as the ideological background of the Premiership or the foreign policy discourse conceptualised into doctrines)[47] and, even more importantly, the foreign policy agenda as it reflects rising national interests together with the additional roles played by bureaucratic institutions or foreign policy elites just makes the necessity of a holistic interpretation of each individual case clearer.

## Factors shaping foreign policy practice

In recent years, especially since the Syrian crisis which led to turbulent conflict and the outbreak of war, the way international and regional politics have been traditionally perceived has needed adjustment. On this basis, this book is useful as it helps to fill large gaps in the current bibliography by assessing new developments that have emerged. To do this, the book will explore the most important factors that have impacted Tehran's and Ankara's foreign policies together with their repercussions on politics in the region, while I will also explain why other factors, though of interest, cannot be regarded as critical but they are rather minor, at this time.

In contrast to the current literature, I will try to analyse and assess specific determinants involved in relation to each event as they arise, rather than pursue a systemic approach to Iranian–Turkish relations like Elik's work concentrating on the narration of historical episodes. Contrary to premises that ideology does not greatly influence the actual practice of agents as it will always be subjected to the upholding of regional influence as the ultimate goal, it is still the ideological background that will often frame the behaviour and, as a consequence, pose certain limitations on a specific practice. Thus, even though the Iranian foreign policy is in practice 'based on a strategic approach against the US hegemony in the Middle East and is not an ideological cause but one based on national and security interests and the balance of power',[48] theoretically at least, foreign policy principles are still considered an important influence as a combination of both discourse and political strategy. It is therefore clear that the various national interests can also constitute an ideational factor and they will be considered as such in my analysis. Although these seemingly contending orientations have often been confused and accordingly labelled 'kaleidoscopic',[49] a closer observation of Iran's revolutionary foreign policy nature indicates that its focus is not complicated or shifting, as has often been perceived, but concrete and consistent, at least in terms of the reforms and changes it periodically adopts which tend to follow the same trends of instigating instability.

In a continuation of Olson's ideas, Elik, who throughout demonstrates a tendency to favour Turkey, does examine the role of ideology and religion but mainly concentrates on the wider context of threat perceptions and security relations while Iran and Turkey are just two of his case studies so that the scope of his treatment is limited.[50] Therefore, this book will distinguish the principles that govern Iran and Turkey as two completely opposite establishments, and discuss them in more depth as another important ideational factor worthy of deeper analysis. In this context, the Iranian Revolution (1979) has been a turning point in mutual relations between the two powers. The chronological order implemented in the book will also provide a useful framework for observing how these factors have had a growing impact on regional and international affairs.

I present Iraq, rather than the Gulf War (1980–1988) per se, as the stand-out factor in terms of its impact on the present since my divisions cover the rise of Iran's Islamic State (1979) until the end of Gulf War I, and the influence of Gulf War II (1988–1991). The rise of the Kurdish factor as a consequence of Gulf War II is also raised as it altered the way the discipline of International Relations is perceived, and generated heated debate over how its interpretation needed to be reconsidered based on the interaction of both state and non-state actors as influential agents. For the same period (1991–2002), the book also underlines the emergence of other non-state entities as a dynamic, and the explicit involvement in world politics of new non-state actors, e.g., the rise of fundamentalist religious groups such as Al Qaeda (القاعدة), or the Islamic State versus other non-state militant actors like Jabhat Al-Nusra or the Al-Nusra Front (جبهة النصرة لأهل الشام). The end of the Iraq War and its consequences (2003–2009) was very much related to the KRG factor, especially with regard to Turkey's governance under Recep Tayyip Erdoğan (2002). Erdoğan was a key figure as he largely succeeded in managing to counterbalance the formerly dominant military control of Turkish politics, and empowered Ankara's relations with the Kurds of Iraq, especially from 2008 onwards, restarting the peace process negotiations for the resolution of the Kurdish issue in Turkey (even temporarily), allowing the PKK movement itself (even unofficially) to take part in the dialogue.

However, the outbreak of the Arab Uprisings and Turkey's direct involvement in Syria's domestic affairs, in line with the US policies of regional democratisation and 'regime change' as provisioned by George W. Bush's Greater Middle East Initiative (12 December, 2002), resulted in a cold war between Ankara and Damascus since August, 2011 disrupting thus their previous cordial relations on the regional level, while on the international level it has fuelled mounting tensions between the US and Russia. Tension was further escalated with the Syrian war, a surprising event, rather than the 'Arab Spring' per se as a systemic factor of regional instability. Within this new Middle Eastern context, still under formation, Turkey's hitherto successful doctrine of non-confrontation with its neighbours started to gradually collapse. This was in contrast to the Iranian dynamic which steadily gained ground as the balance of power between the two powers shifted, and ultimately increased Iranian influence in the region. The cause of this drastic change can be accurately pinpointed to Iran's opportune seizing of the opportunity to exploit the sectarian conflict represented by the well-known Sunni–Shia divide which deepened the MENA (Middle East and North Africa) rift into an abyss. Ankara's disastrous policies served to strengthen relations among the members of the Axis of Resistance, an alliance between Iran, Syria and the Lebanese militant group of Hizbullah, and also resulted in the creation of an embryonic Kurdish entity on its border with Syria.

There is no doubt that the economic factor has been a crucial element throughout as it has provided the only stabilising force in

Iranian–Turkish relations. This relation is built on economic necessity as 'Iran exports gas to Turkey and imports goods (since Gulf War I)'.[51] National security and energy and water issues are priorities for any state or non-state entity; therefore the Euphrates and Tigris Rivers have historically been a major cause of conflict. In the 1970s Turkey cut the flow of water to Iraq by 80 per cent and to Syria by 40 per cent (1975), while in the 1980s Saddam Hussein drained 90 per cent of the Mesopotamian marshes and in the 1990s Turkey was also accused of reducing Syria's water supplies. Today, water is often used as a tactical weapon by IS and the Syrian regime, and there is a widespread belief that water will be the key to those players who gain control of Iraq in the future.[52] Therefore, it is a matter of common sense that issues like these are perceived as another influential ideational factor in the formulation of any foreign policy.

The international powers' involvement in Middle Eastern affairs has also left a tremendous legacy not only on the regional actors' foreign policies, but also in the sense of shaping their identities. However, at the same time, it should be considered that both factors and policies have a symbiotic relation based on their interactions.

On the other hand, although the Palestinian cause has had an indisputable effect on both Iranian and Turkish foreign policy discourses and constitutes one of the two elements of the Islamist foreign policy, the actual support of the Palestinians, in so far as it affects concrete foreign policy practice, may have been intensified in Turkey's case, but in the Iranian discourse it is presented within the wider context of support for national liberation movements rather than as a distinctive foreign policy constituent.[53]

The PLO (Palestine Liberation Organisation, منظمة التحرير الفلسطينية, 1964) officially opened its offices in Tehran on 19 February 1979[54] and later in Turkey on 8 October, 1979.[55] This followed the Shah's departure on 16 January 1979 as the last Persian monarch, fleeing from a civil religious-based resistance with secular elements, instigated in October 1977[56] which later saw Khomeini's rise to power beginning on 11 February 1979. This resulted in a national referendum which led to a new theocratic-republican constitution (1 April 1979) and the announcement of Khomeini as the state's Supreme Leader (December 1979). More recently, and in spite of the

Turkish reaction incited by the incident of Mavi Marmara (2010), Turkish foreign policy has been more proactive than influential as a shaping factor of both foreign policies throughout these periods of change. For instance, the Turkish President's 180° turn in favour of the Palestinians and Turkey's anti-Israeli discourse has not marked any dramatic change in Turkish–Iranian relations. However, it has been criticised by Tehran and others as 'an abuse of the Palestinian issue for the Turkish foreign policy and its interests since in practice Turkey recognises Israel and has intelligence, military and economic relations and agreements with them'.[57] Dr. Ata'ollah Mohajerani presented an explanation for Turkey's actions: 'Erdoğan tried to support the Palestinians because it was a window to the Islamic World.'[58]

Finally, the Syrian crisis and Tehran's alliance with Bashar Al Assad posed dilemmas and challenges for Hamas. The use of the Palestinian Hamas by both Iran and Syria was revealing as it showed that the Iranian alliance with the Palestinian forces was not primarily a strategic alliance. This was perhaps most clearly demonstrated in the Syrian crisis when Hamas chose not to stand by the Syrian President, and moved its headquarters from Syria to Qatar (January 2012). Since then Hamas' strained relations with both Hizbullah and Iran, constitutes a microphage of the broader Sunni–Shia divide endemic in the region following the outbreak of the crisis in Syria.

A potential factor that may well need consideration in the future is the role of Central Asia and the Caucasus in particular, especially 'after the events of 9/11 as an important place in terms of cooperation against terrorism and limiting Russia's influence in the region'.[59] Yet the majority of the current literature and scholarly writings do not deem this to be an important factor in influencing these states' foreign policies in spite of Russia's critical role in the region. This is expressed in Rubinstein's claims about 'Iran's limited role in the power play in the Caucasus' compared to Russia's reluctance 'to abandon its sphere of influence in the Caucasus',[60] while Winrow also asserts that 'Russia is not prepared to allow Turkey and Iran to acquire enhanced influence in the Caucasus and Central Asia at its expense'.[61] Yet, it cannot be excluded when examining Turkish–Iranian interrelations.[62] In addition, Winrow argues that between the period 1989 and 1992, 64 per cent of Iran's arms imports (40 MiG-29s, Su-24s, three submarines, armour, artillery, sea mines and other weaponry) came from Russia.[63]

In the term 'Caucasus' we refer to the Russian geopolitical point of view which recognises three regions: the Central Caucasus (consisting of Armenia, Azerbaijan, and Georgia), the North Caucasus which is part of the Russian Federation (composed of the Southern Autonomous Republics of Russia) and the South Caucasus (including the North Eastern provinces of Turkey and the North Western provinces of Iran). The term 'South Caucasus' is used as a replacement for the term 'Trans-Caucasus'[64] which formerly described the Southern boundaries of the Caucasus prior to independence in the 1990s.[65] The Caucasus (Armenia, Azerbaijan, Georgia) is thus seen as a buffer zone between Iran and Russia.[66]

Ismailov and Papava have highlighted the importance of Georgian–Azerbaijani–Turkish cooperation with the West against an Armenian–Iranian–Russian 'entente' and argue that the Armenian–Azerbaijani conflict has raised the role of Georgia as a critical factor, while the same scholars claim that 'Russia lost ability to control the process of extraction and transportation of Azerbaijani oil'.[67] Indeed, Soviet involvement in the Caucasus had been steadily increasing since 1936 with the division of the region into five republics replacing regional affiliation with national identities as indicated by Peimani.[68] Historically, Russian attacks on Iran in the 19th century ended only with the Turkamanchay treaty (21 February 1828) when Persia ceded several areas in the South Caucasus to Russia, including the Azerbaijani Republic of Nakhchivan (an Azerbaijani region between Southern Armenia and Northern Iran), and 17 other cities in the Caucasus.[69]

The Caucasus is important because of its proximity to the Eurasian states of Russia, Iran and Turkey. The Ottoman Empire fought against the Persians for control over the South Caucasus in the 1600s and again in the 1800s, and there are still thousands of Azerbaijanis and Georgians in Turkey. However, developments in the Middle Eastern region have taken over.[70] The Trabzon Declaration between Azerbaijan, Georgia and Turkey (8 June 2012) raised the importance of the South Caucasus' stability for regional security, which along with the construction of the South Caucasus natural gas pipelines (Baku–Azerbaijan, Tbilisi–Georgia, Erzurum–Turkey (BTE, 21 May 2006) from Shah Deniz (capacity of one trillion cm of gas) in Azerbaijan to Eastern Turkey and oil Baku, Tbilisi, Ceyhan (BTC, opened in May 2006, 1.2 million bbl./d), from the Azeri–Chirag–Gunashli oilfield in the Caspian Sea to the Turkish port of Ceyhan on the South East Mediterranean coast show its economic importance. Other profitable assets include the 2014 Trans Anatolian pipeline from Azerbaijan through Turkey to Europe (TANAP), a $17 billion project expected to reach completion in 2018, the trilateral business forum consisting of Turkey–Azerbaijan–Georgia (TAG-BF), and the proposed Baku–Tbilisi–Kars railway which, especially with regard to its proximity to Iran and Armenia, are indicative of the strategic and financial advantages of the Caucasus as a prospective base from which to control the Middle Eastern region.

This becomes even more important considering Azerbaijan's strategic value for Israel vis-à-vis their diplomatic relations since 7 April 1992 and the February Agreement in 2012 when Azerbaijan signed a $1.6 billion defence deal with Israel that included air defence systems, intelligence equipment and unmanned aerial vehicles. Tehran claims that Baku has given Mossad a blank cheque to conduct operations against Iran from Azerbaijani soil even though the Azerbaijani Foreign Minister Elmar Mammadyarov claims that Azerbaijan will never allow itself to be used in any action against Iran. Vatanka has described Tehran's recent overtures to Azerbaijan as part of a broader effort to limit Iran's isolation and prevent Baku from aiding or joining an Israeli or US military operation against its nuclear programme.[71] According to Shaffer, Baku constructs Israeli drones while on 18 September 2014 Iran shot down an Israeli 'Hermes' drone close to Natanz, which had been launched from the province of Nakhchivan.[72]

Its importance becomes even clearer if the role played by the Nakhchivan Autonomous Republic of Azerbaijan in the Treaty of Moscow (16 March 1921) between Mustafa Kemal and Vladimir Lenin is brought into consideration. Nakhchivan's status cannot be revised without Turkish consent; in effect, a policy against Iran.[73] This allows Turkey to exert pressure and control Armenia *via*

Nakhchivan, while also affording a strategic advantage if it were to be used in any potential confrontation with Iran. Projects such as the Kars–Iğdır–Nakhchivan (KIN), a proposed new train line costing $750 million[74] connecting Nakhchivan, Azerbaijan, and Turkey, could also make Armenia more isolated.

It thus appears that Turkey could potentially take a more active stance in this part of the region, especially considering the role it aims to exert as a key transit state, a point also reflected in Ahmet Davutoğlu's Eurasianist foreign policy discourse. Therefore, while the Caucasus bears its own unique input in regional politics as a factor in the struggle for control of the Middle East as a strategic tool, this role is subordinated to the implementation of Middle Eastern foreign policy in its wider context. Similarly, according to the literature, the Syrian crisis followed by Ankara's 'over active policy of mediating has reduced the importance of the Caucasus region for the Turkish foreign policy'[75] and this means that 'China, Iran and Turkey have remained minor actors in the Caspian region since the breakup of the Soviet Union'.[76]

However, Nakhchivan could play a crucial role in the future, given the Azerbaijani population in Northern Iran and Lezgins in the North of Azerbaijan as well as the establishment of the International South Azerbaijani Turks' National Council by the Azeri Turks of Iran, whose ultimate goal is the independence of the Turks that reside in Northern Azerbaijan. As written by Cemal Mehmatanoglu, the Iranian citizens of Turkic origin number around 35 million, which is roughly half of the Iranian population.[77] Tülümen points out that: 'there are many Azeris among the high clergy in Iran and around 200 Ayatollahs ... Khamenei is [for example] an Azero',[78] while Olson claims that 'Azeris in Iran comprised 75 per cent of the *bazaaris*[79] in Tehran'.[80]

It is thus evident that although the issue of the Azeris and Azerbaijan may not currently be at the epicentre of the states' mutual relations, yet the near future might bring changes that will promote this issue to a significant role as a moderator of Iranian and Turkish politics, especially if the Iranian–US rapprochement failed in the long run. The overthrow of President Yanukovych in Ukraine (21 February 2014) and the release of the US Embassy's cable in Baku

(September 2009) suggesting that owing to the dual track policy of Azerbaijani President Ilham Aliyev, the relation with Azerbaijan was possibly another case that placed 'US interests' in opposition to 'US values' served to strengthen the concerns and suspicions of Aliyev's regime towards the US over what its real intentions are regarding Baku's domestic politics.[81]

There is also the ever-present threat of conflict in Azerbaijan which, although it has recently been Turkified and speaks Turkish, has a large Shia population that leans more towards Iran than Turkey, and therefore could prove a valuable ally for Tehran in the near future in the turmoil caused by any type of transformation in the region. Indeed, according to ISNA (Iranian Students' News Agency, 12 March 2012), the Azerbaijani Defense Minister Saraf Abiev stated: 'We will not allow the territory of Azerbaijan to be used to attack Iran under any circumstances. We want regional security and peace, and believe strengthening military ties between the two countries will guarantee that.'[82] Similar views were expressed in a statement made by the Director of the Yerevan Regional Studies Centre, Richard Giragosian: 'For Armenia, Iran offers an important alternative to closed borders (with Turkey and Azerbaijan) and unresolved conflict as well as an opportunity to overcome Armenia's geographic isolation as a small landlocked state.'[83] In 1993 Turkey closed its border with Armenia after Armenian armed forces occupied 20 per cent of Azerbaijan including the Nagorno-Karabakh region in 1992, whereas in 2007 Iran and Armenia completed their connected gas pipeline. The trade volume between the two rose from $72 million in 2001 to $285 million in annual turnover in 2012.

Despite Baku's assurances, there are still Iranian fears over Azerbaijan's relations with Israel as represented by a $1.6 billion Defence Agreement (2012) between the two countries which could pose a threat against Iran. Other controversial Azerbaijan incidents led to the withdrawal of Iranian representatives in May 2012 vis-à-vis Iranian protests following the burning of pictures of the Supreme Leader of Iran, Ayatollah Ali Khamenei, while Esmail Kosari, former commander of IRGC, made accusations that Baku was collaborating with Mossad and the CIA to assassinate Iranian nuclear scientists.[84]

Reza Altun argues that: 'For now, the Middle East is important [and] unless conflicts in the Middle Eastern region resolve, new developments will not take place in other places.' It is thus deduced that possible future strategic advantages to be gained from Nakhchivan and the other factors that have been raised, are, at least for the present, relegated to the bottom of the agenda.[85]

Another critical issue that is very likely to lead to future confrontation is the importance of water for Turkey, Syria and Iran, an issue that first emerged in the 1920s and continued in the 1990s with the October 1998 crisis between Turkey and Syria. Israel has historically demonstrated a willingness to use military force to guarantee access to water resources, but in 1964 Syria formed plans to exert its own ability to control the flow of water by diverting the Banias River with the aid of the Arab League. This would have caused Israel's water supply to drop by approximately 10 per cent, and so Israel acted to protect this important resource in a series of attacks from 1965 to 1967 that aimed to destroy the Syrian water diversion projects. Its control of the Golan Heights gives it not only a strong military defence position, but also helps protect access to the important water source of the Sea of Galilee, while it is also able to source groundwater from the Coastal Aquifer and the Mountain Aquifer, two major aquifers that actually flow beneath Palestinian territory, namely, Gaza and the West Bank respectively.[86] Water as a means of control to prevent the inner regions of Syria from having an outlet to the Mediterranean Sea was also the reason behind the French granting the Alawis their own state, the 'State of the Alawis' (1920–1936) in the Nusayriya Mountain area.[87]

Similarly, the Southeastern Anatolia Project (Güneydoğu Anadolu Projesi, GAP), which started under the leadership of Süleyman Demirel, is one of the largest river basin development projects in Turkey. It consists of 13 irrigation and hydropower schemes including the construction of 22 dams and 19 hydroelectric power plants on the Tigris and the Euphrates, and is expected to provide around 22 per cent of the state's electricity. It could also potentially resolve the Kurdish issue in the eyes of those who have perceived it as an economic problem for Turkey. Calculations suggest that GAP provides irrigation for an area of approximately 1.8 million hectares of land which allows Turkey – especially the South East – to develop its capacity as an exporter of agricultural goods. Yet there are also concerns that this project in the South East of Turkey could be seen as an effort to eliminate Kurdish culture rather than improve local underdevelopment.[88] This viewpoint has caused Kurdish reactions in South East Turkey to perceive the GAP project negatively as a means of exerting control in the Kurdish areas.

## METHODOLOGY: AN INTERDISCIPLINARY AND COMPARATIVE EXAMINATION FROM A MULTI-ACTOR PERSPECTIVE

In order to deal with such a complex and multi-faceted issue where state and non-state actors are involved, and where different factors influence the relation between Tehran and Ankara, I shall employ the tools of IR discipline. This means that at the same time as pursuing a historical review of Turkish–Iranian relations, I will also touch on political analysis at three levels: the domestic, the regional and the international. The purpose of linking past and present examples throughout the chapter analysis is to demonstrate how the factors I underline as important have remained the same and demonstrate continuity. Accordingly, I will trace their historical roots and analyse my subject-matter through a thematic order based on chronological divisions in order to reveal how events in the present replicate those in the past.

On the domestic level, I will look into the factors that have acted as catalysts to formulate Iran's and Turkey's foreign policies and the parameters that determine relations between the two states, while on the regional level, I will explore the basic policies of Iran and Turkey as well as the ramifications of their interrelation on the region. Finally, on the international level, I will examine how regional and international as well as current developments impact Turkish–Iranian interactions, and analyse each state's relations with regional powers (such as Syria and Iraq), international powers (such as the US and Russia), non-state actors (the Kurds) and international organisations (for example, the EU) in their desire to balance, contain or control power.

The objective of such a comparative study of these actors' relations with both Iran and Turkey is to gauge their effect on the latter's foreign policies. Qualitative data analysis constitutes the main part of this research. I will thus use both primary and secondary sources. The main sources include documents, speeches and interviews with many important regional politicians as well as official statements and news reports by local and international sources. Apart from the literature reviewed in the previous section, my empirical research has also included field-work undertaken in the Turkish Parliament in Ankara, the Kurdistan Region of Iraq, the Qandil Mountains, and the UK. In addition, although the situation in the Middle East has been politically sensitive and increased security measures in Iran have meant that it has not been feasible to visit the country to carry out interviews, nonetheless I was able to interview high-ranking Iranian political figures via meetings in London to achieve the representative views needed to present a well-balanced case study.

The study then raises a series of indicative empirical and conceptual questions:

- What influence does the increasing role played by regional actors in the Middle East have, especially in light of recent developments in the region?
- What are the parameters (both internal and external) that have influenced Iran's and Turkey's foreign policies and their repercussions on a Turkish–Iranian alliance for regional and global politics?
- What is the impact of this interrelation on the policies of both regional states (Syria, Israel, Iraq) and non-state actors (Hizbullah, Hamas, the Kurds), and how does this affect international powers (US) with potential consequences for the regional balance of power?
- What is the effect of the US policy of containing Iran versus the Turkish reaction vis-à-vis the deterioration in Turkish–Israeli relations and the growing relationship of Ankara with Arab states?
- What role do international actors such as the US, Russia or the EU play in the ascension of Turkey and Iran to regional power status in view of the EU and US embargo on Iran's nuclear programme along with American pressure on Turkey to enforce international sanctions against Iran[89] when considered in the light of the strengthening of Iranian–Turkish ties?

- What are the risks involved if Iran continues developing relations with non-state armed groups in the region for both regional and global security?
- What are the consequences of Tehran's and Ankara's meddling in Iraqi and Syrian affairs?

Such questions require scholarly consideration but, to date, current schools of thought have mainly concentrated either on the role of inter-state relations as the driving force behind the international relations system,[90] or pursued a historiographical analysis,[91] while even the most recent offerings still tend to focus on the traditional state security-centred foreign policy perspectives.[92] Thus, apart from the lack of attention paid to the importance of non-state entities in the formulation of foreign policy as they are relatively new players in this capacity,[93] the currently available bibliography also often has a misleading focus on the size of the powers involved, using definitions such as 'middle' and 'small'; for example, Iran is defined as 'a typical state of potential middle power stretching from the Caspian to the Persian Gulf'.[94] One wonders how such terminology can be considered accurate in the light of the changing concept of power in the 21st century as the criteria are relative and the empirical evidence seems to have outgrown the previous theory and completely transformed the conceptual framework as we know it. This can also explain why empiricism has led to the rise of a succession of different schools of thought in IR.

CONCLUSION

In this book, I further enhance my theoretical map which presents International Relations as a complex field of multidimensional interrelations between and among actors at the local, sub-state, trans-state, and state regional and global spheres. In particular, I have drawn attention to the role – both direct and indirect – played in IR by non-state actors, though without *a priori* favouring of either type of actor. The purpose of this book is to contribute further to the study of those dynamics that link and explain patterns of interaction and mutual impact between state and non-state actors. Last, but not least, the current research aims to contribute policy-related findings with respect to the use of regional powers in dealing with non-state groups in the region.

I will thus attempt to draw conclusions with regard to possible trends that have been formative in the Middle Eastern balance of power in the context of Iranian and Turkish foreign policy choices while also looking at additional factors that could advance or impede this relation further. This becomes even more imperative if Iran and Turkey were to form a strong and institutionalised alliance. This case scenario could signify major readjustments in both regional and international politics.

A major strand of the book is its intention to shed light on how regional powers, such as Turkey, interact with other regional (nuclear) powers and act as a bridge between major powers and regional powers, while assessing the repercussions that such a potential interaction between regional state powers could have on Middle Eastern politics. At the same time, it also seeks to examine the key role that non-state actors increasingly play in the foreign policies of stronger powers, examining the implications this can have for the international system in general. Therefore, the study aims to fill the gap in the application of main International Relations theories to the study of relations not only between state actors, but also between states and non-state players.

Accordingly, within this context, I study the correlation of past and current developments, together with regional and international events which have affected this dual relationship, and place it under an extensive scholarly focus that also considers historical aspects and economic, energy and political relations. A chronological order based on thematics is pursued while the historical review aims to link the past to the present so that continuity can be demonstrated.

At the present time with the restructuring of the Middle Eastern region currently in a state of flux, news reports and articles are important sources of topical information which I use to further facilitate the analysis. This is important because no comprehensive scholarly study has yet been undertaken that supports the opinions expressed, but contemporary commentary is relevant and topical in assessing the issues. However, while it is thus understood that the themes under examination may be subjects that have triggered lively debate in the media and widespread comment, substantial research at both the empirical and the theoretical level is still needed.

In addition, there is the imbalance of a dominant state-centric perspective together with an over-emphasis on the security aspects of Turkish–Iranian relations, although, of course, this remains an important consideration, especially when security is a priority for all entities in the international relations system.

To answer the book's main argument, a different kind of approach that reviews all the interconnected elements in order to come up with a reasoned and well-considered analysis is then required. There are increasing scholarly demands for the necessity of 'a flexible and inclusive theoretical framework,' that is, one that incorporates the politics of power and influence but also the role of ideas, interests and domestic restraints. No single theory or level of analysis offers a way of exploring satisfactorily the shifting dynamic of international politics or the international politics of the region ... considering the behaviour of Middle Eastern states in the international system which demands a more ... integrated approach as the region defies attempts at generalisation and resists explanations derived from Western experience [and thus] there is still a gap in the literature'.[95] These are revealing rationales which demonstrate why this book is important in bringing a holistic approach to the politics and relations of the Middle Eastern region.

# CHAPTER 2

# Determinants of Iranian–Turkish Relations: A Historical Review

## INTRODUCTION

Contemporary relations and politics in the Middle Eastern region, especially with regard to Turkish and Iranian foreign policies and their regional strategy, have been largely configured by aspects of identity that can be traced back for centuries. The historical depth of this parameter has a direct relation to its impact as a key element that has been foundational in the identity of the structure and foreign policy principles of modern Iran and Turkey. The root cause of this lies in the past as the inhabitants and, thus, the diverse nations, of the broader Middle Eastern region are essentially the end product of the amalgamation of a series of cultures where one is built on another.[1]

This is certainly the case here as both the Persians, as inhabitants of the region, and the Turkic tribes as immigrants arriving *circa* the 11th century, adopted an accommodating, while also competing, relation that was interdependent as both had need of each other as inhabitants of the same territory.[2] However, the legacy of the Turko-Persian tradition as an intrinsic part of this interaction is indicative as a facilitator of their interrelations, rather than playing a fundamental role in shaping their policies.[3] Contrary to the views generally expressed in the current literature, this chapter distinguishes the Turko-Persian tradition as a factor of unity facilitated by their proximity that at times resulted in a convergence of their spheres of interest rather than being a determinant of their foreign policy practice throughout this period.

It was based on this background that until recently former Prime Minister Ahmet Davutoğlu would emphasise that: 'Turkey and Iran are not rivals but friendly neighbouring countries with common cultural and historical values', raising the need for a 'synergy resulting in increasing bilateral relations, regional peace but also economic buoyancy in Eurasia ... with a new understanding and with a strategic perspective'.[4]

The reign of the Abbasids in the 8th century favoured the elitist customs of their Persian priests (*Barmakids* or *Barmecides*) on the one hand, and the Caliphate's Turkic tribes as servants and soldiers with great political and military strength on the other, and this ushered in an era of co-existence based on a Turko-Persian Islamicate culture.[5] This synthesis of rulers, initially of Iranian origin employing Turkic militias, was preserved under the Samanid Empire (819–999), the first native Persian dynasty following the Arab Islamic conquest. They converted to Sunni orthodoxy and the Turkic tribes they employed composed the majority of their army. Turkic ascendancy in political power at the Samanids' expense and the increasing influence of the scholars of Islam, the *ulama,* as advocates of Sunni Islam and an 'alternative social instrument for the maintenance of public order' continued to grow in strength under the Persianized Ghaznavid (989–1149) and Karakhanid (927–1212) dynasties, but gradually waned with the predominance of the Ottomans in Asia Minor in the 14th century and of the Safavids in Persia in the 15th century.[6]

Although elements of the same Turko-Persian culture were still evident in the rise of the Qajar dynasty (1796–1925), a Persianised family of Turkic origins,[7] the ascendancy of the Safavid dynasty (1501–1736), an Azeri Turkic tribe from Azerbaijan, marked a breaking away from the Turko-Persian past. While originally Sunnis, Persian Safavids under Shah Ismail I (1487–1524) diverted from orthodoxy and at the beginning of the 16th century the Twelver Shi'a Islam was introduced as the Empire's official dogma of faith. The Safavids defeated the Mongols and established a dynasty that lasted

200 years 'to counter the strength of the Sunni Turkmen tribes in Central Asia, the Sunni Mughal Empire in India and the Sunni Ottoman Turks to the West'.[8]

Thus, religious identity strengthened the role of religious ideology as an ideational factor, one that has been ongoing since the early stages of the region's history right up to the aftermath of the Iranian Revolution (1979) and, more recently, the Syrian crisis of March 2011. This factor has undoubtedly had a major influence, and in the Iranian case probably created the structure to a large extent, while also making a considerable but lesser contribution to Turkish foreign policy. Yet the idea of the centrality of the state in politics continues in both cases, even in the paradigm of the Islamic tradition of Iran's theocratic regime with the exception that the state is strongly influenced by Islamic beliefs. In spite of differences in the stance of Iran and Turkey regarding the political role of Islam, this does not affect its position as a structural or institutional feature which remains a constant. Güneş Murat Tezcür perceptively observes that to some extent its presence is a promotion of the notion of guardianship, even though this may be pursued in various ways by different authorities. In Iran's case it is represented through the religious leadership, whereas for Turkey it is via the army. Iran's assumption is that 'the ruling elite has the right to govern by reason of its unique knowledge [as] the authority is restricted by non-elected non-accountable institutions controlled by the guardianship'.[9] Interestingly, the notion of *laicism*, i.e., the model according to which the state controls popular religion, is identical in both the Iranian and Turkish political systems.[10]

As we will observe, although the Islamic Revolution has obviously also acted as a dynamic to some extent, Turkish policies should be interpreted in a more secular context which is reflected in the Turkish need for preservation of the state's secular order, i.e., the principle of Secularism (*Laiklik*), according to which politics is a private matter and religion is separate from it. This stance would become even more evident vis-à-vis Turkey's domestic problems as Islam and the Kurds became regarded as the prime domestic threats following a series of incidents. An example of this was when Necmettin Erbakan was charged with breaking certain laws that guaranteed Turkey's secular

status while another involved a petition made by President Kenan
Evren to the Constitutional Court to repeal the law allowing women
to wear Islamic headcovering at universities (5 January 1989). These
two significant events are indicative of the strain placed on the
secular state at this time.[11]

This is in line with the Iranian view which sees it as important to
weaken any (religious) tendencies in Turkish foreign policy
orientation as confirmed in an interview statement with an
important Iranian political figure: 'If Turkey wants to establish a
Neo-Ottoman Empire then [that] would lead to conflict ... the
Safavid Empire's and European cooperation in the past was aimed
[precisely] to stop the expansion of the Ottomans, a combination of
Turkish Islamism and Turkish nationalism. Therefore, based on
history, Iran and Europe should have good relations today in order
to control the Turkish nationalist Islamist behavior, and stop Turkey
dominating in Central Asia or the Middle East.'[12] Thus, it can be
seen that it is the structures, along with the agents, that are
important in dictating the foreign policy principles of Iran and
Turkey and even at times driving their regional strategies.[13] On this
basis, it is clear that religion constitutes a legitimate tool as far as
implementing policies is concerned, especially in the Safavids' case
where it was foundational in shaping the Empire's structure.

The impact of European influence in the 17th and 18th centuries
heralded the end of the distinctive Turko-Persian tradition. Russian
revisionism and European infiltration into the region, technological
advancement and the discovery of new trade routes to India and
China sounded its death knell as it was swept away by new notions of
modernity such as the nation-state, the rule of (civic) law and the
egalitarian state.

## Sunni Ottoman Empire versus Shiite Persian Safavids: Structural parameters

The second most important period that can be claimed to have
moulded contemporary structures in Iran and Turkey was when the
region was under the authority of Ottoman Selim I (or Yavuz Sultan
Selim) (1512–1520) and Shah Ismail of Persia who brought the
Safavids to power and differentiated them as adherents to Shia Islam.

Selim I was important, not only because of the conquest of Egypt and the expansion of the Empire further eastwards into the Middle East region making him the first legitimate Ottoman Caliph (خليفة, *successor*), but also because it was claimed that he transferred the Caliphate from Cairo to Constantinople.

Selim's reign was marked by a policy of exclusion and cruelty toward non-orthodox Muslim sects. The Alevi massacre in 1514 as heretics because of their support of the Shi'a Persian Empire against the Ottomans gave Selim I the name Yavuz, meaning 'grim'.[14] This cleansing was in response to a number of confrontational incidents including the pro-Shia Rebellion instigated by Şahkulu (the Servant of the Shah) which occurred in 1511.[15] Eventually, the ongoing conflict would turn into a religious war where the two empires fought for power, geopolitical control and regional hegemony. One major event was the Shi'a defeat at the Battle of Chaldiran (23 August 1514), a victory for Selim's policy which aimed to halt the spread of Shi'ism into the Ottoman Vilayets (ولايات, *governorates*). He was a devoted Sunni, a true believer, who was also granted the title of the 'King of the Two Lands (the continents of Europe and Asia), of the Two Seas (Mediterranean and Indian Seas), Conqueror of the Two Armies (European and Safavid armies), and Servant of the Two Holy Cities (Mecca and Medina)' in 1517 by the Sharif of Mecca. The 41-year war between the Ottoman and Safavid Empires was finally concluded by the Peace of Amasya (29 May 1555) which determined their mutual borders.

Whereas the Ottoman leadership was primarily inspired by an inherited Sunni faith which was also partially reflected in its foreign policy, the rise of the Shi'a Safavids incorporated an Islamist ideology that they were prepared to use as leverage to maximise influence in the competition for survival.[16] In one sense, Islam as an ideology per se does not appear to have dictated the foreign policy of either power, but it cannot be doubted that it has played a considerable role as a formative structural factor of the ideational kind. This is helpful in understanding how it was then able to act as a facilitator of the empire's foreign policy and become a significant tool for institutionalisation in the case of the Safavids where the leadership was primarily spiritual, apart from a military chieftain.[17]

Thus, it can be deduced that what shaped the policies of Iran and Turkey were not just the universal tenets upheld by the tradition of Islam, but their interpretations and characteristics reflected variously in the divide between Shi'a and Sunnis and it is these that can be truly considered as structural determinants. Historically, it appears that Shi'a Islam supports 'a tradition of opposition and rebellion to illegitimate holders of authority' in contrast to Sunni Islam's submissiveness to the ruler's authority'.[18] Even when taken out of a religious context, the characteristics of the Shi'ite sect are evident in Iranian foreign policy discourse and practice as a revolutionary force 'supportive of resistance movements which are against hegemony and imperialism' while it is also based 'on a strategic approach dictated by national and security interests rather than on an ideological cause'.[19] As already mentioned, Iran has been identified as an instigator of factional warfare which is based on the way Shia doctrine perceives authority as spiritual[20] so that 'all non-divine authorities other than the Imam and his successors are illegitimate'.[21] The Sunni element can also be seen to have had an impact on the Turkish foreign policy stance as a moderate, status quo power of (mainly) Western influence so even though both 'Iran and Turkey look for a stable region', this is to some extent secondary to their own interests.[22]

This was confirmed in the opinions of leading political figures such as Dr. Ata'ollah Mohajerani, a former Iranian Minister, who stated that: 'The National Iranian foreign policy is realistic based on national interest [as] it is impossible to govern eighty million people based only on ideology. The rule is Islamic according to the Constitution ... but these Islamic decisions are subjected to change according to the security and national benefit of the country.'[23] A high level political figure in Iranian politics added: 'Iran's foreign policy is based on a strategic approach ... it is not an ideological cause but it is based on [its] national and security interests and balance of power and foreign policy is the tool to implement these principles.'[24] On the other hand, Dr. Aykan Erdemir, former MP CHP (Cumhuriyet Halk Partisi) argued that: 'Sunni Islam, not religion or Islam is present today in Turkey' as seen in former Turkish Prime Minister, Ahmet Davutoğlu's attempts to revive 'the New Ottoman Legacy towards the former Ottoman Lands, therefore the focus is on the Middle East, so that we [Turkey] can bring stability and peace in commemoration of the Ottoman era of prosperity and peace and if we [Turkey] can get back to that [our] people will be happy.'[25]

Walking in the footsteps of Sultan Selim I, Recep Tayip Erdoğan renamed the Third Bosphorus Bridge Yavuz Sultan Selim Bridge and initiated a new opening of relations in line with Davutoğlu's 'zero problems' policy with the neighbouring countries. However, this initiative proved unsuccessful, as will be shown in the following chapters.

## THE ROLE OF THE ELITES: ARMY AND *ULAMA* VERSUS ARMY AND AYATOLLAHS

The role of the military, societal and religious institutions within this early historical period under examination demonstrates that agents, either individually as in the Persian case, or as institutionalised entities in the Ottoman context subject to the state control, are determinants that can also explain the formulation of contemporary Turkish and Iranian foreign policies. The Turkish structure of secularism has been strongly linked to the highly centralised system and institutionalisation of the Ottomans. They incorporated the Byzantine (Eastern Roman) army structure and institutions, so that while the Sunna *ulama* were legitimised by the state, they were also subject to the central authority.[26] In contrast, the steady increase of a Shi'a religious elite is observable in Persia, starting from the Safavid period and becoming even more evident during the Qajars' era, as they established financial independence[27] 'through the collection of the religious taxes of *zakat* and *khums*, their control over the *waqf* (endowment) lands [and] their close and profitable relations with the traditional urban merchants, the *bazaar* classes, and the guilds.' This contrasted with the Sunni clergy, who had much less independence as they were subject to the state.[28]

These strata now steadily gaining ascendancy in Persia would later grow powerful enough in the more modern Iran to challenge the state authority represented by the monarchy, and incite the subsequent revolutions, reaching their height with the Iranian

Revolution in 1979.[29] It seems then that the weak institutionalisation
and lack of centralisation in the Safavid Empire that was responsible
for the rise of strong religious tribes is very much linked to the later
roles played by an independent religious elite and the creation of an
army represented by the Revolutionary Guards, established by Iran's
new clerical leadership with the intention of controlling the military
and compelling it to subjection. In contrast, within the Ottoman
Empire the controllable *ulama* elite was subjected to a dominant army
which prevented the clerics from taking control as was the case with
the independent clergy in Iran.

In the case of Iran, the impact of the White Revolution (1963),
which introduced a series of reforms to strengthen the traditional
system, caused the tribal landlords to turn against the regime they
had initially supported and increasingly challenge the Shah's
authority. This eventually resulted in the emergence of two
conflicting centres of power. In the present Islamic Republic of Iran
this is referred to as a duality of power which Dr. Ata'ollah
Mohajerani[30] describes as 'the state as permanent decision-maker
embedded in the Leadership of jurisprudence (Velayat-e *faqih*)' on the
one hand, while on the other is a modern presidential system aligned
to 'the government which is temporary and defends freedom'.[31]
Similarly, it is illuminating how religion is subject to the Turkish
state's authority in Turkish foreign policy and discourse, even in the
case of AK Parti's tenure in office as an Islamist government.
Combining the weight of history with its '2023 vision', Ahmet
Davutoğlu reinforced Turkey's historical commitment to 'integrate
Turkish foreign policy discourse into its national discourse [as any]
gap or contrast between these two ... will make it difficult to carry out
a successful foreign policy'.[32]

How the structural parameters of army and the *ulama* has
managed to preserve the centralisation of the Turkish Republic (1923)
and retain the intrinsic components of the state-control system
inherited from its Ottoman past will be further analysed in the
sections to follow. At the same time a comparison will be made with
the very different role played by the Iranian tribes and the clergy
(مجتهد, *Ayatollahs*, diligent) who have occupied their own distinctive
place in politics.

Reza Shah built his state on military and bureaucratic elements,[33] but the state was never able to exert absolute authority over the Iranian tribes or the clergy's continued independence outside the state's military control. The creation of the Islamic Revolutionary Guards (5 May 1979) further strengthened the existence of the clergy as a separate and distinct entity in the Iranian bureaucracy standing in opposition against the monarchy, and from 1979 onwards the IRGC's (*sepah e pasdaran e engelad-e eslami*) presence was a powerful military force that protected the revolution and the Islamic regime.

TURKISH VERSUS IRANIAN REPUBLICANISM: INTERNATIONAL
INTERFERENCE AS AN EXTERNAL FORCE

In a similar way, external influence has affected the shaping of the Ottoman and Safavid empires. The interference in the formation of their modern versions, and, even more tellingly, on the stage of broader Middle Eastern affairs which reached its climax during the Cold War period, can all be traced back to these early stages of history. Today, the role played by international forces, whether international states or institutions of the international community, stands out as a key determinant of the ongoing transformation of the Middle Eastern state and non-state entities, and thus the fate of the wider region as revealed in the final chapters.

In this context, European expansionism and its impact on the Ottoman and Safavid Empires, especially after the French Revolution in 1789, needs to be analysed. The advance of European influence was facilitated to a large degree by the Safavids' defeat which made modernisation an attractive prospect. Incorporation of European reforms was first implemented by the Ottoman Empire (Tanzimat, 1839–1876), and thereafter by Iran with Abbas Mirzad (1789–1833), the first Persian Prince to introduce reforms to modernise the army and society. However, Mirzad's attempts at progress were unsuccessful. The Tobacco Revolt (1891–1892) clearly showed the decentralised nature of the empire and its inability to oppose the Shi'a clergy, and this would ultimately sow the seeds of the empire's decline.[34] Such Europeanisation attempts or the imitation of a European model must first consider how great its impact will be in the event of serious domestic economic and political crises, which, if not addressed, may result in unsuccessful policies for reforms. Failures in successfully adopting such policies in a modern-day context also serve to explain Turkish and Iranian foreign policy attempts to develop a degree of independence within the period under examination that this book addresses.

External influences that impacted Iran and Turkey included the Anglo-Russian Convention of 1907; Persia's division, linked to its role as a buffer zone and a trade route to India, into spheres of influence between Russia and Great Britain, and, most importantly, the discovery of oil in Iran (1908) which heightened international meddling into regional affairs. These, together with significant landmark events such as the Constitutional Revolutions in both the Ottoman (Young Turk Revolution, 3 July, 1908) and Safavid Empires (1905–1911), the Turkish War of Independence (1919–1923) and the rise to power of the Pahlavi dynasty (1925–1979), shaped the fate of Iranian and Turkish politics up to, and perhaps even beyond, the end of the Cold War.

External interference has been apparent from the very beginning of the creation of the Middle Eastern region into states. According to Fazlhashemi, Shah Ismail turned to Europe after Selim's victory to secure new weapons to face the Ottomans, while the Shirleys, two entrepreneurial English brothers, encouraged the Persian king to start a war with the Ottomans, seizing the opportunity to develop English business links with Iran. As a result, they successfully equipped the army and this allowed Ismail to fight and defeat the Ottomans.[35] In the Iranian case, pursuing a policy that aimed at greater independence resulted in the Islamic Revolution in 1979. The creation of the Islamic Republic of Iran was viewed by Iran as necessary to free themselves of their earlier dependent relations on the West, and follow independent foreign policies instead of being influenced by external directives which had led to international meddling in regional affairs in the past.

In a similar vein, Iranian foreign policy today is also doing everything possible to disassociate itself from past events like the Constitutional Revolution in 1906 which suffered greatly from British and Russian interference. The movement took its inspiration from the Western European constitutional movement of the 19th century and was supported by the *bazaar* merchants and the clergy who had found asylum in the British Embassy, but disillusionment set in when it became evident that, although the British had asked Mozaffar ad-Din Shah (1896–1907) for free elections and reforms in order to contract the Anglo-Russian Agreement in 1907, they quickly abandoned the Constitutionalists in favour of the new Shah Mohammad Ali Shah Qajar. Later on, there was more external meddling with the restoration of Mohammad Reza Pahlavi (1941–1979) to power by British and US interests. This was achieved through the 13 August coup d'état in 1953 as part of Operation Ajax which also resulted in the overthrow of Iranian Prime Minister Mohammad Mosaddegh.

Another case of external meddling concerned the US policy of supplying economic aid to the Shah comprising loans of US $1.3 billion in 1963 and armaments such as F4 jets in 1967. This was because the US feared the threat of Soviet invasion and therefore wanted to place the Shah under obligation so that he would not move towards a more independent position. US concern was that without the strong support of this powerful ally, it could quickly find itself in hot water.[36] Iran also still has bitter memories of other interference including the 1921 February coup by Reza Khan instigated by British diplomatic and military personnel stationed in Iran, a direct Russo-British intervention,[37] the Shah's support of foreign domination with the '1933–1934 new agreement with the Anglo-Iranian oil company that he extended through concessions to 1993'[38] as well as 'US advisors' support of SAVAK in 1957'[39] and Iran's use as a 'US Persian Gulf policy tool', i.e., 'a buffer against the USSR between 1953 and 1978'.[40]

With these issues in mind, Iranian political figures today support the Islamic Republic of Iran's view that the 'US may have interests in the Middle East but not hegemony'[41] and uphold its aim 'as a strategic player to organise all countries in the region so that they strengthen relations against the US and Israel'.[42] On the same basis, the 1987 Iranian doctrine which was reflected in its 'neither East nor West' foreign policy was further interpreted in a statement by Foreign Minister Ali Akbar Velayati (25 November 1987) 'that having relations with countries is different from accepting their hegemony'.[43] Similarly, the contemporary Turkish (Middle Eastern) foreign policy practice and discourse as this was articulated by Ahmet Davutoğlu is dictated by three methodological and five operational foreign policy principles[44] which are also based around the desire for greater autonomy, but in this case operate via a multi-dimensional foreign policy where relations with global actors aim to be complementary.

> We suffer from a perception that other powers design regional politics and we only perform the roles assigned to us … we do not receive instructions from any other powers, nor are we part of others' grand schemes.[45]

Other examples that historically demonstrate Turkey and Iran's growing relations include the 1955 Baghdad Pact (which became the Central Treaty Organisation, CENTO, in 1959) to counter Soviet dominance of the oil-rich Gulf region and the Saadabad Pact Treaty, a non-aggression pact signed between Turkey, Iran, Iraq and Afghanistan in 1937. Further institutionalisation of Turkish–Iranian relations continued through the Organisation of Islamic Cooperation (OIC, منظمة التعاون الإسلامي, 1969), economic cooperation within ECO (the Economic Cooperation Organisation, 1985), the successor to the Regional Cooperation for Development (RCD) established by Turkey, Iran and Pakistan in 1964, the 'Developing–8' (D-8) Group formed by eight Muslim developing countries in June 1997 and, more recently, the Turkish–Iranian Business Council in 2001.

International interference in Turkish and Iranian politics continued throughout the Cold War period but was expressed in diverse ways. US and Soviet rivalry in the Middle East, which escalated during the Cold War period and came to an end with the US predominance in global affairs, also played a major role in formulating Turkish and Iranian foreign policy orientation throughout this period.

An intrinsic component of the US and Soviet discourse was the importance of the oil-rich Gulf region whose protection became central to the policies of both international and regional powers. Iran's proximity to the Persian Gulf gave it a significant advantage and the Shah's better control over domestic politics gave him more leverage over the state's foreign policies in contrast to Turkey's fragile internal situation which constantly demanded attention and left little space to implement an outward-looking and more independent foreign policy. Turkey's political orientation was consumed by its domestic turmoil as left and right wings fought for supremacy at the expense of the development of an active foreign policy stance, a situation which Mustafa Kemal, founder of the Turkish Republic (29 October 1923), also experienced when he was struggling with one-party rule in Turkey.

America initially used indirect military force through covert interventions, but later on was employed in an official capacity through the Eisenhower Doctrine applied in March 1957 where a Middle Eastern state could request aid from US military forces if it was being threatened by armed aggression from another state. It also formulated Defense and Economic Cooperation Agreements with Turkey and Iran aiming to control international communism and use the Middle Eastern region as a buffer zone against the Soviets.[46]

The US gave strong support to Ankara's military element as protectors of the guardianship of Kemal's six principles and especially *laicism* or *laiklik*, and this reached its peak with the US backing of Turkey's first military coup (27 May 1960) against the democratically elected DP (Democratic Party, Demokrat Parti, 1950–1960). This was carried out because of fears that Adnan Menderes' government might overturn the Kemalist order and so action was taken to make sure that Kemal's principles were upheld.[47]

During this period it can therefore be seen that Iran and the Shah's policies had a much greater impact on regional politics, mainly because Turkey had turned its gaze inwards and was absorbed in trying to solve the problems caused by its politically unstable domestic situation. Indeed, the Turkish stance throughout this period is far more reflective of Ankara's domestic problems than any reaction to the Iranian foreign policy discourse and practice. We can also observe that although Republicanism in Iran aimed to liberate Iran from Western control, the goal of Turkey's European- influenced policies was to preserve the unity of the state.

THE INFLUENCE OF THE COLD WAR ON TURKISH–IRANIAN
POLITICS

*Iran and Turkey in the 1950s and 1970s*
## The Kurdish factor
The period from the 1950s and 1960s onwards marks the internationalisation of Middle Eastern politics in the sense that the region
became the focus of attention for international politics. US covert but
direct political interference in the Middle East promoted its liberal
idealist ideology in opposition to Soviet communism. But during
the 1960s significant threats to US regional interests arose, including
the emergence of Arab nationalism and the rise of non-state actors
such as national liberation movements engaging in aircraft hijackings, and Islamic movements, all of which had a major impact on the
regional players. Another more positive example of 1960s change
was Fethullah Gülen's (neo)-Nur movement in Turkey which grew
to become a gigantic transnational Islamic movement based on a
strong network of educational institutions, media (today) and business
organisations both at home and abroad, aiming at a progressive
'bottom-up' restructuring of society through education.[48]

The Cold War was a time of great transformation in the Middle
East region. In Iran the Shah was attempting to create a new modern
state in line with European standards and principles, while Turkey
was absorbed in its efforts to suppress its Kurdish and other Islamist
voices in favour of a consolidated secularist state governed by the
military apparatus. At the same time, the region was affected by the
1973 Yom Kippur War and the 1978 Camp David Accords as well as
the outbreak of the Lebanese civil war[49] which would lead to the
creation and rise of Musa Sadr's Amal movement, and, later on,
Hizbullah (the National Resistance), a Shi'a group fighting Israel and
aiming at the establishment of an Islamic state in Lebanon with
Iranian support. The Lebanese Civil War also allowed Syria to keep
40,000 troops in Lebanon as the bulk of an Arab Deterrent Force in
1976 which marked the start of Syria's interference in the region.

It was this politically volatile environment that ushered in the rise
of a multi-polar regional system interacting with global actors, both
of state and non-state status, a situation that has greatly impacted

international politics today since the course of events in the broader Middle Eastern region has had a major influence on the rest of the world. Multi-polarity has happened not only because international and regional contexts have merged under the impact of globalisation, but also because the role of non-state entities has gained in significance. This has been reflected through their impact on regional developments and their involvement in surprising events with international repercussions.

The importance of non-state entities is epitomised in the role of the Kurds whose influence on the formulation of the foreign policies of Turkey and Iran has been steadily growing. The internationalisation of the Kurdish issue from 1946 onwards brought the Kurds into the spotlight of the international arena. Their presence throughout both the Turkish and Iranian states meant that they were increasingly perceived as reliable allies in regional rivalries in a similar way to the value they had formerly possessed as warriors and strategic partners in the 16th and 19th centuries.

Historically, the Kurdish principalities were also important politically for a number of reasons. They were recognised in their stance as independent entities under the Sublime Porte's authority, the strategic use of Kurdistan's division between the Ottomans and the Persians which was important as a buffer defence zone; the Kurds' coalition with Sultan Selim which resulted in Shah Ismail's defeat on 23 August 1514; and their later collaboration with Mustafa Kemal which facilitated his War of Independence.

The Kurdish alliance with the Turkic nomads against the Byzantine army led them to victory in the Battle of Manzikert (1071) and enabled the Turkification of Anatolia, which laid the foundations of the Ottoman Empire. Again, in 1514–1516 the Ottomans could not have conquered the Mamluk Sultanate without the support of the Kurds, while in the 16th century the Kurds also helped the Ottomans expand to the East to further establish their empire. In both the 14th and 19th centuries the Kurdish Emirates acted as a buffer zone to prevent Persian penetration into the region. In the time of the Safavids, the Ottoman Empire occupied Mosul and Kirkuk and thereafter the Treaty of of Zuhab (Kasr-ı Şirin, 17 May 1639) divided Kurdistan land between Persians and Ottomans for the first time. More recently, Kurdish participation in Mustafa Kemal's War of Independence (1922) determined the trajectory of developments in the Middle East. Finally, the Kurdish role as a key determinant in the politics of the region was even visible in actions such as the reversal of the initial decision made by the Great Powers (i.e. France, Italy, Great Britain, and Japan with the US as a neutral observer) at the post-War Conference at San Remo (19–26 April 1920) to give the Kurds their own state. This offer was withdrawn because of fears of possible repercussions that might affect the powers' regional interests if an independent Kurdish state was created and this influenced their decision to let Iraq keep control of the oil-rich Kirkuk and Mosul areas.[50] In addition, the rise and collapse of the Republic of Mahabad in 1946, which, with some justification, has often been identified as the first episode in the long-lasting saga of US–USSR Cold War relations with regard to Middle Eastern politics, can also be highlighted as another contribution by the Kurds and a determining factor in the regional course of events.[51]

The Kurdish movement in Iraq became increasingly important for US and Iranian Middle Eastern policies. Kurdish support was crucial in the US anti-Soviet strategy to counterbalance the Ba'thists. It also had a key role in influencing Iran, the US's staunchest ally in the Gulf region during the 1970s, where it helped to appease Iran's Kurdish movement and assisted in the facilitation of Nixon's 'Twin Pillars' doctrine (1969–1974) following the US administration 1950s Agreements with both Iran and Turkey. The evolution of the US containment strategy against any regional actor that might jeopardize US interests in the oil-rich Gulf was initially carried out through the support of state actors, but in its second phase non-state entities, such as the Kurds of Iraq were also used to strengthen their case.[52]

This was reflected in the US entering into initial contacts with the Kurds of Iraq and supplying US covert funding of US $16 million to support the Kurdish leader Mullah Mustafa Barzani from August 1969 onwards. Indeed, Kurdish activities during this period were intense, reaching their peak in July 1972 when the Kurdish leadership from Iraq under Idris Barzani and Mahmoud Othman were able to present their case directly to the US government for the first time in an official but covert meeting with the US administration as the result of the Shah's arrangements.[53]

## The Economic Factor

The dynamic of economics was another major determinant. The oil crisis during 1973–1974 had a positive effect on Iran as an oil-based economy, while the strengthening of Ankara's cooperation with Moscow under a three-year Commerce Accord (30 November 1978)[54] seems to have brought the Shah closer to Turkey to counterbalance the Soviet influence. According to the Agreement, Turkey would purchase 1 million tons of crude oil and 500,000 tons of furnace oil in exchange for agricultural products. Turkey's preoccupation with its domestic, economic and political problems vis-à-vis the marginalisation of the left and any oppositional voice along with the increase in Kurdish activities opened the door for greater military intervention in politics. In addition, the subsequent rise of Shi'ism in Iran as another ideology perceived as dangerous for the regional status quo explains the rise of political Islam as a response to societal inequity, corruption and rapid modernisation. The fact that the Pahlavi regime collapsed because of the rebellious religious elites whose traditional authority was at stake is again indicative of the *ulama* formative role in Iranian foreign policy.

## Institutions of Influence: Religion and Military

The historic roles of religion and the military have also been active dynamics in influencing foreign policy objectives. From 1963 onwards, Reza Shah's modernisation policies empowered the state above the influence of the clergy, although this was resisted by the *ulama* who had acted as an independent formative actor in Iranian politics since the 19th century. Accordingly, the clergy together with the *bazaaris* stirred up mass protests in the state's Tobacco and Constitutional Revolutions which led to a new political Islam which would later encourage the political liberalisation of the 1960s and 1970s.[55]

In a similar context, fear of violating the Kemalist order was intrinsically linked with Turkish nationalism which meant that the greater freedom introduced by the liberalisation policies of Suleyman Demirel's Justice Party (AP, Adalet Partisi) were rejected because of the possible consequences on the prevailing Turkish political structure and the state's multi-ethnic society. This resulted in a second

coup d'etat (12 March 1971) to restore the Kemalist order.[56] The coup
was also linked to accusations levelled by the public prosecutor against
the Worker's Party of Turkey (Türkiye İşçi Partisi, 1961), claiming
that it was supporting communism and favouring Kurdish separatism
by stirring up trouble among the Kurds in Iran and Iraq. US
administration interest and involvement in this development behind
the scenes might have also been a contributing factor.

It was during this same period of the first half of the 1970s that
Necmettin Erbakan also established the first Islamist political party,
the National Order Party (Milli Nizam Partisi), banned by the 1971
military coup but re-established under the name of the National
Salvation Party (Milli Selamet Partisi) in 1972, which received
11.8 per cent of the vote in the 1973 general elections. Erbakan as
well as today's AK Parti drew their inspiration from the Ottoman
legacy, and were also both influenced by the Nakşibendi Sufi order
which supplied the ideology behind Erbakan's National View
Movement (Milli Gorus Hareketi) outlined in the 1969 National
View (*Milli Görüş*) manifesto.

## ISLAMIST TURKEY VERSUS ISLAMIC IRAN: THE IMPACT OF FOREIGN POLICY PRINCIPLES

The 1970s saw the rise of Islamic movements as an alternative to a
secular mode of governance in Middle Eastern politics. Perceived
as providing a remedy to socio-economic and political problems,
Islamic movements reached their peak with the establishment of
the Islamic Republic of Iran in the form of a powerful theocracy.
Structurally, an institutionalised clerical rule was inaugurated with
the *Faqih* (jurist) which would acknowledge the supreme power of
Allah as the guide (*rahbar*). However, Güneş Murat Tezcür argues
that this was at the expense of traditional Shi'ite theology and
institutions such as the Assembly of Experts (majlis e khobregan) as
the body to elect the non-accountable *faqih*, the Majlis (majlis e
shura e eslami), the lower house of the Iranian legislature, the
Guardian Council (shura ye neghaban) that ensures compatibility
of the legislation with Islam and the constitution, and the
Expediency Council (majma e tashkhis e maslahat e nezam, 1989)

which arbitrates disagreements between parliament and the Guardian Council.[57] All governmental activities are now coordinated by the Supreme National Security Council (*shura-e amniat-e melli*), while the protection of the Iranian Revolution against possible threats is undertaken by the military institution of the IRGC.[58]

In contrast, the Turkish reaction to the changes brought about by this period led to a third coup d'état in September 1980 which aimed to preserve the Kemalist secular foundations and national unity. A powerful ideological wave was sweeping through the region, most strongly expressed in the influence of Turkey's neighbour, the Islamic Republic of Iran, but also in the establishment of Turkey's Islamist Welfare Party (*Refah Partisi*) in 1983, a development that inevitably impacted Turkey's military element. The creation of a controlled Turko-Islamic discourse was established to counterbalance Communist and other leftist trends, seen as possible threats to the enduring Kemalist status quo, which, in fact, continues to influence Turkish state structures still today.

## The National Interest: A generator of stability

From considering the Islamist element of Iran and Turkey as a determinant, the discussion now broadens to examine how both states' foreign policies have affected their orientation. By considering the progress of events, it was deduced that ideology played only a minor role in the formulation of decision-making in both the Ottoman and Safavid Empires, and that this was also the case in Iranian and Turkish foreign policies. In fact, it can be postulated that the articulation of a coherent discourse has been useful as a frame for the legitimisation of foreign policy choices rather than acting as a driver. This has been reflected in a centralised Ottoman bureaucracy that holds a more Westernised stance in opposition to the decentralised structure of its neighbour Iran where the role of the tribes, the *bazaaris* and the religious elites have been much more anarchic and occupied a distinctive and even independent role in domestic politics.

Indeed, as stated by Recep Tayip Erdoğan's chief advisor, Ibrahim Kalin: 'Throughout the 1980s and 1990s, Turkey continued to have good relations with Iran at the high level even after the revolution [regardless] of the wave of Iranian revolution globally. Turkey was naturally influenced but [it] never gained depth in Turkey due probably also to religious differences vis-à-vis the 16th and 17th century Sunni-Shi'a antagonism in the region. [Of course] there were sympathisers even in Turkey [especially] after the revolution. [In that sense] it had an impact [as] there were students, followers, groups [who] may have tilted towards Iran in their political views, but they never became major actors representing Iranian interests.'[59]

In both cases, Iran under the Shah and Turkey under Mustafa Kemal and his successors, as well as historically under the Ottoman Sultans and the Safavid's Shahs, the instrumentalisation of religion for the sake of the Empire's interests has played a critical role in the formulation of its strategy and impacted both leadership decisions and wider policy-making. Ankara's national interest expressed through the preservation of the regional status quo was explicit in Adnan Menderes' overthrow as a representative of Sunni Islam regardless of his party's electoral success.[60] As it will be demonstrated in the next chapters, another instance which has placed Iran in a more favourable position was the Syrian crisis which demonstrated the need for a carefully maintained balance of power alongside the prioritisation of national security. This Iranian foreign policy principle, which still persists today, was also evident during the alliance between the Shah and the US.[61]

The Shah's 'assertion of dominance and power in the Persian Gulf and the Strait of Hormuz as the principal outlet for Iran's oil and gas exports' as well as Iran's approach to Israel 'for modification of a surface to surface missile' in return for oil concessions in 1977 after Carter refused to prioritise such practical needs are further evidence of Iran's pragmatism to act decisively in its own interests.[62] Iran's rapprochement with the US after 30 years of Cold War tensions was reflected in a change of Iranian foreign policy towards a *détente* aimed to reduce friction between Iran, the West and regional states (such as Saudi Arabia). This too can be seen in the light of favouring Iranian national interest.[63]

## Laicism versus Islamism

It has been observed that it is not just the ideological factors per se that have driven the policies of Turkey and Iran, but the different structures and their related components. The anarchical structure of the Safavid Empire in contrast to a centralised Ottoman bureaucracy was inherited by the Shah. Even during the Constitutional Revolution and subsequent parliamentary periods it was primarily the strength of the religious opposition that led to the formation of Iran's radical structure, especially from the Iranian Revolution (1979) onwards as the next chapter will demonstrate.

In contrast, Turkey's role as a generator of stability (at least until the eruption of the Syrian crisis) was evident throughout the period examined in this chapter, while the state's formation on a Western type of democracy from the 1950s onwards ushered in the multi-party system which was completely different from 'Iran's *sui generis* democracy as an actor [which]works better during times of instability.'[64] Turkey's regional alliances (i.e., Israel and other Arab states) during this period, at least until the outbreak of the Arab Uprisings, cemented the Shah's dominance in the region as a close US ally. However, these different structures have always been, as Osman Korutürk[65] asserts, in essence 'the one completing the other', and this may explain how they have managed to co-exist for 360 years in a relatively stable relationship. Alternatively, this could also be explained by their shared governing principles of prioritising the national interest, maintaining the regional balance of power, and the need for security, especially in the period under the Shah. In this context, both Kemalist Turkey and the Shah's Iran have performed a valuable role, acting like '... bridges in the region as the two main pillars of the regional stability' under the auspices of Western forces.[66]

However, the structural difference between the two is evident in the Turkish bureaucracy's control over the army and the *ulama*, while Khomeini's successful revolution was to some degree related to his ability to control the state's army via the establishment of the Revolutionary Guards. Pragmatism has thus been the main characteristic of Iranian foreign policy, as Osman Korutürk asserts: 'Iran seeks for strength, not for leadership. Once they [Iran] are strong, they can lead the region. They know it.'[67]

## *Hegemony versus dominance*

How foreign policy principles affect the formulation of the Middle
Eastern foreign policies of Iran and Turkey becomes clear when
considering their different approaches, i.e., that 'Iran in principle is
against hegemony ... [but] agrees [any state] may have interests in the
Middle East but not hegemony'[68] while Turkey 'is seeking for
leadership' in the same vein as the Ottoman Sultans.[69] Taking a
historical perspective, it can even be said that Sultan Selim's III claim
for the title of Emperor of the World and the Safavid's struggle for
domination clarifies these two different foreign policy outlooks.
More recently, the 'soft power' principle in regard to cultural and
economic regional expansion adopted by former Turkish PM Ahmet
Davutoğlu as opposed to the new scope of the détente policy adopted
by Iranian foreign policy is another example.

In the following chapters, other key determinants that have
played a part in moulding foreign policy attitudes along the lines of
the Iranian and Turkish paradigms and their impact on the region of
the Middle East will be further analysed.

CONCLUSION

This chapter constitutes the historical foundation on which the
analysis of the following chapters will be constructed. By revisiting
the background as well as looking at the grassroots developments that
took place during these early stages, a framework has been built that
serves to explain and differentiate the contrasting structures of the
Iranian and Turkish political systems. Although, inevitably, they
have been shaped by global events leading to changes such as policies
of reforms in line with adoption of European and Western modes of
governance or in the Cold War period regional developments leading
to internal changes, it appears that domestic crises have also played
a key role in determining events. In both the Safavid and Ottoman
Empires these were not successfully addressed initially, whereas later
on the role of Iran in politics was able to exert more leverage precisely
as Ankara was too absorbed in its own internal tensions to act to
retain and increase its previous influence. Iran's oil-rich resources are
a compelling determinant as they have instigated external

interference, and this has been a dominant shaping factor in Iran and other powers' policies, both in a regional and an international context.

The role of agents did not appear to have a similar effect on the two powers. Whereas the role of the *ulama* or the army might have been instrumental in the continuation of Turkey's structures following the dissolution of the Ottoman Empire, this was not the case with Iran as its *ulama* were anti-systemic and revolutionary in their outlook. Iran's army was also not incorporated into the political structure and thus was not under the absolute control of the leader. As the following chapters will reveal, it is the structural changes that have had a much greater influence on Iran's foreign policies than its relations with Turkey which have been a comparatively minor factor.

The role of the Kurds as an emerging factor for Turkish and Iranian politics can also be found in its infancy in these early stages, just as, more recently, Hizbullah has grown to become a considerable force in regional politics. The analysis also demonstrated that the active and important role of the Kurds of Iraq and their influence on Tehran contrasts strongly with the thus far much more controlled Kurds of Turkey. The role of the leadership in this instance must not be underestimated. However it has a bearing on the relative passivity of Turkey's Kurdish movement which lacked proper organisation until the 1980s, compared to the more dynamic Kurds in Iraq, who were led by the revolutionary Mullah Mustafa Barzani as their figurehead.

The chapter also clarified that ideas and state entities can shape domestic structures to the same extent as the external influence of non-state actors and structures on foreign policy practices. Yet it still seems that the role of structures, whether internal or external, appears to be more powerful than ideas alone, just as the interactions between state and non-state entities have been. The structural role of the army was crucial for the continuation of the Turkish regime, while in Iran the independence of the clergy led to the creation of their own Islamic revolutionary guard corps enabling Basij (سازمان بسیج مستضعفین, The Organisation for Mobilisation of the Oppressed) and the paramilitary forces to act as guardians of the revolution. This would indicate that foreign policy formulation is a combination of differing factors on the domestic, regional, transnational, or international level in any micro or macro analysis. Therefore, in the chapters that follow the text will further examine the role of structures and agents in the formulation of foreign policy decisions, and present a theoretical framework that will elevate the significance of interactions between state and non-state actors in international relations as a compelling alternative to the existing paradigms.

CHAPTER 3

# Turkey–Iran Relations during the Cold War

*The Iranian Revolution had turned the balance of forces in the Middle East 'upside down'.[1]*

Yasser Arafat

## INTRODUCTION

This chapter analyses structural factors and agents as dynamics that have affected Turkish–Iranian relations and their impact on the region within the framework of the Cold War period. The outbreak of the Cold War was itself a determining factor since it signalled a new era of change for regional politics along with intensified levels of external interference, e.g., the US foreign policy of protecting the region from any potential Soviet geostrategic encirclement had been a constant factor since the Vietnam War. US defeat in that war and Johnson's resignation were followed by the electoral victory of Richard Nixon (1969–1974). The international intervention can be traced back to the beginning of this period as a key factor influencing regional foreign policies, following the division of the Middle Eastern region into two camps in earlier decades. Division is also a very real threat today because of growing sectarianism and, specifically, the Sunni–Shi'a divide, an issue that has become increasingly notable in the wake of the Arab uprisings.

As a critical and momentous development, the Cold War undoubtedly helped form the foreign policies of both Turkey and Iran, and reached its peak with the Iranian Revolution (1 April 1979) and the establishment of a theocratic regime in Iran – an Islamic Republic – by Ayatollah Ruhollah Khomeini who became the state's Supreme Leader. This represented a political reorientation as Iran switched from being a key ally of the US to a new position as one of its most fervent adversaries. It also embraced the influential Islamic ideology of Shi'ism, which Iran permeated with its own interpretation following the Safavid tradition, to create a new national dimension of Islam.[2] The impact of the role of the leadership on politics was evidenced by Iran's withdrawal from CENTO (13 March, 1979) and its support for the Palestinian cause. Khomeini's appealing ideology and his anti-imperialist policies were flooded with anti-Zionist elements that regarded Israel 'as the enemy of humanity throughout the world',[3] while anybody who opposed the revolution was also viewed as hostile to Iran.[4] For Turkey, the Iranian Revolution helped to restore its relations with the West, which had suffered from the impact of the 1974 coup d'état in Cyprus and the following US embargo on arms sales to Turkey, incited by US fear of Soviet penetration in the region vis-à-vis the 1972 Iraqi–Soviet Treaty of Friendship and Cooperation and the 1972 Turkish–USSR Declaration of Principles of Good Neighbourhood. Turkey's permission for the transfer of Soviet arms to both Syria and Iraq in 1970 along with Soviet equipment to the Arabs in the 1973 Arab–Israeli War (Yom Kippur War) was further facilitated by the 1972 Declaration of Principles of Good Neighbourhood which lasted until the dissolution of the Soviet Union and, like the 1925 Non-Aggression Pact, which had been renewed for another 10 years on 7 November 1935, encouraged Turkish–Soviet rapprochement.

In this unique environment the Kurdish issue emerged as a critical factor for the formulation of Turkish and Iranian foreign policies, firstly in Iraq, then in Iran where its involvement was increasingly important, and later on in Turkey. The Cold War as a dominant (external structural) determinant explains Soviet pressure on Saddam Hussein to bring Kurds and local Communists into the National Progressive Front (NPF) government with the Ba'ath Party

(18 May 1972) as a condition of the Iraqi–Soviet treaty, another rationale that helps to explain the shift in US foreign policy strategy to ally itself with the Kurds.[5] It was in this setting, and because of Iranian concerns over the Kurdish leadership's negotiations with the Iraqi regime headed up by Mullah Mustafa Barzani vis-à-vis the 1970 Manifesto, that Idris Barzani was invited to Tehran to meet the Chief of Şavak (*Sazeman-e Ettela'at va Amniyat-e Keshvar*, Organisation of Intelligence and National Security) and Israeli representatives. In February 1970, Iranian and Israeli assistance to Barzani amounted to 1,200,000 Iraqi dinars.[6] Undoubtedly, on their side, the Kurds also viewed the need to get some sort of an interactive relation with the US administration as a high priority because the USSR sided with Saddam.[7] This was confirmed in an interview given by Mohsin Dizayee where he stated that in the 1970s the Kurds were in need of US support to counterbalance the USSR–Iraqi alliance.[8]

The outbreak of the Iranian Revolution (1979–1988) was the historic impetus for change in Middle Eastern politics. During the period under examination, it marked a shift for Iran from a pro-Western and secular approach to an Islamic perception of world politics which, combined with the Lebanese Civil War (1975–1989) gradually evolved over three different and distinct phases, still shape and influence Iran's foreign policy discourse today.[9]

The Iranian Revolution was important because it brought about direct Iranian involvement in regional affairs and signalled the onset of a radical foreign policy. The shift was significant as it made the transition from a policy that was heavily dependent on foreign powers towards one with a more 'non-aligned' outlook as reflected in its 'Neither East Nor West' foreign policy principle. Former Foreign Minister Ali Akbar Velayati's interpretation of this in 1986 was that '... having relations with countries is different from accepting their hegemony'.[10]

This period also highlighted the importance of Iraq and Syria as formative factors in Middle Eastern politics, especially in the aftermath of Saddam's invasion of Iran (22 September 1980 – August, 1988), and through Damascus's direct involvement during the first phase of the Lebanese Civil War (1975–1977) and the stationing of Syrian troops in Lebanon from 1976 to 2005 in fulfilment of the Taif Agreement (22 October, 1989, National Reconciliation Accord, اتفاقية الطائف).

The Nixon Doctrine had already resolved that if Iran failed to facilitate US interests in the area, its place would be taken by Saddam's Iraq.[11] Therefore, it is important to analyse how Iraq's role as a determinant before and after the Gulf War influenced Iranian–Turkish relations, while it should also be noted that Gulf War I as a historic episode marked the first significant confrontation to result in regional repercussions involving the triangular US–Iranian–Iraqi relations. Yet, perhaps surprisingly, its impact as a dynamic did not create much of a stir in the mutual relations between Tehran and Ankara. In contrast, Iraq's geo-strategic positioning and economic importance is strongly linked to the Kurdish factor which has become an intrinsic component of its political process. As a result, the Kurdish role in relation to Iraq's federal status has grown increasingly strong right up to the present day, while it has also historically been a fundamental foreign policy component in the formulation of regional foreign policies. Hence, it cannot be disassociated from the Iraqi factor.

The Islamic Revolution in Iran therefore marked a shift in regional politics as Hosseini expressed: 'Iranian foreign policy is based on its Constitution (14 June 1979) which arises out of the regulations of and belief in Islam'.[12] This change radicalised Iranian foreign policy and caused it to turn away from Western values. Its transformed political outlook was expressed through a variety of new or strengthened interrelations. Such examples constitute the Islamic Republic's strong ties with Syria as the only Arab country to support Iran when the US imposed sanctions during Gulf War I. Also with regional non-state actors, including the Kurdish movements, especially those of Iraq and Turkey, which played a role in the formulation of both Iranian and Turkish foreign policies, and finally with the Lebanese Shi'a group Hizbullah, which would later join with Iran and Syria to form the Resistance Axis. An open letter from Hizbullah to the oppressed in Lebanon and the World, assigns the leadership role to Iran.[13] Tehran's involvement with the Kurds under the Shah would also intensify as this chapter will later explain, while Tehran allowed the PKK movement to establish camps close to the Iranian border.

Iran's strategic relations with Syria actually date back to the beginning of Gulf War I when, on 23 January 1983: 'Syrian, Libyan and Iranian ministers pledged support for efforts to support Iran against hostile forces'.[14] Meanwhile, since 1979 Iran and Libya had 'increased their oil prices by more than 10 per cent, breaching the ceiling set by the Organisation of Petroleum Exporting Countries'.[15] At a meeting with Iranian officials in Damascus, Syrian President Hafez Al Assad stated that: 'Syria's ties with Iran were "strategic" and would be maintained in the interest of both countries, despite reports of an impending Syrian–Iraqi rapprochement.'[16]

Indeed, the explicit short-term objectives of Iran's current regional foreign policy were designed to counterbalance Iraqi influence in the region, and maintain its alliance with Syria. Syria was not only important to Iran as its sole Arab state ally during Gulf War I, but also as an avowed enemy of Israel. Syria's firm support has made the Hizbullah movement, geopolitically-speaking, Iran's proxy in Lebanon while also acting as a channel for Iran to Hizbullah. Thus, if the Syrian regime were to collapse, it would signal the end of Iran's ability to exert influence in Lebanon, whilst Hizbullah's aid in achieving Iran's aims through Syria would also possibly stop, not to mention the challenge to Iran's regional policy of de-legitimisation as far as its political opposition to Israel is concerned.[17] Another factor is that Iran still regards Iraq as its natural sphere of influence vis-à-vis the large Shi'ite majority in its population through which it might establish its vision of a 'Shi'ite Crescent'.

Turkey, another multi-ethnic mix, also recognised the new Iranian regime (14 February 1979). Yet this change in Iran's domestic politics had no major impact on Turkish foreign policy towards Iran. Turkish-Iranian economic relations continued in the relatively uninterrupted pattern it has always followed and which still continues today, in spite of US pressures to impose further sanctions on Iran. This continuation can be illustrated by contemporary examples, such as Turkey's policy of the 'gold-for-gas trade with Iran', where Dubai paid Iran 'for its energy imports with Turkish lira' and the Iranians then 'used those lira, held in Halkbank accounts, to buy gold in Turkey' while 'carrying bullion worth millions of dollars to Dubai, where it can be sold for foreign currency or shipped to Iran'. Similarly, 'gold exports to Iran rose to $6.5 billion in 2012, more than ten times the level of 2011'.[18] Thus, it can be seen throughout this period that Iran's relations with Ankara and also within regional and international politics was much more interactive than the rectilinear and Western-oriented Turkish foreign policy, especially as it had become increasingly absorbed in its own domestic problems.

Finally, this chapter examines how Turkish–Iranian relations were formed during the period of the Cold War, particularly between 1970 and 1989, while also analysing the factors that caused these changes, along with their impact on the broader region.

## THE IRANIAN REVOLUTION AND ITS IMPACT ON THE COLD WAR

The second half of the 1970s is identified by a series of landmark developments that had a tremendous impact on the region as far as Iranian–Turkish relations were concerned. Illustrative cases include the reorientation of US foreign policy based on Nixon's 'Twin Pillars' doctrine (1972) which was followed by a third phase in the militarisation of US foreign policy initiated in response to the outbreak of the Iranian Revolution (1 April 1979) and the rise of Khomeini in Iran (1979) together with the Iran hostage crisis (4 November 1979) which was brought to an end by the Algiers Accords (19 January 1981). The Iran–Iraq War (1980–1988),[19] as an outcome also of Iranian radical policies vis-à-vis the hostage crisis, started in the early 1980s, while over almost the same period the Soviet War erupted in Afghanistan (December 1979–February 1989) between the Soviet-led Afghan forces and the multi-national insurgent group, the Mujahideen.

Nixon's 'Twin Pillars' policy of 1972 constituted a security strategy, explicitly employing specific regional states and non-state players as its satellites to preserve the international and regional status quo. US aid to Iran and Saudi Arabia in exchange for preserving the stability of the Gulf can be seen in this context, demonstrated by the Shah buying US $20 billion worth of arms while from 1972 to 1975 the US also tried to block the Soviets in order to reinforce its authority in Iran.[20] This rational policy, which revolved around the careful balance of power, was now replaced by the US foreign policy of 'containment' of both Iran and Iraq following on from the policy of appeasement carried out during Carter's term of office which relied on improved relations with the USSR and less reliance on regional powers. This meant that Iraq was now perceived as the first line of defence against Iranian expansionism.[21] 'Containment' would prove to be one of the most important directions taken by the US government and continues to be the main thrust behind US foreign policy today.

Fearing Iranian domination in the Gulf, the US had to confront both the rise of Khomeini in Iran in 1979 and the Soviet invasion of Afghanistan in December of the same year. The militarisation of US foreign policy duly increased with President Jimmy Carter (1976–1980) assisting 'anticommunist counter-insurgencies', arming 'the opposition group of *Mujahideen* in Afghanistan' and later on supporting 'the Contras in Nicaragua and the anticommunists in Ethiopia and Angola'.[22] The area was seen as vital for US interests as US Secretary of Energy, Donald Hodel (1982–1985) pointed out: 'The Persian Gulf is of great importance to the global strategic balance and to our national interests.'[23] The establishment of strategic bases in Egypt, Somalia (Berbera), Kenya (Mombasa), Oman (El-Messira, Seeb) and Israel, and the creation of the 'Rapid Deployment Force' in the Gulf (consisting of 30,000 US troops) were also indicative of Carter's foreign policy objectives which aimed to put countermeasures in place to halt or at least hinder Iran's rise in power.

The Shah's fall as one of US foreign policy's pillars refocused Washington's attention on Ankara because it feared that if a void was left on the South border of the USSR vis-à-vis the oil-rich Gulf region, a revolutionary Iran might seize the opportunity to fill it. Even though the United States – in order to rid the Middle East of the aggressive regimes of Khomeini and Saddam Hussein – hoped that Iran and Iraq would wear each other out in the struggle for power so that both would lose, it still feared that any power vacuum could potentially be exploited by the USSR.[24] The 1980 Defense and Economic Cooperation Agreement (DECA) was a further US attempt to cement its relations with Turkey as a valuable NATO ally against terrorist acts and other regional threats, the most important being Iran, which had ceased its support for the US after the Iranian Revolution. US policy took advantage of the devastating Turkish economic crisis to strengthen the bond between the two states, promising $2.5 billion for five years in exchange for securing US access to intelligence facilities on Turkish soil to replace the ones lost in Iran.[25]

President Carter's State of the Union address (23 January 1980) that 'any attempt by any outside force to gain control of the Persian Gulf region [would] be regarded as an assault on the vital interests of the United States [in the Middle East], and such an assault [would] be repelled by any means necessary'[26] reveals the move away from his former policy of appeasement, whereas the increasing importance of the Middle Eastern region can also be explained, from a geopolitical perspective, by the US pursuit and ultimate success of its goal of achieving the encirclement of the Soviets. US 'containment' of both Communism and Khomeini's Islamism (as another expansionist ideology), with the support of Saddam's Iraq, would continue right up to the eve of Gulf War I, while the Iranian Revolution also acted as a catalyst for increased US effort in the region.[27] In economic terms, the US need for oil, despite its self-sufficiency since the 1950s, was another consideration, reflected in Kissinger's testimonial stating that 'oil imports in 1977 had reached 50 per cent [a greater part of which stemmed from the Middle East]'.[28]

It can therefore be seen, as Reagan's conservative policies would also later reveal, that US sanctions against Iran can be traced back to this period and were primarily imposed because of the hostage crisis rather than the Iranian Revolution. This was also the underlying reason why the restrictions were not removed in spite of the 1981 Algiers Accords. This was illustrated in a statement made by Dr. Ata'ollah Mohajerani:

> The first US sanctions were imposed because of the hostage crisis as, even after the revolution, the Embassy of the US in Iran was still active [whereas] since Autumn 1978 secret contacts between the US administration and the Revolutionaries were taking place.[29]

After November 1979 Carter ordered a freeze on official Iranian bank deposits and other assets in the US estimated at $6 billion,[30] and on 7 April 1980 he also announced a series of sanctions against Iran that included the breaking of diplomatic relations, the invalidation of all visas issued to Iranian citizens for future entry to the US, prohibition of exports from the US to Iran and a formal inventory of Iranian government assets to facilitate processing and paying claims against Iran.[31] However, the impact of the Iranian Revolution on Turkish–Iranian relations was exaggerated. In March, 1982 Turkey, although it was considered a close US ally, 'signed with Iran a $1.8 billion barter agreement [according to which] Turkey would exchange food in return for 60–100,000 b/d of Iran's oil',[32] and Iran agreed to supply Turkey with gas and made an agreement to build a pipeline (10 September 1982).[33] In addition, on 4 December 1986, Turgut Özal firmly denied that there was any surge of Islamic extremism in the country.[34]

Contrary to scholarly claims that perceive the Iranian Revolution[35] as a driver in bilateral relations with Turkey and a shaping factor in their mutual policies towards each other, I argue that the impact of the revolution only appears to have produced short-term repercussions on Iran's relations with Turkey, even when the latter had to deal with the potential threat represented by the Iranian Revolution. The 1980 coup in Turkey was a continuation of the Turkish coups d'état of 1960 and 1971 respectively, and mirrored Turkey's own domestic turbulence and its need for survival in order to confront the leftist and Islamist trends of the 1970s (thereby imitating world politics and the Cold War divisions into Right and Left) in favour of the dominant secular order.[36] At the same time, Ankara would face the issue of the PKK (*Partiya Karkerên Kurdistani*, Kurdistan Workers' Party), established in 1975, which, due to its geographic location and radical ideology, leaned more towards Iran. Iran responded by not only pledging direct support to the PKK, but also acted as a facilitator to channel aid and support from other players to the PKK movement.[37]

The mobilisation of the PKK movement in 1984 quickly gave it a significant role in Turkish politics to such an extent that Ankara's foreign policy agenda started to prioritise the Kurdish issue, thereby increasing the Kurds' importance as a determining factor in shaping the mutual relations of Iran and Turkey. However, Turkish–Iranian relations did not change in any dramatic fashion throughout this period. As analysed earlier in Chapter 1, the consistency in Ankara's foreign policy prior to 1979 and during this period should be ascribed to the dominant role of the army as the safeguard of the state's Kemalist principles:

Globally, of course, there was a revolutionary wave and Turkey was
naturally influenced by it, but it never gained depth. Even in Turkey
there were sympathisers after the revolution who might have tilted
towards Iran in their political views, but they never became major actors
representing Iranian interests.[38]

It is also on this basis that Turkey's various diplomatic crises can be
explained. Thus, whereas in Turkey the 1970s were marked by the rise
of Islamism long before the Islamic Revolution in Iran, the 1973
Turkish elections led to the formation of a coalition government.
This was between the National Salvation Party (*Millî Selâmet Partisi*,
NSP, 1972), the successor of the banned National Order Party
(Millî Nizam Partisi), which was headed up by Necmettin Erbakan
and received around 12 per cent of the popular vote, and Bülent
Ecevit's Republican People's Party (*Cumhuriyet Halk Partisi*, CHP)
which won 33.3 per cent of the popular vote.

During this period when the National Front Government was in
power up until 1978, Turkey improved relations with both the USSR
and the Middle East and advocated a more independent foreign
policy outlook. It embodied elements of Bülent Ecevit's New Security
Concept and aimed to develop good relations with the neighbouring
states and become less reliant on the West, a stance reinforced by the
Cyprus crisis in 1964 and Turkey's military intervention in Cyprus in
1974. Turkish foreign policy's Arab rapprochement should also be
viewed within the context of the increasing rise of the Left and the
Islamic ideology's key role as a dynamic alternative. Bozdağlıoğlu
argues that: 'Turkey played up Islamic identity [also] when the
economic difficulties of the 1970s caused by the oil crisis required
rapprochement with the Middle East.'[39]

The deteriorating relations between Ankara and Washington
were expressed in President Johnson's letter of 1964, which warned
against Turkish involvement and stated that the USA would not aid
Turkey even in the event of a Soviet attack on the country.[40] On
15 May 1978, Ecevit declared that the Soviet Union did not constitute
a threat to Turkey, and thereafter a Soviet–Turkish agreement
(December 1984) for natural gas in return for Turkish goods and
services was drawn up.[41] This was an evident counterbalance policy
following the US Congress arms embargo imposed on Turkey from

February 1975 to September 1978 in response to Turkey's 1974 invasion of Cyprus and which resulted all together in greater Turkish–Soviet cooperation and improved relations with the Arab neighbouring states, while it also explains Turkish efforts to reduce any tensions with Tehran. In June 1979, US Congress also reduced aid to Ankara vis-à-vis Ecevit's rejection of the US demand to allow U-2 spy planes to overfly Soviet territory from Turkish bases in violation of the SALT II arms agreement.[42] As an Islamist, Erbakan was in favour of strengthening relations with the Muslim world through all possible means.

The opening of the PLO offices in Ankara in 1979 should be viewed in a similar context as a furthering of Turkish attempts to build good relations with neighbouring Arab states.[43] It thus seems that Turkey was trying to play the role of mediator in its relations between Arabs and the Israelis, a stance which was increasingly necessary in view of its growing dependence on foreign aid since the early 1950s.[44] Likewise, the 1979 Camp David Accords fostered good relations between Turkey and Israel although the Iranian regime opposed the agreement as it hoped to maximise regional power and exploit any vacuums in the Persian Gulf region. The shifting nature of Ankara's Middle Eastern orientation can therefore also explain the military intervention of the 1980 coup that followed.[45]

At this point, Turkey was combining an Islamist outlook with a Kemalist/secular foreign policy orientation, irrespective of who was in power, although its policies were still strongly influenced by the army which had a predominant role in Turkish politics. As a result, on 24 February 1983, Erbakan is said to have been sentenced to four years' imprisonment, convicted of attempting to establish an Islamic state.[46]

Through events like these the Islamic Revolution, as a form of internal structural change influenced by external developments and, to some extent, by the stalemate between the secular modernising mode of governance and the revolutionary and leftist waves in the region, would leave its own stigma with regard to Turkey. Nonetheless, the continued struggle between domestic secular forces versus leftist trends, which was only occasionally expressed through Islamism, would continue to provide the best explanation for Turkish developments.

However, there certainly seemed to be a strong link between the 1980s coup in Turkey and the revolutionary nature of Iran's new regime after the fall of the Shah, which ignited fears of the potential threat of revolution spreading further into the region. Saddam's invasion of Iran was partly instigated by, among other rationales, Tehran's aspirations for the unification of all the oppressed under its leadership alongside Khomeini's efforts to export the revolution, which to a certain extent was achieved. Khomeini's vision was clear: 'We should try to export our revolution to the world. We should set aside the thought that we do not export our revolution because Islam does not regard various Islamic countries differently and [Islam] is the supporter of all the oppressed peoples of the world.'[47]

The Islamic Republic's tendency to deepen the politics of sectarianism in the region as a prime objective to achieve dominance in the Gulf Region has also been another element of friction. This foreign policy attitude in the aftermath of the Iraq War (March 2003) became even more explicit especially through its support of Shi'ite militias and other revolutionary movements. Iranian involvement in regional politics appears to have ultimately elevated Iran's present-day status. According to former Ambassador Turgut Tülümen, Khomeini was furious with the West for its historical role in breaking the unity of Islam under the Ottomans through the collapse of the Ottoman Empire, insisting that 'this union [had] to be recreated but he did not emphasise who should do it. Since the initiatives for exporting the revolution there is no doubt that what he had in mind was union of all Muslims under the roof of Shi'ism.' As Tülümen noted, there is a strong belief among the Turks that 'the Shiite–Sunnite rivalry is, in reality, an artificial separation for the purpose of undermining, if and when necessary, the powerful Turks on the West'.[48] This same notion of sectarianism has also been highlighted by Iran's Supreme Leader, Ayatollah Khamenei, who expressed his concern that one of the immediate effects of the instability caused by the collapse of the Arab order could be to deepen sectarian divides in the region and escalate existing sectarian conflicts.[49]

Similarly, in August 1981, Prime Minister Hossein Mousavi would confirm that one of the objectives of Iran's foreign policy was 'to carry the message of Islamic revolution to the world' in line with its vision of disseminating the Islamic ideology worldwide.[50] The Iranian Revolution and Khomeini's ascendancy had relatively little effect on Ankara, but it did bring Turkey back to the American fold as far as the broader regional picture was concerned. Iran was not strong enough, militarily or ideologically, to export the revolution in the absence of any political ideology, especially as Iran is Shiite while the majority of the Middle East is Sunni. Moreover, Iran's eight-year war with Iraq had absorbed and exhausted its capabilities to fulfil Khomeini's desires in this respect.[51] However, the Iranian Revolution did constitute a threat to Turkey in the sense that it proved that the masses could overthrow a dictatorial regime and allow the Islamists to take over as was demonstrated in the first period of the Arab Uprisings.

Within Turkey, the emergence of Islamism, as represented by the National Order (Milli Görüş),[52] was to a great extent a response to the threats posed by leftist or communist ideologies, as had been the case in Iran, while opposition to Turkey's increasingly secular authoritarian modernisation was another factor.[53] This position was most obviously expressed through the Turkish–Islamic synthesis where the Turkish nationalism dictating preservation of the state's Kemalist principles combined with Islamic elements. It is said that this synthesis was responsible for the creation of the Fethullah group and other components of it,[54] and it is interesting that even later, under Turgut Özal (1983–1993), Turkey continued to court the Islamic constituency through actions like Özal's pilgrimage to Mecca (July 1988), the recognition of the PLO (January 1975), receptions for Yasser Arafat in November 1979 and March 1986, and Özal's support of legalisation for the wearing of the headscarf by Muslim women in universities.[55]

Özal's liberalism was expressed through an assertive foreign policy along the same line that today's AK Parti has formulated its own foreign policy discourse and practice. According to the *New York Times* (2 March 1980), Turkey and the US signed an agreement that would enable the latter to use 12 bases and installations in Turkey in return for military and economic aid to Turkey.[56] Throughout the 1980s, Turkey's foreign policy context was to a great extent dependent on Özal's activism and focused on liberalisation policies

aimed to break the state's isolation which had been the result of
Erbakan's openness to the Islamic world including rapprochement
with Iran and Libya.[57] Özal himself affirmed on 10 November 1983
that his plan was to emphasise growth and encourage an aggressive
(pro-Western) foreign policy.[58] This was clearly evident in Turkey's
foreign policy towards the Caucasus and the Caspian regions where it
was competing with Iran to try and win influence.

A Cold War attitude continued even into the second half of the
1980s vis-à-vis the Economic Cooperation Protocol (15 December
1986)[59] between the Soviet Union and Iran, while it also affected the
differing ideological perceptions of Left and Right wing parties in
Iranian politics. This was observable in their contrasting attitudes
expressed through a Conservative, 'Right wing' dominated by the
clergy and the Supreme Leader, Khomeini on the one hand, which
regarded itself as an expert on foreign policy issues, while on the
other President Bani Sadr belonged to the Freedom Movement of Iran
(نهضت آزادی ایران, Nehzat-e Azadi-e Iran, FMI, 1961) and represented a
Centre Left type of party which opposed continuing the war with Iraq
from 1982 onwards. This group had split from the National Front of
Iran (جبهه‌ی ملی ایران, Jebhe Melli Irân), a secular Iranian nationalist
movement founded in the 1940s by Mohammad Mosaddegh which
was actually a coalition of parties.

At this point, I want to clarify why the scholarly preoccupation
with the division and strict classification of the Iranian political
parties has to be set to one side as these considerations are of little
importance for regional politics, especially as far as the foreign policy
and the role of the *faqih* during this period is concerned.

The problem with this rigid academic approach is that differing
views could emerge even within the same factions, so that dividing
lines laid down between religious-nationalists (*milli mazhabi*),
reformists (*islahtalabi*) and religious-revolutionaries (*mazhabi*) became
blurred, as is still the case today, making it impossible to lay down
arbitrary divisions. The same caveat holds true for Turkey where there
also were and are both secular and Islamist Nationalists and Liberals.[60]

Similarly, the National Front in Iran was an assortment of
ideological fluctuations since it consisted of Liberals (Iran Party,
1946), Socialists (the Toilers Party of the Iranian Nation), Islamic

Liberals (the *Mojâhedine Eslâm*) and the Tehran Association of Bazaar Trade and Craft Guilds. In the same way, the Second National Front in the 1960s, a more religious and radical group led by figures such as Dariush Forouhar, held a different position from the Third National Front which consisted of religious-Nationalists (*milli mazhabis*) and *mazhabis* (the FMI), the Iran Nation Party (*Hezb-e Mellat-e Iran*), and the Society of Iranian Socialists led by Khalil Maleki who had not been part of the Second National Front owing to his involvement in the Tudeh Party.

The Communists were represented throughout the 1950s by the Tudeh Party of Iran, the Organisation of Iranian People's Fadaian majority (*Fedayan-e Khalq*), initially a guerrilla movement that in the 1970s advocated the overthrow of the Islamic regime in Iran, and the Communist Party of Iran of which Ebrahim Alizadeh was one of the founders, a particularly influential organisation in the 1980s. The Nationalists in Iran belonged to the National Resistance Movement of Iran founded by Shapour Bakhtiar, while Abdul Rahman Ghassemlou led the Democratic Party of Iranian Kurdistan (DPIK) and the Party of the Iranian Nation (PIN) was headed up by Dariush and Parvaneh Forouhar. We could also argue that the Freedom Movement – a Liberal Islamist movement – has found a natural successor in the more recent Green Movement founded in 2009 as both represent umbrella-type organisations that have gathered Liberals, Islamists, Nationalists, and even (later on) Reformists.[61]

It is this factionalism in addition to the constant movement of political candidates from one party to another that makes any scholarly attempt to present a concrete and well-ordered categoris-ation of Iranian political parties so difficult, especially as it seems that a lack of institutionalisation is something that the leadership in Iran actively encourages.[62] Daryaee argues that competition has existed even within the same factions; for example, the Marxist Left, the pro-Soviet Tudeh Party, the Islamic anti-clerical Left, and the other regional ethnic groups.[63] Likewise, ideological variety from liberal to radical exists even in the same party of Conservatives or within the clergy and the liberal-radical Islamists, or later on the Reformists to the extent of partition which helps to explain the loose cut of Iran's political system. This factionalism and ideological fluctuation that

demonstrate the inevitability of change in Iranian politics has been
so intense that the Supreme Leader, Ayatollah Khamenei (3 June
1989), divides threats into two broad categories; those emanating
from within the ranks of the revolutionaries and those planned by
external enemies.[64]

The political controversy that had existed in the 1980s between the
Conservative and (Islamist) Liberal camps as two opposing poles of
friction was now succeeded by a conflict between the Conservative
camp represented by Khamenei 'who was talking about a Cultural War'
and the more Reformist Akbar Hashemi Rafsanjani (1989–1997) who
supported Ali Hosseini Khamenei (4 June 1989) as Supreme Leader
despite his religious credentials. Although he did advocate rapprochement with the Arab states, he also wished to work towards improved
relations with the West and the European Union, refused Khomeini's
fatwa against the British author Salman Rushdie and was in favour
of a deal to end the economic sanctions in Iran which had been
imposed because of the perceived threat of its nuclear programme.
In the same context, it would not be practical to try and impose a rigid
scholarly focus on, for example, Rafsanjani's ideological orientation
as he was affiliated with both the Combatant Clergy Association
(جامعه روحانیت مبارز, 1977) and the Executives of Construction Party
(*Hezb-e Kaargozaaraan-e Saazandegi*, حزب کارگزاران سازندگی).

The same conflict that later on caused friction between the two
main parties within the Iranian political system, i.e., between the
Conservative and Reformist camps, was still observable even under
Mohammad Khatami's Presidency (2 August 1997 to 3 August 2005)
until the hardliners succeeded Reformists in the contest for power
against the Conservatives with the election of Mahmoud Ahmadinejad (2005–2013). More recently, the balance of power has shifted
back to its former parameters once more, i.e., between the Reformist
camp under Hassan Rouhani (3 August 2013) and the Conservatives
and this is still ongoing. Recent attacks and disruption of a number of
speeches and gatherings by Reformist groups in Iran in the lead up to
the 2016 parliamentary and Assembly of Experts elections are
indicative of this persistent tension over power dominance.[65]

Today, the nuclear issue offers a useful paradigm that demonstrates how existing views are split among the Conservative

establishment so that hardliners, although affiliated with a specific circle within the security regime, will sometimes hold views that clash with the official stance of the Iranian Revolutionary Guard Corps (IRGC), a staunch alliance to the Supreme Leader.[66] However, even apart from the leadership, influential decisions are increasingly being made among certain circles within the Conservative alliance in combination with the policies of the security and intelligence services.[67] The factional conflict of this period between the government and the state – a duality of power – and also with its militant clerical organisations, continues today in ongoing arguments between government and the army, supported by the state with the Supreme Leader at its head.

Iran's lack of institutionalisation and weak state-society ties, as analysed in Chapter 2, form a complete contrast to the Turkish military civil bureaucracy which is rooted in the Ottoman system of power transmitted via a centralised authority. These two widely different political modes of governance constitute the structural parameters that would continue to influence the period under examination.[68] As argued earlier, the rise of the revolutionary element that forms Iranian politics today is linked to Iran's social transformation throughout the 1960s and the societal reaction it provoked in the second half of the 1970s incited by religious Shi'a segments of the society.

To explain the persisting factionalism in Iranian politics in its simplest terms, one need look no further than the clash of Right and Left wing ideologues, with Iran tradition represented by the Conservatives and its historically based societal structure as analysed in Chapter 2. Likewise, the Shah's failure to recognise the importance of the financial and organisational autonomy of the *bazaaris* (the merchants and artisans located inside the *bazaars*), as a vital societal stratum, was a key factor in the mobilisation of the opposition which found its legitimisation in Islam. Thus, when the Shah attempted to exert control over the *bazaars* and tried to eliminate their independence and privileges in the 1970s, it led to the initiation of the Revolution. More than 30 per cent of all imports were destined for the *bazaars*, and the 500,000 or so *bazaaris*, controlled Iran's non-hydrocarbon exports (such as carpets and dried fruits) through which they maintained their economic power. The *bazaaris* also had close links to the clergy to such an extent that prosperity of the *bazaar* also meant prosperity for the religious establishments and, as creators of charity organisations, Islamic banks, health clinics, and religious schools, they often paid the salaries of the workers and civil servants.[69] Thus, the rationale upon which the Revolution was built is easily comprehended, although societal dissatisfaction in Iran and the repercussions of the Revolution also had an international dimension.

The situation in the aftermath of the Revolution (1979–1982) was particularly complicated as 'the situation of the Revolution in Iran meant it was not ready to fight Iraq'[70] as all the parties involved were competing to maximise their power through the use of force. However, although there were Marxist groups, liberal Islamists and Nationalist Movements (The People's Mojahedin of Iran, Mojahedin-e-Khalq, 1965), the Conservatives were still the main decision-makers in Iran, especially in the aftermath of June 1981 when the clergy-dominated faction supported by Khomeini prevailed over the Islamic Liberals and other mujahidin and radical forces in Iran.[71] Khomeini's dismissal of Bani-Sadr as President also marked the end of the Mojahedin-e-Khalq in Iranian politics who 'found safe haven in the Kurdistan Region [while] most Marxists fled to the Soviet Union'.[72]

The beginning of the Revolution paved the way so that throughout the 1980s, and in spite of the presence of Liberal-Radical Islamist factions in Iranian politics who stood against Khomeini along with the Nationalist movement, the majority of parliament were followers of the 'Conservative line', or, more accurately, the Imam as Dr. Ata'ollah Mohajerani explained: 'The majority of parliament, the media, the ayatollahs, and the Expediency Council along with the Revolutionary guards (basij, سازمان بسیج مستضعفین, The Organisation for Mobilisation of the Oppressed)' were supporters of Khomeini.[73]

It is thus understood that Islamic values – as another ideational factor dictating Iran's foreign policy principles – would determine the parameters of its political discourse and, consequently, its relations with Turkey as the previous chapter also showed. Yet foreign policy practice remains primarily pragmatic and firmly entrenched in the realm of *realpolitik*. A year before his death, Ayatollah Khomeini declared that 'state interests [*maslahat*] have priority over sharia and the religious law is applied in cases of conflict between them'.[74] This means that any division of Iranian–Turkish relations into set periods,[75] or any attempted categorisation of the various political trends based on the intense factionalism in Iranian politics would appear complicated.[76] Initially, it seems possible to argue that there are obvious divisions, starting with three (conservatives, pragmatists, and radicals), succeeded by two (pragmatist/Reformist wing versus the Conservatives-ideological purists identified by the Supreme Leader), but such a categorisation of the Iranian political elites in the post-Cold War era is quite risky considering, firstly, that change is inherent in Iranian politics which periodically seems to alter course into different kind of trends, and, secondly, that divisions and dichotomies also often emerge even within these same factions.[77]

The fact thus that Iranian foreign policy per se can be identified as an assemblage of different shades of political views, either idealist and realist elements or a Reformist and more moderate leaning[78] helps to explain why each camp seems to be driven by a need to pursue both approaches, and often seems to swing from one end of the spectrum to the other.

The Soviet–Afghan War (1979–1989) should be perceived in a similar context of realism, and this has been also responsible for Tehran's policy of helping Shi'a rebels to fight the Soviets so that the establishment of a regime hostile to Iran is avoided.[79] On 10 November 1982 the Iranian Deputy Foreign Minister, Ahmad Azizi, 'announced a proposal to end the Soviet occupation of Afghanistan which included the replacement of Soviet forces with an Islamic peace-keeping force'.[80]

The Soviet–Afghan War and its developments not only alerted Iran, causing its Ayatollah, Khomeini, to condemn the Soviet intervention and pledge 'unconditional support' for Muslim insurgents in Afghanistan, but also the US and Turkey.[81] The Turkish reaction to the Soviet War in Afghanistan brought Ankara closer to the American bandwagon through a Defense Cooperation Agreement that would regulate the status of US installations in Turkey and define the scope of US military aid to Turkey.[82] This period is of considerable importance, as US National Security Advisor Zbigniew Brzezinski would state in March 1980, that the hostage crisis and the Afghanistan problem were among the rationales that made US relations with Iraq imperative.[83]

## NON-STATE ACTORS AS FACILITATOR OF STATE FOREIGN POLICY

It is clear from Chapter 2 that foreign policy principles have affected Iranian and Turkish behaviour, and that this has also been shaped by the role of the leadership. Apart from the role of internal and external structural factors in the formulation of foreign policy, which is considerable, the impact of state foreign policies upon non-state entities and vice-versa, or interactions between state and non-state actors as the facilitators of regional (and international) politics, would appear to play a steadily growing role in its effective application.

### The role of Hizbullah and the PKK factor

Ali Akbar Velayati, speaking from his position as Special Advisor for International Affairs to the Leader of Iran, Ayatollah Sayyed Ali Khamenei, emphasised Syria's key role in the region in resistance against crimes perpetrated by Israel. Certainly, if Syria had not supported Hizbullah logistically, Hizbullah and Hamas would not have won the 33-day war (Lebanon War, 2006) and the 22-day war (The Gaza War, 2008–2009) against Israeli assault. Mahmoud Othman reinforces this view, arguing that Hizbullah is important in two ways: providing support to Al Assad's regime and acting as a deterrent to the threat of Israel.[84] Velayati's statement thus underlines Syria's significance as a critical factor and a key player at the centre of the Middle Eastern region as will be demonstrated in Chapter 6.[85] Had it not been for Hizbullah, the role of Iran in Lebanon would also have been far more restricted.

The Shi'ite community in Lebanon was politically active through the Amal Party, but the aftermath of Israel's 1978 invasion of Southern Lebanon, which aimed to remove the PLO forces north of the Litani River, fuelled the rise of Hizbullah, a radical resistance movement that gradually transformed into a professional guerrilla force and a political party. According to Baer, historical ties between Iran and Lebanon's Shi'a groups can be traced back to the Safavids (1501) when envoys were sent to Lebanon 'to recruit Shi'a clerics to teach Iranians the tenets of their sect'.[86] Norton also notes that: 'Most of its leaders were trained in Najaf and Karbala in Iraq under the watchful eye of Iran's ambassador to Syria, Ali Akbar Mohtashemi.'[87]

Even though Hizbullah per se has not been an immense influential factor in Turkish–Iranian relations, it has played a significant part in facilitating Iran's foreign policy as well as promoting the Axis of Resistance, which started in 1985 with its alliance with Syria and Iran against Iraq, which would increasingly have a major impact on current Middle Eastern affairs. Hizbullah's 'hostages' policy' in Lebanon following the hijacking of TWA Flight 847 in June 1985 in return for US weapons for Iran, and its attacks against the US Embassy in Beirut (April 1983) after its intervention in South Lebanon (August 1982), which resulted in the withdrawal of the US in February 1984, can both be viewed within the context of the movement's alliance with Iran in resisting both the US and Israel, and are also significant examples of the promotion of a radical and destabilising foreign policy.[88] At the same time, as far as the organisation of the Axis of Resistance is concerned, instances such as the 1987 conference on liberation movements and Hizbullah groups at Tehran University, which also included representatives from Iraqi opposition parties, the Kuwaiti and Lebanese Hizbullah and the Bahrain Liberation movement, further indicate Iran's strategic orientation.[89]

Iran's provision of a safe haven for the PKK was linked to Tehran's perception of it as 'a resistance movement in Turkey fighting for independence',[90] and scholarly claims have indicated that the funding and arming of the PKK was provided by the Revolutionary Guards.[91] Turkey's Prime Minister, Bülent Ecevit, also accused Iran of '... supporting the PKK vis-à-vis the hosting of PKK's sixth annual congress in Urmiya, February 1999 [and] Iran's intelligence cooperation with PKK against Turkey'.[92] All of these are telling incidents with regard to the key role played by the PKK which later chapters will discuss in more detail. In this context, Reza Altun, co-founder of PKK and Executive Council Member of KCK, explained

PKK's alliance with Iran as tactical. On the one hand, Iran wanted to control PKK and use the alliance to exert pressure and push its policies forwards, while, on the other, PKK wanted support in its struggles against Turkey, and therefore needed to establish political relations with different regional states, and Iran was one of the most important of these in terms of influence.[93]

Through interactions like this, it is clear that Iran's alliance with non-state actors has been an intrinsic as well as a consistent feature of the regional policy promoted by Tehran, especially during periods of stability. Indicative examples include the Shah's policies during the 1970s in favour of Iraq's Kurds, the Hizbullah movement in Lebanon, the establishment during Gulf War I of the Supreme Council for the Islamic Revolution in Iraq, known as the Islamic Supreme Council of Iraq, and the support of existing groups such as the Dawa Party (Party of the Islamic Call, حزب الدعوة الإسلاميه) and its militias, the Badr Brigades (the Badr Organisation, منظمة بدر), especially in the aftermath of the Iraqi War (March 2003).

### The Kurds of Iraq: A key determinant

Both the Kurds and Iraq have been important factors in shaping Turkish–Iranian relations, the seeds of which can be found in this period as the following chapters will show. Massoud Barzani, former President of the Kurdistan Region (KR), stated:

> The Kurds have been part of this competition and conflict. For us the period following 1979 and the Shah's removal was one of the biggest events in our history. Whoever or whatever was leading to this change, we would support it. This had led to close relations with the Islamic Republic of Iran.[94]

Kurdish cooperation with Iran after the Shah developed in intensity because the Kurds shared a long border with Iran, and thought that the longstanding Kurdish issue could be solved with Iran's cooperation. A well-known Kurdish political figure, Mahmoud Othman presented a succinct overview of the situation:

> We made mistakes in evaluating these contacts, thinking that they would solve the Kurdish issue but the Kurds were wrong. The Kurds overestimated these contacts and they paid the price.[95]

The changes that the Iranian Revolution brought into the region in the 1970s and especially the period following the Algiers Agreement (1975) weakened the Kurdish movement in Iraq, which was really still in its infancy and in the first stages of formation. However, in the following decade of the 1980s, both the Kurdish movements of Iraq and Turkey would significantly grow in influence to become formative agents in Turkish and Iranian foreign policy behaviour. Viewed as agents of instability and change rather than unity, their role as influential dynamics made them an important consideration in the planning of regional strategies that aimed to eliminate the possibility of their internal fragmentation which could otherwise pose a threat to regional stability.

The Kurds per se appear to represent the apple of discord between Tehran and Ankara as they hold out the opportunity of a broader sphere of influence and control. This is more than ever evident today, especially taking into consideration Iraq's Shi'a majority, the oil reserves of the Kurdistan Region in Iraq (KR), the rise of PKK's power in three major areas of Kurdistan, the de facto self-determination of Syria's Kurds, and the Kurdish movement's aspirations for independence, competing for regional dominance.

It is interesting to observe how during the 1970s the US administration contained Iraq in favour of Iran as dictated by Nixon's Twin Pillars doctrine (1969–1974), fearing Saddam's regional domination because of the Iraqi–USSR alliance (1972). Then, from 1984 onwards, the empowering of Iraq received support at Iranian expense (National Security Directive 139, 5 April 1984). It was even reported that 'American intelligence agencies provided Iran and Iraq with deliberately distorted or inaccurate intelligence data [to further] Reagan's administrations goals in the region.'[96]

This was the period during which the second stage of US relations with Iraq's Kurds evolved, starting with simple US–Kurdish contacts in the form of economic aid in the 1960s which would eventually develop into the first covert but official US relations with the Kurds of Iraq (June–July 1972). It was at this historic 1972 meeting arranged by the Shah between Idris Barzani, Mahmoud Othman, Richard Helms, Director of the CIA, and Colonel Richard Kennedy, Deputy Assistant to the President for National Security Council Planning, that the Kurds were finally able to present their case directly to the US government for the first time.[97]

Helms and Kennedy were authorised by Dr Kissinger 'to express the sympathy of the US government for the Kurdish movement under Barzani ... noting that the presence of the Kurdish representatives in his office was proof of our position to consider their requests for assistance'. Helms explicitly expressed his desire:

> To continue the relationship with the Kurdish movement which had been officially initiated; however, US aid to the Kurds would have to be channelled 'either via Iran or Israel'. On their side, the Kurds requested 'autonomy and continuance of direct secret contacts', believing that Kurdistan 'albeit small, could be exploited as an effective tool to reverse Soviet expansion in the area'.[98]

Details of US aid to the Kurds amounting to US$16 million would later be leaked by *Village Voice*, an American magazine, through its publication of the Otis Pike Committee Report (19 February, 1976), entitled 'The Report on the CIA that President Ford Doesn't Want You to Read'.

It is thus evident that the role of the Kurds in Iraq has been instrumental in facilitating Iranian and US foreign policy in the region, with the Kurds seen as 'a useful tool for weakening Iraq's potential for regional adventurism' according to Pike's Report.[99] Although such developments were primarily a by-product of the Cold War and the course of regional events, the Kurdish role in shaping the foreign policies of both the Iranians and the Turks gradually increased, reaching its peak with the strategic importance of Turkish–KRG institutionalised relations since 2008[100] while Iran also views the Kurds as crucial: 'The Kurds of Iraq are the main element of Iran's foreign policy.'[101]

However, the question can arise why the US chose to aid the Kurds in Iraq rather than those in Syria, Iran or Turkey. This is so for a number of reasons. First, as a key actor at the heart of Middle Eastern politics, Iraq was important for international politics in the region as a counter-balance to Iran's Shi'ism and the Soviet Union's communist ideology. Interestingly, the National Oath (28 January 1920) in the last term of the Ottoman Parliament outlined the potential territories that the new Turkish state should include as

Kirkuk, Mosul, Alexandretta (Hatay), Antakya, Kars, Ardahan, Batum and Aleppo with the Aegean Sea described as 'open sea' and provisioned for a referendum in Western Thrace.[102] At the same time, the geostrategic location of the Kurds along the Iranian, Turkish and Syrian borders represents a strategic threat for the regional states that are confronted with the formation of Greater Kurdistan. Historically forming a buffer zone between the Ottomans and Safavids, and now acting as a bridge between them and the Arab world, the Kurds today have seen their role upgraded, especially with the on-going process towards the settlement of Kirkuk's status, and the revival of the Kurdish movement in Syria following the outbreak of the Arab Uprisings. In this context, as explained in Chapter 2, the role of interference, whether in its regional form or as a type of external meddling, has been a critical element of Turkish and Iranian politics dating back to its early history.

Furthermore, inter and intra Kurdish political differences, especially throughout the 1980s in view of the PKK–PUK coalition (1987–1989) against KDP and vice-versa, were used by both Iran and Turkey to serve their interests. Indeed, the Kurdish element has been instrumental in the wider context of Iraq as a driver in the development of Turkish–Iranian relations as well as in the facilitation of their regional policies.

Finally, according to a secret memorandum of the State Department, Iraq itself had been placed right at the top of the US foreign policy agenda since 1946 and was considered a vital foothold in the Middle East to such an extent that US standing in the entire area was dependent on the attitude of Iraq towards the US. Iraq's pivotal geo-strategic and economic importance for America's Middle Eastern policy had also been raised by Kennedy's Ambassador in Iraq as well as the Former Deputy Secretary of Defense, Frank Carlucci.[103] Moreover, according to one Ba'athist official, '... the party had come to power on an American train' after the overthrow of the Hashemite monarchy in Iraq.[104]

As far as Iranian–Turkish relations are concerned, Gulf War I has been a significant historical episode and determinant but, contrary to the dominant arguments in the literature which reference the Gulf War as the key influence, I believe that its effect, though important, is of less significance than generally presented. In this book I attempt to demonstrate that two of the main predominant factors for both Tehran and Ankara were actually Iraq's impact and the Kurdish movement as intrinsic components that cannot be disassociated.

## IRAQ AS FACTOR UNDER THE PRISM OF GULF WAR I

During the 1980s, the Cold War framework was still in evidence and was reflected in the foreign policies of the Iranian and Turkish states. At this point, the role of Iraq as an influential and rising factor in the mutual formulation of Turkish–Iranian relations needs to be discussed in its own right and not within the more frequently referenced determinant of Gulf War I cited by the scholarly literature, since any controversies between the two during this period were related mainly to Iraq and not to the war itself. This was in contrast to events such as Turkey's downgrading in diplomatic relations to second secretary level (2 December, 1980)[105] because of Israel's annexation of Jerusalem. This did not have any dramatic impact on Turkish–Iranian relations, although it should also be noted that Sharon, the Israeli Defence Minister, declared (29 May 1982) that 'Israel's sale of $27 million in weapons to Iran was made with the "full knowledge and agreement" of the US government.'[106]

The 'Irangate' revelation in 25 October 1986 (when Reagan confessed that the US had sold arms to Iran and transferred the money to the Contra guerrilla army fighting the Sandinista of Nicaragua, believed to have been leaked to Lebanese newspapers by Ayatollah Hussein-Ali Montazeri,[107] a candidate for the Supreme Leadership), was the most representative paradigm of how revolutionaries put ideology aside in order to promote their own security and interests. As Parsi explains: 'Iran's rhetoric against Israel did not match its actual policy [as] Iran was secretly dealing with Israel which provided Iran with tires for Phantom fighter planes [and] weapons for the Iranian army', against the context of the state's periphery doctrine.[108] Similarly, the most important of Iran's interests lay in protecting the survival of the Revolution. On the US side, Reagan excused US provision of small shipments of material to Iran as an attempt 'to begin a "new relationship" with Iran'.[109]

Meanwhile, the rise to power of Turgut Özal and his Motherland Party (with a majority of 211 seats in the elections of 8 November 1983) can, like the swift trajectory of the AK Parti, be regarded as a turning point in Turkey's politics (including its Kurdish policies), especially when compared to the policies applied prior to the military junta. Firstly, and contrary to claims generally made in the literature, the role of Iraq in tandem with Gulf War I clearly had a considerable effect on the course of Iranian–Turkish relations.

The war posed a security dilemma for Turkey as, if Iraq lost the war, the power vacuum this created could be exploited by Iran. Therefore, both Iraq and the Gulf were considered important for US economic-strategic policy because of their vital role within the region. This explains US support for Iraq which was viewed as an alternative policy for maintaining the fragile regional status quo owing to Iraq's undisputed status as the arbiter responsible for the pricing and supply of Persian Gulf oil.[110] Therefore, it was the economic benefit to the United States from the oil pipelines (through which two million barrels per day flowed from Iraq through Turkey and Saudi Arabia) that was also considered to be at stake.[111] It is probably for this reason that documents in the National Security Archive at George Washington University record that after 1983 the United States changed the orientation of its foreign policy from the dual containment of both Iran and Iraq to the containment of Iran with Iraq's support.[112]

This gives rise to a series of considerations that need to be weighed. Turkish–Iranian relations did not change during the war but were characterised by a steady unaltered reality: 'Turkey was Iran's one of the largest trading partner in 1983', while immediately after Özal's electoral victory, the two economic partners renewed their Regional Cooperation for Development trade agreement (12 January 1984).[113] This stronger degree of economic cooperation was a natural outcome of the Gulf War as the Strait of Hormuz was closed and the sanctions imposed by the US on Iraq prevented any goods reaching Tehran through the Persian Gulf.

Under these circumstances the relations between the two powers became much closer in the 1980s, giving rise to the consideration of Iraq's potential as a key regional ally. This was reinforced by a series of events including the Autonomy Law of 1974 negotiated between Saddam and the Kurds, Saddam's empowerment since his 1972 alliance with the USSR, the nationalisation of Iraqi oilfields (1972), the 1973–1974 oil crisis and inter-Kurdish cooperation between KDP and PKK in 1982 together with the role of Iraq as a Shi'a force in the Gulf. Iraq's growing influence alerted both Turkey and the US administration. The US–Iraqi rapprochement in 1984 in tandem with Özal's principle of Turkism are two factors that help to explain Turkey's growing need for socio-political and cultural cooperation, primarily for economic reasons but also because of the importance of Iraq's oil-rich Kurdistan Region for Turkey's foreign policy.

As the main objective of his strategy, Özal's liberalisation policies had a strong economic focus driven by his desire for cultural domination throughout the region, which aimed to accommodate all the various ethnic and political groups, including Iranians or Kurds, and bring them beneath the umbrella of a broader Turkism.

However, as Olson points out, Rafsanjani would accuse Ankara of 'planning to seize the Kirkuk oil fields' by carrying out Turkish incursions into Iraq in 1986 and 1987, taking advantage of the 'Frontier Security and Cooperation Agreement' between Turkey and Iraq (February 1983), and the 'Border Security and Cooperation Agreement' (October 1984), along with a 'Security Protocol' contracted between Ankara and Baghdad that allowed raids on PKK encampments in the KR in the fight against PKK rebels.[114]

Turkey had occupied Mosul and Kirkuk during the Safavid era and throughout Gulf War I Tehran cooperated with the Kurds in Iraq. Özal therefore allied himself with Iran, believing that the US would also establish some sort of 'good relations with Iran [since] if Iran lost the war, anti-Khomeini forces would move quickly to overthrow the Iranian government', and thereby restore the status quo ante.[115] Yet the Iranian strikes against oil centres at Kirkuk and Mosul on 23 September 1980 also caused Özal growing fears that Iran might re-capture Kirkuk.[116]

Such concerns were especially evident later on with the IS threat to capture Erbil (September 2014), which was seen as the new oil exploration capital but also due to other geopolitical rationales directly related to its discourse for the creation of the so-called Caliphate. The

Iranian state responded immediately by sending troops to fight IS in Iraq, a move that provoked US involvement although America's initial response had been neutral.

Such developments do not seem to support scholarly assumptions to the effect that 'a deterioration of relations' would have been witnessed without the Gulf War, or arguments that the geopolitics of the war by itself constituted 'incentives for Turkey and Iran to deepen cooperation'. Equally, there is a lack of substantive evidence for the further claim that 'Turkey's decision to cooperate with Iran was an attempt to prevent Tehran from falling into the Soviet sphere',[117] especially in the light of Bülent Ecevit's declaration on 15 May 1978 that the Soviet Union was no longer a threat to Turkey, and the later 1984 Accord signed between Turkey and the USSR for Soviet natural gas 'in return for Turkish goods and services'.[118] Therefore, such claims seem vague and insubstantial.[119]

For Özal, expanding economic relations with Tehran served his liberalisation policies as he attempted to diversify Turkey's energy supply, upgrade its status as an energy corridor and increase its political status. In addition, since there were no extra fees involved, Iranian gas was cheaper and a good solution to Turkey's own energy needs.[120] For Iran, which was suffering from the US embargo and from eight years of constant war, Turkish trade was a necessity.[121] During the same period, Iran agreed to supply Turkey with natural gas and to build a pipeline between the two states.[122] Between 1983 and 1985 Turkish–Iranian trade amounted to US$230 million, making Turkey Iran's third most important commercial partner. Turkey also traded with Iraq during the war, importing up to 60 per cent of oil for use in Turkey from Iraq.[123]

At the same time, Iraq depended heavily on Turkey's control of the 'downstream water' supplies. In this respect, Turkey was also important to Iran as it needed to use Turkish ports in the Black Sea and the Mediterranean 'for strategic imports' during the war.[124] Within the period under examination, the Damascus security and economic cooperation protocols between Damascus and Ankara were also put in place when Özal visited Syria in July 1987 to discuss an increase in the downstream volume of water received by Syria.[125]

The status quo fitted well with Turkey's desire to eliminate any regional threat that would hinder its aim of regional domination through economic and cultural means (i.e., by the application of a 'soft power' policy). Ankara's wish to have good relations with its neighbours, including Iran, was also in line with its goal of joining the Europeanisation process, having made an application for membership of the then European Economic Community (EEC) in 1987. In addition, the Turkish state was doing everything possible during Özal's term in office to absorb any leftist influences domestically, which was expressed both within the concept of a Turko-Islamic synthesis as well as through President Kenan Evren's support for the idea of establishing a 'Communist party in order to prevent their penetration into political parties'.[126] Similarly, the promotion of Islam was intended to bridge this gap in society. However, the Cold War mentality was first and foremost the determinant of Iranian–Turkish relations, a factor that also facilitated the increasingly popular notion of Turko-Islamism – in other words, the elevation of Turkism via Islamism as promoted throughout the 1980s by Turkey's intelligentsia (Aydınlar Ocağı–the Intellectuals Association). On this basis, the Turkish desire to eliminate any rising regional power and especially its chief competitor, Iran, explains Özal's quest for assurances on a six-day official visit to China (2 July 1985) that '[They] would not supply arms to Iran'.[127]

## EXTERNAL INTERFERENCE: THE US ROLE VERSUS SOVIET INFLUENCE

This section examines the US 'dual containment' policy versus US backing of Turkey's secularist wing in relation to the military coup and the US–Turkish Defense and Economic Cooperation Agreement of the 1980s, the rise of Ronald Reagan's Presidency in the US (1981–1989), and the effect of Neo-Conservative ideology on US–Iranian relations as well as on Iran's Russian and Syrian foreign policies. It also suggests ways in which Gulf War I affected the regional balance of power as reflected in the Iraqi–Turkish economic partnership throughout the 1980s, Soviet support for Iraq and US aid dispensed to both parties. The role of the US in the region was often one of intervention. In contrast, Soviet influence, although significant, was not great enough to counterbalance US regional influences. This may have been partly because the USSR was bogged down in Afghanistan where it had lost morale, fighting against an oppressed people, which caused doubt about its military competence and incited rebellion against authority. Thus, for the Soviets, Afghanistan was another Vietnam, which they in turn had to confront.

The role of external interference as a determining factor in both the Iranian and Turkish foreign policies could be traced right back to when the Iranian and Turkish states were first created, while it increased further under the rule of the Shah. In his memoirs, the Shah confirmed the US contribution to his overthrow in January, 1979, 'by sending a US general "with the clear purpose" of neutralising the Iranian Army so it would not fight on the regime's behalf'.[128] External interference was also evident during the 444-day hostage crisis that started in November 1979 and through the Iranian discourse (12 September 1980) which maintained that the hostages would be freed if the US would guarantee both political and military non-intervention. As a regional state power, Iran, for the first time in contemporary history, had the capacity to exert pressure on the US and influence US foreign policy, which it did to such an extent that the US hostage crisis ended only when Reagan was inaugurated as President (20 January, 1981). The pressure felt by the US was evident in Carter's order to freeze official Iranian bank deposits and other assets in the US,[129] although a few months later he had changed his tune, stating that 'he looked forward to establishing normal relations with Iran in the future and regretted any misunderstandings between the US and Iran'.[130]

Thus, the seizing of the American Embassy in Tehran by Iranian radicals had an explicit impact on the American Presidential elections and Republican Reagan's electoral victory. However, in spite of allegations of an October Surprise deal thwarted by Republican interference in the Iranian hostage crisis through an alleged Paris meeting that took place in 1980,[131] a bipartisan House panel concluded that 'there is no merit to the persistent accusations that people associated with the 1980 Presidential campaign of Ronald

Reagan struck a secret deal with Iran to delay the release of American hostages until after the election'.[132]

Yet the fact that Reagan was victorious (21 January 1981) and the hostages were released almost immediately afterwards has raised considerable speculation. A number of scholarly arguments support the belief that 'the timing was arranged in such a way that the release took place only when Reagan had been sworn in' with Ibrahim Yazdi claiming that: 'Khomeini knew that releasing the hostages would cause Carter to win the election and Reagan to lose. [In that sense] Iran wanted to show that Khomeini could determine political outcomes in the US just as [the US had done in Iran] done in 1953.'[133] Similar views were expressed by Fadhil Merani who believed there was 'a "prolongation plan" according to which [Iran] kept the hostages longer to punish Carter as [US] wanted to invade and take part of Iran but failed. The hostages were then freed the same night that Carter lost the elections.'[134] However, on the Iranian side, Dr. Mohajerani said that 'it was just a mistake of Iran that the hostages were not released 2–3 months before the elections that made Carter look a lame duck'. It was because 'Iran had not understood the power structure in the US, there was an information gap and Khomeini thought that Carter would not do anything against the Islamic Republic. Khomeini did not distinguish between Reagan and Carter.'[135]

Perhaps the main lesson that can be taken away from the hostage crisis is that it is representative of the enduring objective of the Iranian regime to force external powers outside the Middle Eastern region to pay attention to it as a force to be reckoned with and to impose, through change, its own power as a regional arbiter in support of a radical agenda. This can be seen right up to the present day in the outlook of Iran's foreign policy which has upheld a revisionist role as a force for change ever since the post-Shah era. This anti-Western discourse, which was the outcome of the Iranian Revolution, was not a new phenomenon, but a reactionary policy that arose out of the region's historical past and the regime's need (based on article 152 of the Constitution) for survival and emancipation against any hegemonic or unjust control.[136] It was this stance that formed the Western perception of Iran as radical, especially as it became increasingly difficult to engage in dialogue on a mutually acceptable way forward between the two actors.

Back in the 1970s, the regime already feared the possibility of an attack by the US. The agreement between Abbas Taj, Iran's Minister of Energy, and the Soviet Union (5 October 1979) for the construction of a power station in Isfahan following the construction of the first nuclear power plant in Bushehr in 1974 are practical reflections of this ideological anti-Western Iranian discourse.[137] In a speech in Tehran, Khomeini labelled Carter 'the enemy of humanity and pointed to the futility of US economic or military coercion'[138] while also stating that 'the hostages would be freed [among others] if the US guaranteed political and military non-intervention in Iran'.[139] According to Tülümen, 'Khomeini preferred to fight [against] everything related to the Western values which [were] responsible in his understanding, for all the sufferings and the corruption encountered in Iran.'[140] The rise of the Mojahedin-e-Khalq, who supported Khomeini against more moderate forces and 'called for national mobilisation to prepare for possible US invasion' is a case in point.[141] Such examples clearly indicate that Iran views a stable Middle Eastern order very differently from the way it is regarded by international powers and, more specifically, the West or Iran's regional allies such as Turkey.

External interference was decisive in determining the outcome of Gulf War I. The 'dual containment' of Khomeini's Shi'a Islam (seen as another expansionist ideology) and Saddam's Iraq was evident through the 'dual policy' of Jimmy Carter's administration (1977– 1981) which supplied arms to both Iraq and Iran because of fears that the USSR would gain ground in these countries.[142] The US rapprochement with Iraq and a shift in the containment of Iraq policy via the Kurds was a consequence of the need to replace Iran as a US-friendly bastion in the Gulf after the fall of the Shah. US concerns had grown steadily as Iran's former support of the Twin Pillars dogma gave way to the rise of Khomeini and this led to the US administration's belief that 'an Iraqi defeat would be contrary to the US interests'.[143] It was this period of the 1980s that would usher in the contemporary trend of 'on/off' US policies towards both Iran and Iraq.[144]

ECONOMICS OF WAR: IRANIAN–TURKISH ECONOMIC AND
POLITICAL ALLIANCES

> *Should Iraq collapse, the installation of a revolutionary Shi'ite regime in*
> *Baghdad would raise the Iran-Syrian axis [which] would threaten not only the*
> *Gulf region but also Jordan, Israel and the US interests in the Eastern*
> *Mediterranean. [Thus] destabilisation would open opportunities for increased*
> *Soviet influence in the region.*
>
> 1986 Congressional Report[145]

Turkish–Iranian relations and, in particular, their economic dimension has pursued a steady and unaltered rectilinear policy that has
continued up until the present day. However, during this period, Iran
was going through a very difficult time with pressure from Iraq, the
'arms-for-hostages policy' scandal, US sanctions resulting from the US
Senate ban on the import of Iranian crude oil along with other
Iranian products,[146] internal disputes, damaging incidents such as
the assassination in Vienna of Abdul Rahman Qassemlu, the leader of
Iran's Kurdistan Democratic Party (13 July 1989), and its pressing
need for economic interdependence which would lead to the
deployment of yet another 'imports-for-oil policy'. All these factors
explain the necessity for Iran's deliberate courting of strong
economic relations with Turkey.

The Turkish–Iranian protocol (14 January 1987) concerning the
construction of a pipeline to transport Iranian crude oil from Iran's
installations at Ahvaz to Dortyol is another illustrative case,[147] as the
Iranian economy had suffered a further blow with the Saudi cut
in production in 1986 which caused oil prices to fall and resulted
in a dramatic drop in Iran's oil revenues (1986–1987), thereby
making the finding of economic relief imperative for the regime in
Tehran.[148] The economic shortfall was exacerbated still further when
Reagan imposed further restrictions (27 October 1987) on US high-
technology exports to Iran.[149]

## The shifting balance of power

The end of Gulf War I (September 1988) came following the
acceptance of UN Resolution 598 (20 August 1988) that called for a
cease-fire, and the establishment of the status quo ante bellum, but
the repercussions for Iran were severe. Indeed, as Mehdi Bazargan,

leader of the Liberation Movement in Iran, confirmed, the war with Iraq had hurt 'the economic, political and military interests' of Iran.[150] In contrast, Iraq emerged as a victor and Saddam Hussein's political reputation was enhanced, even though the Iraqi economy was exhausted. On the Kurdish side, the Kurds of Iraq were disorganised and marginalised following the 'Anfal [The Spoils] Campaign' that the Iraqi regime had carried out against them which had inflicted great damage. The huge significance of Iraq and Syria in regional politics positioned them as central elements in the wider field of Middle Eastern politics, a role that has even greater influence today as will be explored further in the following chapters.

The collapse of the Soviet Union followed by the emergence of a unipolar international relations system which would later shift to multi-polarity, was both detrimental and a key element in transforming the regional setting. The death of Ayatollah Khomeini (3 June 1989) which was followed by the succession (4 June 1989) of President Ayatollah Sayyed Ali Khamenei as Supreme Leader (*Rahbar*) of the Revolution, signalled the transition from the first Revolutionary period to a Republican era from 1990 onwards. It was also during this period that President Akbar Hashemi Rafsanjani, who had won the 28 July 1989 elections, appointed, Hassan Rohani as Secretary to the Supreme Security Council (12 October 1989). The dissolution of the Soviet Union and, in particular, Iran's defeat created opportunities for Turkey to take advantage of the weak balance of power to grow stronger and assert its authority in the region. Although there were other factors to consider, like US pressure on Saddam's Iraq and Russian pressure on Turkey via the Kurds,[151] this did not hold back Turgut Özal who intensified his pursuit of an active and Western-oriented foreign policy.

On the other hand, Supreme Leader Ayatollah Khamenei did not deviate from Iran's radicalised foreign policy. The swift rejection of talks with the US (14 August 1989) was followed by Rafsanjani's release of an 18-page government document, setting out the country's internal and external foreign policy goals based on the principle of 'Neither East Nor West'.[152] The Taif Agreement also made Syria the dominant power in Lebanon and this further boosted the Tehran–Damascus–Hizbullah Resistance Alliance.

Incidents such as Turkey's foreign policy reaction to the Israeli invasion of Lebanon (6 June 1982), Iran's support of Hizbullah (1982) and the correlations stemming from the relational triangles of Turkey–Israel–Iran and Turkey–Iraq–Iran are all indicative of the region's interdependence and explain how structures (material or ideational) shape foreign policy. One instance of this was Turkey's downgrading of its diplomatic ties with Israel to the second secretary level (30 November 1980) vis-à-vis the latter's annexation of East Jerusalem, while Özal's improved relations with the Arab world was partly because of Turkey's need of support in the Cyprus issue. Moreover, the 'soft power' elements represented by Özal's broader activist policy only altered in the 1990s when strategic relations with Israel were dictated primarily because of its perception of Syria as a security threat. Syrian pressure on Ankara in view of PKK's asylum to Abdullah Öcalan after the coup d'état in Turkey on 12 September 1980, PKK fighters joining the Syrian side in the 1982 Lebanon War, and issues concerning the rights to water supplies from the Euphrates and Tigris rivers reflected in negotiations such as the 1987 Syrian–Turkish Protocol are also indicators of mutual interdependence in regional politics influenced by both state and non-state agents.

In spite of Iran's political and economic isolation and its disputes with Turkey over the Kurdish issue (as well as the PKK issue), both states maintained their bilateral economic cooperation which reached its peak in 1985. The influential role of non-state players, such as the Kurds in Iraq, also continued to shape regional politics, a key determinant which has continued up to the present day.

CONCLUSION

So far the study has illustrated the continuation of a series of factors that have played an important role in formulating the foreign policies of Iran and Turkey throughout their history. I have made a case for a dynamic relation between the two, which has been identified by a degree of consistency, despite the various changes inherent in the Iranian socio-political system.

The Cold War period gave rise to a number of other factors whose influence is evident even in today's politics in the Middle Eastern region. This period was important as it set the framework for the Turkish and Iranian foreign policies to develop and unfold, and, as such, constitutes a critical external structural determinant that has shaped them both. Iranian factionalism and the hard-core pro-Western Turkish policies have also been explained along the same lines. It has been shown that the rise of any new ideological innovation such as Communism or Islamism or Khomeini's Islamic Revolution that might jeopardise the regional balance of power or the status quo ante, specifically of the Gulf region, was perceived as a threat and, as a consequence, increased external interference. Therefore, it can be clearly demonstrated that changes in the US Presidency were linked to regional developments.

The Iranian Revolution generated a fear of regional expansion and actually did also have international dimensions. Yet, at the same time, it could equally be considered as more the result of domestic structural changes created by societal dissatisfaction and domestic turbulences than a universal effect. Here, we can observe a link with Chapter 2 as the events of this chapter reinforce how a system's domestic structures can impact strongly on foreign policy behaviour, especially given that the religious element can form the foundation of national identity as in the case of Iran. Thus, it was no surprise that the societal stratum, which had its own distinctive impact, would undergo a repositioning following the outbreak of the Revolution.

It was also observed that the traditional role played by agents/guardians (i.e., the army), as in Turkey's case, was a means to retain the same foreign policy directives based on unitary *statism*. Another finding was how after, but also before, 1979 the role of internal agents, other than external actors, had grown in importance and in their impact on the formulation of foreign policy. In the case of Iran, this reached its peak with the fragmentation of its former political direction and the consequent prevalence of factionalism.

Another perception is that the impact of the Iranian Revolution on Ankara's foreign policy was no greater than that of the Cold War per se. This was deduced by analysing key factors such as Erbakan's rise in power prior to the outbreak of the Iranian Revolution, the succession of coups d'états which mirrored similar events during

the Cold War period and the risk, within this same context, that
the PKK movement carried for Ankara as a formative player in its
policies. The potential for achieving the realisation of Greater
Kurdistan, and its important geostrategic location between Meso-
potamia, Europe, the Arabian Peninsula, Iran and the Caucasus,
transformed the Kurds, particularly those of Iraq and the PKK, into
critical and possibly key players in regional politics. It was no
accident that the Kurds of Iraq were considered as a basic element of
Iranian foreign policy, especially given its interest in expanding its
influence in Iraq.

An important new insight gained from examining the Cold War
period was that I uncovered two emerging factors that were critical
in the formulating of Iranian and Turkish politics. As discussed in
more detail in the following chapters, Iraq and Syria were driving
forces in, rather than the result of, that war and, subsequently, so
were their Kurdish entities which were considerable determinants in
the formulation of the foreign policies in Iran and Turkey. The
confrontation of a potential Kurdistan, as well as the orientation of
both Iraqi and Syrian foreign policy, would very much determine the
extent to which Tehran or Ankara was likely to fulfil their objective of
peace and security in the region according to their value systems and
leadership direction. For example, Saddam Hussein and Gulf War I
actually averted this contingency of the threat that a potential export
of the Iranian Revolution could have posed.

Following on from Chapter 2, it was shown how Iranian and
Turkish foreign policy principles evolved before and after the Iranian
Revolution, and how this affected the stance of both actors during
Gulf War I. Turkey maintained economic relations with Iran in order
to serve its own foreign policy objectives through the use of its so-
called 'soft power' principle, an enduring strategy Ankara still uses
today. It thus gained the advantage by preparing itself to fill any
vacuum that might arise from this unstable period. Again, this is
something the Presidency of Turkey is still trying to accomplish in
today's unsettled circumstances.

The strategic importance of Iraq replacing Iran in its former role as
the bastion of US foreign policy was clearly demonstrated through
the politics applied during the Afghan War, while the establishing

of the roots of the Axis of Resistance can also be traced back to this time. Gulf War I was also critical for Syria which grew strong and powerful under the leadership of Hafez al-Assad. It viewed Iran as a potential and future reliable ally, and thus this period marked the foundations of a deeper alliance between Syria and Iran.

Referring to the period from 1979 onwards as a landmark era inevitably turns the spotlight onto Iran as the epicentre of change and the focus of regional and international attention. Its outlook and policies provided a direct contrast to the set and pro-Western Turkish foreign policy outlook identified by a greater focus on its domestic policies in contrast to comparatively minor changes in shaping its foreign policy practices.

In spite of the repercussions of the Cold War and the differing impact these had on Turkey and Iran, and given that they belonged to entirely different ideological camps, their economic relations remained stable, due possibly to their structural similarities vis-à-vis consistency, as analysed above. In both cases, although the precise nature of the power behind the state varies, represented by the army in Turkey or the Ayatollahs in Iran, it is nonetheless the state that remains the dominant decision-making actor. However, in the case of Iran, *realpolitik* and the prioritisation of the national interest prevailed, while the attempts made from Khomeini onwards to break with the historical past and minimise external interference, can to a great degree be held responsible for what is internationally perceived as the evil perpetrated by the state. In Turkey consistency was guaranteed through its relations with the West and foreign aid, whereas in the case of Iran the pre-Shah period was replicated, which also gave a sense of continuity.

Attention was also drawn to the fact that the consistency of Ankara's foreign policy prior to 1979 and during this period could be ascribed to the dominant role of the army in safeguarding the state's Kemalist principles, and the use of Islam to fight any leftist or communist ideology. On the other hand, in the Iranian case, the inherent change in the political system by its very nature relied heavily on the use of an Islamic army to protect its theocracy. It was further observed how the leadership's beliefs in both the Turkish and the Iranian cases could act as a significant influence in the formulation of foreign policy. Finally, the principles governing the Iranian and Turkish establishments as ideational factors were clarified, including the importance of regional episodes as structural factors. The roles of Iraq, Syria and the US as regional and international state actors were reviewed in the context of external interference, along with examining how the Kurdish movement as a non-state entity also had a significant impact on the formulation of Turkish–Iranian politics. The nature of these factors, the reasons for their development and how they subsequently progressed will gradually be revealed in the following chapters.

# CHAPTER 4

# Turkish–Iranian Relations in the 1990s: The Impact of Gulf War II and the Consolidation of the Kurdish Status

*Iran and Turkey are two important countries who need each other as a bridge in the region as two main pillars of the regional stability.[1]*

Osman Aşkın Bak

## INTRODUCTION

Throughout the Cold War period, and more importantly during the 1980s, a series of considerations like the rise and development of political Islam vis-à-vis the Iranian Revolution, alongside the communist ideology, the hostage crisis (4 November 1979 to 20 January 1981) and the Afghan War,[2] were widely perceived as threats for the Western Alliance camp and accordingly further strengthened the US foreign policy's focus, which aimed at establishing a balance of power to preserve the regional status quo. At this time, US policy-makers tended to favour Iraq while pursuing Iran's containment via US intervention at Iranian expense in the second half of Gulf War I, including the controversial shooting down of an Iranian aircraft in July 1988.

Gulf War I was the first important confrontation with regional repercussions involving the triangular US–Iranian–Iraqi interrelation. Thus, while the US was supportive of both combatants at the beginning of the War, the balance after 1983 shifted in favour of Saddam's Iraq. US economic strategic interests in the Gulf and the broader Middle East area prompted US support for Iraq as an alternative policy for maintaining the fragile regional status quo.[3] The US wished to see a stable and internally secure Iraq 'as the first line of defence against Iranian expansionism'[4] since a continuation of the War would pose 'serious problems for the US economic and security interests in the free world'.[5] The end of Gulf War I (September 1988) was achieved with the acceptance of UN Resolution 598 (20 August 1988), which called for a cease-fire, and the establishment of the status quo *ante bellum* although at Iran's expense. Even though the United States – in order to rid the Middle East of the aggressive regimes of Khomeini and Saddam Hussein – was interested in the mutual exhaustion of Iran and Iraq 'so that both should lose', it still feared that any power vacuum could potentially be exploited by the USSR and therefore it was important that 'their nations would be left intact'.[6] Gulf War II, marked by Saddam's decision to invade Kuwait on 2 August 1990 and the extermination of the Kurds, crystallised the US administration's determination to remove Saddam from power as a threat to vital US interests in the area, a stance indicated by the Iraqi rhetoric of George W. H. Bush and Colin Powell from 1989 onwards.

The US decision to ally itself with Kuwait against Saddam[7] was the result of the US perception of Saddam as a danger to the region based on a number of concerns vis-à-vis Iraq's revisionist policy which could endanger the regional status quo. These included US awareness of Iraq's chemical weapons capability– which the Western powers had originally helped to develop, the regime's violation of human rights with regard to Kurdish persecution which amounted to genocide, Saddam's military strength following Gulf War I, his autocratic nature and harsh policies as well as Saddam's rhetorical threats against Israel and the Gulf States. Such concerns heightened in 1988 after the three-phase 'Anfal' (The Spoils) campaign[8] carried out to punish Kurdish support for Iran during Gulf War I. The regime's violation of human rights in persecuting the Kurds amounted to genocide and caused the US administration considerable alarm.

US fears of Iraq's aspiration for regional domination and the dualism of US foreign policy discourse were key factors in the US foreign policy objective of restraining Saddam. The US also had deep concerns over oil production if Saddam continued unchecked as 'the invasion of Kuwait would allow Saddam to control 10 per cent of the world's oil supply'[9], while regional hostilities were also exacerbated by Kuwait's hopes of forcing Saddam to the bargaining table in order to extract a truce from him that would include 'Rumeila drilling rights and a non-aggression pact' with US backing.[10] In addition, Kuwait increased its oil production by 40 per cent, which resulted in falling oil prices and thus put economic pressure on Saddam.[11]

The post-Cold War period undoubtedly signalled US dominance and its monopolisation of the international relations system while the demise of the Soviet threat paved the way for a new era in global politics as US foreign policy now began to turn away from its policy of dual containment of Iran and Iraq towards the containment of Iraq through regime change. This shift marking the fourth change in US foreign policy involved the direct use of force in order to deal with the emerging regional challenges.[12]

The presidential target of regional stability for the benefit of the United States on the one hand, and the US administration's growing belief from the early 1990s onwards that 'Saddam Hussein saw the end of the Cold War as an opportunity to pursue his own expansionism'[13] on the other, were key influences in shaping the US Iraqi policy, which focused on replacing Saddam. On 18 June 1990, Saddam reportedly informed a meeting of the Islamic Conference in Baghdad: 'we will strike at [the Israelis] with all the arms in our possession if they attack Iraq or the Arabs'. He declared 'Palestine has been stolen' and exhorted the Arab world to 'recover the usurped rights in Palestine and free Jerusalem from Zionist captivity'.[14] Fiery speeches like these fuelled US fears that Saddam's threats against Israel and the Gulf States would bear fruit, while there was also a growing awareness of the difficulties of controlling Saddam as Iraq renewed its aspirations for regional domination. All this made the US foreign policy objective of restraining Saddam Hussein imperative including US-backed attempts to overthrow him from within.[15] However, the US appears to have continued its economic relations with Saddam's Iraq until the very last moments of Gulf War I (2 August 1990 – 28 February 1991) as the Bush administration apparently approved \$4.8 million in advanced technology product sales to Iraq and \$695,000 worth of advanced data transmission devices right up to the invasion of Kuwait (2 August 1990). At the same time, further restrictions on the activities of the Kurdish movement were imposed by regional inter-state alliances, which acted as a counterbalance to the Israeli–Turkish coalition as well as US–Turkish relations.[16]

It is within this context that this chapter observes and further explores the development of the factors examined in previous chapters in order to demonstrate their continuing relevance in the context of the post-Cold War period. During this period the Islamic Revolution maintained its importance as a major structural factor in the second Republic (1988–1991) as demonstrated by the rise of the Reformist camp in Iranian politics. The chapter also reveals how foreign policy principles, the basis on which Iranian and Turkish policies were formulated, had their own distinctive effect during this period just as they had during Gulf War I on the stance taken by Turkey and Iran. The impact of Gulf War I – in terms of Iraq's influence and Turkey's interaction with Tehran – also continued in the post-Cold War context, but this time centered on the Iraqi crisis which became the key factor in the formulation of Turkish–Iranian relations and regional politics.

During this same period, the economic dimension of Turkish–Iranian relations was very important, just as it had been during the war. Iran faced a difficult economic situation compounded by the drop in oil revenues (1986–1987), the various US economic sanctions and its earlier listing as a state supporting terrorism in January 1984, while the economic costs of the conflict for Turkey increased pressure on Ankara to cooperate with Iran in the energy sector. This, together with the conditions in the North of Iraq (today's Kurdistan Region), played a key role in fostering Turkish–Iranian cooperation.[17] Turkish and Iranian foreign policies shared a focus on limiting Kurdish aspirations for independence and keeping

Iraq integrated, while they were also united in confronting Kurdish uprisings and pressurising a Saddam already economically weak due to the economic embargo on Iraq after the war. These combined aims inevitably led to a Turkish–Iranian strategic rapprochement.

While Ankara seemed to show a greater interest in Iraq's domestic politics (although Tehran has recently consolidated its plans for political control over Baghdad including seeking opportunities to benefit from the oil reserves belonging to Iraq)[18] there was still no leverage or concrete outcomes that favoured either state in so far as their influence on Iraq was concerned. However, the Kurdish factor continued to be a major source of concern for both states and therefore occupied much of the Turkish and Iranian political agenda during this period.

In relation to economics, it made excellent sense for Turkey to continue supporting Iran in the light of the US economic embargo on Iraq straight after the war and the no-fly zone established in both the north and south of the country which further strengthened the Turkish–Iranian objective of strategic cooperation. However, Turkey also made sure it seized every opportunity to promote its own economy and foreign policy, and although heavy costs had been incurred by the war, amounting to around $40 billion, it used the situation to its advantage by preparing to fill any vacuum that opened up during this period of considerable instability. This was shown in Turkey's determination to forge wider alliances as demonstrated on 28 November 1992, when the foreign ministers of Afghanistan, Iran, Turkey, Azerbaijan, Kazakhstan, Turkmenistan and Pakistan met in Islamabad to sign the founding charter of the Economic Cooperation Organisation (ECO) and form an economic bloc.[19]

However, this era could justifiably be called the decade of the Kurds as their influence was found right at the centre of regional developments from the onset of Gulf War II onwards where they played an influential role in regional and international foreign policies, especially with regard to the creation of the Kurdistan Regional Government in Iraq in May 1992 and the dominant role played by the PKK. This involved inter and intra-Kurdish fighting which threatened to jeopardise the security of the regional state powers and resulted in external interference vis-à-vis US mediation, including Turkey's failed attempt to bring about a resolution of Iraq's intra-Kurdish disputes in 1998 on the basis of the Washington Agreement (1998) and its involvement in Abdullah Öcalan's capture (Kenya, 1999). The arrest of its leadership marked 1999 as the most significant year for the PKK.

The increase in US involvement could be viewed as indicative of a 'proto-stage' leading to the development of US interactive relations with the Kurds of Turkey, which, in turn, had the potential to encourage forms of governance, such as, for instance, a federal model which, if Ankara chose to adopt it over the next decade, might serve as a means of resolving the turbulent on-going peace process between Turks and Kurds in Turkey.

Two other developments during this period were the increasingly important role played by the Caucasus, while Iran's nuclear issue also came to the forefront of international politics, causing a massive shake up of the existing political chessboard, especially after 1992, but neither of these had any dramatic impact on the relations between Turkey and Iran.


THE IMPACT OF GULF WAR II ON TURKISH–IRANIAN RELATIONS

*The role of the leadership as reflected in foreign policy discourse and practice*

The 1990s marked a season of dramatic global shifts in power with the demise of Soviet power in favour of a US-dominant unipolar international relations system, but it was also a decade when the Iranian and Turkish political systems experienced major domestic changes.

This change in Iran began with Ali Hosseini Khamenei becoming Iran's Supreme Leader following the death of Khomeini (1989) and the election of Akbar Hashemi Rafsanjani as President for two terms (1989–1993 and 1993–1997). It was also reflected in the increasing dominance of the Reformist faction that opposed the traditional outlook of the Islamic elite by advocating a more pluralist Islam[20] with a primary focus on contemporary culture, post-modern epistemology and technological advancement. However, Iranian foreign policy had changed very little in essence and still followed the same well-trodden revolutionary paths with its continued use of asymmetrical tactics and weapons. For example, when Iran was excluded from the Middle East peace negotiations held in Madrid in October 1991,[21] Tehran organised its own conference at the same time in order to demonstrate its opposition to the process, while in 1992 Rafsanjani would reassert Iran's claims to the islands of Abu Musa and the Tunbs, proclaiming that its neighbours would have to 'cross a sea of blood' to reach them.[22]

For many years the Iranian political system had been based around a structural dualism reflecting the institutional and ideological differences and power struggle between the traditional Islamic system represented by *velayat-e faqih* and the presidential system, so that the political tensions arising from this continued to be very much in evidence during the 1990s. Dr. Ata'ollah Mohajerani summarised the situation: 'the gap between the two continued to be a major force in shaping Iranian politics with Rafsanjani focusing mainly on issues of economic reforms [*refah e eqtesadi*], industry, culture and infrastructure, while Khamenei concentrated on the Culture War with the support of the state's military forces'.[23]

One of the first conflicts of this antagonistic dualism during this period occurred when the Minister of Culture and Islamic Guidance, Seyyed Mohammad Khatami, was dismissed and replaced by Ali Larijani in 1992, who was also subsequently removed to make way for Rafsanjani's appointment of Seyed Mostafa Agha Mirsalim, a conservative anti-Western Islamist, in 1994.[24] According to Seifzadeh, this was part of Rafsanjani's continued efforts to oust the radical left from powerful institutions such as the Revolutionary Guards Corps during his first term as President, but his attempts met with failure.[25] During his second presidential term, opposition towards him grew with the conservatives condemning his modernist agenda and failing to cooperate with him even though Rafsanjani had supported and strengthened the Supreme Leader's constitutional power at the expense of the Presidency.

On the Turkish side, the national elections on 20 October 1991 voted Süleyman Demirel's centre right True Path Party (DYP, *Doğru Yol Partisi*) into power, but although it had tripled its representation to 178 seats, this was still not sufficient for a party majority and therefore led to a coalition government (21 November 1991–25 June 1993) with the Social Democratic Populist Party (SHP, *Sosyaldemokrat Halkçı Parti*). However, this coalition had very little effect on the orientation of Turkish–Iranian relations as further analysis of Turkish foreign policy decisions later in the chapter will reveal.

The electoral victory of Necmettin Erbakan's Welfare Party (*Refah Partisi*, RP) on 24 December 1995 with a lead of 21.38 per cent paved the way for the rise of political Islam in the region, especially as it coincided with the landslide victory of the Reformist Seyyed Mohammad Khatami in becoming President (22 May 1997), winning a staggering 69 per cent of the votes in spite of obstacles posed by the traditionalism of the state's more conservative wing expressed through the Supreme Leadership. Both leaders embraced more democratic ideas and were committed to bringing change in the political landscape.

Khatami's landmark proposal for 'A Dialogue among Civilizations' broke Iran's isolation and opened up a new chapter in Iranian politics through a different kind of policy aimed at the 'reduction of tensions' (*tashanoj zadaei*).[26] The new willingness to be open rather than opposed to the West was highlighted in the Tehran Declaration (11 December 1997) at the end of the global Islamic summit forum on 9 December 1997 which focused on the need for cooperation, dialogue and positive understanding among cultures and religions and rejected the ideology of confrontation.[27]

Accordingly, Khatami instigated the renewal of negotiations between Iran with the US, causing US President Clinton to view Khatami's appointment as a real opportunity to make headway with Iran. Khatami also improved relations with the Arab World, bartering a beneficial trade agreement with increased cooperation in the power and power-generating sectors between the two countries (1998), and followed this up with the historic Security and Military Agreement (2001) with Saudi Arabia. He even improved Iran's relations with the EU, both in political terms and as a trading partner, and carried out constructive visits to a number of European countries.

*The role of Iraq: External mediation and direct use of force*
Gulf War II marks a historic moment in regional and international politics as its contribution to the formulation of the foreign policy of both regional and international powers was highly significant. It facilitated the US decision to shift the emphasis of its Middle Eastern foreign policy to include the direct use of force, and also underlined the role of Iraq as the key determinant in subsequent developments in the region including its crucial impact on the trajectory of Turkish–Iranian relations and on Turkey's foreign policy decisions per se. There can be no doubt that these structural changes, along with the rise of the new Russian Republic in 1991, and the turbulence caused by perennially thorny problems like the PKK and the Kurdish issue in Iraq, together with the emergence in the foreign policy discourse of the problem of terrorism (1990) and the nuclear issue (1992) in the aftermath of the Cold War, were responsible for creating an overall sense of chaos and uncertainty. This unstable political landscape explains the Turkish Presidency's new activism under Turgut Özal (1989–1993) with foreign policy decisions formulated in direct response to the new political changes affecting international relations.

The Iraqi foreign policy within the context of Gulf War II was critical for Turkey's re-entry into the Middle Eastern political arena while Ankara also wanted to forge closer relations with its neighbouring states of Iran and Syria.[28] It was on this basis that Turkey initiated tripartite negotiations with Syria and Iran in Ankara on 14 November 1991 to discuss regional developments. Certainly, the need for regional allies and the filling of any potential gap left behind as a result of the repercussions of the war in Iraq were matters of pressing importance for both Iran and Turkey.

However, this new political setting which both Iran and Turkey were striving to control to their advantage was also the outcome of the dissolution of the former Soviet Union, which impacted Turkey's relations with the Transcaucasus. For example, one result of this was the US–Turkish agreement to increase aid to Central Asia and the Transcaucasian Republic even though at this point Russia was still dominant while both Turkey and Iran occupied relatively minor roles as discussed earlier in the literature review.[29] Other outcomes showing Turkey's greater influence included Turkish and Armenian governments signing an agreement in 1992 in which Turkey agreed to supply Armenia with power[30] while later the same year President Özal ordering the blocking of Armenia's export route to the Black Sea to scare Armenia into abandoning its war with Azerbaijan over Nagorno-Karabakh because of Turkey's cultural, linguistic and historical links with Azerbaijan.[31]

Meanwhile, Rafsanjani concluded 14 agreements in Baku including a memorandum on Principles of Friendship and Cooperation in October 1993.[32] In pursuit of cooperation, Rafsanjani also held a four-day meeting with Turgut Özal in Turkey in July 1989, shortly after his election as President.[33] This was followed by successive meetings between the Turkish and Iranian sides, including key meetings between the Turkish Prime Minster Yıldırım Akbulut (1989–1991) and officials in Iran (28 February 1990)[34] as well as between President Rafsanjani with Turkish Interior Minister Ismet Sezgin (14 September 1992)[35] to work on plans to fight the PKK rebels, resulting in assurances from Iran's Interior Ministry that Tehran would neither support the PKK nor allow its rebels to enter Iran through its borders with Iraq.[36]

Iran's main problem was the altered orientation of the US administrations' foreign policy from the dual containment of both Iran and Iraq to concentrating its containment focus mainly on Iran from 1983 onwards (for which it enlisted Iraq's support according to documents in the National Security Archive at George Washington University).[37] Iran was under considerable pressure because of US administration's policies against Iran, including the State Department's annual report on terrorism which listed Syria and Iran as nations supporting terrorism (30 April 1990).[38] These developments, along with Tehran's fear that Turkey might be gaining an upper hand in the region, influenced Iran's decision to build alliances with regional states to counterbalance Ankara's post-Soviet influence as an emerging regional power. The result was that Iran turned towards the Caucasus, which also led to the establishing of diplomatic relations with Armenia.[39] For the first meeting of the ECO convened in Tehran, the former Soviet Central Asian and Transcaucasian Republics were also invited[40] while Turkey (9 May 1990) held its first public meeting with Israeli officials in ten years vis-à-vis the situation in Iraq.[41]

Relations with the US continued to be difficult as the US also had major concerns about Iran's nuclear capabilities resulting in an IAEA team led by Jon Jennekens travelling to Iran (6 February 1992) to investigate allegations that Iran was developing nuclear weapons.[42] However, this proved to be an erroneous assumption as the team finally concluded (12 February 1992) that Iran's nuclear programme was entirely peaceful.[43] Another factor affecting US–Iranian relations was the issue of partisanship even within the US bureaucracy itself. Parsi would later reveal that although the State Department and National Security Advisor, Condoleezza Rice (2001–2005), had wanted to open talks with Tehran, this was hindered by the White House who were mostly anti-Iranian.[44]

Iran's international standing deteriorated still further because of its radicalism and acts of violence, such as the assassination of Prime Minister Shapour Bakhtiar in Paris (6 August 1991), and the killings of Dr. Sadeq Sharafkandi, leader of the KDPI (Democratic Party of Iranian Kurdistan, *Partî Dêmokiratî Kurdistanî Êran*), Fattah Abdoli, Homayoun Ardalan and their translator Nouri Dehkordi at the Mykonos Greek restaurant in Berlin (17 September 1992). The German court's verdict on 10 April 1997 implicated both Supreme Leader Grand Ayatollah Ali Khamenei and President Ayatollah Rafsanjani in the attacks, asserting that the murders had been carried out with their knowledge, and this played a large part in the EU's subsequent decision to loosen ties with Tehran in 1997.[45]

Saddam's invasion of Kuwait and the US decision to ally itself with the latter because of US fears that Iraq's revisionist policy might endanger the regional status quo reflected a growing concern about the stability of the surrounding regions. This resulted in the proclamation of the Damascus Declaration (18 June 1991) by Egypt, Syria and the Gulf Cooperation Council (GCC, 25 May 1981) which was created in response to Gulf War I, Iraq's hostility and fears of the Iranian Revolution's expansion into the Gulf region – although it was never implemented.[46] According to National Security Directive No 45 (20 August 1990), the Iraqi invasion of Kuwait was to be condemned as a threat to vital US interests in the area

(UN Resolutions 660 and 662 respectively). Under UN Resolution 661 the United States would impose economic sanctions on Iraq to prevent any damage to oil supplies from Iraq and Kuwait, while National Security Directive 54 (15 January 1991) confirmed that the US would not hesitate to use military force against Iraq if it jeopardised vital US security interests, such as access to Persian Gulf oil, or the security of key US-friendly states in the region like Israel.

'Operation Desert Storm' – a US offensive aimed at the liberation of Kuwait that lasted for six weeks – was directed with the view that the occupation of Kuwait constituted an act of hostility and was therefore a threat that needed to be eliminated. More specifically, UNSC (United Nations Security Council) Resolution 688 (5 April 1991) called on Iraq to end Kurdish suppression and to provide the Kurds with humanitarian aid as there had been a grave humanitarian crisis caused by the flood of Kurdish refugees across the borders of Iran and Turkey in the aftermath of Gulf War II. It was the combination of the massacre of the Kurds by the Iraqi air force, the mass exodus of two million refugees who feared a second Halabja and increasing pressure from the media that KR's Prime Minister, Nechirvan Barzani, believed 'obliged both the US and Turkey to support the Kurds of Iraq'[47] which led to the creation of a no-fly zone that prevented Iraqi air forces from flying over Northern Iraq above the 36th Parallel so that the North was effectively isolated from the rest of the country. In addition, the subsequent 'Safe Haven' scheme (24 April 1991) imposed on Iraq by the US, Britain, France and Turkey provided increased protection for Iraq's Kurdish population. However, the Kurds in the North and the Shi'ite in the South of Iraq took advantage of the war situation to instigate an uprising, although it was suppressed the following day, a course of action that the US accepted as necessary.[48] However, this development led to further crises in the Kurdish and Shi'ite regions.

Massoud Barzani explained that: 'The rebellion was a Kurdish initiative while the US only [became] involved later on ... [the] US had informed both Iraq and the Kurds that in the case of a Kurdish attack, the Kurds will be held responsible for the consequences ... However, if the Iraqi regime attacked first, the US would respond immediately.'[49] On the US side, the President defended US actions:

'[the] US should not bear the guilt of suggesting that the Iraqi people take matters into their own hands, with the implication being given by some that the US would be there to support them militarily, since that was not true'. President George H. W. Bush did, however, suggest that '... it would be good if the Iraqi people would take matters into their own hands and kick Saddam Hussein out and I still feel that way and I still hope they do', although he added: 'I do not concede encouraging an exodus.'[50] The decision not to assist the Kurdish rebellion seems to have stemmed from the reluctance of the US administration to embark on an 'all-out' meddling in the Middle East that would keep US military forces occupied exclusively with Iraq and thus deprive the United States of an active presence in other parts of the world.[51] Therefore, despite President Bush's keen desire to 'get Hussein out of there ... for the tranquillity of Iran—Iraq'[52] the United States did not support the uprising in March 1991.[53]

Gulf War II between the Iraqi and the coalition with the allied forces reached its end on 28 February 1991 marked by the Safwan agreement (3 March 1991). A series of directives by George H. W. Bush (1989–1993) that clarified the US foreign policy's stance towards Iraq, setting out the Iraqi obligation to destroy its chemical and biological weapons (under UNSCR 687 of 3 April 1991), and putting in place the continuation of sanctions against Iraq (provided for by UNSCR 661), which resulted soon afterwards in the creation of the Iraqi no-fly zone (NFZ) (UNSCR 688 of 5 April 1991) and lasted up to 22 May 2003 under the UN Resolution 1483.

Iran absorbed the refugees, while Turkey chose to resettle Iraq's Kurds back in their native region. As a result, Turkey took responsibility for providing the Kurds with a costly and intensive relief programme involving 15,500 tons of supplies, known as Operation Provide Comfort, renamed Operation Poised Hammer (in 1997), and later Operation Northern Watch. Saddam's refusal to comply with UNSCR 687 which called for a ceasefire against the Kurds as well as inspection of Iraq's 'chemical, biological and missile capabilities', reinforced the US conviction that Iraq was indeed engaged in attempts to acquire materials for a nuclear weapons programme.[54]

Gulf War II and Iraq's position thereafter were important considerations for both Turkey and Iran amid fears that a divided and fragmented Iraq could cause regional instability, facilitating the rise of the Kurds and possibly the potential empowerment of the Kurdish movement. Therefore, Özal joined the UN embargo on Iraq following Gulf War II even though the stakes involved were much higher for Turkey than Iran leading to enormous financial losses due to loss of trade.[55] However, Turkey may have hoped to gain compensation for its loss as Olson noted that Hashemi Rafsanjani, the Majlis speaker between 1980 and 1989, made continuous claims throughout the 1990s asserting that Ankara was planning to capture the oilfields of Kirkuk.[56]

Gulf War II saw more involvement from Turkey and the international community than Iran, but it still had a significant impact on Turkish Iranian relations as Gulf War II made it necessary for Turkish and Iranian foreign policies to cooperate more closely. The two states were drawn together by shared concerns over the Kurdish issue, although this was mainly in relation to the activities of the Kurdish movement in Iraq and the role of the PKK in Turkey, as Iran's Kurdish movement had been relatively well controlled since the Shah's policies in the 1960s. However, the Kurdish issue and its security implications had also risen to become one of the top priorities in regional foreign policy agendas, and had already resulted in a number of meetings between Iranian, Syrian and Turkish foreign ministers such as the August 1994 meeting in Damascus.

Rafsanjani's pursuit of a policy of détente, and, more importantly, economic interdependence were also critical parameters, especially in the light of the devaluation of Iran's rial in the 1990s and Turkey's growing energy needs. Therefore, it was a natural step for Turkish President Demirel to enter into cordial relations with Iran. In 1994 Demirel attended a ceremony in Iran to mark the start of construction for the Iran–Turkmenistan pipeline, and in the same year signed a 30-year gas supply agreement with Turkmenistan President Saparmurad Niyazov.[57] Özal was motivated by the thought that Iraq, particularly the oil-rich northern part, could become a considerable sphere of influence if Turkey could get control, the idea being that it could then be potentially incorporated into a confederate mode of governance. The *Financial Times* would later reveal that the US and Turkey had agreed on a plan (23 September 1996) which would allow Kurds and Turkmen groups to take control of Northern Iraq.[58]

Finally, the continued preservation of a dual policy of expanding relations with both the European Community vis-à-vis Turkey's EC application (14 April 1987) and the Muslim world in view of its proximity to the Middle East can again be discerned in the same context of Turkish activism during the post-Cold War era. Throughout this period, Turkey adopted a *realpolitik* stance and used this to develop advantageous relations that would result in economic and security benefits. This dual track policy became even more essential in the new order created by the demise of the USSR and Gulf War II when the political circumstances led to a widely held belief that Tansu Penbe Çiller (1993–1996) was in charge of the West and Erbakan in charge of the Islamic world.[59] However, attempts to solve the Kurdish issue continued. Karayılan asserted that Erbakan sent Abdullah Öcalan in Damascus a proposal for the political solution of the Kurdish issue based on the federation model,[60] while Çiller had also suggested that the Kurdish issue in Turkey could benefit from a solution similar to Spain's ETA model (*Euskadi Ta Askatasuna*, Basque Country and Freedom, 1959), to which Doğan Güreş responded with the claim that there was no Kurdish problem in Turkey – only a problem of terrorism.[61] Murat Karayılan asserted that Israel's stance on the Kurdish issue in Turkey was in favour of non-solution as it was in Israel's interest to perpetuate the problem because while Turkey remained in a state of constant conflict fighting the Kurds, Ankara would continue to need assistance and support from Israel and the US.[62] Nevertheless, Israel did enter into an agreement with the army generals to provide 50 guided air-to-ground missiles for Turkey to use against the PKK in 1996–1997 and also trained the Turkish pilots.

Turkey's trump card, which it has continued to play with some success in its Middle Eastern foreign policy, is its view of itself (in contrast to the military structure stance of the traditionalists) as the gateway to Europe which has made prioritisation of its Europeanisation process and its vision of becoming an EU member an intrinsic part of its political process. However, the fact that

Turkey was only recognised as a candidate country in 1999 (Helsinki Council, 10 December) and that the launch of accession negotiations to join the EU only started in December, 2004 also shows the importance Turkey attributes to its dual policy towards Central Asia, the Caucasus (especially in the first half of the 1990s) and the Middle East throughout this period. Osman Aşkın Bak's statement reflected this:

> In Central Asia we have been ahead of Iran since the 1990s ... Turkey has close relations with Azerbaijan and an active presence with Azeris speaking Turkic making up more than 40% of Iran's population.[63]

The arrival of Bill Clinton in the US Presidency (20 January 1993 to 20 January 2001) coincided with an ideological radicalisation of US foreign policy discourse which continued George H. W. Bush's 'direct strikes' policy and reinforced the same policy aims of dual containment of both Iran and Iraq. An example demonstrating the policy in action was the instrumental role played by AIPAC (American Israel Public Affairs Committee) in the successful lobbying for the passing of the Iran–Libya Sanctions Act of 1996 (ILSA) with secondary economic sanctions on foreign companies (mostly in the oil sector as stated in D'Amato Law)[64] investing in Iran and Libya.[65] Another was the Iraq Liberation Act (1998) for regime change along with the maintenance of UN economic sanctions as well as Senate approval of the Foreign Oil Sanctions Act of 1995 (20 December) which imposed sanctions on foreign companies investing more than $40 million in Iran's oil industry.[66]

In addition, a House and Senate Conference authorised an $18–20 million agreement for covert operations against Iran while the FY1996 Intelligence Authorisation act (HR 1655, PL 104–93) included about $14 million more than requested for strategies aimed at changing the regime's behaviour. The FY1998 legislation provided $4 million for a new broadcasting service Radio Free Iran run by Radio Free Europe/Radio Liberty (RFE/RL) and another $4 million for radio through FY1999 provided by the omnibus appropriation of HR 4328 (PL 105–277). As far as the trade ban was concerned, the August 1997 amendment (Executive Order 13059) was put in place to prevent US companies from knowingly exporting goods to a third country for incorporation into products destined for Iran.[67]

The main components of the US foreign policy agenda at this time were to assist Israel to become a self-sufficient power so that it would no longer need American economic or other types of aid, the containment of Iran, the strengthening of US–Turkish ties, and the continuation of US–Saudi relations regarded as particularly important for its role as a major oil-importing resource, and thus a good market for American products.[68] Iran's role continued to be contained even though the IAEA (International Atomic Energy Agency) inspection team's investigations had reported that Iran's nuclear programme was entirely peaceful (12 February 1992)[69] because the US still had concerns following claims that a North Korean cargo ship had allegedly been carrying Scud missiles for Iran and Syria (9 March 1992).[70]

## Dimensions of political economy

Meanwhile, in the economic field, cooperation between Turkey and Iran continued to address their mutual energy needs throughout the 1990s by committing to the construction of a $23 billion gas pipeline construction for the delivery of natural gas over a period of 23 years, a long-envisaged project that was finally given the go-ahead in the Blue Stream agreement (December 1997) with the aim of steadily increasing the bilateral merchandise trade volume to $2.6 billion per annum.[71] As the agreement dealt with purchase and not investment, it was not considered to transgress the US law passed on 5 August penalising companies investing $40 million per year in Iran or Libya.[72]

However, in all of this the importance of the post-Cold War political setting involving the dissolution of the USSR and the major role played by Russia in the progression of both Turkish and Iranian foreign policies and economies needs to be taken into account as a key factor. Considering the catastrophic events that had affected it, the reawakening of Russia seems to have happened quite rapidly with its activities from the 1990s onwards giving it an increasingly significant role in the Middle Eastern region, especially after the Ukraine crisis (November 2013), and the eruption of the Syrian crisis

(March 2011), a topic that will be further analysed in subsequent chapters.

On 25 January, 1993, the Ministry of Foreign Affairs under Andrey Vladimirovich Kozyrev announced the Concept of the Foreign Policy of the Russian Federation, which stated that Russia would take responsibility for ensuring stability in areas previously controlled by the former USSR.[73] This authority was demonstrated when Russia imposed restrictions on both Iran and Turkey concerning their activities in the Transcaucasus (discussed in Chapter 1) while Russian support continued to be vital for both states. Russian arms in exchange for Iranian oil and natural gas had been a mutually beneficial trade-off[74] and Iran and Russia were also united in their foreign policy concerns regarding US efforts at containment. Iran's potential as a prospective partner was also evident in its ability to balance US and Turkish influence in Central Asia and the Caucasus as Tehran shared Moscow's opposition to transferring Central Asian gas to Europe via the Trans-Caspian pipeline and through a Russian–Iranian alliance it could potentially exert political pressure on Turkey.[75]

In addition, Russia viewed Iran as a useful ally to confront regional threats in the battle for influence in the Gulf.[76] Accordingly, the twin factors of promoting the national interest at the same time as keeping an eye on security concerns within the surrounding states prioritised a policy of rapprochement between the two states which, for the time being, overcame any differences in policies and attitude. The 1990s was thus a period of continuous cooperation in various forms for Russia and Iran, mainly because they shared concerns on how the renaissance of the Kurdish role would impact the region together and what its potential ramifications on regional foreign policies might be.

Two incidents indicative of Russia's facilitating role in the region were Moscow's 1994 hosting of the PKK conference and the creation of Kurdish House in Moscow, which was established to assist Kurds struggling against the Turkish regime, by the Confederation of CIS following a meeting with Kurdish representatives (January 1995).[77] The Russian–Kurd as well as Russian–Iranian alliances were opposed by US intervention in February 1995 which aimed to support the

Baku–Ceyhan pipeline and thereby contain Iran and Russia in order to prevent them dominating future pipeline decisions, a course of action that aptly delineates the triangles of power formed in this period.[78] The values of regional interdependence and mutual collaboration were clear and resulted in outcomes like the strengthening of the Israeli–Turkish alliance under a series of agreements in 1996,[79] Russia and Iran's economic cooperation in the fields of energy, oil, gas and transportation in 1996[80] and the Iran–Russia MoU on 4 October 1997.[81]

## *KRG and PKK: Determinants of foreign policy*
## Kurdish relations with Iran and Turkey

The value of the Kurdish role for both Persians and the Turks (as outlined in Chapter 2) can be traced back through history. Abbas, the Chairman of the Kurdistan National Assembly (KNA) and the organisation's Washington DC representative highlighted Kurdish importance, 'the only buffer zone that can prevent new Ottoman or Persian Empires is the Kurds. The only way to promote and secure minorities is by supporting the Kurds.'[82]

The 1990 First Kurdish National Congress in Paris with Jalal Talabani, Massoud Barzani, and Murat Karayılan was interrupted with a summons from Washington to Talabani followed straight afterwards by a meeting with Özal to try and deal with the crisis developing in Iraq. The events that followed saw the emergence of the Kurdistan Regional Government (KRG) in Northern Iraq (May 1992) as a consequence of Gulf War II and the humanitarian crisis which marked the renaissance of the Kurdish movement in the Middle Eastern region and also re-injected a sense of unity into Iraq's Kurdish movement. The US policy supporting regime change in Baghdad along with the stabilisation of the KRG as a semi-independent state sowed the seeds for a new era in international relations. This change also prompted the re-awakening of the Kurdish movement in Turkey, particularly through the activities of the PKK movement, the next link in a chain of Kurdish insurgencies occurring throughout the 20th century; namely, Sheikh Said's Revolt in 1925, the Agri Dagi revolt in the Mount Ararat region from 1926 to 1930 and the Dersim Revolt between 1936 and 1937. It also foreshadowed the mobilisation of the Kurds in Syria in response to Abdullah Öcalan's decade-long stay in Syria following the 1980 coup d'état in Turkey.[83] However, the role of Turkey in these changes was also crucial as it helped consolidate the status of today's Kurdistan Region and made a major contribution to the Kurdish renaissance.

Murat Karayılan indicated that the Chief of General Staff, Necip Torumtay, was strongly opposed to an invasion of Northern Iraq and in favour of joining the US coalition forces in the war against Iraq, but this plan was never implemented as the Turkish General resigned. Özal's decision to support the US coalition against Saddam Hussein was in part influenced by the possibility of annexing the parts of the Kurdistan Region described in the National Oath (*Misak-ı Millî* of 1920) as discussed previously in Chapter 3.[84] In addition, the element of Özal's foreign policy discourse founded on the principle of 'Turkism' also aimed to prevent any negative repercussions in relation to Turkey's Kurdish problem caused by the claims of Iraq's Kurds in the light of the policy of 'neo-Ottomanism' as Turkey wanted to avoid obstacles that might prevent its possible annexation of the oil-rich northern regions of Iraq or a federation with the Turkmen and the Kurds in Iraq under Turkish auspices. It was considerations like these that influenced the way Ankara chose to play its role in post-Cold War politics, in addition to its status as a member state of NATO.

Özal's foreign policy was constructed to provide a way out of the state's isolated position and create opportunities to increase Turkey's economic and cultural domination.[85] Therefore, although the Premiership recognised the existence of a 'Kurdish problem', its primary focus was to set in motion a series of actions that would transition Turkey from a conservative state to one that was much more liberal in its attitudes. This, in turn, resulted in more lenient policies towards the Kurds including lifting the ban on the Kurdish language (1987) and repealing Law no. 2932 to legalise Kurdish publications and permit broadcasting of Kurdish programmes of 60 to 90 minutes duration (August 1992), along with the teaching of Kurdish as a recognised second language in the Turkish application for European membership (1987).[86] Although the direction of Turkish foreign policy from 1923 onwards had regarded Turkey as heir apparent to the Ottoman Empire, Turkey did not attempt to reposition itself or try and find a new role in the post-Cold War era, and this stance was reflected in Turkish foreign policy. Instead, it behaved in the same way as its neighbouring states, and, like Iran, took the safer option of continuing to expand its role and influence without compromising the security of its position in the newly emerging political landscape.

Throughout this period, it seems that the role of the Kurds was formative in determining foreign policy strategy as mutual striving to solve their Kurdish issues had pushed Tehran and Ankara towards a cooperative interrelation rather than hostility, even though at times each would still accuse the other of stirring up Kurdish insurgency within their individual states. Accordingly, Iranian and Turkish rapprochement at this time focused mainly on the formation of security committees concerned primarily with the situation of the Kurds in Iraq along with Iranian and Syrian involvement in the Kurdish issue in Turkey. However, this could sometimes cause confrontation; for instance, when Turkey accused Iran after the PKK was supplied with arms from Iran and Armenia via Nakhichevan (a landlocked enclave of the Republic of Azerbaijan).[87] On the domestic front, Kurdish voters were seen as a highly valuable asset vis-à-vis the Social Democrat Populist Party's (SHP) recognition of the Kurds[88] and therefore a prize both sides eagerly desired to win to gain the advantage. As far as the role of the Kurds in Syria in the period under examination is concerned, there were no concrete relations or developments relating to it in either the Iranian or Turkish foreign policies prior to 2003 or as a result of the Iraq War.

The 1991 negotiations held in Ankara between the Kurdish delegation led by Jalal Talabani and Özal to lobby for the continued presence of an allied strike force in Turkey[89] were the start of a series of continuous meetings reflected the growing influence of the Kurds. In 1992, Massoud Barzani and Özal discussed the PKK's role along the borders and the pressing issue of constant Turkish raids against PKK camps in the Kurdistan Region such as the severe offensive on 12 August 1993, and Operation Hammer in June 1997, which resulted in the deaths of hundreds of Kurds,[90] while in 1996 Massoud Barzani also met with the US Assistant Secretary of State for Near Eastern Affairs, Robert Pelletreau, and Prime Minister Çiller to further discuss Iraqi—Turkish border security.[91]

US relations with the Kurds of Iraq were also growing stronger at this time, starting from limited contacts in the form of economic aid (August 1969) which then developed into an official but covert US–Kurdish relations in July 1972 and finally extensive official and overt interactions in 1992. Although the creation of the KRG in 1992 started from a humanitarian basis, regime change had always been a primary objective for the region in the US administration ever since the Gulf crisis caused by Saddam Hussein's Iraq. This was responsible for the Washington invitation (through Danielle Mitterrand's mediation) extended by the US administration to the Kurdish delegation (Jalal Talabani, Ismet Sherif Vanly, and Kak Fatah) to visit the US. One key consequence of this meeting was that Özal also invited Talabani to Turkey, although Kurdish negotiations were overshadowed by severe inter and intra Kurdish conflicts which dragged on to 1998 in a prolonged season of disruption caused partly by external interference.[92]

In 1993 Talabani also acted as the intermediary between Özal and Öcalan at the Beqa'a Valley of Lebanon and was directly responsible for delivering Özal's proposal for a ceasefire (later followed by a series of ceasefires, including those of November 1995 and 1 September 1998) and the opening up of a potential political process to resolve the Kurdish issue in Turkey. The outcome was a major step forward with an important meeting between Kurdish representatives, from PUK and KDP parties, in Tehran in October 1995 to discuss reconciliation between the two parties.[93] Although both Iran and Turkey had meddled in intra-Kurdish fighting and played one Kurdish movement off against the other,[94] the previous Özal–Öcalan dialogue in 1993 was viewed by both sides as a lost opportunity where the first possibility of a feasible political solution of Turkey's Kurdish issue in the post-modern era had been allowed to slip away. The new willingness to reconcile was the fruit of Özal's more democratic Kurdish policy, but negotiations were severely affected by Özal's death on 15 April 1993 just one month after the opening discussions. Although Karayılan would argue later on that Erbakan suggested a political solution to deal with the Kurdish issue based on the federation model,[95] it was not long before negotiations broke down.

In the violent year of 1994, Foreign Minister Faruq Al Shar of Syria met with his counterparts Mumtaz Soysal of Turkey and Velayati of Iran in Damascus to discuss regional matters and the situation in North Iraq as a result of the earlier Damascus meeting (19 January 1993) between Prime Minister Demirel and President Al Assad of Syria to end its support for the PKK[96] following the February 1993 meeting between Velayati, Hikmet Cetin and Faruq Al Shar.[97] Similar meetings continued over the next few years with Turkey and Iran issuing a declaration to prevent PKK members crossing from Northern Iraq to Iran on 16 June 1994,[98] while on 24 October 1996 Iranian Vice President, Hassan Habibi, and Turkish Prime Minister, Tansu Çiller, met in Ankara[99] to discuss Turkish and Iranian operations against PKK camps in Iran.[100]

In the light of the continuity of Turkish–Iranian cooperation, 1997 could be called the year of Iran in view of its extensive activities and deepening relations with Turkey. This interdependence, particularly in the field of economics, was linked to the severe economic crises affecting the two states, which in Iran's case was caused by the negative impact of continuing US sanctions while Turkey's economy was threatened by political instability and galloping inflation, which even a series of rigorous disinflation policies (April 1994, 1998–1999 and February 2001) had failed to remedy.

However, throughout this decade even economic issues had less impact than the on-going Kurdish issue for Turkey and Iran. It was the main focus of both Iranian and Turkish foreign policies, and also acted as a catalyst in the development of stronger regional alliances forged to unite against what was seen as a disruptive influence in the region. The Kurdish issue limited Turkish attempts to implement an active foreign policy toward the region and weakened its previously central role. Interestingly, the dynamic of Iranian–Kurdish relations, while inversely proportional to Turkish–Kurdish relations during this period, also experienced its own changes in the 21st century as subsequent chapters will analyse.

It was Ankara's determination to play an active role and achieve control in regional developments that led to its unsuccessful reconciliation efforts in October 1996, known as the 'Ankara Process', a course of action that ended in direct intervention by the US and a formal peace treaty, the 'Washington Agreement', on 17 September 1998. This was not the first time the US had acted as mediator. On 19 June 1992 the US with Saudi backing had given its support to the Vienna meetings between the Kurdish parties, the KDP and PUK, which led to the formation of the Iraqi National Congress (INC, 87 members), created with the purpose of driving Iraqi opposition against Saddam. On 27 October 1992 the first meeting of the INC was convened in Salahaddin (Kurdistan Region) and all Iraqi opposition groups (including Shiite political figures), were represented. The Salahaddin Conference consolidated Vienna's aims, organised Iraqi opposition and established the status of the Kurds in the post-Saddam era while also ratifying the Resolution on Federal Law passed by the Kurdish parliament.[101]

Turkey took on the role of mediator in the long-term rivalry between the KDP and the PUK (May 1994–September 1998), an inter-Kurdish struggle for power between the Kurdish movements of Iraq. Kurdish politics and the Kurdistan Region thus clearly had an effect on both Turkish foreign policy and regional politics. Indeed, Turkey's relations with the KDP throughout this period were encouraged through alliances between Syria, Iran, the PKK and PUK whose close ties with Tehran remained strong.[102] Yet, Reza Altun explained that:

> PKK was fighting Turkey [and therefore] the main aim was to carry struggle inside Turkey; relations with different states – among others, with Iran, were essential. However Iran-PKK relations were tactical and not strategic. Iran wanted to control PKK and use it in its policies while on the other hand PKK wanted political relations with the states of the region. Therefore, PKK approached Iran.[103]

## The Kurds: A balancing factor

Before and after Gulf War I, the balancing role of the Kurds of Iraq was demonstrated through the Shah's continued support, which lasted right up to the Algiers Agreement of 1975, and even today the Kurdistan Region of Iraq continues to constitute a major element of Iran's foreign policy.[104] The current role of the Kurds, specifically those of Iraq, is of vital importance in relations between Turkey and Iran.[105] For Iran, exerting influence via the Kurds or through the use of their territory to cause instability in Iraq has been a vital element in maintaining the balance of power in its favour. At the same time, giving support to the PKK in Turkey has been a way to exert pressure and have leverage on the crucial issue of water sharing from the Tigris and Euphrates Rivers[106] while it also served as a means to express displeasure over Turkey's choice to support the Middle East peace process in opposition to Tehran.[107]

Abdullah Öcalan's 'Safe Haven' in Syria established for over a decade since 1989 was a landmark in Syria's Kurdish policy towards Turkey, and also represented the alliance of the more radical Axis in the Middle East consisting of Syria, Iran, the PKK, PUK and Hizbullah, although this could be subject to change according to the dominant interests of each group. Öcalan's 'exodus from Syria', i.e., his expulsion (9 October 1998), was defined by Murat Karayılan (6 May 1996) as part of an international conspiracy begun in 1992 which aimed at the PKK's extermination. It involved several assassination attempts against the PKK leadership, who were regarded as an increasing threat for regional states, especially following Iraq's creation of the KRG, while both Iran and Syria turned against the PKK when it seemed that the movement was becoming too strong with the formation of its central executive committee and leadership council at the PKK's 5th Congress (Haftanin, 8 February 1995).[108]

For their part, Syria and Turkey were trying to avoid conflict over the PKK issue and also water sharing, which was the main issue of controversy between Damascus and Ankara, especially after Turkey announced plans to launch a large irrigation project – called GAP – in May 1993 that would further deplete water resources for Syria.[109] The worsening of Ankara's relations with Damascus was partly responsible for the new military training and education agreement that Turkey signed with Israel in February 1996. The 20 October 1998 Adana Agreement that stopped an imminent Turkish war against Syria was yet another indicator of Syria's long-held policies aimed at peace. Damascus' refusal to be drawn into any war situation over the previous 30 years allowed its military and economic dynamics to remain comparatively intact, and this was certainly a factor in the Syrian regime's ability to withstand the pressures in the first stages of its March 2011 crisis, although this grew more difficult as the situation escalated into a full-blown war.

GULF WAR II AND ITS AFTERMATH: THE ROLE OF THE KURDS

Gulf War II is chiefly important for two reasons – the beginning of an
era of regime change in regional politics following Saddam Hussein's
capture and execution (November/December 2003) and later on for
the Arab Uprisings (December 2010). At the dawn of the 21st century,
both Iran and Turkey were relatively empowered, considering the
difficult adjustments required by the new post-Cold War political
setting, while from 2001 onwards the political map of the Middle East
was undergoing dramatic change. In Iran's case, the US Secretary of
State Madeleine K. Albright made a speech in New York in June
1998 calling for Iran to join the US in drawing up a road map to
normalise relations between the two states (17 June 1998) while US
sanctions on Iran also relaxed (17 March 2000). This was reflected
in Albright's speech given before the American–Iranian Council on
17 March 2000:

> President Clinton and I welcomed the new Iranian President's call for a
> dialogue between our people .... Now we have concluded the time is
> right to broaden our perspective even further ... today, I am
> announcing a step that will enable Americans to purchase and import
> carpets and food products such as dried fruits, nuts and caviar from
> Iran ... Second, the United States will explore ways to remove
> unnecessary impediments to increase contact between American and
> Iranian scholars, professional artists, athletes, and non-governmental
> organisations ... Third, the United States is prepared to increase efforts
> with Iran aimed at eventually concluding a global settlement of
> outstanding legal claims between our two countries.[110]

However, this seeming change of attitude should be viewed within
the wider context of the US Iraqi policy of containment and regime
change, already in place in the early 1990s. The 17 September 1998
Washington Agreement that ended the Kurdish civil war in Iraq
with the aim of uniting KDP and PUK Kurdish forces against
Saddam[111] should also be taken into consideration. In addition,
the US administration was reluctant to open many fronts when
Washington was suffering constant blows directed against its
embassies around the world, signaling the commencement of the
war on terror.

It is helpful to place the temporary easing of US–Iranian relations which was a consequence of Iran's greater openness and the close cooperation between Riyadh and Tehran in 1997 and 1998 within the context of key regional events. The most significant of these were the establishment of the Taliban Emirate in Kabul in Afghanistan and the rise of the Taliban, which represented serious security threats to Iran as demonstrated in the killing of Iranian diplomats in September, 1998 as well as the Taliban's deployment of 25,000 troops along its borders with Iran[112] in September of the same year to deter Iran from carrying out military action. This was in response to their belief that the Taliban had committed genocide against the Shi'ite Hazara community in Mazar-i-Sharif.[113] US–Iranian relations improved in the face of this common enemy and US foreign policy's considerations of Iran as an essential ally in its support to end the civil war in Afghanistan (1996–2001), a process begun by the invasion of US forces in 2001.

Iran's help was considered all the more valuable as in January 1999 the Shi'a Supreme Council for Islamic Revolution in Iraq (SCIRI, 1982 renamed in May 2003) had rejected a US offer of aid to finance opposition groups in their efforts to topple Saddam Hussein.[114] The SCIRI leaders based in Iran declined the offer, partly because they did not want to collaborate with the INC,[115] but possibly also because the Iraqi Shi'a feared retaliation from Saddam in response to the killings in the village of Dujai, North of Baghdad, in 1982.

The role of Turkey as a NATO ally was also upgraded because of its important position in relation to US policy in the region.[116] The US administration regarded democratic Turkey as a strategic role model for the states surrounding it, and viewed it positively:

> Turkey as a model of integrated peace, prosperity and strength in the 21st century [which] the US has to help so that other countries of the region can follow the same paradigm as the guarantor of regional stability.[117]

Furthermore, the unexpected rise of new surprising threats in the post-Cold War era such as the 9/11 terrorist attacks on New York increased the US need for regional allies. The recognition of the Turkish state's key role in implementing US regional policies, and its political importance for US foreign policy, was also demonstrated in the post-Saddam era as will be further discussed in later chapters. Accordingly, the US view was that Turkey held the position of:

> Important, moderate, pro-Western ally ... a buffer against a resurgence of Russian aggression ... a potential outlet for Caspian Sea energy resources [and] an alternative to Russian and Iranian threats ... for US policy initiatives in the region.[118]

On this basis, the US granted military and economic aid to Turkey,[119] supported the country's accession to the European Union (EU), and also gave the green light for Turkish operations in the North of Iraq in pursuit of Kurdish rebels (according to the official state discourse) from October 1991 onwards to eliminate the PKK (a course of action that cost Turkey US$10 billion per annum). This gave Turkey permission for anti-PKK initiatives like sending 15,000 Turkish troops to invade the North and attack PKK forces on 7 April 1999,[120] and an agreement with Iran (13 August 2000) for military cooperation against PKK forces.[121] However, in spite of US warnings prohibiting any Turkish military operations inside Northern Iraq in pursuit of Kurdish rebels (i.e., PKK forces) for fear of regional instability, the first Turkish military strike was made against the PKK on 2 December 2007 with Turkish parliamentary approval (November 2007).[122]

Throughout the 1990s, Turkey went through a time of extreme domestic instability with successive weak governments and a series of coup d'états ending with Erbakan's enforced resignation on 18 June 1997 following the 28 February 1997 memorandum of the Turkish Armed Forces via another 'velvet', i.e. covert, coup[123] which aimed to reestablish the Turkish secular order and abolish any Islamic radical trend. This policy resulted in a new government led by Bülent Ecevit at the head of the Democratic Left on 18 April 1999, a popular decision enhanced by the extra votes he managed to win after announcing the capture of Öcalan, leader of the PKK.

During this decade, both Iran and Turkey signed agreements with Russia and the US, reflecting the high priority each placed on national interest so that maintaining the regional balance of power was considered more important than forming a unilateral alliance. For instance, in spite of Turkey's long-established trading relations with Israel, Ankara was critical of Prime Minister Binyamin Netanyahu's policy towards the Palestinians as well as his statement that 'a military alliance between Israel and Turkey could be the foundation for a new regional framework' (7 September 1998) as it implied coercion.[124] However, Turkey had turned to its old ally Israel in drawing up the December 1996 agreement, asking for aid in upgrading its fleet of F-4 Phantom jets at an estimated cost of $650 million, and as the political instability continued it strengthened its military and economic ties with Israel.[125] This emphasis on regional stability together with a leaning towards independence in the foreign policies of both states was largely responsible for shaping their regional status, while the way both resolutely avoided being exploited against their interests is a characteristic often demonstrated by rising major powers.

A series of events from 1999 onwards paved the way for Kurdish empowerment in the 21st century. Massoud Barzani, former President of the Kurdistan Region of Iraq, pointed to notable developments in relations between the US and the Kurds since 9/11 indicative of international Kurdish interaction and recognition coexisting alongside a foreign policy agenda and practice that now increasingly recognised their importance to the region.[126] The continued US Iraqi policy aimed at undermining Saddam with the support of the INC throughout this period also served to strengthen the US–Kurdish alliance[127] while Öcalan's capture under US auspices (15 February 1999) marked the third US direct involvement in the region's Kurdish issues and the first in Turkey's Kurdish issue which effectively launched the 'proto-stage' of an interactive relation with the US administration.[128]

Finally, the capture of Abdullah Öcalan in Nairobi, Kenya in 1999 was instrumental in opening a way for the resolution of Turkey's Kurdish issue. The arrest of the PKK leader empowered the Kurdish movement to such an extent that ongoing peace talks between the Turkish government and the Kurds, begun directly afterwards, still dominate the Turkish political agenda. Moreover, contemporary accounts reveal the importance of this single incident in opening the way for the US administration to make advances in its struggle with Iraq through adopting a policy of regime change with Ankara's support. To set this in motion, the US allegedly signed a protocol with the Turkish government (4 February 1999) agreeing that they would hand over Öcalan to the Turkish authorities in exchange for concessions in Turkish Iraqi and Kurdish policies. However, the US also sought a commitment from Ankara to give Öcalan a fair trial and not just execute him, while they also called for rights for the Kurds.[129] Later on, Öcalan would claim that his departure from Syria and subsequent capture were part of a well-organised NATO plan set in motion with Russian collaboration in order to obtain credits from the International Monetary Fund, while he also identified the main organiser as Sandy Berger, Special Assistant to the US President for National Security Affairs together with cooperation from David Irvin, Director of Mossad. This suggests that the roles of Greece and Turkey were minimal, since it is clear that the US was largely responsible for the execution of the plans. In this context, Kenan Evren's statement that 'Öcalan was sent to us' is particularly revealing of the roles played by Israel and the US.[130]

Öcalan's capture opened up a new chapter in Turkey's Kurdish issue as well as in regional politics. It reinforced the discourse about the need for democratisation in the Middle East through the Kurdish issue, and his claims that the 21st century would of necessity involve a democratic confederation where the Kurds could look forward to playing a leading role that would elevate their status without changing regional boundaries.[131] Members of the PKK also emphasised the need for the Kurdish issue to be settled by bringing Turkey's confrontational foreign policy to an end in order to gain Turkey's acceptance for the proposal submitted by the PKK's 7th Congress (20 January 2000) advocating the potential resolution that the two nations should be synthesised into one within a Republican democracy.[132]

CONCLUSION

This chapter demonstrated the impact of Gulf War II as a structural determinant on regional politics, and illustrated the role of Turkish–Iranian relations as a springboard for the major geopolitical changes that followed. The chapter focused on the 1990s with particular emphasis on the post-Gulf War II period, and traced Iraq's impact as a crucial factor in shaping both Turkish and Iranian foreign policies vis-à-vis the political landscape existing at the time. It is also very probable that the Iraqi developments provided the impetus behind the increasingly turbulent events that reached their climax with the outbreak of sectarianism in the region.

Furthermore, it was explained how the Kurdish issue became the main catalyst of the 1990s in formulating Turkish and Iranian foreign policies towards the region. The underlying factors behind this view of the Kurdish contribution as a critical dynamic in vital issues concerning Middle Eastern politics, e.g. important issues like oil, water and regional security, were also explored. At the same time, the chapter looked at the dynamics of political relations concerning the Kurds and, in particular, the way the power triangle between Turkey, the Kurds and Iran facilitated closer Turkish–Iranian relations. Another important factor discussed in analysing the escalating importance of the Kurds concerned the rise of the KRG in Northern Iraq in May 1992 which elevated the Kurdish status and highlighted the Kurds' key role as influencers in Iraqi as well as within regional foreign politics.

Through analysis of contributory events it is suggested that the Kurds' change of status was primarily caused by external interference and mediation from a variety of sources. These ranged from powerful state entities, vis-à-vis the role of France in the Iraqi case with regard to the Kurdish issue, to international institutions and organisations such as the EU which played a major role in incidents like the steps taken to counter the perceived threat of Iran's nuclear capabilities as the following chapter will demonstrate. In addition, the role of the US administration was revealed as a major determinant in foreign policy making, including its various bureaus and lobbies which helped to determine presidential decisions and policies. This is also related to the foreign policy makers' central role in shaping strategies. Paul Wolfowitz's stance as Under Secretary of Defense for Policy in the 1990s along with the Department of Defense and the Vice President in tandem with the Jewish lobby are key examples of cases influencing US foreign policy implementation during George H. W. Bush's Presidency.

Perhaps most importantly, this chapter presents a comprehensive overview of the Kurdish role in regional and international foreign policies during this period, beginning with the first direct US intervention in the Kurdish issue, which then spearheaded the US policy of regime change in Iraq. Thus, the US alliance with the Kurds can be seen as a formative and stabilising factor in the post-Saddam era, a role which seems to have been in preparation since 1992. This can be surmised from the long-standing involvement of US foreign policy as a facilitator of the Kurdish cause and promoter of the resolution of the Kurdish issue(s) in the Middle East through constant and direct interventions aimed at restoration of the Kurds' autonomous structures and status in the region throughout this period.

Since the 1990s, this has become even more visible as demonstrated by US support of the Turkish model (at least until the outbreak of the Syrian crisis) as an example of modern state governance within the Islamic context of the Middle Eastern region. This has resulted not only in a sense of reconciliation and a willingness to work with political Islam and accelerate an Islamist version of governance on the Turkish political scene, but also support for the resolution of the Kurdish issue as dictated by US vital interests in the area which Turkey appears keen to assist.[133] Moreover, US policies facilitated the rise in power of political Islam in Turkey, a state of affairs that would once have seemed very unlikely.

Considering this development, it would be quite ironic were the resolution of the Kurdish issue to take place through the settling of the role of Islam as these have been the two most sensitive issues in Turkish political history, and both, until very recently, were viewed as threats.[134] It is interesting that the rise of the AK Parti (the Justice and Development Party, *Adalet ve Kalkınma Partisi*) as an Islamist party in power on the one hand, and the Kurdish issue's vigorous resurrection in politics on the other, has led to an emphatic call to the Turkish state to address the resolution of its Kurdish issue. However, such an approach is essential to resolve the long-standing hostility expressed towards the Kurds by many adherents of Turkey's secularist stance.

It cannot be denied that it was the Kurdish factor that elevated Turkey in the post-modern era and gave it a leadership role in sorting out the entangled foreign policies relating to the region, while concerns over security linked to the national interest have also increased its standing. In one sense, taking into consideration the way Iran's status has come under considerable pressure by external forces (namely the US and IAEA's inspections) it could even be claimed with some justification that Turkey has been the most active regional actor during this period.

However, the pivotal role of the US and Russia's influence in the region, which has been steadily increasing since 1990, has been particularly important with regard to Turkish–Iranian relations, although this interrelation has been more of a cooperation within the energy and military sectors. The paradox is that this US and Russian connection to Middle East politics (revived once again in today's Syrian crisis) and, in particular, its relation to Turkish–Iranian interactions was also affected by Kurdish policies in the region in tandem with surprising events like Abdullah Öcalan's arrest, resulting in an increased need for Turkish–Iranian interdependence.

Finally, this chapter constitutes the ground to understand the aftermath of George W. Bush's Presidency (20 January 2001–20 January 2009) and the events of 9/11, an exciting new framework of international relations started to evolve. The next chapter will show how a number of key factors such as the election of Bashar Al Assad to the Syrian Presidency following the death of his father Hafez Al Assad (20 June 2000), the continuing domination of international foreign policy agenda by non-state entities and the steady growth of Iranian and Turkish interdependence would further impact Iranian and Turkish relations as regional politics entered a period of significant change.

# CHAPTER 5

# The Iraq War and the Rise of Non-state Actors (2001–2010)

INTRODUCTION

When considering the Iraq War (March 2003) and its consequences, the beginning of the 21st century is important for three main reasons. First, the emergence of unexpected and shocking events, particularly the terrorist attacks on the World Trade Center in the heart of New York on 11 September 2001, created an environment that triggered a bold shift in US foreign policy heavily influenced by George W. Bush's new US doctrine with its emphasis on the New World Order in the post-modern era.[1] Secondly, the subsequent War on Terror, although actually a continuation of the US foreign policy's fourth change under Bill Clinton (1993–2001), signalled a major change in direction as the previous limited use of US force was now expanded into overt and more aggressive involvement in the Middle East. The moving from occasional attacks to the use of 'pre-emptive all-out' force was probably the most controversial part of the interventionist and prohibitively expensive policy instigated by George W. Bush. Its effect was that the Joint Resolution for the 'Authorisation for Use of Military Force against Iraq' (16 October 2002) gave the US Iraqi policy the go-ahead, even though it contradicted previous UN resolutions.[2]

The impact of the US foreign policy's change towards greater militarisation, following Gulf War II, was remarkable as, rather than acting as a pre-emptive, it would actually stimulate terrorism as demonstrated by the growth of Al Qaeda, a religious fundamentalist non-state actor, and the rise of al-Maliki in Iraq as the next chapter will further analyse. Thirdly, the US containment of global terrorists, whether among state or non-state actors, and the ideological radicalisation of the US foreign policy discourse with regard to the Iraq Liberation Act (1998) under Clinton's Presidency following George W. Bush's direct strikes policy[3] resulted in a fundamental review and re-shaping of US foreign policy agenda to make combatting terrorism a priority, placing it right at the centre of Bush's hardcore foreign policy agenda. Clinton, who was already struggling to deal with the implications of the failed terrorist attacks in New York in 1993, informed George W. Bush at a meeting held on 2 December 2000:

> 'You will find Bin Laden and Al-Qaeda are by far your biggest threat. One of the great regrets of my presidency is that I did not get him for you because I tried to.'[4]

Just a week before the events of 9/11, Donald Rumsfeld, Secretary of Defense, announced the administration's first National Security Directive (Presidential Directive No 9, 4 September 2001), which stated that the US needed to 'eliminate Al-Qaeda and related terrorist networks using all elements of national power'.[5] In the aftermath of 9/11, he declared: 'freedom and democracy are under attack ... this will be a monumental struggle of good versus evil ... but good will prevail'.[6] Certainly, the fear of terrorism would continue to influence and guide George W. Bush's foreign policy agenda throughout his tenure of office.

9/11 legitimised US interaction with state and non-state entities to combat terrorism. A degree of relations had already existed under Clinton's presidency, but the new directives consolidated the importance of the role of alternative non-state actors in applying foreign policies and helping to shape developments in the international system.[7] One example of this was the role of the Kurds in Iraq, previously discussed in Chapter 4, which increased in the aftermath of Gulf War II, and would become even more influential in the 2000s when the Kurdistan Region (KR) consolidated its status. In fact, the Kurds of Iraq had been playing an increasingly central role in the US policy of Iraq's containment since the 1970s.

According to Alexander Haig, the US President's Deputy Assistant for National Security Affairs (1970–1973) under Nixon's Presidency (18 July 1972),

> 'US covert support to the Kurds would not only avert a direct Soviet involvement and a hostile Iraqi regime, but as well ... would prevent a Turkish reaction while US could place its US officials there.'[8]

This was beneficial for the Kurds as Mohsin Dizayee explains: 'the Kurds in the 1970s were in need of US support to counterbalance the USSR–Iraqi alliance',[9] particularly after the USSR signed an agreement with Iraq to establish naval facilities in the port of Umm Qasr, an action which prompted a US declaration of the Gulf region as highly important in terms of its strategic value.[10]

Following the example of the Kurds in Iraq, other non-state actors, such as the PKK movement from 1984, and especially from 2002 onwards, would also exert greater influence as events in the region continued to boost their status leading to further expansion and growth of political power as this chapter will demonstrate. One example of this increased status was Iran's mediation as the central state player in the region, in the 2001 peace negotiations which aimed at achieving unity between the PKK and PUK, a case indicative of the growing influence that the PKK and the Kurds exert on regional foreign policies.[11]

The Iraq War and its aftermath, a period of immense change extensively researched in my previous studies,[12] stands out as a landmark event. Triggered by external, mainly US, interference in Iraqi affairs, it served as a critical parameter that would pave the way for the region's ongoing transformation, and thus create a pivotal momentum for regional politics and the formulation of regional foreign policies including those of Iran and Turkey. Gulf War III was also strongly influential as it acted as a structural determinant with a major impact on Turkish–Iranian relations, signalling the onset of regional sectarian conflict which increased regional instability. At the same time, the outcome of the war created favourable conditions for the rise of Iran as a formative factor in regional politics, a position of influence that Iran still holds today, although it remains to be seen whether this development will lead to further regional repercussions.

Beyond any doubt the rise to power of the AK Parti (*Adalet ve Kalkınma Partisi*, the Justice and Development Party, 2002) in the elections of 3 November 2002, following the state's financial crisis under Ecevit's government, turned a new page for Turkish politics and, to some extent, Ankara's Kurdish policies too. The banning of the Islamist Virtue Party (*Fazilet Partisi*, FP, established in December, 1998, and successor to *Refah Partisi*) in June, 2001 resulted in a split that led to the rise of Erbakan's Felicity Party (*Saadet Partisi*), and Erdoğan's Reformist Party (Justice and Development).

The AK Parti has certainly had a degree of success, managing to counterbalance the power of the military which, along with its paramilitary wings, had long acted as the safeguard of the state's Kemalist nationalist discourse, thus preventing it from achieving ultimate control vis-à-vis the latter's conflicting opposition to the government's Islamic rhetoric. Initially, Erdoğan's charismatic leadership together with other socio-economic and external factors were viewed positively by voters and led to successive victories for the party with overwhelming majorities of 42 per cent on 28 March 2004 and 46.6 per cent in the national elections on 22 July 2007 followed by an even greater increase in votes by 49.8 per cent in 2011 while a similar result of 49.5 per cent was achieved in the November elections of 2015.[13] In spite of the government's current shift away from its initial programme and policies, this rise of an Islamist party in the Turkish political scene was significant, not only because it satisfied the US regional policy for the promotion of a 'moderate' Islam, but also because it marked the second change of direction (following Turgut Özal's policies) that made considerable efforts towards liberalisation through a series of reforms launched with US support.[14]

Erdoğan's commitment to the goal of EU membership for Turkey, the rewriting of the 1982 Constitution, the maintaining of the Kemalist principle of secularism, the end of the era of *coups d'état* in Turkey[15] and the resolution of the Kurdish issue through addressing 'the economic justice and identity related grievances as well as security issues' were the building blocks of the PKK's role in Turkish politics, and even today are major concerns in AK Parti's agenda.[16] Erdoğan's initiatives throughout this decade made it clear that Turkey was committed in its determination to follow a path towards democratisation, and this resulted in a new identity for AK Parti as the party of 'Conservative Democracy'.[17]

AK Parti's 'Conservative Democracy' ideology and Erdoğan's understanding of conservatism[18] did not just mean the conservation of established institutions and relations, but the importance of the protection of core values and principles in tandem with the pursuit of progress. He stressed that using religion as a political instrument militated against a peaceful society, political diversity, and, ultimately, even religion itself. For him, the AK Parti vision was to synthesise local and universal values, balancing tradition and modernity, morality and rationality.

There are many different trends within the Islamist groups in Turkey, including advocates of secularism, leftist democrats, and other movements with varying degrees of involvement in politics,[19] a pattern replicated in the diverse political circles found in Iran described in previous chapters which invite comparison as Demirci asserts that the 'Revivalist movement' that tries to reconcile traditional Islam with modernity to which the İskenderpaşa Community belongs, actually embodies similar values to Erdoğan's principles.[20] Erdoğan emphasised that:

> [Our government] demonstrates that a religious person can protect the idea of secularism. In the West the AKP is always portrayed as being rooted in religion. This is not true. We can speak about the place of Muslims in modern society and their contribution to a modern way of life. The accommodation of democracy within AKP's Islamic character is not only compatible with the democratisation of the country but is also followed by reforms for the sake of such democracy.[21]

However, Erdoğan did not adopt the 'common good of the *ummah*' from Islam as his guiding principle, but rather claimed to have adapted this to fit with the demands of the 21st century via participation in social, and, subsequently, political affairs. It is in this context that the ideology of egalitarianism can be implemented. Such an idea is not only the mission of Islam, but a basic humanitarian need for the survival of all civilised societies. Thus, when talking about the Justice and Development Party (AK Parti), we refer to a political movement with Islamic roots operating within the framework of a secular system while respecting the boundaries between religion and state although these have become less defined as time goes on.[22]

For Iranian politics, this decade was divided into two periods. The parliamentary victory of the Islamic Iran Participation Front (Jebheye Mosharekate Iran-e Eslaami) in 2000 with 150 seats (out of 290) ceded to Seyyed Mohammad Khatami (1997–2005) changed history for Iranian politics as the state moved into a period of unparallelled openness vis-à-vis Khatami's famous proposal of a Dialogue Among Civilisations. Interestingly, this development followed a similar pattern to AK Parti as it opened with a promising first stage that aimed to marry secularism with the Islamic tradition alongside an increasing European orientation as expounded in the third Reform Package (August 2002). However, while Erdoğan achieved a successful counterbalance to the Kemalist forces with his domestic policies, the enduring institutional differences in Iran meant that any discourse operated by Khatami had to first meet with the approval of the Supreme Leadership's policies.[23] In contrast, the second half of the decade in Iran was a period of revolution introduced by the Iranian President Mahmoud Ahmadinejad (2005–2013) which caused concerns for the US administration because of its controversial stance on key issues.

The same factors explored in previous chapters also had a strong influence in the context of the Iraq war and the consequences which followed. This chapter will now proceed to examine the part these factors played (whether structural, internal, external, material or ideal-based, state or non-state entity related) and discuss the ways they shaped and developed Turkish–Iranian relations during this period.

## THE ROLE OF IRAQ IN THE FORMULATION OF TURKISH–IRANIAN RELATIONS: POLITICAL AND ECONOMIC CONSIDERATIONS

*We are facing a two-generation war. And start with Iraq ....*[24]
Steve Herbits (Adviser to US Secretary of Defense, Donald Rumsfeld)

The beginning of the 21st century constituted a landmark for regional politics as it heralded a new era of change. The monopolising of the US foreign policy agenda by the urgent need for the containment of global terrorism created pressure for the United States to respond to events that resulted in unexpected threats worldwide.

Attention focused primarily on Iraq, which continues to preoccupy more the Turkish and to a lesser extent the Iranian foreign policy agenda, resulting in unparalleled military expenditure and signalling the peak of US external interference in the Midde Eastern region thus far, following a course of high-level political force encouraged under George W. Bush's Presidency. Bush made the controversial decision to override the UN and declare war against Iraq and Saddam on 20 March 2003, an act of aggression that marked the fifth change in US foreign policy. In addition, this period was remarkable for the intensity of explicit US interactions with non-state actors, which had a significant impact on regional politics and International Relations discipline.[25]

The reason given for the Iraq War which aimed to liberate Iraq from Saddam's autocracy was the US allegation against Saddam based on the supposed threat posed by Iraq's possession of WMD (Weapons of Mass Destruction). The US decision to declare war represented the peak of the United State's interventionist policy which institutionalised the use of force, and thus initiated a new phase in the US relations with the Kurds of Iraq. However, Bush's policy seems to have been based on a 1992 Defense Planning Guidance foreign policy document which referenced Iraq and North Korea as primary case studies and had been unearthed by neo-cons during Bush's administration.[26] Originally drafted by Paul Wolfowitz and prepared by the US Defense Department, it was re-submitted by Dick Cheney after being leaked to the *New York Times* and the *Washington Post* (1992–1993).

The revised document called for the US to be prepared to take unilateral action, although there was no mention in the draft document of taking collective action through the United Nations. However, what was important was the 'sense that the world order is ultimately backed by the US' and that it 'should be postured to act independently when collective action cannot be orchestrated'.[27] US Military General Wesley Clark seemed to confirm this when he spoke of a *policy coup* initiated by members of the Project for a New American Century (PNAC), citing a confidential document handed down from the Office of the Secretary of Defense in 2001 that outlined an entire restructuring of the Middle East and North Africa.

Significantly, the document allegedly revealed campaigns to systematically destabilise the governments of Iraq, Somalia, Sudan, Libya, Syria, Lebanon and Iran.[28] In addition, a letter to Bush (20 September 2001) signed by a number of conservatives and neo-conservatives including William Kristol, Perle and Solarz working as part of the neo-conservative think-tank, the Project for the New American Century, suggested that the US must capture or kill Osama bin Laden, attack Afghanistan, target Hezbollah, consider striking Iran and Syria, fully support Israel 'in its fight against terrorism', end all assistance to the Palestinian Authority, and greatly increase military spending along with the provision of full military and financial support to the Iraqi opposition in order to overthrow Saddam Hussein, whether or not evidence linked him to 9/11.[29] Another evidence of this change of strategy was that since September 2001, Congress had appropriated US$602 billion for the wars in Iraq and Afghanistan according to the Congressional Budget Office.[30]

Whether or not the United States had already discussed, since February 2001, the invasion of Iraq at the first National Security Council meeting with the intention of distributing Iraq's oil resources (the second largest in the world, according to US Treasury Secretary Paul O'Neill)[31] is ultimately of minimal importance. US desire to remove Saddam from power in the aftermath of Gulf War II, as indicated by George H. W. Bush's and Colin Powell's campaign against Saddam's Iraq – begun in 1989 has been evident vis-à-vis US support for the formation of the Iraqi National Congress (INC) and its series of conferences held from the 1990s onwards. Richards Haas, Director of Policy Planning Staff at the State Department, claimed that 'the decision was already set by July',[32] while in his speech to the National Convention of the Veterans of Foreign Wars (26 August 2002) Vice President Dick Cheney spoke of designs against Saddam.[33] What was, however, of crucial importance was the rise of Iraq as an enduring factor in the formulation of regional, and, consequently, Turkish–Iranian politics. In this context, one can explain Iran's rapprochement with Russia (12 March 2001), together with the preservation and strengthening of its relations with Damascus based around mutual cooperation on security and energy issues linked to the Iranian–Russian agreement (25 December 2002) for the construction of an $800 million nuclear reactor near the Southwest port of Busher[34] which also resulted in the strengthening of Iranian–Chinese relations (20 April 2001).[35]

During the early years of the 21st century, the process of establishing regional alliances was gradually taking shape. Iran's isolation was already increasing, although the seeds of a strengthening Iranian–Syrian axis could also be traced during this decade, sealed by successive meetings emphasising the need for cooperation.[36] At the same time, the role of Turkey was being upgraded through Ankara's expansion of its foreign relations, and its continued interest in Iraq, probably more than in Tehran at this stage, which was reflected in economic benefits received from Iraq linked to the bilateral agreement for economic integration with Baghdad (10 July 2002). Other factors in its improved position were the role of the Turkish military in Agfhanistan; for instance, as part of the international security force in Kabul (30 June 2002), and, later on, its involvement in Iraq's Kurdistan Region (KR). Turkey was already well on its way to becoming a key player, and this was in large part due to its strongly motivated ambition to fill any gaps left by regional imbalances, especially after Saddam's overthrow.

Turkey's role was further strengthened by the US need for regional allies to help it pursue its regional policies. The Middle Eastern political arena consisted mainly of states with a Muslim orientation, and therefore the AK Parti was the ideal candidate for promotion as 'a shining example of a democratic and moderate Muslim positive force in the Middle East', a choice that fulfilled the criteria of the US Middle East Partnership Initiative (11 December 2002). Turkey was viewed as crucial in helping to implement reforms within the region such as the US democratisation project and its foreign policy doctrine of stability, the two prime objectives forming the backbone of US policies towards the Kurds in the 21st century.[37]

Turkey was also perceived as a regional ally that could fulfil the important role of acting as a counterbalance to the Islamic Republic of Iran's strong ties with Syria and non-state actors in the region, including the Lebanese Shi'a group Hizbullah and the Palestinian Islamist movement Hamas, which together formed what Iranian and Syrian leaders called the Resistance Axis. Iran's close alliance with the Palestinians and Hizbullah had often been demonstrated as in the case of the ship *Karine-A* belonging to the Palestinian Authority which was captured in the Red Sea, and subsequently discovered to be transporting Iranian weapons (4 January 2002). According to the US State Department's 2008 Country Reports on Terrorism, Syria also allowed Iran to use its territory as a transit point for weapons bound for Hizbullah and provided Iran with an entree into the Levant, allowing it to project its power far beyond its immediate borders, becoming a threat to Israel.[38] Yet, what the US administration could not foresee was that the potent combination of Tehran and Shi'a empowerment in the aftermath of the Iraq War would eventually force Turkey to enter the conflict.

On the other hand, Iran's isolation in the sense of its regional status as a reactionary power confronting the American hegemonic role in the Middle Eastern region did not alter much, in spite of Iran's constructive role in helping to preserve Afghanistan's stability with the formation of its interim government at the Bonn Conference (December 2001) following the removal of the Taliban forces from power by the US in October 2001 (which had also been achieved with Iran's cooperation).[39] Moreover, Iran pledged $530million for Afghanistan's reconstruction at the January 2002 Tokyo Conference.[40] However, it was hard to bridge the gap between the two with the US target of geostrategic control of the Middle Eastern region aimed at counterbalancing potential competitors such as China and Russia seemingly in direct contrast to Iranian rapprochement with these competitor states.

The fundamental differences between the US and Iran brought the former closer to Turkey, although Turkey also needed US support vis-à-vis the 2001 financial crisis that had forced the country into the International Monetary Fund (IMF) bail-out programme, thereby accelerating Ankara's Europeanisation process. George W. Bush's notion that Iran along with Syria and Iraq were states that sponsored terrorism and thus formed an 'axis of evil' further crystallised US foreign policies against it. Moreover, US concerns were reinforced by the White House's suspicions (December 2002) of Iranian nuclear capabilities. In spite of Bush's objection to the Congressional Syrian Accountability Act (4 September 2002), the law was successfully passed on 20 November 2003 (PL108–75),[41] a result that clearly indicates the role of bureaucracy in foreign policy-making over and above the will of the Presidency. It demonstrated the highly influential role of the neo-conservative rhetoric responsible for US hard-core policy in the form of sanctions against Syria, which were put in place to force Syria to choose between forming an alliance with the US or standing against it.

The imminent approach of Iraq War not only raised Iraq's profile so that it would dominate the formulation of regional politics for years to come, but also heralded Turkey's shift to a pro-active foreign policy practice and discourse. Although they had previously had limited interaction, Iran drew closer to Turkey because they shared a similar focus on their spheres of interest and internal problems. However, the issues experienced with Iraq had heightened concerns and fears regarding the issue of Iran's nuclear potential within the international community, and from this period onwards the situation grew increasingly tense.

George W. Bush's decision to go to war with Iraq was not just about the perceived threat linking Saddam's Iraq with the events of 9/11, or Saddam's supposed possession of WMD, or even his authoritarian behaviour, which was growing increasingly uncontrollable, but also the pressing need for the United States to secure its economic superiority in the post-Cold War era through control of the region's energy resources. As stated by Saddam Hussein[42]: 'The weapons inspections would show that the US was only looking for a way to seize Iraqi resources'. Chief UN Weapons Inspector Hans Blix also told the UN Security Council (9 January 2010) that: 'Inspectors had found no smoking gun evidence that proved Iraq continued with a secret weapon progam.'[43] Similarly, in November, 2009, Muhammad El Baradei, Director-General, would publish an IAEA report stating that: '... Nothing serious' was found at the Qom nuclear plant in Iran.[44]

Turkey was interested in the possibility of becoming a participant alongside the US in the event of war against Iraq, primarily because of its financial stake in Kirkuk and its oilfields. In exchange for its support,[45] Turkey asked the US for an aid package[46] to compensate for its previous losses during Gulf War I which had amounted to $40billion. Indeed, following the seizure of Kirkuk from the Kurds (10 April 2003), the US had assured Turkey that the Kurdish forces would be required to give up control of the oil-fields once US control was established,[47] while the US army also announced that it would start to pump oil from North Iraq to Turkey at a rate of 200,000 to 300,000 b/d (August 2003).[48] However, much to Erdoğan's disappointment, the Turkish Parliament voted against supporting the US deployment of troops in preparation for war against Iraq, with the rejection of the US motion submitted on 1 March 2003 requesting access for more than 62,000 US troops to operate from Turkish bases and ports in the event of a war with Iraq, a response that would largely dictate the post-war trajectory of Turkish foreign policy. It is said that the generals' decisive role in turning down the US request was largely responsible for the failure of the government policy's to reach the majority needed for approval with the negative vote winning by 264 to 250 (1 March 2003). This severely limited Turkey's role in backing the US strategy of regime change in Iraq, although later on limited US access to Incirlik Air Base was permitted. The loss of potential aid and loans from the US worth $30 billion resulted in a 5 per cent drop in the Turkish lira against the dollar (3 March 2003). Aykan Erdemir asserted that the main reason for Turkey's negative parliamentary vote against sending American troops to Iraq via Turkish soil 'was CHP holding against the bill'.[49] Indeed, Turkey's deep state,[50] in contrast to the government's position, opposed any attack or intervention in Iraq that could facilitate the continuation of the existing US foreign policy which had created a de facto Kurdish state in the North up to 2003. Aykan Erdemir commented on the political situation at that time: 'Erdoğan saw that as one of his biggest defeats and punished all those who voted against the bill so that they are now out of politics.'[51]

However, Turkey's role remained important, and its status as a regional player was upgraded in the aftermath of the war. This was further strengthened through its acceptance of the principle of Iraq's federal structure (19 June 2004) and the autonomy of the Kurdistan Region. One example of this was Syria's approach to Turkey as a

consequence of the US House of Representatives' sanctions against
Syria under the Syrian Accountability and Lebanese Restoration Act
(HR 1828) in November 2003 which resulted in the two states signing
a security agreement on 17 December 2003. In addition, Turkey
played the role of mediator between Israel and the Palestinians
(February 2006) when it urged Hamas to renounce violence, while it
also tried to negotiate peace talks between Syria and Israel (2008) as
described by Buthaina Shaaban on 23 April 2008: 'Turkey mediates
secret negotiations between Israel and Syria.'[52] However, the peace
process broke down in 2000 in view of the Israeli raids in Gaza
(December) and over disagreements about the extent of the Israeli
withdrawal from the disputed Golan Heights.[53] Later on, Turkey also
initiated a mediation between Iraq and Syria on 31 August 2009 vis-à-
vis Iraq's accusation that Syria was involved in the 19 August Green
Zone bombing in Baghdad.

The Syria–Turkish rapprochement dates back to January 2001
when Syrian military officers travelled to Ankara to propose that
relations be fully normalised[54] which was then followed by 20
memorandums of understanding and protocols signed regarding the
fields of economy and trade within the scope of the High Level
Strategic Cooperation Council formed between Turkey and Syria in
September 2009. The Free Trade Agreement (1 January 2007)
increased trade volume between Turkey and Syria to $2.5 billion in
2010 with Turkish imports from Syria and Turkish exports to Syria in
2010 amounting to $663 million and $1.85 billion respectively.[55]
Relations between the two states developed further with the Syrian–
Turkish Defense Agreement of 27 April 2009[56] while in 2010 a MoU
on electricity transmission provided Syria with Turkish exports of
nearly 1 billion kilowatt-hours of electricity, amounting to a turnover
of almost $100 million. The goal of this interrelation was to become a
successful 'model [that] will not only develop bilateral ties but will
also have an effect in changing the unfortunate fate of this region.
No disorder or external factor will be able to cast a shadow on our
relations with Syria',[57] although, in view of the former Turkish
Prime Minister Davutoğlu, then acting as Minister of Foreign
Affairs, this aim soon ran into problems as the following chapter
will further analyse.

In contrast, Iran had played a limited role in regional politics, mainly because of EU and US pressures to curtail its nuclear program during this period together with the perpetuation of US economic sanctions, while it also had to deal with domestic institutional differences. Ayatollah Khamenei's decision to change the power structure in Iran by giving more authority to the Expediency Council and Parliament over the Presidency (1 October 2005) launched a new period in Iran's revolutionary republic vis-à-vis the election of Mahmoud Ahmadinejad to the Iranian Presidency (25 June 2005) with 62 per cent of the votes.The first head of state received by Iran's new government in August 2005 was Bashar Al Assad who had been elected as president of Syria after the death of his father Hafiz Al Assad in June 2000. The strengthening of Iranian–Syrian relations as part of the Resistance Axis continued and became organised throughout this decade as both faced the same threats; namely, the US and Israel. This led to the creation of an Iranian–Syrian Supreme Defense Commission[58] formed on 16 June 2006 as a response to US funding supporting foreign and domestic opposition.[59] Russia also proved to be an ally, ruling out sanctions against Iran and supporting its peaceful nuclear programme.[60]

Another major concern, alongside Iran's nuclear issue and its relations with the West, was the resolution of its Kurdish issue,[61] a matter of pressing importance affecting the whole region, but, in particular, Iran's existing relations with Turkey.

## NON-STATE ACTORS IN IRANIAN AND TURKISH FOREIGN POLICIES: THE KURDS AS A FORCE FOR CHANGE

So far, the examination of Turkish–Iranian foreign policies in relation to their domestic changes and regional as well as international developments has demonstrated how (ideational and material) structures have shaped the formulation of their policies. Likewise, it is interesting to observe how the role of non-state entities has also had an impact on state foreign policies. In the case of the US, the role of Al Qaeda was detrimental. As a result, Iran pursued, and still continues to base, a great part of its foreign policy on its reliance on multiple non-state actors together with the continuation of its interference alongside Turkey in Kurdish politics. This example is again indicative of the critical role that the Kurds play as an intrinsic part of four different regional foreign policies; namely, Iran, Syria, Iraq and Turkey.

The Kurdish role as a key factor able to influence regional policies during this period, including those of Turkey and Iran, was intensified in the post-Gulf War III political setting. The US policy of regime change and the need for an Iraqi balance of power led to an official and direct – albeit undeclared – US Kurdish policy regarding the Kurds in Iraq in the 21st century, a continuation of the 1972 covert but official and 1990s direct interactions. The institutionalisation of the Iraq Kurds' relations with strong state powers such as the US led to the KRG's rise to a position where it could act independently as a semi-autonomous entity linked to its increasing empowerment since 2005.

Indeed, 2005 was a particularly significant year as the transition government that restored Iraq's sovereignty prepared the ground for a permanent constitution alongside a referendum (15 October 2005) which recognised the role of the Kurds as central. The 2005 elections for a National Assembly, the KRG's elections for a new constitution (30 January 2005) and the establishing of a permanent Iraqi government (15 December 2005) followed by the rise of Massoud Barzani as the President of the Kurdistan Autonomous Region (12 June 2005) and Jalal Talabani's election to the Iraqi Presidency (7 April 2005) all demonstrated the increased importance of the Kurdish role after Saddam's fall (9–10 April 2003). The first KNA unification vote (October 2002) and, later on, the KDP–PUK unification agreement (21 January 2006), as well as the Congressional Defence Authorisation Bill (FY2008, HR 1585, September 2007) that recognised Iraq's federalism and the Kurdish districts as legal entities, further revealed the continuing progression of the KRG's role in stabilising Iraq.

The institutionalisation of US–Kurdish relations was now strongly linked to the Kurdish issue and US foreign policy interests as for the first time US foreign policy directed its efforts to work directly with the Kurds and their cause, rather than responding to the Kurdish issue purely on a humanitarian basis as before. This change enabled the KRG to pursue its de facto independence with US support and had a positive impact on the Kurdish movement as a whole with the outcome that this non-state entity was elevated into a player of strategic importance. This institutionalised interaction was sealed with energy, military and other strategic deals which then paved the way for the KRG's expansion of its relations with other regional states including Iran which reasserted its control through the Shi'ite bloc in Baghdad, while at the same time enhancing recognition of the Kurds through their foreign policy agenda and practice.

George W. Bush's official White House invitation to Kurdish President, Massoud Barzani (25 October 2005), the first high-level official meeting (1 May 2008) between Prime Minister Nechirvan Barzani of the KRG and, on the Turkish side, Ahmet Davutoğlu, Senior Adviser to the Turkish Prime Minister, Murat Özçelik, Special Coordinator of Iraqi Affairs at the Turkish Foreign Ministry, and Derya Kanbay, Turkish Ambassador in Baghdad (April–May 2008) represented a move towards greater cooperation and interaction, including an agreement to find a peaceful solution to the PKK issue in Turkey. These events, together with another invitation extended by King Abdullah bin Abdulaziz of Saudi Arabia to the KR's former President, Massoud Barzani (12 March 2007) and Barzani's December 2015 visit to Riyadh, were all cases that represent an official recognition of the KRG, the Kurdish role as foreign policy makers, as well as the increasingly influential role the KRG was beginning to play in both Turkey's Kurdish and Iraqi policies and in Iranian foreign policy towards Iraq in the light of Iran's support to the Iraqi federal government. Such actions were influential in building the foundations of the series of historic meetings that still continue today.

The development of a US Kurdish policy to bring order to the chaotic situation that existed after the fall of Saddam, and help maintain Iraq's internal stability along with the Kurds' strategic importance in preparations for the war where their help was regarded as crucial, indicated a major change as external interference swung towards support for the Kurdish cause in Iraq for the first time, and, as a result, gave the progression of the Kurdish issue a massive boost. The first session of the Kurdish parliament (4 October 2002) held with the participation of Colin Powell and Danielle Mitterrand was followed by a series of INC meetings between the Kurds and the US (namely, INC's third conference in July 2002, the New York meeting in December 2001, the London Conference in December 2002 that prepared the ground for participation in the 2003 War, and the Salahaddin meeting in February 2003), that effectively drew up a 'road map' for liberating Iraq from Saddam.[62] The rise of the Kurdish role in Iraq was also very much linked to the Turkish parliament's refusal to ally itself with the United States against Saddam which meant that:

> US–Kurdish relations after 9/11 were characterised by new developments since the Kurds had become, for the United States, a major part of the liberation of Iraq and a front against terror, whilst their role [was also] important for the democratic rebuilding of Iraq as well as for Iraq's political processes' as stated by the President of the KR.[63]

The Kurds' strengthened position made them important economic players vis-à-vis the KRG's Petroleum Law (19 June 2007) and subsequent oil contracts with foreign (including American) companies. After the historic meeting between former President Massoud Barzani and Turkey's former Prime Minister Erdoğan on 4 June 2010, the former Turkish Foreign Minister, Ahmet Davutoğlu, stated that Turkey 'views its relations with Iraq and especially with the Kurdistan Region as important and wants greater economic integration with the KRG'.[64]

Turkey's request asking President Barzani for 'mediation for a peaceful solution to the Kurdish question in Turkey' during his visit to the US was followed by the 2008 Trilateral Mechanism set up between Turkey, the US, Iraq including the KRG with the aim of developing cooperation in order to eradicate the PKK in Iraqi territories. These policies further revealed the KRG's key role as a political and strategic player.[65] However, the empowerment of the KRG was not viewed entirely favourably by the Turkish government. Kurdish demands such as the 'normalisation' of Kirkuk according to Article 140 (§2) via a referendum (initially planned for 15 November 2007 but still pending today), and the later 27 April 2007 statement threatening military intervention in the Kurdistan Region based on a so-called 'midnight memorandum' (an 'e-memorandum' published online that was subsequently made public by the state's military elite) were seen as issues. Such incidents and, more importantly, the unsuccessful 'electronic coup' exposed Turkey's domestic problems which were reflected in the AKP's attempts to stabilise its power and control over the state's military apparatus. However, Ankara's main fear was the threat posed by further KRG empowerment, especially if a potential incorporation of the oil-rich region of Kirkuk after the fall of Saddam went ahead. From Turkey's viewpoint, this would be a disastrous outcome as it would cause serious obstacles for Turkey's increasingly desperate attempts to control its own Kurdish issue.[66]

It is only from 2008 onwards that the Turkish government has seemed to finally accept the post-war status quo as a permanent reality, an inevitable consequence of its struggle caused by internal pressures and the contest for power between Turkey's military structure (and the deep state) in opposition to its elected government as disclosed by the Ergenekon scandal.[67] The Head of Foreign Relations in the KRG described the process:

> [As a] change [that] was not easy and it took a while to happen as Turkey might not have been ready to accept that Baghdad would not have full control of the area and was dealing only with Baghdad until 2003. Therefore, there was no direct interaction [between Ankara and KRG] for a certain time.[68]

At first, Turkey tried to deal directly with Baghdad through the establishment of consulates in Mosul and Basra (2008–2009) with 48 agreements and MoUs (memoranda of understandings) relating to energy and other economic issues signed in Baghdad in November 2009,[69] while the High Level Strategic Cooperation Council established with Syria in 2009 was another initiative aimed at expanding bilateral relations. However, in June 2009 the first oil export from the KR to the Turkish port of Ceyhan took place.[70] Improving Turkish–KRG relations also appeared to have had a positive impact on Turkey's Kurdish strategy as Erdoğan announced $12 billion for projects in the South-east region (12 March 2008).[71] This would be very much an evolving process as the 'Kurdish Initiative' in 2009 followed by the Oslo talks of the same year between the PKK and Turkey's National Intelligence Organisation (MIT, *Milli Istihbarat Teşkilatı*) which negotiated three protocols on how to settle the Kurdish issue in Turkey as well as the stages for a political solution which is still ongoing today.

During this same period, Iran appears to have shared a similar viewpoint to Ankara as both states wanted to influence developments in post-Saddam Iraq with Iran focusing – apart from the KR – on the South where most of the Shi'ite population were located, whereas Ankara's interests clearly lay in the North. However, Iran's foreign policy was not particularly pro-active despite concerns over its own Kurdish issue, as its agenda was predominantly preoccupied with the US dual containment policy directed against Iran and its nuclear issue in view of the United Nations Security Council sanctions against Iran on 23 December 2007 followed by a number of others that were unanimously approved by the UNSC on 24 March 2007.

However, Iran had still another reason for concern. The continuation of the US troops' occupation in Iraq 'was Iraq's main problem' according to Supreme Leader Ayatollah Ali Khamenei as Iran feared a potential attack following the overthrow of the Iraqi regime.[72] Iran's perception of US hostility was also boosted by Executive Order 13224 (15 August 2007) in which the US labelled Iran's Revolutionary Guard Corps, the 125,000 wing of the Iranian armed forces, as 'specially designated global terrorists' vis-à-vis Iran's aid to insurgents in both Afghanistan and Iraq as well as its support for destabilising actors in the Middle East as a whole.[73] These US suspicions were seemingly confirmed by the increasing strength of the Resistance Axis through the deepening of the Iranian–Syrian alliance following the 10 October 2007 oil agreement, which further reinforced their economic partnership, while another runaway parliamentary victory for the conservative wing in Iran won 71 per cent of the seats on 14 March 2008.[74]

The PKK element was another important factor in regional politics as it stimulated both Turkish–KRG and KRG–Iranian strategic cooperation, with Iraqi Foreign Minister Hoshyar Zebari proposing a joint intelligence base in Erbil manned by Iraq, Turkey and the US (23 January 2009) as well as KRG–Iranian cooperation on the PJAK matter and the opening of Iranian consulates in Erbil and Suleymaniya (13 February 2009).[75]

The year 2007 was particularly critical as the Turkish–PKK conflict escalated to such an extent that the Turkish parliament approved a motion (17 October 2007) allowing troops to cross the border into the KR and take part in military strikes against PKK rebels on 2 December 2007. The capture of PKK leader Öcalan in Kenya (1999) did not affect the movement as much as Turkey had hoped, and Turkish fears of the impact of PKK's empowerment upon its domestic situation vis-à-vis the Iraqi developments increased after the election results of 22 July 2007 when Kurds standing as independent candidates gained 23 seats as members of the Democratic Society Party (DTP). Indeed, Turkey's Kurdish parties historically had a long interaction with Turkish politics and often caused serious concerns for Ankara, mainly because of their close affiliation with PKK, which is viewed as a terrorist organisation.[76] However, although the PKK was the main Kurdish movement in conflict with Turkey, Ankara failed to recognise the considerable changes PKK had undergone since 2000, at least so far as the politicisation of its cause was concerned, and the achievement represented by the movement's partial completion of its third stage in spite of its pursuance of a sometimes changeable discourse or practice.

In the aftermath of the Iraq war, new Kurdish parties/organisations arose in the Kurdish regions. In Turkey these were Kongra-Gel/PKK (2003) and the Koma Komalen Kurdistan (KKK, 20 March, 2005), renamed Koma Civaken Kurdistan (KCK, Democratic Confederation of Kurdistan) in 2007.[77] In Syria, the PYD (the Democratic Union Party, *Partiya Yekîtiya Demokrat*, 2003), which with its military wing the YPG (the People's Protection Units or People's Defense Units, *Yekîneyên Parastina Gel*) played a key role in the fight against terrorism, particularly in more recent clashes with IS (Islamic State) including the bloody conflict of January 2013 when the PYD confronted both the Free Syrian Army (FSA) and IS in the town of Serêkaniyê (Ras al-Ayn). Such events are strongly representative of the contributing influence of the Kurdish movement in Syria as an embryonic, yet considerable, dynamic that plays a deterministic role in the future of Syria, a topic which will be further analysed in the next chapter. In the Kurdistan Region of Iraq operated the Kurdistan Democratic Solution Party (KDSP), while Iran had the PJAK, a Kurdish guerrilla movement known as the 'Party for Free Life'. PJAK's main goal was a democratic Iran, which it was trying to achieve through armed struggle (with its first attack against the Iranian military taking place in 2004). This meant that PJAK was considered a serious threat, described by Reza Altun as an 'establishment which brought tensions between PKK and Iran'. Reza Altun further explained the nature of the various Kurdish parties affiliated with the PKK:

> All these parties are not PKK [but] inter-related paradigms. There is a unity but each has its own separate agenda and strategy based on their situation and sociopolitical conditions. They are all united because they all accept Apo as their leader and agree with his strategies. However, each part [is identified by] different sociopolitical needs and methods for struggle.[78]

Murat Karayılan, acting leader of KONGRA-GEL/PKK, asserted that the US urged PJAK members to leave the PKK and form an independent organisation with the aim of possibly making official American relations with PJAK. However, PJAK did not accept the American offer.[79] Undoubtedly, there was also a tactical relation between Iran and PKK as interactive partners within the context of Iran's foreign policy through which it exerted pressure on Turkey via its use of non-state actors. Reza Altun argues that: 'Iran wanted to control PKK and use it in its policies while, on the other hand, PKK wanted political relations with states in the region and therefore approached Iran.'[80]

THE IRANIAN VERSUS THE TURKISH MODEL

*Energy politics*

> *Iran and Turkey know there is paradigmatic unity between them.*
>
> Reza Altun[81]

In spite of the fact that the constitutions of Turkey and Iran followed essentially different models, the foreign policy orientation of both states was in favour of empowering their geostrategic role and thus stabilising their political influence in the region. Therefore, despite the ups and downs of their relations over the years and their political differences as two diverse entities in the region following very different forms of government based around their own distinctive interests and economic gains, they both came to the realisation that the formation of alliances with regional state and non-state actors was an essential tool for their geostrategic survival.

On this basis, the economic level of interdependence between Iran and Turkey had always remained high, but in the period following the Iraq war, their interrelation founded on mutual objectives of achieving regional survival and expansion in tandem with the successful meeting of their energy needs became more intense. Since the start of Turkish imports of natural gas from Iran, and the establishment of the Turkish–Iranian Business Council in 2001, Turkish investment had climbed steadily from $3.5 billion in Iran's South Pars megafield capacity, the equivalent of 1900 trillion cubic feet of gas, to $10.2 billion in 2008. However, it should also be noted that at this point Iran and Turkey were involved in a 25-year agreement between the two countries arranged in 1996 in which Iran had pledged to supply Turkey with 10 billion (b cm) of gas annually.

Iran was Turkey's second largest supplier of natural gas (16–18 per cent) after Russia, and also a major supplier of oil (30–32 per cent of imports in recent years). In 2002, the two states completed a pipeline connecting the gas fields of Tabriz to Ankara, which continues to provide Turkey's current supplies today.[82] The annual bilateral trade volume for gas reached its peak in 2010 at $10.6 billion,[83] while Iran also offered Turkey price concessions on its oil imports. Iran increased its gas exports to Turkey by 50 per cent in 2010 to 8.25 b cm and reportedly reached the 10 b cm commitment level in 2011. The Turks have sought to increase this supply even further (to 16 b cm annually), but the high price of Iranian gas, uncertain supplies, and the frustrations of doing business in Iran have created difficulties in achieving this. Therefore Iran and Turkey are not always in agreement; for instance, when the issue of gas transit and the development of the Caspian Basin arose, Turkish and Iranian interests seemingly diverged with Iran refusing to support the Trans-Caspian pipeline, which aimed to supply Central Asian gas to Europe via Turkey in favour of a preference for other alternatives routes to European markets while Turkey opts for its establishment as a corridor for Central Asian energy supplies to Europe.[84] In the same context, Flanagan argues that 'Russian efforts to control the flow of energy from the Black Sea and Caspian Basin regions threats [the very] ambition of Turkey to play a key role in expanding the East–West energy transit corridor – even as it further develops its own North–South energy axis with Russia.'[85]

Iranian–Turkish cooperation also steadily increased from this period onwards in a number of other areas, as one of the most important being Iran's role as Turkey's fifth largest trading partner. The total bilateral trade volume for Turkey increased five-fold from 2000 to 2009 to eclipse $16 billion in 2011 with Iranian exports to Turkey, particularly energy, accounting for over $12 billion of that total. In 2010 the two governments made a pledge aiming to push expansion of trade between them up to $30 billion, a course of action that they agreed to facilitate by opening more border crossings.[86]

According to Uslu, nine meetings at the ministerial level were concluded in 20 December 2008, while the International Monetary Fund Directory of Trade Statistics (DOTS) stated in 2009 that the volume of trade between Iran and Turkey was $5.63 billion with Turkey's exports to Iran amounting to $1.87 billion while its imports (mostly energy) were $7.84 billion.[87] In 2009 alone, Ankara imported 5.1 billion cubic metres of natural gas from Iran, a 35 per cent increase over the year before. In February of 2010, Turkey announced it was prepared to link its Northeastern port city of Trabizon with the Iranian port city of Bandar Abbas by a pipeline, and this was probably responsible for the Islamic Republic increasing its gas exports to Turkey by 98 per cent from 20 March to 5 May compared to the same period in the previous year. In July 2010, Javad Oji, Head of the state-owned National Iranian Gas Export Co and Turkey's ASB Co, confirmed that Iran and Turkey had signed a contract to build a 660-kilometre pipeline crossing Turkey from Iran in spite of the rise in international sanctions against Iran.[88] In February 2010, the Central Bank of Iran approved the establishment and operation of a Turkish-owned bank in Bandar Abbas, while, in the same month Iran signed a customs memorandum of understanding with Turkey that opened up the Bazergan, Khoy, Saro and Maku border points for trade.[89] Flanagan points out that:

'Two significant growth areas in economic relations have been Iranian investment in, and travel to, Turkey. Iranian firms are increasingly operating in Turkey as a way to access international markets in the face of a more restrictive business climate in Dubai and other Gulf states due to sanctions. More than 1,470 Iranian firms were operating in Turkey at the end of 2010, up from only 319 firms in 2002. Turkish banks have also positioned themselves as an acceptable international intermediary for financial transactions between the Islamic Republic of Iran and states such as India that do not want to infringe on US sanctions. Iranians now constitute the 4th largest group of foreign tourists in Turkey thanks to visa-free travel with nearly 2 million visitors in 2011 adding to the growth in Turkey's robust tourism sector'.[90]

The greatest example of just how interdependent Iranian–Turkish relations had become during this period could be seen in the Turkish response to the United Nations Security Council (UNSC) Resolution 1929 (9 June 2010) following UNSC 1737 (2006), 1747 (2007), and 1803 (2008) which further strengthened the sanctions against Iran in protest at its nuclear program. Turkey as a non-permanent member of the UNSC voted against the resolution as did Brazil with the Joint Declaration by Iran, Turkey and Brazil on Nuclear Fuel in May 2010. Turkish State Minister Cevdet Yilmaz went even further when he talked about a 'golden age' opening in Turkish–Iranian relations that recognised the two states as 'friend and brother' countries. On 2 March 2010, Turkey and Iran signed a memorandum of understanding boosting industrial and commercial relations between them, while Iranian supplies to Turkey reached an average volume of 18–25 mil c/m of gas per day.[91] Finally, on 10 June of the same year, Turkey agreed to create a free trade and travel zone with Syria, Lebanon and Jordan.[92]

*Foreign policy and security*

The 'Turkish–Iranian paradigmatic unity'[93] lay primarily in Ankara's desire to achieve historic, domestic (namely, democracy and the development of freedom), economic and foreign policy restoration.[94] To further this goal, Ahmet Davutoğlu's *Strategic Depth* doctrine (2001) proposed an interactive policy for Turkey as an initiator and mediator of peace and stability in the region which would be reflected in Turkey's pursuance of a proactive foreign policy founded on three key principles: orientation towards Europe, strategic dominance and maximisation of its security.[95]

Davutoğlu's doctrine and its Turkish foreign policy discourse provoked some debate over its justification from both Neo-Ottomanist (*Yeni Osmanlıcılık*) and/or Eurasianist viewpoints. AK Parti's will for regional hegemony, a principal characteristic of AK Parti's foreign policy behaviour, although essentially a legacy of the 1923 Turkish state, as a deviation from the long-held beliefs and aspirations of the Ottoman Empire, has little in common with the latter's strength to hold the state together.

According to the literature, Eurasia was conceived as a geographical space where ethnic Russians, Turkic peoples and Mongolians resided so that Eurasianist discourses were generally perceived as relating to the Turkic countries in Central Asia and the Caucasus, and therefore Eurasianism implied the creation of a non-Western Eurasian space based on a regional economic integration model. This was a complete contradiction of Kemalist Eurasianism which promoted a nationalist perspective and hostility towards any pro-Western policy in the Eurasian space, instead favouring alliances with Russia, China and Iran where Turkey would feel a secure and welcomed partner.[96] Yet, even within these contexts, and bearing in mind Erdoğan's objective to expand further into Central Asia and the Caucasus and strengthen Turkey's influence in the region, Turkey's foreign policy orientation was to a great extent shaped by a Western framework and operated within it, and this meant that it would not reject a unipolar Western hegemony.

The Turkish reality was a foreign policy that combined various attitudes and characteristics including Kemalism to preserve the national identity, and this influenced Turkey's decisions to cooperate with Georgia in an agreement of military assistance and cooperation in 1999, with Georgia and Azerbaijan in the Trilateral Security Agreement representing Turkish–Georgian–Azerbaijani cooperation in January 2002, and also the 24 December, 2010 agreement with Iran and Azerbaijan to combat crime, terrorism and local conflicts.

The year 2008 was one of historic importance, marked by official Turkish recognition of the KRG, improved Turkish relations with

Syria, the renewal and strengthening of the rapprochement with Iran and a more active Turkish foreign policy towards the increasingly isolated Iran. However, in a broader context, 2008 was also the start of the economic crisis in Europe, while during the same period the 2008 Russia–Georgia war revived Russia's Eurasia foreign policy activism, which opposed what it saw as US and NATO interference in the Middle East and Eurasia.

To restore its influence in the Middle Eastern region, it was obvious that Russia needed Syria as Moscow's naval base at Tartus was essential for Russia to expand into the East Mediterranean. To achieve this, Russia was prepared to do whatever was needed in order not to leave Syria to either Turkey or the West, and therefore in 2008 the Russian parliament voted to release Syria from three-quarters of the almost $14 billion debt it owed Russia.[97] The PKK could also be relied on to play a supportive role in implementing Russian policy in the region, given that 88 per cent of mines and 85 per cent of rocket launchers used by the PKK were of Russian origin.[98]

Turkish–Iranian understanding was established first and foremost because of Iran's crucial need for regional allies that it could depend on to help counterbalance US and EU pressures relating to its nuclear issues as since 2003 the EU3 diplomatic initiative (UK, France and Germany) had been pushing Iran to close down its nuclear enrichment programme. At the same time, Iran had to deal with Iraq's sectarianism, and especially the exclusion of the Arab Sunni element from the administration, which presented an existential threat right on its doorstep, while another pressing concern was the continuous threat posed by the presence of US troops along its borders. The US administration's favouring of Turkey at the expense of Iran following the Iraq war, increased Iranian fears for the future, so that Tehran viewed with suspicion the US policy's successive interventions aimed at restoring democracy.

The year 2009 was a turning point for Iranian politics as it flagged up the radical nature of Iranian foreign policy following the 12 June elections, where the results giving Ahmadinejad a 62.63 per cent lead were hotly contested. The election's outcome caused public outrage and ultimately led to the launch of Hussein Mousavi's Green Movement. The Leadership believed that the massive protests (18

September 2009) of more than 100,000 opposition supporters protesting the re-election of Mahmoud Ahmadinejad (5 August 2009) despite the hard-liners' warnings, were engineered by the West, and this, together with the discovery of uranium traces in the area around Al Kibar village by UN inspectors (5 June 2009),[99] combined to place US–Iranian relations at a crossroads where mistrust and suspicion were rife.[100] This perception of US determination to control Iranian influence in the region was aggravated even further by the visit of Israeli Foreign Minister, Avigdor Lieberman, to Brazil (21 July 2009), the start of a ten-day official tour of South American countries to 'curb Iranian influence'.[101]

Circumstances throughout this period certainly seemed to favour Turkey above other regional actors as a key player with growing influence. This role was demonstrated through a number of events such as Erdoğan's decision to play the Palestinian versus the Israeli card, and move away from its thus far cordial relations with the latter to draw closer to the Arab and Muslim world. Changes of direction favourable to Palestinian interests were subsequently carried out via Turkey's activism in the Middle East process, its major part in resolving Iran's nuclear crisis, the launch of a 'Kurdish Opening', initially introduced as the 'National Unity and Brotherhood Project' in 2009, and the government's adoption of a harsh rhetoric in relation to its Israeli policies. Already since 2004 Turkey publicly had denounced the Israeli assassination of Sheikh Ahmed Yassin and Israeli policy in the Gaza Strip, while on 29 January 2009, Erdoğan walked off the stage at the World Economic Forum in Davos, Switzerland, after exchanging bitter words with Israeli President Shimon Peres following the 2008 Israeli offensive in Gaza known as the Gaza War or Operation Cast Lead (27 December–18 January). In 2010 Turkey also withdrew its ambassador in Tel Aviv; following the massacre of around ten Turkish peace activists when Israeli commandos raided a Turkish aid ship taking part in a humanitarian mission to break the siege of Gaza.[102] It was this event that caused the meeting of Deputy Prime Minister Bülent Arınç with the Syrian Head of State, Bashar Al-Assad (28 February 2010) to discuss the Gaza issue.

The multi-dimensional nature of Turkey's foreign policy was linked to the regional uncertainty and its domestic problems, but also the AK Parti's objective of survival which it attempted to achieve by increasing Turkey's relative autonomy versus the US and EU.[103] It was in this context that Ankara made approaches to Iran and Russia such as the 7 August 2009 agreement for the contruction of a Russian–Turkish gas pipeline,[104] a move which made sound economic sense as Turkey was heavily dependent on Russian natural gas which accounted for two-thirds of gas imports into the country.[105]

In May 2010, the Turkish and Russian governments also signed an agreement to cooperate on the construction and operation of four 1,200 megawatt Russian-design VVER power reactors at Akkuyu in South Western Turkey. The Russian state-controlled Atom-StroyExport was commissioned to construct the plants, paying all the $20 billion construction costs with a prospective operational date sometime between 2016 and 2019. The terms of the Akkuyu agreement, including Russian training of Turkish personnel in plant operations, opened the door to further cooperation relating to the development of Turkey's nuclear power sector. Currently, Turkish businesses have invested more than $7 billion in Russia while Turkish contractors have completed projects in Russia worth $33.8 billion.[106] However, during this period Ankara appears to have recognised that without the resolution of the Kurdish issue in Turkey and an increase in its ability to influence its Arab Muslim neighbours, its goal of transformation into a formative power in the region would be impossible. According to Murat Karayılan:

'The Turkish state was in direct dialogue with the PKK from September 2008 to June 2011. Turkey's main problem is the Kurdish issue. Ankara cannot claim that it is a democratic state and realise any opening to the outside world unless the Kurdish issue is resolved.'[107]

*Taraf* recorded that 'negotiations were also held in 1996–1998 between the Turkish General Staff and PKK'[108] in an attempt to resolve the problems. At the same time, this period also saw DTP's closure on 11 December 2009 and the formation of the BDP party, its successor, on 18 December 2009. Erdoğan continued to make concentrated efforts to circumvent the state's military structure, achieving a measure of success with the rejection by Turkey's highest court of a closure case against the AKP in July 2009. He also made positive steps in changing public opinion towards the acceptance of a potential (con)federal resolution of its Kurdish issue. The insecurity in the region was aggravated by George W. Bush's policies, which were part of his 'Greater Middle East Initiative' (announced on 12 December 2002) and the 'Greater Middle East' map, prepared by Lieutenant-Colonel Ralph Peters and published by the *Armed Forces Journal* (June 2006).[109] The fragile situation was also not improved by Syria's unsuccessful attempts to approach the US administration via visits such as that of Syria's Deputy FM Faysal Makdad to Washington (1 October 2009).

Therefore, it can be concluded that the year 2009 acted as a catalyst in setting the course for both current and future developments. On the one hand, there was a sense of cooperation and high level rapprochement among some regional powers – namely, Iran and Turkey, and Iran and Iraq with Syria. But, on the other, US administration plans for regional transformation linked to George W. Bush's administration, the neo-cons focus on the protection of Israel's security, and the short-lived optimism regarding Barack Obama's pacifist policies, created unprecedented chaos within the region.

During this period, Obama's Presidency did not seem to introduce any particular shift or changes into the US foreign policy discourse and practice.[110] Obama had initially followed relatively 'soft' policies reflecting a more positive approach towards Iran, a continuance of the policy of engagement and rapprochement he had adopted since 2009. Examples of his stance were that he 'waited until 23 June 2009 to condemn the violence in Iraq'[111] and also made a historic call to Hassan Rouhani (2013) in the first direct communication between American and Iranian leaders since the 1979 Islamic revolution, but this did not prevent Congress voting to impose gasoline sanctions in record time following AIPAC pressure. Parsi summed up Obama's objectives thus: 'Obama had recognised and favoured diplomacy with Iran, [was an advocate of] limited enrichment, opposed Israeli settlements on Palestinian territory and signaled that regime change was no longer an American objective [in the context of his discourse] to renew US relations with the Muslim World.'[112]

However, in a January 2010 memo, Secretary of Defense Bill Gates warned that the US lacked a coherent, long-term plan to deal with Iran's steady progress towards a nuclear capability.[113] Perhaps this warning influenced Obama as later on he seemed to change track, approving US intervention in Libya in 2011, sanctions against Iran (2010, 2011), and supporting the opposition of the Palestinian Authority's bid for statehood through the National Security Council (NSC, September 2011), a *volte face* to such an extent that scholarly works claim that 'Washington has changed Obama far more than [Obama] has changed Washington.'[114] Likewise, Khamenei, in a 2009 speech in Mashhad responding to Obama's New Year's message, 'stressed Obama's inability to change US foreign policy, arguing that the real decision makers in Washington were unknown. Structural factors would overpower Obama.'[115] Therefore, scholars have perceived Obama's reaching out to Iran during this period as 'genuine but short lived'.[116]

US foreign policy's much stronger focus on the War on Terror and Obama's continuation of his predecessor's policy together with his greater involvement in domestic politics left US Middle Eastern policy at an impasse caused by presidential indecisiveness and the lack of concrete foreign policies, other than military means.[117] Obama's historic speech at Al Azhar University in Cairo on 4 June 2009 aiming to mend US relations with the Middle East seemed to have been forgotten in his later UN speech (25 September 2012), which stressed the need for the containment of a nuclear-armed Iran, and the need to protect Israel and the Gulf's security alongside the importance of maintaining stability within the global economy.[118] Similarly, on 3 May 2010, the American President renewed the sanctions on Syria imposed by former President Bush[119] along the same lines as the Foreign Operations Appropriations Act, FY2006, signed by the President as PL 109-102 (14 November 2005) which repeated previous bans on US aid to Syria, although it also contained a provision authorising at least $6,550,000 for programmes supporting democracy in Syria and Iran.[120] However, these sanctions seemed to contradict the view expressed in the US State Department's *Country Reports on Terrorism, 2004* which stated that 'Syria has cooperated with the United States and other foreign governments against Al

Qaeda and other terrorist organisations, while discouraging signs of
public support for Al Qaeda.' Earlier, US Assistant Secretary of State
William Burns also told a congressional committee on 18 June 2002
that the cooperation the Syrians had provided in relation to Al Qaeda,
even if it was in line with their own self-interest, had saved American
lives. According to a more recent news report, Syria helped unravel a
plot by an Al Qaeda group in Canada, which aimed to attack US and
Canadian government installations.[121] However, Syria was not the
only state subjected to US sanctions as on 1 July 2010 President
Obama also signed tough new sanctions against Iran into law, which
penalised foreign companies trading with Iran.[122]

## IRANIAN–TURKISH RAPPROCHEMENT: INTERNATIONAL AND REGIONAL STRUCTURES

Throughout this period, Turkish rapprochement with Iran was clearly
evident. As Iranian Foreign Minister Manouchehr Mottaki declared in
2010: 'Turkey is familiar with Iran's position which can help others to
understand Iran better.'[123] According to the Turkish New NSC
Document, the Red Book (2010), Iran no longer wanted to be seen as
a threat.

The peak of Turkish–Iranian relations in 2010 should be viewed
within the broader context of Turkish–Iranian needs which
essentially created an interrelation built on necessity. Turkey's
economic recession in 2001 had highlighted the need to increase
its exports[124] as a profitable market for Turkish goods[125] while Iran
was suffering from isolation due to its nuclear crisis. The huge
transformation going on within the regional environment also
opened up new opportunities, while Turkey's foreign policy of 'zero
problems with neighbours' and a complementary agenda of leadership were other contributing factors. From Osman Korutürk's
perspective, the situation was promising:

> 'Iran is our opening to Central Asia and we are their opening to
> Europe and beyond … AK Parti is seeking for leadership in the region
> but Iran is more rational and pragmatic and they seek for strength not
> for leadership. Once they are strong, they can lead the region. They
> know it.'[126]

On Iran's side, this mutually important relation should be perceived within the broader context of Iran's foreign policy priorities, which were focused on no longer being in isolation so that they could once again engage in regional politics, and, as a result, expand their influence via strong and multiple alliances. Iran's deepening inter-relation with Turkey was an important step in achieving this. Osman Aşkın Bak stated his belief that: 'Turkey can play an important role for Iran to join the international community.'[127] Gulf War III was a golden opportunity for both players to penetrate further into the region, and Iran, in particular, benefitted significantly. However, this did not cause any rifts in relations between the two states. Arshin Adib-Moghaddam explained the situation:

> 'Turkey and Iran are too embedded within each other to be separated or to act antagonistically. This interdependence is not merely apparent in terms of mutual security concerns that a common border inevitably brings about, it is also lodged in the cultural tapestry that holds the Iranian-Turkish dialectic together.'[128]

At the same time, in spite of Turkey's economic need to diversify in order to meet its energy requirements and its desire for regional allies for hegemony, Ankara's links have always been strongest with the US vis-à-vis the US–Turkish 2006 strategic vision document which embodies historical US–Turkish relations stretching back over many years.[129] The fact is that specific interests will dictate regional interactions and cause fluctuations in the balance of power both within and outside the region, and this is true even in the case of revolutionary powers such as Iran. Examples demonstrating this include a report in *Middle East Online* (26 August 2008)[130] stating that, according to figures published by the US Department of Agriculture, Iran bought more than 1.17 million tons of wheat from the US between June and August 2008, while, more recently, Tehran also completed a nuclear deal with the US administration on 14 July 2015.

EPILOGUE: TOWARDS A CONCEPTUAL ANALYSIS

This period points out the evolution of the same contributory factors outlined in previous chapters, and clearly demonstrates their continuity under the prism of an intense rapprochement between Iran and Turkey dictated by their foreign policy needs and objectives. This was largely due to external material structural (and surprising) events including 9/11 and the subsequent US intervention in Iraq as well as ideational structures vis-à-vis the War on Terror rhetoric which was a foundational component of George W. Bush's US Presidency.

Internal material structural factors reflected in domestic changes and developments also exerted great influence as was clearly demonstrated in both Iranian and Turkish politics during this period. In strong contrast to US–Iranian relations and domestic politics in Iran, Erdoğan's foreign policy opening to both the Western and Middle Eastern world enjoyed the US backing. In spite of doubts about Erdoğan's political orientation and objectives, the lack of any other charismatic leadership together with the rise of political Islam in Turkish politics as an appealing discourse to the masses made the US administration favour Erdoğan's Turkey with its new model of 'moderate Islam' above Iran so that it rose to become the key player in the region. During this period, Ankara's need for domination, based on the theoretical background of its foreign policy and the dogma of (economic and foreign policy) 'restoration' related to its 'Ottoman Syndrome' was also clearly apparent. However, while its policies clearly reflected elements of ideational structures, the evidence also indicates strategic security as another prime consideration in terms of preserving the state's borders and keeping its territorial integrity intact, rather than just directing its focus towards perpetuating Turkey's political survival.

One important, and somewhat surprising, outcome highlighted by this chapter was the way US Iraqi foreign policy advanced Turkish foreign policy goals up to 2010 far beyond those of Tehran. One reason for this could be that Ankara's foreign policy discourse formulated by Ahmet Davutoğlu and implemented throughout this period arguably exerted a greater influence on international and regional politics in terms of activism and regional cooperation than that of Iran. Yet, the Iraq war and the course of events that later unfolded also proved beneficial for Iran, whose importance and role appears increasingly interesting as the next chapter will further elaborate.

US military presence –and US interventionist policies thereafter – played a key role as a catalyst in stimulating the expansion of Turkish–Iranian interactions, especially as both states shared a desire to preserve their security, extend their influence and ultimately achieve regional dominance.

The period from 2007 onwards following the White House's decision to disengage militarily from Iraq through disarmament and regime change (28 February 2003) was particularly significant and had great impact on the region.[131] Although the US foreign policy of war in Iraq still continued, it now experienced a complete change of direction, transforming into a sectarian war with such a strong focus on fighting the War on Terror that the ideology of the Islamic state rose to take centre stage in regional politics, as the next chapter will further examine.

The impact of these regional and international determinants on Turkish and Iranian foreign policies ultimately favoured Turkey's foreign policy, especially as Iran's room for manoeuvre was severely limited owing to a number of considerations. The main reason was Iran's increasing isolation reinforced by the continuing arms and economic embargo while it was also facing difficulties owing to the fragmentation of its internal political situation into centres of power with conflicting interests (the policies of the military and the conservative wing on the one hand, and the government on the other). In addition, Iran had to contend with continued US and EU pressure to shut down or at least limit its nuclear programme. In contrast, Ankara, a staunch US ally, pursued a pro-active policy and took advantage of the emerging vacuums of power offered by the post-war political landscape. However, the severity of the Turkish economic crisis of 2001 and Iran's isolationist position raised the pressing issue of (economic) survival. This caused both Turkey and Iran to recognise the necessity for stronger regional and international alliances and to turn towards each other.

The role of the leadership as a critical ideational structural determinant in the formulation of politics would also strongly influence events, yet no more than the role of the institutions per se. The rise of George W. Bush and his conservative and pre-emptive policies led to the US foreign policy's further radicalisation, taking in the form of excessive militarisation as it placed terrorism firmly at the centre of the international agenda. Likewise, the radicalisation of Iranian politics in its second term vis-à-vis Mahmoud Ahmadinejad's revolutionary, anti-Western and anti-Israeli discourse, a major factor in fuelling US suspicions, led to the initiation of a US policy to curb Iranian influence in the region. Erdoğan's strong leadership and his ability to maintain a skilful balance was also critical in Ankara's policies for rapprochement with the Middle East, including Iran, as he ensured that the preservation of Turkey's Europeanisation orientation and its Western alliance remained intact in its foreign policy agenda. However, Erdoğan's leaning towards the school of thought rooted in political Islam was the underlying reason for apparent contradictions such as Erdoğan's denial of his longtime staunch ally Israel to formulate a foreign policy that expressed outspoken support for the Palestinian cause and Hamas.

Iraq, through the prism of the Gulf Wars over the last decades, emerged as perhaps the most critical factor in the formulation of both Iranian and Turkish politics as their policies had to respond to ongoing developments in Iraq. The aftermath of the Iraq war confirmed the importance of Iraq as a perpetuating dynamic signalling the onset of regional transformation in the Middle East as multiple centres of power were created and regional foreign policies seized the opportunity to reshape the regional balance of power, hoping not just to improve and stabilise their status but also increase their influence via a more competitive environment. There is no doubt that the outcome of the developments made at this time will still have the power to determine future politics and how the New Middle Eastern order will be reconstructed for many years to come.

Therefore, I argued the role of the Iraq war as a structural factor that gave both Iran and Turkey a chance to maximise their gains through the reshaping of the regional balance of power, enabling Turkey to upgrade its role in international politics and Iran to emerge from its isolation as the following chapter will further explain. Thus, Iraq was a determinant in the rapprochement between Iran and Turkey, but, even more importantly, acted as a catalyst in shaping Turkey's foreign policy so that it was able to expand its role in the region and significantly upgrade its position in line with its aim to become an important Middle Eastern power. In addition, the overriding factors of the UN resolution and the US Iraqi war stimulated further Iranian–Turkish relations as both took steps to maintain and increase their influence in order to become major participants in the post-Saddam political setting.

A key factor in closer relations between Iran and Turkey was the major economic benefit for both states, particularly in the area of energy supplies. However, Turkey's efforts for unilateral economic standing regarding the pipeline initiatives and its support by the West contrasted strongly with Iran's isolation and depleted economic status with the exception of Khatami's short-lived opening which had initially seemed to promise so much. It was this scenario that led to the strengthening of the Axis of Resistance as an organised way to neutralise the threats posed by international efforts to pressurise Iran and also Syria in the aftermath of Rafiq Al Hariri's assassination by a car bomb in Beirut (14 February 2005).

Another indispensable dynamic that we have considered in this analysis of Middle East and international politics has been the influence exerted by the foreign policies operated by non-state entities. For the US, the main threat was posed by Al Qaeda and was linked to terrorism, while for Iran and Turkey it was the Kurdish case with its longstanding historical implications – a determining factor in their mutual aim of achieving stability and eliminating tensions on the Iranian–Turkish borders. Both Iran and Turkey were particularly alarmed by the re-emergence of the Kurdish issue, although the employment of non-state actors in Iranian foreign policy had traditionally constituted a means to implement and facilitate its goals in the region, for example, through Hizbullah. This tension would escalate vis-à-vis the rise of the Kurds of Iraq, now also viewed as a potential energy power as the next chapter will reveal.

The international recognition and consolidation of the Kurdish status in Iraq as well as (from 2005 onwards) the rising role of Syria's Kurdish constituent and the drastic developments in Turkey's Kurdish status were ultimately strengthened by US Iraqi foreign policy. US Middle Eastern policies facilitated the Kurds of Iraq from

2006 onwards in gaining a much greater role in the formulation of regional and international politics by means of Kurdish cooperation with Iran, the Kurds' institutionalised relations with the US and Turkey, and their key role at the forefront of the fight against international terrorism. The embryonic but nonetheless dynamic role of the Kurds in Syria in the aftermath of the Arab Uprising's outbreak also served to prove that non-state actors can have their own impact on the formulation of both state and regional foreign policies. Certainly, in the case of Turkey and Iran non-state actors constitute the epicentre of the axis of their foreign policies as will be further argued in the following chapter. This was also demonstrated in the increasing role of non-state actors and institutions such as the EU as it was the non-state actors' actions that led to the EU's gradual involvement in Middle Eastern politics, a situation that has become even more intense today with the rising threat posed byAl Qaeda and IS. This outcome is indicative of the inevitable interaction between the different levels of analysis (domestic, regional and international) along with wider local–regional–national–global interactions.

CONCLUSION

This chapter has analysed the key factors influencing Turkish and Iranian policies throughout this period, while also considering their conceptual implications. Building on the premises set out in my previous work,[132] I raised the role of both material and ideational structures and their interplay, observing them in relation to EU–Turkish and EU–Iranian relations linked to democratisation and nuclear *desiderata*, Iranian institutions and the US administration as a determinant in the formulation of regional politics. I have also examined the role of specialised government departments and lobbies, such as the powerful Jewish lobby, and discussed how they have impacted on the formulation of policies (mainly in an Iran context). In addition, I analysed their interaction with the role of political agents such as the Kurds in Iraq from 1992 and the Kurdish 'silent' revolution in Syria from 2004, and also looked at the way Hizbullah became a key player in the Resistance Axis following the

Israeli invasion in Lebanon, and the impact of regional states as seen in Iraq's deterministic role in shaping both the Iranian and Turkish foreign policies.

On a conceptual level, the impact of ideas and beliefs that stem from different actors (state or non-state) highlight both the importance of the leadership (as shown in the case of George W. Bush, Recep Tayip Erdoğan, Ayatollah Khamenei, Mahmoud Ahmadinejad and, more recently, al-Maliki in Iraq), and of the unit – in the sense of the role played by both the individual and groups of individuals in the formulation of decision-making, and, consequently, foreign policy making. In this sense, the examination of the ideologisation of political or Islamic aims have also made clear the influential role of ideas and beliefs in shaping foreign policy to achieve the objective of the balance of power.

To summarise, the rationales for the Turkish–Iranian interrelation built on mutual necessity were primarily analysed on the basis of their economic interdependence combined with security and thus political motivations vis-à-vis the increasing impact of the Kurdish factor, the continuing threat on their borders, and the growth of their strategic interactions achieved through successive meetings which resulted in the development of much closer cooperation. Turkey's rapprochement with Iran also reflected the Turkish foreign policy need to steadily develop an independent foreign policy trajectory and enhance better relations with the Arab world (including the MENA countries) for the goal of regional dominance. This shows that the formation of regional alliances according to national interests is more prevalent than has perhaps been realised, and that interactive relations based on economic criteria can be enduring in the face of potential conflicts as has been demonstrated in the case of Iran and Turkey. As far as the Iraq factor is concerned, it seems to have explicitly paved the way for the 'Arab Uprisings' era, although the fruit of this has been a phase of intense instability and disorder.

There can be no doubt that the progression of these structural (ideational and material) factors stimulated prejudice in the US and other powers towards Iran and created the circumstances for Turkey to be seemingly favoured above Iran as far as the regional landscape was concerned, while the growing isolation imposed on Iran was a primary factor in stimulating the Turkish–Iranian rapprochement which reached its peak in 2010.

From 2010 onwards, and especially after the US withdrawal in 2011, the region would undergo a time of great change vis-à-vis a series of landmark events along with their ramifications, including increased pressure on Syria and the rise in Iraqi power of the Shi'ite element as a consequence of Nouri al-Maliki's appointment as Prime Minister. These issues continued to contribute to the ongoing regional crisis as will be further discussed in the next chapter.

CHAPTER 6

# Turkish–Iranian Relations under the Lens of the Syrian Crisis: A New Era for Middle Eastern Politics

*This historical conflict continues in a new form ... the New Middle East is being formed in the wake of what is happening between Iran and Turkey.*[1]

Reza Altun

## INTRODUCTION

This chapter sheds light on the latest developments following the post-Saddam era which was remarkable for two outstanding events – the outbreak of the Arab Uprisings (December 2010) and immediately afterwards the withdrawal of US forces from Iraq – at least, in the form of a military presence, adapting instead into an observer although still reserving the option to use limited force. The aftershocks of these developments would intensify from 2011 onward right through the Syrian crisis, an event which would actually cause even greater turmoil in the politics of the region and ultimately stimulate ethno-ideological and socio-political differences in the form of sectarianism, although, somewhat surprisingly, it would leave regional economic relations relatively intact. Turkish–Iranian relations as seen through the lens of the Syrian uprising on 15 March 2011 are particularly interesting at this point as Syria acted as the decisive factor guiding the subsequent divergence between the policies adopted by Iran and Turkey. As agents of two very different camps, their approaches were in stark contrast as summed up in the following statement from Osman Askin Bak, former co-chairman of the Turkey–Iran Parliamentary Friendship Group: 'Turkey cannot support Bashar who kills thousands of people while Iran thinks Syria is a shield for them against Israel.'[2]

This chapter argues that the Syrian crisis and thus Syria per se, rather than the Arab Uprisings (or 'Arab Spring' as it is often optimistically referred to in the literature), along with the continuing impact of the series of important dynamics detailed in earlier chapters has been the real influence behind Turkish and Iranian foreign policies and acted as the catalyst for their role in bringing about the new and unprecedented change that the region is currently experiencing. Thus, it is Syria that emerges as the overriding factor in the way Turkish–Iranian foreign policies are formulated, and this is especially true of its role in provoking conflict and disrupting Turkey and Iran's long-established historical relations which had been steadily improving over the last ten years or so.

The Iraq war had a dramatic effect on regional foreign policies as it left a significant power vacuum in its wake that even now regional forces are still struggling to fill. This was more evident after the withdrawal of the majority of US ground forces which in turn was followed by a series of strategic mistakes including perhaps, most significantly, the lack of any real plan for how a united Iraq would take up the reins of government again. This vacuum created opportunities for Iranian foreign policy to get deeply involved in the Centre and South of Iraq, control the federal government in Baghdad and stir up sectarianism over a prolonged period. One of its dimensions was the creation of a Shi'a armed group, the People's Mobilisation Forces, known as the Popular Mobilisation Units (PMU, الحشد الشعبي Al-Hashd Al-Sha'abi), in the fight against the Islamic State (داعش, IS) that was eventually incorporated by law (19 December 2016) in the state's official army.

Beginning with the Iranian army's successes in Iraq, the continued support of Bashar al-Assad and the perpetuation of his rule in an attempt to strengthen the Axis of Resistance from Baghdad to the

Sana'a vis-à-vis the Houthis' rebellion on 21 September 2014 all serve as indicative examples of how Iran has emerged as a formative regional actor with a multi-dimensional foreign policy centred on change at both regional and international levels.

Therefore, Iran's traditional foreign policy alliances with non-state entities combined with the rise of the Islamic State proved advantageous for the Syrian regime as it coincided with the critical period where Bashar al Assad's regime was striving for survival. It also assisted Iranian foreign policy in its continued pursuit of controlled chaos and instability which had served Iran so well thus far in its attempts to advance its position and role in regional politics. Developments in Syria also elevated the role of the Kurds in Syria in a similar way to that of the Kurdish movement in Turkish politics as both supported tactical alliances with Damascus and Tehran and this impacted Iranian and Turkish foreign policies. A similar view was expressed by Ibrahim Kalin, the chief advisor to the Turkish Presidency: 'solving the Kurdish Issue in Turkey will have a positive influence on the Kurdish population in Iran and also in Syria. That's why it is welcomed by everyone.'[3]

However, at the time of writing, Turkey's Kurdish policies have taken a different direction that diverges widely from Erdoğan's earlier 2013 speech in Diyarbakir which created hope for peace vis-à-vis the welcoming of Kurdish leader and former KR President, Massoud Barzani, and Erdoğan's recognition of the meeting as 'historic' and a 'crowning moment'.[4] A sharp shift increase in Turkey's Kurdish policies of persecution has been noticeable from 2015 onward due to Ankara's prolonged pressure in the face of the imminent rise of a second Kurdistan Region on its borders with Syria which would further threaten Turkish ability to maintain control of its domestic situation.

Another example of the way Syria impacted Iranian foreign policy was the confirmation by Hassan Nasrallah, leader of Hizbullah, of his support for President al-Assad in the fight to retain his rule against the uprising (30 April 2013).[5] The Syrian crisis led to intensified Iranian supervision of the Hizbullah fighters operating in Syria.[6] In a televised interview with the Al Manar TV channel (25 August 2015), Bashar al-Assad would state that: 'the power of Iran is the power of Syria, and a victory for Syria is a victory for Iran ... We are on the same axis, the

Axis of Resistance.'[7] President al-Assad's message in this interview which was shortly afterwards followed by Russia's direct interference in the regime's struggle for survival, does not only indicate signs of weakening in the regime, but also the Sunni camp's progression as a particularly strong power in the region since they heavily outnumber Shi'a forces. This increasingly means that any peace process in the Middle East which fails to take account of them is almost certainly doomed to failure. This was reflected in the December 2011 Washington meeting when al-Maliki told Obama: 'If the region's Sunnis backed by the Arab Gulf States try to roll back gains made by Shi'as, we will all become Hizbullah.'[8]

The rise of Islamic State as a successor of Al Qaeda in Syria and thereafter in Iraq to become the main focus of regional conflicts has elevated the importance of Iran even more as its involvement has been directly responsible for upsetting the regional status quo and bringing instability. Whereas the Arab Uprisings had a detrimental effect on Arab society and its regimes and led to the weakening and ultimate dismantling of some of the most important Arab states in MENA, this was not the case with the Kurds. The importance of the Kurdish status increased in Syria and strengthened in Iraq despite KRG's prolonged economic crisis due to the dramatic fall in the price of oil (2016) – the main source of income for the KR and the continuation of the federal government's withholding of the federal budget payments to the KRG (since early 2014). The Kurdistan Region has so far continued to represent an oasis of stability – despite the severe repercussions of the border-violating coup on October, 16 2017 in Kerkuk following the KRG's 25 September Referendum – in the heart of the Middle East. The Kurds' political and geostrategic role has become increasingly significant, a factor which has caused IS and its supporters to view them as prime targets vis-à-vis the latter's confrontation against primarily Kurdish and Sunni areas in Syria and Iraq.

Thus, Iraq's weak structure and the power vacuum that opened up allowed IS to invade Iraq and, in particular, target the Kurdistan Region, which with its geostrategic location rich in oil fields offers a valuable source of potential funding. However, Iran also views the KR as important because of the need for Kurdish collaboration and support for the Shi'ite-dominated federal government in Baghdad.

Moreover, Kurdish populated areas not only supply 'a safe haven border in the South of Iran that can give Tehran a safety margin of 2,000 kilometres away from the Turkish border to the Gulf' but also offer Iran credibility on the international stage 'because if the Kurdish issue can reach a resolution, Iran will finally be able to approach the international community and claim to have solved an important issue', i.e. the Kurdish issue. The Kurds are also considered vital for the Turkish economy which is 'in need of the Kurdistan Region as it is important for Turkey to have the Kurds to export [our] oil as we have only Ceyhan after the closure of Baniyas terminal'.[9] This need to win the Kurds as allies expressed by Fadhil Merani was further confirmed by Aykan Erdemir who stated: 'For Turkey, relations with the KR are very important.'[10]

The current unsettled situation in the Middle East, reflected in a number of ongoing conflicts, has inevitably strengthened the role of the army, particularly in its role as the representative and safeguard of the Supreme Leader's authority in Iran, while in Turkey the army has historically occupied a powerful position in terms of its influence within the Turkish state. In Iran it is clear that the Islamic Revolutionary Guards Corps, together with its offshoots, continues to play much the same role as it always did. In Khamenei's Eid Al Fatr Speech (18 July, 2015) four days after the Iran nuclear deal (14 July 2015) which aimed to limit Tehran's nuclear programme in exchange for economic sanctions relief, his remarks seemed intended to aggravate the Basij militia's opposition to the US with a pugnacious statement that 'even after this deal, our policy toward the arrogant US will not change'.[11] On 18 June 2017 the Islamic Revolutionary Guards Corps (IRGC) decided to utilise its most advanced capabilities – Zolfaghar mid-range ballistic missiles with an approximate range of 700 km – against hard-to-reach IS targets in Syria's eastern Deir Ezzor province.[12] In the case of Turkey, bureaucracy continues to play a conciliatory role, for even though the army currently plays a limited role in Turkish political life, its historic legacy and Erdoğan's need to retain the advocates of the nationalist/military wing as voters means that it continues to shape the state's political political decisions. This has been even the case in the KRI (Kurdistan Region of Iraq). The rise of the Islamic State, as another surprising event, elevated the status of the peshmerga forces that constitute the official army of the KR.[13] IS's offensive attack on 9 June 2014 against Mosul, a key area that determines the control of the Iraqi–Syrian border as a strategic point, primarily the Sunni areas in Iraq, and the group's advancement within a brief 15-day period (1–15 August 2014) towards Kurdish territory some 40 km Southwest of Erbil (6 August 2014) changed the course of events into a unique war. This new type of asymmetric warfare (the war on terror against the IS) supported by advanced weaponry, while gradually consolidating their status, upgraded the military role of the Kurds as a considerable military security force that enjoyed global recognition and that was positioned on the frontline of the international anti-IS coalition. Indeed, the peshmerga forces' cooperation on an equal level with strong state entities through a succession of direct high-level meetings, such as the US Chairman of the Joint Chiefs of Staff, General Joseph Dunford (April 2016), and President Obama's Envoy for the Global Coalition to Counter the Islamic State of Iraq and the Levant, Mr Brett McGurk (19 June 2016), in addition to the cooperation between the Iraqi army and the Kurdish peshmerga forces against IS are indicative of their significance as the main security apparatus of the KR, in the same way that the forces of the People's Protection (or Defence) Units (YPG) have fought against the IS in Syria have been unique.[14]

This reinforces one of this book's primary arguments, which concerns the equally influential role played by non-state entities such as religious extremist groups, nationalist movements and military organisations or institutions. Likewise, the impact of the EU and its institutions have had a tremendous effect on the formulation of Iranian politics vis-à-vis the severe restrictions imposed by economic embargos on Iran, while NATO's stance towards Iran is particularly interesting when compared to the cases of Libya and Syria, which have resulted in two completely different attitudes, the first expressed through vigilance and the second by indecision. Other major influences include the US as well as powerful regional states like Qatar and Saudi Arabia.[15]

The crisis in Syria started as a revolution, and turned into a civil war that has engulfed the whole of the region, acting as the precursor of a new global war that seems as if it will continue until the final reshaping of the Middle Eastern region (following the secret 1916

Sykes–Picot Agreement). However, at the same time it has provided a golden opportunity for regional and international competition to exploit the resulting power vacuum with each power trying to gain the upper hand through its regional allies vis-à-vis US sanctions against Russia as well as the interference of the Gulf States, and in particular Qatar and Saudi Arabia, in Syria's domestic affairs.[16]

The Syrian crisis granted Russia a means of reviving its determinant and influential role in the Middle Eastern region and helped it make a comeback on the regional political scene. Vladimir Putin's Russian foreign policy platform for the 21st century depicted in his 'Foreign Policy Plan of the Russian Federation' focused on the West's role of intervention and the way that often meant imposing its own values, which not only muddied international relations but also undermined the role of the UN. In response, Russia decided to appropriate a role as a counterbalancing power and use it to act as a regulator to promote revival of the global economy and prevent an all-out military intervention by the West.[17] Consequently, since 2014 Russia has been seeking to revive its alternative to NATO, the Collective Security Treaty Organization (CSTO), that originally began as a military exercise near Kyrgyzstan codenamed 'Unbreakable Brotherhood'.[18]

The role of external interference, dating back to the early historical stages of the formulation of these Middle Eastern states, including Iran and Turkey, has always been a two-edged sword and especially in its current evolution into interventionist policies which have sometimes had a disastrous effect, weakening the already fragile regional balance of power and condemning it to enduring sectarian conflict. However, this external interference could not have gained such momentum without the help of the surprising events in the region as mentioned in earlier chapters. The rise of IS and its activities as well as regional and international developments together with domestic developments, like the ascendancy in the Iraqi Premiership of al-Maliki, can be said to have opened the Aeolus' ox-skin bag containing the great winds, acting as a driving force in regional politics and causing it to explode into further internal sectarianism.

The Syrian uprising led to a severe and continuing crisis, which, along with Baghdad's increasing sectarianism, were both exploited by

Iran and, to a lesser extent, by Turkey. This, together with the policies introduced by Barack Obama, would tilt the regional balance of power – even if only for a short term – in Iran's favour, while Turkey found itself struggling with a problematic foreign policy hijacked by Erdoğan's proactive policies, especially in Syria where the underlying hope was that Bashar al-Assad would shortly suffer the same fate as Qaddafi. Ankara convinced itself that if Turkey was the first to point out al Assad's need to pursue reforms, a potential Muslim Brotherhood alliance would grant the Turkish Premiership the regional leadership among the Sunni in the Middle East with Turkey as its axis. The first conference of Turkic-speaking states – namely, Azerbaijan, Kazahkstan, Kyrgykstan and Turkmenistan – in Istanbul (15–16 September 2012), and also the creation of the Syria Democratic Turkmen Movement, a Syrian Turkmen Platform 2012 whose first meeting was hosted by the former Turkish Foreign Minister (15 December 2012) with the purpose of creating a Turkmen assembly in the aftermath of the Syrian uprising, can both be perceived as attempts to acquire a leading role for Turkey in this context.

Thus, the Syrian crisis would prove the Trojan horse for Turkish foreign policy with seemingly costs for Erdoğan's political future as was the case with the failed 2016 coup d'état that followed. By August 2011 it was very clear that Turkey had become an enemy of the Assad regime, retaliating to the Syrian military shooting down of a Turkish warplane that apparently violated Syrian airspace (June 2012), with the creation of a war situation culminating in a demonstration of power and Ankara's 'taste the water' policy. Turkey's Syrian policy represented a complete turnaround from the rectilinear foreign policy of rapprochement Turkey had pursued from 2004 onward following a series of agreements on Water Resources (2008), Free Trade (2004) and Visa arrangements (2009). The subsequent collapse resulted in the repositioning of Iranian–Turkish relations as a necessary counterbalance to the breakdown in Syrian–Turkish relations.

## THE SYRIAN FACTOR

The importance of Syria as a key actor in regional politics due to its geostrategic location as Turkey's gateway to the Gulf, and its crucial position as an Iranian ally in the heart of the Middle Eastern region, had already been witnessed during 1957 (August–September) when a former Syrian crisis had been a catalyst for the Anglo-American Working Group's attempt to find a solution based on its 'Preferred Plan'. According to this plan,

> –the US and UK administrations worked to forestall communist influence in Damascus through covert actions to overthrow the government as the main objective was to remove the Soviet influence in Syria. The Secret Intelligence Service and CIA would then gather the Syrian opposition groups in Jordan under the aegis of a Free Syria Committee with Aleppo being the initial seat of the Committee. The aim was not to bring any change in Syria's independence or integrity but if any sentiment for a form of association or federation with Iraq would emerge this was to be encouraged as with the Iraqis talking of instigating a tribal uprising in Syria, political prisoners would be freed in Mezze prison and the Muslim Brotherhood's potential for civil unrest could have been exploited so that border incidents between Syria and Iraq or Jordan could serve as pretexts for military action under Article 51 of the UN 'self-defense.[19]

The plan was never executed, but it is very interesting nonetheless as it is indicative of how foreign agents are able to manufacture the fall of a government through internal pressures and/or outside military intervention. According to his memoirs, US President Eisenhower himself stated that Turkey wanted to invade Syria, but was put off by the strong reactions of the Soviet Union with Nikita Khrouchtchev openly threatening Turkey with repercussions should the invasion go ahead.[20] Interestingly, this same scenario – but in this case linked to the Syrian Civil War – has recently been played out again.

The aftermath of the US withdrawal from Iraq led to regional turmoil, and this was exacerbated by the failure of Turkish foreign policy to calculate regional developments leading to failure in its objectives, both concerning its intended rapprochement with its neighbours, and its desire to become the leader of the Sunni camp in the region. In fact, Turkey's placement of Syria at the epicentre of its foreign policy allowed Iran to expand even further into the region and consolidate a successful regional and international foreign policy that supported its goals of swaying the regional balance of power in its favour, bringing Russia into the ring as an active player to counterbalance US dominance in the region, and, finally, drawing international attention away from its domestic problems. The pinnacle of its political endeavours would be the completion of a deal resolving its nuclear issue with the international community which it continued to pursue despite fears of a potential rebound.[21] However, this Iranian triumph – even if it would prove short-lived in the years to come – could never have been accomplished without a series of events that paved the way for its success.

Firstly, Turkish foreign policy's downgrading of its relations with one of its strategic partners – Israel – signalled the onset of the failure of its 'zero problems with the neighbours' policy vis-à-vis the Israeli attack on 31 May 2010 when around ten people were killed on the *Mavi Marmara* Turkish ship carrying pro-Palestinian activists to Gaza, leading to the expulsion of the Israeli ambassador from Turkey in early September 2011.[22] This resulted in a Turkish rapprochement with Syria leading to a boosting of trade between the two states, although this would ultimately prove short-lived as it too became a victim of the breakdown in relations between Turkey and Israel.[23] Ahmed Davutoğlu, Turkey's former Foreign Minister, presented an overview of the situation between Turkey and Israel:

> Turkey downgraded its diplomatic relations with Israel to the minimum level and suspended all military ties following the attack carried out by Israel in the international waters against a humanitarian aid convoy by NGOs on 31 May, 2010 in which 10 Turkish civilians lost their lives. No official agreement has been concluded in the fields of energy including the defense industry between Israel and Turkey.[24]

It is also significant that after the Israeli campaign against Gaza (July 2014) Turkey held three days of mourning to show solidarity with the Palestinians. The final breakdown in Turkish–Syrian relations occurred after a highly unsuccessful Turkish visit to Damascus (August 2011) where Erdoğan and Davutoğlu attempted to interfere in Syria's domestic affairs by calling on President al-Assad to 'step down for the sake of the Mideast peace'[25] and tried to convince the Assad regime to adopt a real plan for reforms. This colossal failure sounded the death knell to Erdoğan's foreign policy vision, which, in turn, jeopardised the Turkish foreign policy of domination in the region. The US radar system that Turkey agreed to host in Malatya

Kürecik province in September 2011, as part of the developing missile defence system in Europe, also affected Turkey's relations with Iran in spite of Erdoğan's assurances that: 'The radar base in Turkey is a NATO concept and if Iran interprets it in a different way that is their decision … Unless Turkey is attacked we will never allow Iran to be attacked from Turkish territory.'[26]

In spite of scholarly arguments citing Turkey as an agent of containment,[27] the proactive stance adopted by the Turkish government in favour of an interventionist policy against Damascus was aimed less at containing Iran and more at the expansion of Turkish influence to fill the power vacuum created in a post-Saddam and potentially post-Assad political setting. Turkey believed this goal could best be served through a tripartite alliance that would bring Ankara together with other powers to form the main axis of a Sunni–Muslim Brotherhood-oriented democracy with Erdoğan reported by the Anatolian News Agency as stating: 'We proposed a three-way system here. This system could be a trio of Turkey–Egypt–Iran [or] a second system could be Turkey–Russia–Iran [and] a third system could be Turkey–Egypt–Saudi Arabia'.[28] However, the Arab world was unwilling to follow a new Ottoman leadership when a predominantly Sunna superpower like Saudi Arabia already existed, and nobody was really sure whether Bashar al-Assad would actually be overthrown at this time, while other issues like the deposed former Egyptian President Mohammed Morsi (July 2013) being sentenced to death by the Egyptian authorities, and rising domestic fronts fuelled by an increase of votes for the Kurds, also caused concern. It appears very difficult that great powers would allow a controlled Syria by a single regional player to emerge in the post-Assad era.

The failure of Erdoğan's foreign policy goals throughout this period can be further explained by the persistence of the government's initial efforts to 'continue to work very hard in order to make possible the political transformation in Syria' as stated by Ahmed Davutoğlu.[29] This was represented by Turkish direct involvement from 1 April 2012 onward in the organisation and support of the Syrian opposition, namely the Friends of Syria in Istanbul (following the 24 February 2012 inaugural meeting in Tunis), known as the Syrian National Council, a Muslim Brotherhood majority organisation, the Free Syrian Army (FSA) and later on different fundamentalist Islamist groups that would join in demanding al-Assad's overthrow. These latter groups would later split in terms of their allegiance (24 September 2012); for instance, 13 organisations announced that they no longer recognised the SNC as part of the FSA Supreme Military Council formed at Antalya in December 2012 and called for unity based on Sharia (Jabhat Al Nusra, Tawhed brigade, Shour Al Sham, Islamic brigades), which further complicated the situation and turned relative order into chaos.[30]

The intensification of sectarianism in Iraq under al-Maliki's rule along with the rise of IS and the elevation of the Kurdish status in Syria increased opportunities for Iran to implement its political agenda. The election of Hassan Rouhani to the Iranian Presidency (4 August 2013) allowed the Islamic revolutionary government to pursue a less reactionary policy and thus present a different face as a moderate Islam taking stock of the effects caused by the continuing economic pressure suffered by the state over the previous three decades.[31]

Certainly in this situation, Erdoğan completely failed to accomplish Turkey's aim to 'use its growing role in the Middle East to mediate between the newly-elected Obama administration and Iran'.[32] However, this lack of success may also be partly explained by AK Parti's failure to form a single-party majority government in the parliamentary elections of 7 June 2015 since no party received enough votes. Thus, the weaknesses of Turkey's foreign policy granted Iran a golden chance to act as a mediator almost right from the beginning of the crisis 'prepared to use all means available to it to help Turkey improve its ties with Syria'.[33] Such developments allowed Iran to change the regional balance of power in its favour for the first time since 2002, support AK Parti's rise in power and also realise a diplomatic but pragmatic victory in view of the nuclear deal agreed on 14 July 2015 in Vienna between the Islamic Republic of Iran and the P5 + 1, i.e., the permanent members of the UNSC and the EU. It was a political turning point for Iran as it now occupied a dominant and decision-making role backed by Russian support in most of the burning issues faced by the region.

## The role of external interference in the Syrian crisis

In spite of the promise of Obama's new Presidency during its first term (2009–2012), which had seemed to offer a new beginning for relations between the Muslim world and the United States (Cairo speech, 4 June, 2009), while also depicting a will to follow a new policy of disengagement as far as the Middle Eastern region was concerned, the President's second term of office (2012–2017) demonstrated that no matter how willing Obama was in the intention to move away from his predecessor's policies, his policies would continue to follow the linear nature of the US foreign policy, and therefore remain, in essence, unchanged.[34] Already, in his 2010 National Security Strategy, Obama was arguing in favour of 'diplomacy, but if necessary the use of force' as tools for the achievement of his strategic goals.[35] The US President then further institutionalised the use of force on the basis of Bush's National Security Directive 26 (NSD, 2 October 1989) as well as NSD45 (20 August 1990), which incited the direct use of force and repeated traditional American security interests.[36] In 2011 Barack Obama led an allied military intervention in Libya without consulting the US Congress, relying on extensive use of drones rather than a massive military presence on the ground and proceeding with the support of the international community. The US has rarely acted unilaterally in its military decisions without seeking consensus from the international community.

It was with the consensus of the UN and NATO that Obama would intervene in Libya (2011), sanction Iran (2011), and oppose the Palestinian Authority's bid for statehood through the National Security Council (NSC, September 2011). However, Obama's focus in his UN speech (25 September 2012) on the containment of a nuclear-armed Iran and the importance of security for Israel and the Gulf in balance with the stability of the global economy reveal the perpetuation of traditional US foreign policy goals in the region. With the outbreak of the Arab Uprisings, Obama issued the Presidential Study Directive 11 (PSD-11) in 2010 ordering officials 'to study ways of promoting change in the Middle Eastern countries [since] the Obamians saw the events … as the beginning of transformational changes … and a new era [where] authoritarian leaders like Ben Ali and Hosni Mubarak were no longer forces for regional stability. Their regimes were shaky [therefore] the US could serve its own long-term interests by identifying itself with the forces for change (that is, the Muslim Brotherhood).'[37] For the first time, Obama intervened directly to put pressure on Egyptian president Mubarak's regime to resign, claiming that a policy serving both 'idealism through the pursuit of democratic change and realism would win popular support in a country of strategic importance'. Obama went before TV cameras to announce that he had told Mubarak that an orderly transition to a representative government 'must begin now' and when reporters asked the White House press secretary Robert Gibb what the president meant by 'now', he replied: 'Now means yesterday'.[38]

In the aftermath of the Syrian uprising, Secretary of State Hillary Clinton took the same line, demanding openly that Bashar al-Assad be deposed from the Presidency, claiming that 'Syria cannot develop into a democracy that respects human rights as long as Mr. Assad is in power.'[39] In the same vein, on 18 August 2011 the US President would mark the US policy of 'regime change' in Syria with an official declaration of the US priority that 'For the sake of the Syrian people, the time has come for President Assad to step aside.'[40] Barack Obama's directive EO 13582 (18 August 2011) ordered the US Treasury Department to freeze Syrian assets in the US, banning the import of petroleum products produced in Syria together with a prohibition against US citizens operating or investing in Syria.[41] Obama declared a new self-defence strategy in his 'War without End' West Point Speech (28 May 2014), that would target the war against terror, support external intervention to aid Syria's neighbours; namely, Jordan, Iraq, Lebanon and Turkey, and act in cooperation with Congress to aid those elements standing in opposition against al-Assad's regime and the terrorists by every means in its power.[42]

US discourse and practice thus appears to demonstrate that the Middle Eastern region has continued to hold the same level of importance for US interests as it strives for economic survival against giants such as China or Russia and attempts to ensure the safety of Israel, making it imperative to pursue engagement as a pre-requisite for US Middle Eastern foreign policy. This means that Obama did not manage to change direction towards the pacifist foreign policy based on disengagement that he originally envisioned, instead ending up in a Catch-22 situation where he has had very little choice in the policies he has eventually had to adopt, which were ultimately dictated by his indecisiveness and inability to act promptly. This lack of strong leadership would cost the US dear as it led to the escalation of the post-Arab Uprisings drama. In that sense, it is evident that external intervention not only continued but also intensified with the revival of Russian involvement in Syrian and Middle Eastern affairs. Scholarly remarks, such that 'Obama came into office planning to cut military spending [but he found] himself increasingly bogged down in exactly the kinds of geopolitical rivalries he had hoped to transcend', are indicative of the way US foreign policy operated in the region independent of the Presidency.[43]

This becomes even more evident in the competition for energy, as Vali commented:

> The oil market is so vulnerable that a shortage or high price in one corner means higher prices everywhere else. If the Asian states lose their Middle Eastern supply, their demand for oil will not go away, [but] it will push prices higher. Thus, we may cut our imports of Middle Eastern oil further but we must still keep viewing stability in the region as a vital American interest. [Moreover] China's trade with Iran has grown to $45billion in 2011 and with Saudi Arabia, $50billion. BP forecasts that between now and 2030, 95 per cent of the increase in world demand for oil will come from China and India (and India by 2030 could overtake China as the world's most populous country). Without US leadership in the Middle East, the region's future will be left to China and Russia or to Turkey, Iran and Saudi Arabia.[44]

Furthermore, the shift of influence to the Persian Gulf and the respective roles of Iran and Turkey along with the imbalance that the Iraq War created in the regional balance of power, especially between Sunni and Shi'ite forces, is an issue that the US is only now beginning to rectify starting with the nuclear deal, while the changing fortunes of the Middle East players and especially the Syrian crisis have opened the field to Russia, and given it another chance to re-enter regional politics as a key actor.[45] Vali made a succinct summary of the situation: 'the US is not ready to accept the Iranian revolution [while] the Persian Gulf is surrounded by a Shi'a majority in Iraq and could challenge Saudi Arabia for primacy as an oil exporter. Saudi Arabia has 262 billion barrels of oil reserves [whereas] Iraq's oil reserves vary between 144 to 300 billion barrels and Iran's are about 136 billion.'[46] This huge capacity for oil production is what makes the Kurdistan Region in Iraq so important.

The pinnacle of external intervention was undoubtedly the strong support controversially given by Russia to the regime of Bashar al-Assad in Syria. In a speech to the Heritage Foundation on 6 May 2002, John R. Bolton, Under Secretary at the time, grouped Syria with Libya and Cuba as rogue states supporting international terrorism and intent on pursuing the development of WMD. On 9 October 2002, Bolton told the Senate Foreign Relations Committee that 'we remain very concerned that nuclear and missile programs of Iran and others, including Syria, continue to receive the benefits of Russian technology and expertise'. In his briefing for the Subcommittee on the Middle East and South Asia on 16 September 2003 Bolton would again voice particular concern over a range of Syrian WMD programmes that had come to his attention in an attempt to exert further pressure on Syria so that Assad destroys its WMD and ultimately surrender.[47]

The sharing of Russian technology with Syria involved constant meetings such as that attended by Ali Habib, Chief of Staff of the Syrian Armed Forces, in Moscow on 3 October 2005 to discuss maintenance and modernisation of Syrian equipment by Russian experts as well as Syrian purchase of ammunition,[48] the Russian agreement to write off 73 per cent of Syria's debt (2005)[49] and the Russian veto blocking UN action against the Syrian regime, while at the same time giving strong support to al-Assad, were all indicative of the institutionalised relations between the two partners.[50] Indeed, Russian Foreign Minister Sergey Lavrov admitted in early September 2015 that 'Russian planes are sending to Syria both military equipment in accordance with current contracts and humanitarian aid'[51] while participation by Russian forces in military operations in Syria in support of government troops was also noted by observers.[52] This explicit alliance was confirmed by al-Assad himself in a recent interview when he stated that his major allies – namely Russia, Iran, and Hizbullah – had been 'beyond loyal' since

Syria's revolt broke out in 2011 in contrast to the 'the United States [which] abandons its allies, abandon its friends'.[53]

Russia's goal of rebuilding and reviving its role in the region by means of alliances based on common interests with powers like Syria and Iran, was an implementation representative of its strategy to counter US dominance in the Middle East. Such alliances were crucial, as demonstrated in the case of Algeria, which has become one of Russia's biggest defence customers. Delivery of 14 Russian-made Sukhoi fighter jets (2 billion rubles ($30 million) per unit) to Algeria in 2016 and 2017 was agreed between the two states, while Algeria's previous purchases included 44 of Russia's heavy multi-role Su-30MKI fighter jets with a total of 44 planes delivered in the period from 2006 to 2010. Sergei Chemezov, the head of Russian defence technology holding company Rostec, confirmed that a further Algerian Su-30 contract was signed in the spring of 2015.[54]

Russian alliances like these are notable for their enduring and strategic nature, a quality also reflected in its foreign policy making, whereas US policies in the region have suffered a serious setback. Russia has now introduced five new foreign policy principles which include the right to intervene in neighbouring states, defend the honor and dignity of its citizens, revise borders, and demand a sphere of influence in Eurasia as a whole. This stance in tandem with its determination to act as a counterbalance to the United States and NATO[55] explains Russian relations with Iran which has been a key factor in assisting Moscow to rebuild Russian status in the region as a major regional power. Interestingly, this disproves the myth that weaker states always depend on stronger ones as reality has proved that bigger states can also be influenced or even determine their role from weaker ones. This notion ultimately challenges traditional International Relations concepts as terms like big/small and strong/weak are now often interchangeable.

However, even in this context it should be made clear that the foundation of such interrelations is still driven by national interest. Volker pointed out that Syrian–Iranian interactions have also been 'largely a marriage of convenience, based on a commonality of interests that will persist as long as both parties are isolated. Damascus and Tehran do not have the same agenda. As one high-ranking Syrian official put it to me, we want a peace process, they don't.'[56] Similarly, Putin's initiative to sign 11 cooperation agreements with Erdoğan (2012) including a $20 billion nuclear power plant built in Akkuyu on the Turkish Mediterranean coast is another example of how such agreements are actually motivated primarily by national interest, the real driver behind most, if not all, foreign policies. Russia is already Turkey's number one trading partner for Russian gas and oil, while Turkey is also dependent on Russian gas for its electricity production. Erdoğan has confirmed that both states share a goal to raise bilateral Turkish–Russian trade to exceed $100 billion – a figure up by nearly $40 billion from 2012.[57]

President Vladimir Putin and former Turkish Prime Minister Tayyip Erdoğan entered into an agreement to start jointly working in Syria during the former's visit to Istanbul on 3 December 2012. Their attitude of mutual cooperation was revealed by Putin at a joint press conference with Erdoğan when he stated: 'We share the same views about what is going on in Syria', which in effect was saying that both nations regarded political change in Syria as necessary. Putin's spokesman Dmitry Peskov commented further on Syria's situation in a 5 December statement in Ashgabat when he said that the 'exit or the continuation of the Assad regime is absolutely not a must'. The statement though was mistakenly read by Erdoğan to mean that the continuation of the Assad regime as the only state in the Middle East and Mediterranean providing a military base (in Tartus) for Russia was no longer relevant. This mistake would cost him dear and the Friends of the Syrian People conference held in Rabat, Morocco on 12 December 2012 would signal the eventual breakdown of an unsuccessful Turkish Syrian foreign policy which, Turkish sources revealed, was entirely based on political misconceptions, as Erdoğan assumed that Russia would support al-Assad's removal.[58]

For Turkey, its relations with Russia was very important as Ankara's economy relied heavily on Russian imports of natural gas which accounted for 70 per cent of its needs, leading to a $20 billion deal investment in Russian power plants. Indeed, in May 2010 Turkey signed a deal with the Russian state-controlled firm Atomstroyexport to build a four-reactor, 1.2 gigawatt nuclear power plant at Akkuyu on the Mediterranean. The plant is both owned and operated by Russia and aims to eliminate the need for a Turkish indigenous enrichment process for nuclear fuel. The plant started construction in 2013 and is scheduled to be commissioned in 2021.[59] Iraq also signed a $4.2 billion agreement with Moscow for 13 Russian helicopters – Night Hunter –as well as 40 Mi-28N and Mi-35 helicopters in 2013 for border surveillance as part of its counterterrorism strategy.[60] These are just a few examples that indicate the extent of Russia's growing involvement in the Middle Eastern region.

In contrast, US foreign policy has been dogged with confusion and found itself at an impasse after President Obama's failure to follow his foreign policy of 'reset to Asia-Pacific' policies and the administration's decision to turn its focus onto domestic politics. This led to a gradual 'disengagement' from the Middle Eastern region, which, with Syria acting as the catalyst, was a prime factor in Russia's increased role of influence. The US only realised it had taken its eye off the ball when Russia took advantage of its successful Russian–Syrian foreign policy to take on the role of main ally of the Axis of Resistance.

Traditional US foreign policy towards the region can be identified as linear, as its main goal is the preservation of the regional balance of power which, to date, has served US interests well. To try and maintain this, the US responded straight after the nuclear deal with Iran by entering into a 'buffer zone' agreement with Turkey (16 August 2015). The proposal was for a safe zone about 40 miles wide, stretching for 68 miles along the Turkey–Syria border from the town of Jarabulus to Marea, and eventually reaching as far as the outskirts of Aleppo. Although the buffer zone was not realised, it still holds its own tactical significance and constitutes a representative example of the way in which US Middle Eastern foreign policy tends to be conducted following a *quid pro quo* approach. The plan appeared to be that US–Turkish and coalition air strikes would combine to attempt to clear the area of IS fighters.[61] State Department spokesman, Mark Toner, explained: 'The US and Turkey have decided this zone will be occupied by the Free Syrian Army and can only be used by forces sworn to overthrow the legal government in Damascus.'[62]

The general assumption was that Turkey and the US could at some point move into Syria in alliance with GCC states and, in particular, Saudi Arabia in response to political developments; for example, as a pre-emptive measure to block the attempts made by the Syrian regime, backed by Moscow and Iran, to control Sunni areas such as Aleppo, which at the time of writing seems unrealistic given divisions within the GCC itself. The Free Syrian Army was indeed completely reorganised since 2014 by the Turkish intelligence forces to become an organisation accountable to Erdoğan and the Saudi–Qatari trainers assisted by American contractors. The majority of those initially involved with the FSA accepted an amnesty from the Damascus government or joined al Nusra or ISIS forces. It is believed that this new aggressive move was fuelled by desperation based on the improved relations between Russia and Saudi Arabia and recent inroads made in the previously frosty relations between Saudi Arabia and Iran. However, Saudi Arabia has now allegedly stopped giving material support to IS in Iraq and Syria, leaving that organisation to fend for itself.[63]

Erdoğan has also had his own issues to deal with as he needs to address pressing domestic concerns such as the Kurdish issue and the friction with the Gülen movement as well as issues posed by Syria and the Kurds on Turkey's borders in addition to the constant threat of an IS confrontation. Thus, the leaked information, possibly relayed by Syrian intelligence after successfully managing to penetrate the Turkish system, of a conversation between Turkey's former Prime Minister Ahmed Davutoğlu, National Intelligence Organization (MİT) Hakan Fidan, Foreign Ministry Undersecretary Feridun Sinirlioğlu, and Deputy Chief of General Staff, General Yaşar Gürel, with Turkish officials admitting the possibility of staging a Syria attack to 'make up a cause of war', has caused greater damage, while also revealing the lengths to which Turkey will go in order to remove its perceived enemy, Bashar al-Assad.[64]

The Geneva I and II Conferences on Syria which took place on 30 June 2012 and January/February 2014 with the aim of resolving the Syrian crisis did not meet with political success. Thierry Meyssan blamed this on the length of time spent trying to partition Iraq and Syria with Turkey's participation based on the 'Juppé plan', later known as the 'Wright plan', which has been ongoing since March 2011. Meyssan revealed that Alain Juppé, the French Minister for Foreign Affairs, secretly proposed support for Ankara's candidacy to the European Union and help in solving its Kurdish problem if Turkey would join France in its war against Libya and Syria. In June 2012, General John Allen also apparently plotted with General David Petraeus and Secretary of State Hillary Clinton to sabotage the Geneva agreement between Washington and Moscow for peace in the Near East. The Clinton–Allen–Petraeus trio appears to have staged a second operation in December 2014, which managed to disrupt the Moscow Conference by again promising the Muslim Brotherhood that they would implement the 'Juppé–Wright plan' which resulted in the Syrian National Coalition's refusal to engage any further in peace negotiations.

General John Allen, known for his opposition to the agreement with Iran, was Erdoğan's contact for the creation of the 90-mile wide 'no–fly' zone over Syrian territory, which was also created with the aim of setting the 'Juppé–Wright plan' in motion.[65] However, this resulted in even more Iranian cargo planes and shipments of arms to Syria (March 2011)[66] and an atmosphere of increased hostility vis-à-vis Syrian downing of Turkish RF4 military aircraft (June 2012), which was not improved by the creation of a Russo–Syrian military Commission (August 2015). Matters escalated still further following the mutual cooperation agreed between Moscow and the White House in Washington, which concerned the removal of Patriot missiles, installed by NATO and stationed in Turkey since January 2013.[67] Although the aim of this was to prevent the Syrian Air Force from deploying on the frontier, Meyssan explained that what actually happened was that it facilitated occupation by Islamic State, signalling another political victory for Iran. This, in turn, meant that the agreed US–Turkish de facto 'safe zone' (July 2015) along the Turkey–Syria border had to be postponed.[68] Turkish foreign policy demand for such a zone was a clear indication of Ankara's concern for the boomerang-effect that IS attacks could have on its own territory, both directly and from within.

A change of direction in regional politics seemed to be on the horizon with President Obama favouring a steady 'disengagement' versus Russia's direct presence in Syria[69] which has been further strengthened by Russian supremacy within the Axis of Resistance framework. US foreign policy's dilemma was expressed through a turmoil situation when a considerable number of Democratic lawmakers were raising questions over whether toppling Syria's Bashar al-Assad should still be a priority considering the steady gains by Islamic State. Senator Jeanne Shaheen, D-NH, remarked:

> I think we've come to a point where we should be reassessing what our strategy [should be] with respect to Assad and Syria and the conflict there. I don't have the answer on me about what I think that should be, but I really think we're at a point where we need to reassess, because what we've been doing so far is not working.[70]

The role of Iran in this case has been critical because it seems that political instability spread from Iraq to Yemen. Thus, in spite of the continuation of steady progress in Iran's bilateral relations with Turkey with the aim of establishing joint committees on bilateral issues,[71] the post-Arab Uprisings environment has significantly weakened the influence – although not the traditional role – of Turkey's Middle Eastern foreign policy in contrast to Tehran's growing importance as a powerful intermediary in both regional and international politics. Iran has been directly involved in Syria considering Iranian Foreign Minister Mohammad Javad Zarif's meeting with both President Bashar al-Assad and Hizbullah leader Hassan Nasrallah to agree a revised four-point plan for political transition as well as a series of secret Iran–US talks begun in 2011, which has resulted in the 14 July 2015 nuclear deal.[72] In addition, the US–Moscow Agreement, which weakened Turkish influence in Syria following the direct involvement of Russia after Bashar's TV interview (25 August 2015), indicated that the regime's power was diminishing and that it was now finding it much more difficult to continue fighting. This situation could intensify once the Arab Gulf States have finished sorting out Yemen, as they can then start to refocus on Syria and turn their attention to bringing some sort of resolution to the post-Assad environment. The growing inclination of Arab Gulf States such as Qatar or Saudi Arabia to encourage opposition groups and take a lead in the settlement of the post-war political setting in Syria seems to reflect general Middle East support for this course of action[73] aimed at curbing the growing Iranian influence in Syria and within the region.

Indeed, it seems very unlikely that Moscow would ever allow the IRGC to dominate the entire theatre of operations in Syria, especially with regard to the strategic position of the Russian naval base in Latakia on the Mediterranean coast. This has probably influenced Russia's decision to have a direct military presence in Syria and is indicative of its determination to get actively involved in the region. However, although Russia would probably prefer to be solely responsible for preparing Syria's plan of transition rather than sharing the role with Iran, Moscow is also very aware that at this stage it needs Tehran as a valuable economic and strategic partner just as Iran needs Russia in case of a future US incursion into Iran. This makes the two powers' cooperation in formulating Syria's political transition a strategic necessity, especially as Russia is aware that the restoration of its influence has been comparatively recent and owes much to the failure of Turkish foreign policy which, by adhering to its role as a staunch US ally, let Russian armed forces move in to sort out the situation in Syria rather than getting involved. Yet Russia's partial withdrawal of its forces from Syria (initially in March 2016 in order to increase its presence again following the intensification of the war and thereafter in January 2017) and its policies of controlled use of power clearly illustrates the extent to which Moscow is aware of the sensitive balance of power in Syria and the fragile nature of Damascus' internal political situation but possibly that Bashar al-Assad is also militarily secure.[74]

Following Obama's refusal to change US strategy in Syria (November 2014), US Defense Secretary Chuck Hagel and Army General Martin Dempsey, the Chairman of the Joint Chiefs of Staff, made the US position clear, stating in a Congressional hearing that the focus would still be on helping Iraqi forces defeat the Islamic State of Iraq and the Levant (ISIL) inside Iraq, rather than a US Syrian policy of ousting President Bashar al-Assad.[75] This has had the effect of gradually bringing al-Assad closer to Russia through the Axis of Resistance with Russia occupying a growing role in regional politics as it has evolved to become the only international player that can offer a constructive role in drafting and supervising a transitional plan for Syria's post-conflict future.

The Axis policy also has implications for Iranian survival as, through it, Iran can attempt to control the end result of a predetermined plan for regional transformation, as publicised in information gathered from US maps, which outlines a possible reformation of the region and hinting that Iran's containment is high up on the long-term US agenda. The strengthening of the Axis of Resistance policy might very well indicate that Iran could be the next US target after Syria.

## *The Army: A continuous institutional power*
The implications of the role of the military and its power (as an institutional structure) in both the Iranian and Turkish cases are multi-faceted. In Iran, the role of the army continues to play the same role described in Chapter 2, but since the Islamic Revolution it has now been given ever-increasing importance. This has resulted in the establishment of an Islamic military stratum to the extent that Iran today has become a crucible of military might, a change of direction from its previous orientation, which was much more secular. In contrast, the military has historically had a strong presence and leading role in Turkish bureaucracy, and, although AK Parti has managed to counterbalance the army's power to some extent, the latter still has a degree of control vis-à-vis its electorate power, which partly explains the Turkish government's tendency to opt for 'dual track' policies, e.g. in its Kurdish policies, as it needs to choose a path that satisfies both Turkish internal secular and nationalistic circles of power as well as the Kurdish side. However, Ankara's covert support to opposition forces, like FSA,[76] together with charges that Turkey's Syrian policy was aiding other non-state fundamentalist Islamist groups ranging from Jabhat Al Nusra (جبهة النصرة لأهل الشام), to Ahrar Al Sham, for instance, altered its regional image as a Muslim democracy and, at least, demonstrated its replacement with an Islamic bureaucracy.

In addition to the domestic sphere, the need for survival often makes the possession of large strong armies imperative, both on a regional and international level. The outbreak of the Arab Uprisings and the rise of IS along with other linked (fundamental) non-state entities that may arise in the course of the continued restructuring of the Middle Eastern region has increased the need for strong armies that can either liberate or preserve territories, not just to protect their own interests but to pursue a wider policy of maintaining the regional status quo. Thus, a potent and mighty army constitutes perhaps one of the main tools in maintaining security and establishing foreign policy. One prime example of this was the gathering of armed forces that came together to strengthen the Axis of Resistance formed in the late 1980s and early 1990s, which followed a dual policy that aimed to control Israeli pressure in the region and, at the same time, counterbalance the US dominance that had been in ascendance up to that time.

Armies are essentially structures that make winning possible. This was clearly demonstrated in the recent achievements and strategy of the Iranian army, which, in cooperation with Hizbullah and Bashar al-Assad's forces, took advantage of the rise of IS to penetrate further into the region. Likewise, Russian cooperation and the imminent delivery of advanced S-300 air defence missile systems for deployment at Jablah, the base the Russians have built outside Latakia for the intake of Russian troops to protect the Iranian military air facility at Ghorin, south of the port town of Latakia, the Russian MiG-31 interceptor craft standing by at the Mezza airbase at Damascus airport, and the giant Dmitri Donskoy TK-20 nuclear submarine to the west, all bear witness to the radicalisation of current politics and the extent to which the army continues to play a key role in the formulation of foreign policy. One extreme example of military power is found in Iran where the Iranian Revolutionary Guards Corps (IRGC) constitutes a state within a state.[77]

In the Turkish model, the role of the army is a parameter that must be considered in any formulation of domestic politics as it possesses considerable influence, which often swayed voting percentages in successive electoral campaigns. In the past Turkey has been dominated by its military/deep state power structure but Erdoğan managed to counterbalance this to some extent, although he has not succeeded in completely eradicating it (as was evident from the 15 July 2016 coup d'état), and therefore continues to need to win their electoral vote. However, the Gülen movement is gaining increasing control over the state's bureaucracy to the extent that it could even, in time, take over the powerful role of the old military structure as a US card of international pressure for the government of AK Parti. As its stance is in opposition to the secularists who also have many followers, it seems likely that Gülen will probably undergo transformation into a meta-deep state model positioned against the liberal forces.[78]

Turkey's current situation has been referred to as being 'in the middle of a process of institutional rebalancing'[79] but in the case of the military this is unlikely to bring about any real change in its position as, in the light of recent events, it still seems that the army and its historic legacy will continue to be a part of Turkey's political framework for the foreseeable future. However, in the case of Syria, it appears that Turkey also needs the support of the Free Syrian Army to keep control of its borders, especially in a post-war political theatre characterised by the gradual disintegration of IS and the FSA's own distinct role in the post-conflict Syrian political arena. Likewise, the role of the PKK and its military wings in both Turkey and Syria have continued to play a critical role in Turkish–Iranian relations, while the strategic locations of Turkish military bases, especially Incirlik, have been crucial for the US in its fight against terrorism and the threat posed by IS. However, bases used for smaller-scale operations, such as the Bashir airfield in Harir outside Erbil, have the potential to become much more significant and may in time take over some, or all, of Incirlik's role. The significance of these bases in routing skirmishes like that of August 2014 when IS were only 30 km from the outskirts of Erbil, make the reasons for US foreign policy prioritisation of Turkey abundantly clear.

## KURDISTAN BETWEEN IRAN AND TURKEY: IMPLICATIONS OF THE WAR ON ISLAMIC STATE

The Kurds first played a significant role as catalysts in deciding the Middle East balance of power as supporters of the Oghuz Turks in the battle of Manzikert (1071), which led to the occupation of Anatolia by the Turkic tribes under the leadership of Alp Arslan,[80] while Kurdish territory also created a buffer zone between the Ottoman and Safavid empires in the former's favour. This also acted as a formidable barrier against Iranian penetration into the region, particularly during the period between the 16th and 19th Kurdish Emirates, while later the Kurds would fight in Mustafa Kemal's War of Independence (1922). Most recently of all, their continuing importance in contemporary Middle Eastern affairs has been highlighted by their strategic role in the fight against IS. The Kurds of Iraq have also been valuable as allies of both Iran and Turkey – in addition to the Iraqi foreign policy – and at times been able to use their influence to achieve desired political outcomes. From 2000 onwards the KRG has also been a major player in US Iraqi foreign policy for 'regime change', serving as a very useful partner in the Iraqi context of preserving security as a de facto independent regional non-state actor. In the twin roles of defender of the borders between Iran and Turkey and frontline fighter in the war against IS, the Kurds have been crucial in influencing transformation within the region.

It is evident that the importance of the Kurdish factor in Iranian and Turkish Iraqi foreign policies will steadily increase in coming years as an indispensable dyamic in the equation of regional restructuring outlined by US and Israeli foreign policies[81] (in cooperation with other powerful states of the international community, namely France and Germany) which seeks to find an answer to the instability and chaos incited by Iranian foreign policy. The current US foreign policy emphasis on prioritising Iraq and the Kurds is clearly demonstrated through US participation in the issue of the Kurdish Presidency (2015) and its foreign policy's growing involvement in the KR's domestic political processes. Indeed, in 2014 President Obama himself clearly stated that the US has economic and political interests in the Kurdistan Region.[82] Sharing the same view, Fadhil Merani explains that '1992 is a landmark in Kurdish–Iranian relations as it is witnessed a shift to relations directly with the Foreign Ministry since relations before was only limited to the level of the Revolutionary Guards.'[83]

The significance of Kurdish–Iranian interactions vis-à-vis the secret April/May 2015 meeting in Erbil between representatives from the Kurdish government and Iran is one of many recent pieces of evidence showing that 'both sides today are trying to find a common language to solve the problem'.[84] Another interesting factor has been the institutionalisation of Turkish–Kurdish relations from 2008 onwards, which reached its peak with former Turkish Minister of Foreign Affairs Ahmet Davutoğlu's reference to the KR as 'Kurdistan' and also the use of the term 'leader of Iraqi Kurdistan' to refer to Massoud Barzani, a momentous step forward in their previously troubled relations.[85] Moreover, Erdoğan himself apologised on behalf of the state (23 January 2011) for the killings of more than 13,000 Kurds by the Turkish military using aerial bombings and poison gas during a Kurdish rebellion in Dersim which took place between 1936 and 1939. Such developments demonstrate that the Kurdish situation has dramatically changed and that what now exists is a circular, rather than triangular, interactive relation between the US, Turkey and the Kurds with Iran at its epicentre, acting as a regulator of domestic and regional affairs.

This circle – in the sense that all these (regional and international) powers portrayed are of equal importance in determining the regional balance of power – originally started with the rise of the Kurds as reliable partners in the US facilitation of the Iraqi policy of 'regime change', a process aimed at establishing the region's transformation, which began with the overthrow of Saddam Hussein and will be concluded with its eventual return to effective self-government. In this process the role of the Kurds is formative as the Kurdish issue has long been a cause of conflict, and therefore its resolution will impact both Iranian and Turkish foreign policies while also fulfilling a core goal of the US Middle Eastern Initiative dating back to the pre-Iraq war period.

Figure 6.1 below demonstrates the role of the foreign policies pursued by Iran, Turkey, the US and, more recently, Russia (currently reviving its sphere of influence in Middle Eastern politics) in relation to the Kurds as part of the international relations system and shows how these actors, both of state and non-state status, appear equally important through symmetrical circles of influence as far as the impact of their policies on each other is concerned. However, Iran and Turkey remain central regional powers, although Iran holds the more dominant role right at the epicentre of the current course of events vis-à-vis its more direct, interactive and revolutionary role in political affairs in contrast to Turkey's more problematic foreign

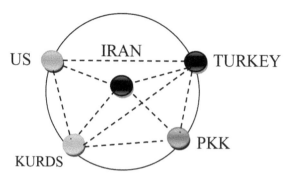

FIGURE 6.1 A model for multi-dimensional interactions in international relations. The diagram illustrates the multi-dimensional interactions formed between different central state and non-state actors in international relations. In the circle as well as the existing powers (or in their place) there could also be different regional and international powers such as Russia or Syria.

policy, currently in stalemate. Finally, the diagram highlights the crucial factor of Kurdish participation, which is evidently active as can be seen from the way it forms triangular relations between the different powers.

The role of the PKK in the Middle Eastern transformative process is absolutely crucial. Turkey is aware that a non-solution to its Kurdish issue, whether within a federal structure or any other mode of self-governance (such as the model of democratic autonomy – *Özerklik* – suggested by the Kurds in Turkey),[86] will always act as an impediment to Turkey's objective for regional dominance. So, for Turkey making peace with the PKK must be seen as a key element in resolving its domestic situation and achieving security on its borders. For Syria, the PKK is an intrinsic part of the political process and the reformation of the state in the post-Assad period. For Iran it is a critical ally, not only with its role supporting multiple non-state actors (i.e., Iran established relations with the Palestinian Islamist movement Hamas, especially since the July War (حرب تموز, 2006) until the outbreak of the Syrian crisis), but also because it has played a vital part in the implementation of Iran's foreign policy practice within the wider axis of the Resistance policy held by Iran, Russia and Syria.[87]

As PKK has a presence in both Syria and Iran, Iran perceives the PKK as potentially a destabilising power and, therefore, as Uslu summarises, since 'there is no neighbouring state for Iran to build an alliance with, Iran will build alliances with non-state actors'. Uslu points out that Turkey's moderate Islamic model – backed by the US – is 'a direct challenge to the Iranian model', so the Kurdish areas in Syria and Turkey are important 'as a new corridor between Iran and Syria'. This argument not only explains the Iran–PKK 2011 agreement[88] but also incidents like the alleged release of Murat Karayılan in August 2011 after negotiations with the Iranian security forces who had captured him following information from the National Intelligence Organization (MİT), an event which took place a few days before Turkish airstrikes on Qandil.[89] Reza Altun summarised the agreement Iran reached with the Kurds:

> In 2011 Iran wanted to eliminate PJAK but later changed its mind. PKK was the intermediate and mediated between the two sides. The ceasefire that followed meant that Iran would not attack the region where PJAK was influential and the latter would not conduct any attacks on Iranian forces. One factor that forced Iran to make this settlement was its own political situation as it had many potential border conflicts with Afghanistan, Pakistan and Syria. That's why it did not want to have a regional conflict on its own land and that is how the ceasefire came about.[90]

Fadhil Merani emphasises the PKK's ability 'to use that relation [with both Iran and Turkey] to put pressure on both [at a time] when Iran seeks to establish itself as an international player and Erdoğan is forced by his mistakes to adopt the Muslim Brotherhood's policies and as a Big Brother to take on the regional leadership'.[91] Certainly, as far as Iraq is concerned, the role of the Kurds appears to be the only link keeping the state united until a time comes when such a situation in Iraq might no longer be sustainable. For the international powers, the Kurds serve the goal of regional transformation while for the Kurds themselves, inter- and intra-Kurdish cooperation and commitment to the consolidation of separate autonomous regions appear the only way to fulfil the aims they have struggled to achieve for so long. This situation explains Turkish fear of Iran's capability to threaten Turkey's security as well as Iran's concern for its own internal problems in view of the presence of PJAK (the Party of Free Life of Kurdistan, پارتى ژيانى ئازادى كوردس) within its borders that has the potential to destabilise them or, at least, create constant problems on its borders. Indeed, the Kurdish issue has been, thus far, the main constituent of Iran's security cooperation with Turkey as almost 39–40 per cent of its multinational society consists of different ethnicities (Azeri, Kurds, Lurs, Arabs, Baluchis, and Turkmen).

The way the Syrian crisis has repositioned the central focus back to the Middle East has revived Cold War alliances and allowed Russia to reclaim zones of influence in the region, and this has strengthened the future role of the Kurds as intrinsic players in this process of transformation even further. The PKK–Iranian alliance came at a time when Syrian–Turkish relations were breaking down, its lowest point represented by Erdoğan's call to Assad to 'finally step down' for the sake of peace in the region.[92] From 2004 onwards, the PKK's role increased and intensified vis-à-vis the formation of PJAK (پارتى ژيانى ئازادى كوردستان, Free Life Party of Kurdistan) under the auspices of the PKK movement and the rise of Rojavayê Kurdistan (Western Kurdistan, 11 November 2013) in the North East area of Syria. Sedat Laciner clarified the situation: 'Russia, Iran and Assad's Syria see PKK as among the most important tools for stopping Turkey in the region.'[93]

The second renaissance of the Kurds via the developments in Syria and the announcement of the Kurdish Cantons following the example of the Kurdistan Region in Iraq resulted in the empowerment of the Kurds in Syria from 11 July 2012 when YPG (the People's Protection Units, July 2015) began to advance and take over control of the North-Eastern areas from the regime. The possibility of a second Kurdish state being established in Syria, following the fight against the IS, raised Turkish fears over their own Kurdish population and changed the direction of AK Parti's initial commitment, which had aimed to accelerate the peace process by taking steps to close the door on domestic conflict. Instead, Turkey revived its traditional Kurdish policy by continuing the war against the Kurds. This meant that Ibrahim Kalin's stance that: 'A new course has started in Turkey's Kurdish issue since 21 March, 2013, and that solving the Kurdish issue in Turkey will also have a positive influence on the Kurdish population in Iran and in Syria'[94] was rapidly replaced by Turkish President Abdullah Gül's position that: 'Turkey cannot permit *a fait accompli*; there is no question of accepting such a thing in Syria'[95] in response to the rise of Rojavayê Kurdistan (Western Kurdistan, 11 November 2013) in the North East part of Syria.

This change of direction implies, firstly, that not all political circles in Turkey (especially the nationalist-Kemalist wing) are ready to accept a potential co-existence with the Kurdish movements, and, secondly, that Erdoğan himself has to face up to the implications of a dual reality.[96] Accusations that it was the Gülen movement that was responsible for bringing the secret negotiations at Oslo of summer 2012 into the public eye are indicative of the many voices in Turkey that still oppose the peace process and its political resolution, while in February 2013 the ongoing Erdoğan/Gülen war endangered the arrest of MİT director Hakan Fidan for acting as a participant and mediator in the negotiations.[97]

The failure of the 'Friends of Syria' platform – a Turkish initiative – and the formation of the Syrian National Council (SNC) over the summer of 2011 following Turkey's warning that called on Syria to make urgent reforms (Davutoğlu's trip to Damascus on 9 August 2011) were instrumental in empowering the Axis of Resistance. Indeed, Iran exploited the regional turmoil and the situation in neighbouring Iraq which became increasingly unstable. This was as a result of al-Maliki's decision to give the order for the unilateral deployment of forces, namely the Tigris Operations Command, in Kirkuk and Diyala[98] following incidents such as the confrontation of Sunni politicians who were accused of planning terrorist attacks against Shi'ites with the alleged consent of Sunni Vice–President Tariq Hashemi (December 2011).[99] Subsequently, even more inflammatory actions took place, including Baghdad's refusal to give permission allowing a plane carrying Turkish Energy Minister Taner Yıldız to land in Erbil which brought Iraqi–Turkish relations into further crisis.[100]

The anxiety that the continuation of Kurdish fighting against IS caused Turkey was increased by the 11 June 2012 Hêwler Agreement which was reached after a meeting that unified the People's Council of Western Kurdistan, PYD, and the Movement of a Democratic Society for Western Kurdistan (TEV-DEM) with the Kurdish National Council backed by the KRG. It was a development that deeply concerned the Turkish administration because its own allegiance lay with the Syrian National Council formed in Turkey and supported by the Syrian Muslim Brotherhood. This opposition body suggested military intervention in Syria and opposed the Kurdish policy of self-governing by electing local committees, but also chose to set itself apart from the Syrian National Coordinating Body for Democratic Change, which, in turn, did not attend the 'Friends of Syria' conferences in Tunisia (February 2012) and in Istanbul and Paris (April 2012).

In response, the Kurdish Supreme Committee (*Desteya Bilind a Kurd*, 12 July 2012) was set up in Erbil with an agreement between PYD and the Kurdish National Council in Syria (consisting of 16 Kurdish political parties, KNC, 26 October 2011), the whole process being carried out under the mediation of President Barzani with the aim of decreasing tensions and bringing the Kurdish movement together. However, this cooperation has still not properly materialised, in spite of the Kurdish leaders' recognition of the necessity of its creation. Selahattin Demirtaş analysed the situation:

> If Kurds are able to unite as one around their common interests, it will be easier to find democratic solutions to the problems they face in the countries in which they live. For these reasons, we're involved in developing warmer relations with the Kurdistan autonomous region [of Iraq] and other Kurdish regions. We see the warmth reciprocated from the other side, and this pleases us. Barzani's call on the PKK to lay down its arms must be understood within the framework of his desire to see the Kurdish issue in Turkey move toward a democratic solution. He has never made a one-sided call. While calling on the PKK to lay down its weapons, he also calls on the Turkish government to work for a political, peaceful solution to the Kurdish issue.[101]

Therefore, I would argue that the unity of the Kurdish movement lies in the role and policies of the PKK, which is the key to unifying the Kurdish movements in Iraq and Syria as interconnected paradigms. The KRG is also important as the first Kurdish de facto state-entity with regional and international recognition and established relations, while PKK not only has an enduring interrelation with the KRG, but a presence in both Iran and Syria as well as a role in the on-going peace process in Turkish politics. The power of its relations

with Iran and other revisionist forces in the region combined with
the KRG's balanced relations with both Ankara and Tehran would
greatly strengthen the already important role of the Kurds in Syria
and work positively to consolidate the Kurdish status in the Middle
Eastern region. However, this would only be possible if all the entities
involved united their energies towards the same goal.[102]

At such a political crossroads, it seems critical for Turkey to
continue the efforts and progress towards a successful resolution of
the peace process, which started in 1993 during the Presidency of
Turgut Özal and continued between the Turkish state and PKK leader
Abdullah Öcalan in İmralı and Oslo throughout the period between
2009 and 2011 as Turkey increasingly recognised the dangers of
isolation.[103] Turkey's deteriorating foreign policy relations have
contributed to the rise of greater empowerment for Iran, especially
with regard to the inclusion of Russia in its Axis of Resistance policy.
Iran's regaining of its place in the regional balance of power has been
achieved mainly because US Iraqi policy has favoured Tehran and
thus changed the balance of power to its advantage. It is this that has
given Iranian foreign policy precedence over Turkey.

At the same time, in contrast to Iran, Ankara has struggled to adapt
to differing political circumstances, as in the case of its relations with
the Kurds. The dramatic increase of the Kurdish vote from 6.1 per cent
in 2014 under BDP's (*Partiya Herêman a Demokratîk*, Democratic
Regions Party or Peace and Democracy Party) leadership to 13.1 per
cent in 2015 when the People's Democratic Party (HDP, Partiya
Demokratîk a Gelan) overcame the 10 per cent threshold needed to
enter parliament and became the first Kurdish party to do so, gave the
Kurds exactly the same number of seats (80) in the Turkish parliament
as the Nationalist Movement Party (MHP). This clearly showed a
change in mood towards the Kurds with the public recognition of their
valuable role as partners in Ankara's peace process leading to its further
liberalisation and the establishment of democratic rule in contrast to
its unstable politically past. However, Ankara has continued to identify
the Kurdish issue with the problem of terrorism despite many years of
negotiation with the PKK leader, leading Turkey to withdraw from
foundational agreements that would have set changes in motion
relating to constitutional guarantees in line with the Dolmabahçe

Palace agreement (March 2015) and resulted in significant progress towards resolution of the Kurdish issue.[104] It thus seems that Turkish proactive foreign policy has been caught in its own trap as a result of its direct meddling in Syria's domestic affairs, which left it with 'zero neigbouring allies'.[105] The seriousness of its position is indicated in the statement made by Iranian Chief of Staff Major General Seyed Hassan Firouzabadi in the early stages of the conflict that 'it will be Turkey's turn if it continues to help advance the warmongering policies of the United States in Syria'.[106]

The hypothesis, that the role of the Kurds with their strategic location right in the middle of the geopolitical map of the region will continue to be crucial, primarily stems from the impact of their foreign policies on regional and international states. However, Iran's current position of favour should not be taken for granted as there is always the possibility of disintegration. This could lead to a shift into different modes of governance; for example, Turkey might choose to follow the example of Iraq as a result of the changes in the region. The strengthening of the Iranian opposition, via the agreement for cooperation between the Revolutionary Organization of the Toilers of Kurdistan (Komala) and the Democratic Party of Kurdistan (KDP) in August 2012, albeit of minor importance, certainly seems to indicate a leaning towards this direction.

In this context, the Kurds stand out as valuable partners, especially when considering the growing levels of US–KRG strategic cooperation as demonstrated by House Resolution 1654 which authorises 'the direct provision of defense articles, defense services, and related training to the Kurdistan Regional Government, and for other purposes' vis-à-vis the IS threat. In addition, House Resolution 1736 passed by the House Armed Services Committee authorises the provision of $715 million for security assistance to Iraqi forces combatting IS with 25 per cent of the funds released directly to Kurdish peshmerga and Sunni forces.[107]

*Energy politics: The Kurds – a bridge between Iran and Turkey*
Since the onset of the Syrian crisis in March 2011, and also as a result of Turkey's meddling in Syria and increasing economic pressure on the Islamic Republic of Iran, the need to win Kurdish cooperation, not only as an important alternative political and strategic ally, but

also a catalyst for energy and economic partnerships, has become more and more evident. For instance, Russian Rosneft concluded a series of agreements in the oil and gas sectors with the KRG during the 21st St Petersburg International Economic Forum (2 June 2017).

The strategic importance of KR has indeed been recognised by global foreign investors such as Exxon Mobil (which first signed oil deals with the KRG in November, 2012),[108] Chevron, Gazprom, Aspect Energy, Marathon Oil Corporation, Hillwood International Energy, Hunt Oil and Prime and Murphy Oil, all of which operate within the region.[109] Another factor has been the steep decline in Turkish energy trade dealings, which used to surpass US$1 billion annually, but 2012 saw GDP growth drop to 2.1 per cent while in 2013 the rate of decline increased to 4.1 per cent.[110] This was a drastic change compared to the high figures achieved during the period from 2002 to 2011 and has been of great concern for the Iranian economy as it remains dependent on its oil exports.[111] The KRG's Ministry of Natural Resources oil report stated that it had exported 18,105,734 barrels of crude oil (an average of 584,056 barrels per day), that is 18.1 million barrels of oil by December 2015, through the Kurdistan pipeline network to the port of Ceyhan in Turkey'.[112]

The role of the KR has great geopolitical and strategic importance. This has been clearly demonstrated through its institutionalised relations with the US vis-à-vis President Barzani's successive visits to Washington DC (in April 2012 and on 3–8 May, 2015) where he was received by President Barack Obama as head of state, while it has also developed important relations with Turkey and Iran. Turkish–Kurdish–Iranian relations have not been only limited to security cooperation meetings between the KR's PM Nechirvan Barzani and the Islamic Republic of Iran's border guard General Commander, General Qasem Rezai[113] or political interactions, but also the fields of economy and energy as expressed in Barzani's statement: 'Turkey is an important country for us in all aspects. We want Turkey to be more active in the energy field because Turkey is our access to the outside world.'[114]

Energy is a rich resource for Kurdistan as it sits on an estimated 45 billion barrels of oil and three trillion cubic metres of gas[115] with current oil production reaching around 600,000 (bpd). To maximise its profits, the KR built the first direct export oil pipeline in 2013, capable of delivering 1 million barrels of oil per day by 2015 to the border with Ankara. The Taq Taq-Khurmala (approx. 300 km) pipeline, from the Northern Taq Taq oilfields, connects Khurmala and Tawke (Zakho/Dohuk province) oil fields to the border in Pishkhabur, linking into the Kirkuk–Ceyhan pipeline on the Turkish side so that the Kurds can carry out independent export of their oil to Turkey's Mediterranean port of Ceyhan.

The construction of a second pipeline for gas was also agreed at the Caspian Gas Forum in Istanbul (2013). KR's Minister of Natural Resources, Ashti Hawrami, outlined plans for expansion: 'the region plans to export 10 billion cubic metres (bcm) of natural gas to Turkey over the next two years, but this may slip to 2019'.[116] The Kurdistan Regional Government Ministry of Natural Resources Oil Export Report recorded that the KR exported 18,461,357 barrels of crude oil (an average of 595,528 (bpd)) in October/December 2015 through the Kurdistan pipeline network to the port of Ceyhan in Turkey.[117] The Kurdistan Region exported a total of 19.2 million barrels of oil via the Ceyhan pipeline with around $400 million deposited with Turkish state lender Halkbank. In September, 2014, Reuters also reported another lucrative energy market for the KRG with at least 3 million barrels of Kurdish oil on ships heading out to Asia.[118]

Iran is the KR's second-largest trade partner (after Turkey) – with a value of trade around $8 billion in 2014 and $12 billion in 2015 with the expectation that bilateral trade will increase to $20 billion.[119] Accordingly, it decided to follow Turkey's example with an agreement to construct a 180-kilometre gas pipeline inside its territory, reaching to its border with the Kurdistan Region to fuel power stations in Kurdistan with Iranian gas, while another pipeline would be used to transport Kurdish fuel to Iran. Abdulla Akreyi, the Head of KRG–Iran relations, summarised the process: 'We agreed on building two pipelines (2014) from Iran to Kurdistan. The second one is for the KRG to export crude oil to Iran, in return for which Iran will supply 3–4 million litres of refined oil fuel for the power stations (in the Kurdistan Region) and natural gas.' Rostam Qasemi, a former oil minister heading up the Iran–Iraq economic development committee, concluded that: 'The Kurdistan Region is in need of 25 million cubic feet (Mcf) and Iran can supply that volume.'[120]

The KRG's independent oil exports have been providing the KRG with around $700 million a month since 24 June 2015, when the KRG started selling Kurdish oil independently of Baghdad, in spite of Baghdad's opposition. The latter has retaliated by withholding the Kurdish share of the profits received, estimated at around $1 billion a month in February 2014[121] in spite of Kurdish suggestions that the UN (and Baghdad) is welcome to take on the responsibility for supervising them.[122] In addition, Baghdad faced declarations of autonomy, both indirectly and directly, from many of its provinces such as the claims asserted by Anbar, Diyala and Salahaddin in 2011 and 2012 which al-Maliki rejected. It is quite evident that the reality in Iraq today is no longer a desire for a unified Iraq, but at least a confederated Iraq consisting of into separate regions.[123]

In spite of the steady advance of Turkish–Iranian economic relations, political tension still remains high as the two powers occupy different camps regarding their stance on the Syrian war. Hassan Rouhani's statement that: 'Iran and Turkey are the most powerful countries in the region and Ankara seeks to increase the level of economic ties with Tehran to $30 billion by 2015'[124] loses validation when the two states remain at odds over the crucial issue of their regional political interests. To resolve this, an agreement that brings unity must somehow be reached between the two in line with the vision of figures such as Tunser Kilic, General Secretary of NSC, who wants Turkey to move towards an alliance with Russia and Iran.[125] However, political actions like the international economic embargo on Iran and Turkey's gold-for-oil scheme, an operation in opposition to the US FY 2013 National Defense Authorization Act (including new sanctions prohibiting the transfer or sale of gold),[126] together with the $20 billion estimate of the bilateral trade in 2012 seem to be setting a different course when compared to their current foreign policy choices as well as their geopolitical agenda.

## The Kurdish role in the Iranian and Turkish responses to the Syrian crisis

Iran has contributed to the preservation of the Syrian regime vis-à-vis Iranian support of Damascus at the beginning of the Iran–Iraq war and has a vested interest in playing a role in the post-Assad political setting, both in Syria and in the wider region. Iran's hostile perception of US views and policies is demonstrated in the statement given by Yahya Rahim Safavi, the advisor to the Supreme Leader and the Joint Chiefs of Staff, that 'the Americans think they must have a presence in West Asia and North Africa to ensure the survival and security of the Zionist regime and to create a strategic rival in confrontation with Iran – this rival is Turkey'.[127] However, this viewpoint contrasts with former US ambassador Ryan Crocker who states: 'US military intervention would likely not produce a better outcome in Syria and that the Barack Obama administration should focus on a "post-Assad" but not a "post-Alawite" future.'[128] This is in stark contrast to Turkey, which has tried to point out reforms to the Syrian regime, an interference in Syrian domestic affairs that has had disastrous results, leading to the severing of diplomatic relations, and an increase in support for the Syrian opposition and, more seriously, religious movements like Jabhat Al-Nusra (جبهة النصرة) or the Free Syrian Army. Among other events that have damaged Turkey's reputation, there have been reports of jihadists being accommodated in Antakya until 2012 and then transferred to Syria via the village of Guvecci and Yayladag town as well as the damning disclosure of Turkey's role in weapon shipments to the opposition and reports of militants crossing its border, while it is also alleged that 3,500 tons of military equipment have reached Syria through Turkey.[129] Salih Muslim Mohammed, former leader of the Democratic Union Party (PYD) further discredited Turkey when he stated that, '... based on documents from 2 September 2012 Turkey was planning to stir up unrest and get the Kurds to relocate to Southern Kurdistan [Kurdistan-Iraq]'.[130]

Turkish foreign policy has certainly been ineffective in addressing the problems created in the onset of post-Arab Uprisings period while another issue centres on the ongoing internal controversy between Erdoğan and Gülen because the former supported a political solution to Turkey's Kurdish issue which Gülen resisted. Later on, the complete abandonment of negotiations with the Kurdish leadership was another false step as it resulted in the growing empowerment of the Kurdish movement. This, along with successful Kurdish policies in both Syria and Iraq supporting the fight against terrorism and, specifically, the confrontation of IS, has brought the Kurds out of the shadows and placed them at the epicentre of regional developments. Turkey had thought it could deliver a solution to the Syrian problem as reported by analyst Kaan Dilek in *Taraf* (2012), making reference to 2007 when 'Israel had detected and blown up Syrian nuclear infrastructures and at that time, although the US wanted to put pressure on Syria, Turkey held them back, saying that we are going to convince Syria'.[131] Apparently, it could not live up to its promises as Ankara did not succeed throughout this period in forming the necessary alliances to become leader of the region and was therefore unable to implement its proposed Syrian foreign policy given the Russian presence that limited the scope of Ankara's policies and the freedom of manoeuvre in Syria. Yet, the 15 July 2016 unsuccesful coup d'état marks a U-turn in Turkish politics and in particular in Turkey's foreign policy as Erdoğan managed in a short period not only to change the orientation of its foreign policy that became more receptive followed by domestic changes in the leadership such as Ahmet Davutoğlu's disposal, but also improve Ankara's relations especially after the crisis in Russian–Turkish relations.[132]

The result of the success of Kurdish policies was increased standing in the international community, perhaps best summarised in the US view expressed by US Defense Secretary Ash Carter of 'Kurdish fighters as a model of the kind of force needed to defeat Islamic State'.[133] He continued: 'the Kurds are acting, and because the Kurds are capable of acting, we are supporting them, and that is successful'.[134] The Kurds' importance for Iran has also been demonstrated in their ability to exert a degree of control; for example, Iran's request 'to allow Iranian weapons transfers to Syria, was rejected by Barzani', underlining Iran's need of support from the PKK.[135] Indeed, the Kurdish empowerment from 2012 onwards has been reflected in its growing status in the region via a series of events including the preservation of the Kurdish status in Syria, KR's independent oil sales from May 2014 onwards,[136] the strengthening of EU relations with the KRG invited to attend and contribute alongside Iraqi authorities in the EU–Iraq talks (May 2015) and the opening of the EU liaison office in the Kurdistan Region (23 August 2015). In the 2015 meeting with KR's Prime Minister, Nechirvan Barzani, and the EU delegation, praised the role of peshmerga forces for 'having been able to repulse the Islamic State terrorist organisation, IS, and protect the region's population consisting of various religious and ethnic backgrounds'.[137] For Turkey, the Kurds constitute both a direct and indirect threat vis-à-vis the repercussions that the peace process and a political resolution would have on Turkey's state structure as well as the Kurds' crucial role in protecting the Turkish border and their involvement with Iraq.

It is thus clear that the main obstacle the Kurds have to confront lies within the Kurds themselves. Lack of inter- and intra-Kurdish cooperation[138] and controversies between different groups[139] have continually placed the Kurdish discourse for independence in jeopardy. This needs to be speedily resolved so that the peace process in Turkey can continue[140] as it will facilitate Syria's Kurds in their attempts to consolidate an autonomous status, rather than continuing to rely on external players and other regional neighbouring states to stabilise and promote their current position. For this to happen, the role of PKK in bringing about the institutionalisation of Kurdish status in Turkey is critical while the commitment to the Dohuk Agreement (22 October 2014) must be honoured if the threat posed by IS is to be overcome. Other positive moves in this direction would be the consolidation of the Kurdish status in Syria with the long-awaited resolution of the Kurdish issue within the Syrian borders,[141] the 'normalisation' of Kirkuk according to Article 140 (§2) where the Kurdish population currently stands at 51.3 per cent according to a 2015 KRG survey,[142] and the replacement of the Baniyas–Kirkuk oil pipeline damaged by a US bombardment back in 2003. These factors, in addition to the crucial settling of the dispute over Mosul's future, constitute strategic points that could accelerate Kurdish progress towards their long-awaited self-determination.

CONCLUSION

Henry Kissinger used to say that the Arabs cannot make war without Egypt and they cannot make peace without Syria. The US Iraqi foreign policy from 2003 onwards paved the way for the reshaping of the Middle Eastern region which is still changing as the Arab (Sunni) states at its centre weaken. The Iraq war acted as a catalyst for regional imbalance and this was exacerbated by al-Maliki's policies favouring Iran, but the impact of the Arab Uprisings on the region also instigated the onset of the Kurdish reawakening, and the potential consolidation of Kurdish status in Iraq, Turkey, Syria and Iran. However, for further progress to be made, the Kurdish movement must put aside inter- and intra- Kurdish differences, whether ideological or tactical.

Notable during the period discussed has been the steady strengthening of existing historic Iranian–Turkish relations based on mutual economic benefit. Yet, more recently, the interaction between Ankara and Tehran has been severely affected by the rise of the Syrian crisis, a factor dividing regional and international players which has resulted in Ankara and Tehran supporting opposite sides. Hence, the role of the economy as a connecting factor between the two powers is, to some degree, contradicted by the differences in their actual foreign policy agendas.

In both Turkey and Iran, the role of institutions plays a major part, and this is particularly true of the army, which has undergone a revival in importance as a result of the regional crisis. It continues to influence foreign and domestic policy decisions, both positively and negatively, and this enhances its status as a critical structure within government. Erdoğan has, to some degree, succeeded in counterbalancing the military apparatus in Turkey, but this does not mean that AK Parti has eliminated it, or even managed to gain total control. In Iran the IRGC has dominated the political scene with its shows of strength and exploited its key role as the main pillar supporting the Supreme Leadership's power. Yet, this supremacy could still be challenged as Iranian foreign policy's use of multiple groups to consolidate its power may signal the onset of internal division. Rouhani's proposal for a Referendum in the Republic's 39th anniversary of the Islamic Revolution in order to bring the people together is indicative of this. Tehran appears to have trained Muqtada al-Sadr's Mahdi Army, the 'Special Groups', and, more recently, 'the emergence of a new Shi'ite militia in Iraq in the form of "Saraya Al-Khorasani" [Khorasani Brigades]', named after Iran's Supreme Leader, Ayatollah Sayyed Ali

Khamenei (who is alternatively referred to as Sayyed Khorasani), in the fight against the Islamic State (IS).[143]

The Syrian crisis, and in particular the crucial role of Syria in terms of its importance as a geostrategic centre in the region as well as its major contribution to the energy industry, has ensured the return of Damascus to the forefront of regional petroleum policies, especially with regard to the Baniyas pipeline. At the same time, the struggle of al-Assad's regime for survival has brought Russia back into the ring as a major player in the Middle Eastern region and revived its role to such an extent that it has been able to adopt a policy of direct interference and use of force in the region, stepping into the gap left by the US vis-à-vis Barack Obama's 'disengagement' policy following US withdrawal of ground forces from Iraq and the distressing lack of any clear US strategy regarding Iraq's future.

Tayyip Erdoğan attempted to carry out policies to form a 'Middle East Quartet' by joining with Egypt, Saudi Arabia and Iran (July 2012), but his efforts were unsuccessful. Later on, Turkey's decision to support the Syrian opposition, ranging from the Free Syrian Army, which included Muslim Brotherhood supporters, to fundamentalist religious groups, was largely responsible for Iran overtaking Turkey in terms of political advantage. It achieved this by gaining powerful allies through the formation of the Russia–Damascus–Tehran axis.

Yet, it is very unlikely that Russia will ever let Iran and the IRGC take entire control of Syria, while the widely different objectives held by Syrian and Iranian foreign policy also make this unlikely. The Russian–US agreement that gave the green light to Moscow to intervene directly has shown the high stakes that a post-Assad environment could have on Iranian foreign policy, and this seems to indicate that therefore curtailment of Iranian influence is just a matter of time. The statements made by the Supreme Leadership Ayatollah Ali Khamenei of, on the one hand, the idea of a 'heroic flexibility' that 'is not opposed to diplomacy', and, on the other, emphasising that Iranian resistance to hegemony should be sustained, reflect the Iranian regime's potential concerns over its status.

Unless a stronger Turkish–Iranian alliance can be achieved, it is the role of the Kurds, as they continue to seek stability and consolidation of their status in this transforming era, that stands out as a unique example of a non-state entity with an enduring impact on Turkish and Iranian foreign policies. This is indicated not only through the effect Kurdish strategies have had in helping to establish security in a volatile situation, but also due to the strong economic ties between these three powers as inter-dependent actors.

It is clear that the Middle Eastern region and, in particular, core states like Syria and Iraq are greatly influenced by the role and policies of international players whose interference has been sustained. This has not just been limited to external interference but also increased regional pressures such as Turkish and Qatari initiatives to form the National Coordination Committee (NCC), an umbrella group of leftist, nationalist and Kurdish factions founded in June 2011. The interference of such groups invariably impacts on the formulation of Iranian and Turkish foreign policies, although these represent two opposed positions with the former primarily seeking the continuation of the struggle against US hegemony and the latter pursuing policies which reflect a US orientation in its role as a NATO ally and pro-Western partner. Indeed, the first overseas speech Barack Obama delivered as US President was from the Turkish parliament (6 April 2009).

In this scenario it is perhaps surprising that it has not been the outbreak of the Arab Uprisings that swept through the entire MENA region, but the Syrian crisis that has been the primary factor of change, causing huge upheaval in Iranian and Turkish foreign policies and seismic shifts in the balance of power in the region. This crisis has deepened owing to the lack of organised opposition in confronting the Syrian crisis and the absence of effective strategies aimed at resolving the issues emerging from the shape of a post-war future for Syria. US indecisiveness delaying prompt action and the victimisation of the Kurds have contributed further to this instability.

However, the rise of a common Islamic threat, IS, which mainly targeted the Sunni and Kurdish areas, had a positive effect in unifying the Kurdish movement vis-à-vis the hopes raised by the Kurdish Supreme Committee and the strengthening of KRG foreign relations regionally and internationally, culminating with agreements to construct oil and gas pipelines with both Iran and Turkey and operate independently of Baghdad. Yet, a series of conditions still act as impediments to a unified Kurdish regional policy. Overcoming quota issues in Kurdish political representation, domestic and external plans for the KR's dichotomy under the pretext of conducting the Kurdistan Referendum that would only unite again (possibly temporarily) Iran and Turkey against the KRG despite the overwhelming majority of the 93 per cent of the votes that backed the territory's independence from Baghdad and the part played by power politics and ideological differences are evident. In reality, the road to Kurdish self-determination appears to inevitably lead to a confederate mode of governance (with the exception of Turkey) as federalism has proved to be a failed enterprise, i.e. one that is not just limited to local autonomy as the more leftist wings would prefer, but includes constitutional rights enabling the Kurds to act as equal partners in a democratic system, within (or without) present borders and state structures.

Nonetheless, a positive outcome appears negotiable as, in essence, convergences of opinion outnumber the divergences which are mainly concentrated on power politics in line with the historical trajectory. Kurdish inter- and intra-cooperation is critical, but should be forth-coming as the Kurds represent a valuable stable ally that could be of benefit to the neighbouring states, especially considering that those who target and form the most productive alliances (which includes the Kurdish element), will inevitably emerge from the regional turmoil as stronger and more influential players. Although at the moment there is a situation of instability in the heart of the Middle East where the Kurds are located, the Kurdish movement in Turkey, and, more specifically, the PKK can use this situation to facilitate Kurdish unity, developing relations with other Kurdish powers and their allies to maximise advantage for the Kurdish movement as a whole. Moreover, this is almost certainly only a temporary disorder. Although Iranian foreign policy tactics have continued to stir up instability in the region, this is becoming increasingly unsustainable in view of the current progression of events.

Interestingly, it seems that the dynamics introduced by inter-national, regional and domestic factors appear to have greater influence in changing the direction of Turkish and Iranian foreign policies towards the region than *vice versa*. This also means that, as interaction of multiple state and non-state actors develops to take on different roles, the complexity of regional politics will also increase, and this will progressively affect the independence of non-Arab states such as Iran and Turkey. Therefore, the role of factors that impact on their policies is critical when examining the broader political landscape inside and outside the Middle East since 'the New Middle East is being formed [also] through what is happening between Iran and Turkey'.[144] Factors of greater weight could also stem from both the external structural environment and emergent domestic crises as when states pursue aims to formulate more independent foreign policies they may also become more vulnerable and prone to instability.

To summarise, the main findings of this chapter show clear indications of a wave of change sweeping through the broader MENA (Middle East and North Africa) region, which has turned the spotlight onto Syria as the exceptional factor in bringing change, just as Iraq did earlier, while also highlighting the rising role of the Kurdish determinant during this period and beyond. Meanwhile, the series of civilian or militarised uprisings baptised 'Arab Spring', which started on 17 December 2010 in Tunisia, is still continuing in the more recent Syrian and Yemeni crises. Like 9/11, the 'Arab Spring' was a totally unforeseen event and constituted a milestone in international politics, changing world affairs so that the region would never be the same again. The drive of domination rather than cooperation as the prime goal of the region's foreign policy can only bring further dichotomy, and this means that unless Turkey and Iran can reach a compromise that lies in, but also goes beyond their mutual cooperation for economic survival, which at present is their sole lifebelt in a sea of uncertainty, the chasm separating them will get deeper and they risk a permanent rift in their relations.

The considerations we have presented so far will reach their conclusion in the next and final chapter where the empirical evidence provided throughout the book will be extensively examined to present theories and concepts regarding the role of unforeseen events as catalysts for change. The increasing pressure of domestic, but more importantly, external conditions and their impact on the period under examination will be further analysed. The chapter will also examine the key role played by the interaction between state and non-state actors (particularly the influence exerted by the latter in state foreign policies) and the way that such interrelations have often been shaped by their own foreign policy interests.

# CHAPTER 7

# Conclusions and Conceptualisations

## INTRODUCTION

This book has focused on a long period starting from the genesis of both Turkey and Iran until the end of Barack Obama's Presidency and the unsuccessful coup d'état in Turkey that signal a new cycle of changes that awaits to unfold and mark a new period of analysis which requires a comprehensive and in-depth study in its own right.

This series of developments that synthesise a new political setting, both regionally and internationally, also includes the rise in power of a controversial US Presidential figure, Donald Trump (20 January 2017) placing right at the heart of the US foreign policy the major goal of containing the spread of radical Islam.[1] Furthermore, it consists of Hassan Rouhani's re-election with 57 per cent in the Iranian Presidency (5 August 2017), following the 19 May 2017 elections and the battle between a formal alliance comprised of reformists, centrists and pragmatists (symbolised by Khatami, Rouhani and Rafsanjani respectively), and the conservatives/ principalists.[2] In the case of Turkey, the 15 July 2016 coup heralded a new era for Turkish politics to the extent that it constitutes a landmark with the pace of change reaching its peak with the newly-established presidential system following the 16 April 2017 Turkish referendum with 51.41 per cent 'yes' to 48.59 per cent 'no' vote.

Similarly the Kurdish 25 September referendum in the Kurdistan Region of Iraq with the question–'Do you want the KR and the Kurdistani areas outside the Region's jurisdiction to become an independent state?' – that garnered a 'yes' vote of 92.73 per cent changed the course of events in the Middle East.[3] The harsh response of the Iraqi Federal Government with an invasion in Kerkuk in cooperation with Iran and a certain circle from the opposition forces, in particular, the Kurdistan Patriotic Union (PUK), exposed the Iraqi revisionist agenda, revealed the plans of the opposition in the KR and uncovered the increasing role of Iran in Iraq.

Turkish and Iranian participation in the Astana Summits (24 January 2017), the fourth and fifth round of the Astana Process talks on Syria (3–4 May and 4–5 July 2017) aiming at the creation of four 'de-escalation zones' on the ground in the same vein as the seventh round of Syrian peace talks in Astana (30–31 October 2017) in addition to the sixth Astana Summit (14–15 September 2017) with a focus on Idlib province, as well as their engagement in international meetings on Syria's peace talks (i.e., Geneva Conferences) respectively continue to confirm the rising importance of both Iran and Turkey as intrinsic elements of the change currently unfolding in the Middle Eastern region.[4] Their historic influence on the region in the past has continued into an active role in the present with direct involvement in the cases of Syria (i.e., on 24 August 2016 Turkey, in an effort to prevent the unification of Kobani and Afrin, launched a military operation together with the Free Syrian Army (FSA) in Syria, known as Operation Euphrates Shield) and Iraq in confronting IS. In one sense, IS represents a new threat but the phenomenon constitutes an escalation of the same kind of religious extremism in different form that can be traced back in the recent past. It is very likely that such phenomena can emerge again in the future in different forms and types as an outcome of political actions instigated by different members of similar radical groups of religious orient in the broader region.

Turkey and Iran are increasingly seen as major players in the region, and this has been reinforced vis-à-vis the transitional nature of the conflicts from the international to the national, and even on a local level. As indispensable allies, their foreign policies are able to influence and facilitate international powers' policies towards the region and in a global context. At the same time they can take advantage of regional structures to interact with non-state actors in order to promote their aspirations for influence or expansion on both a regional or international level. This combined regional and international focus places Iran and Turkey right at the centre of the international relations system and its developments.

One of the main reasons why this book is important is because its analysis presents a comprehensive overview of the onset of revival for both the Turkish and Iranian foreign policies and the part they have played in facilitating regional restructuring. At the same time it highlights another key factor, the role of non-state actors through the case the Kurds and the impact of their continuous efforts to consolidate their status mutually on both Turkish and Iranian foreign policies. The increasing importance of the Kurdish status, mainly in Iraq and Syria, that has transformed the Kurdish factor as a central actor responsible for bringing change into the regional political setting, has raised further concerns in both Ankara and Tehran. This has been evident through the Syrian peace talks and Russia's proposal of a draft constitution supportive of an assembly of (autonomous) regions and thus Syrian federalisation.[5] It has been also the case vis-à-vis the 25 September 2017 Independence Referendum by the KRG as well as US explicit support for the Kurds in both Syria and Iraq in the fight against the Islamic State as intrinsic part and the main frontline in this anti-terror war. US cooperation with the Kurdish-led Syrian Democratic Forces (SDF) in Syria (i.e., in Raqqa – 6 June 2017) as well as with the peshmerga forces in Iraq in the context of the anti-IS coalition campaign and the latest battles including Hawija and its surrounding villages, following the liberation of Mosul (July 2017), Tal Afar (August 2017) and other areas stand out.[6] Certainly the Kurds today continue to represent the apple of discord between Tehran and Ankara given their critical role in both states' efforts to maximise their regional power.

All the themes explored in these chapters revolve around the impact of non-Arab states together with the role that non-state entities play in regional politics, which is an insufficiently examined topic in the field of IR. Consequently, the book has attempted to demonstrate that the nature of the subject matter under analysis is not merely an inter-state or a bilateral issue, but one of significant importance simply because even though 'the present state of conflicts in the Middle East goes beyond Turkey and Iran, [they are also] being conducted through them as main (f)actors in the emergence of new political forms in the region'.[7]

The book then concentrates on the exploration of the prime factors (rather than the minor ones that have the potential to evolve into determinants in the future as explained in Chapter 1) involved as catalysts in influencing the formulation of Turkish and Iranian foreign policies toward the Middle East. The study of Turkish–Iranian relations analysed throughout the chapters has aimed to demonstrate their continuity and connections based on their historical relations stretching back many years, but also examine the changes that have occurred within these parameters from 1979 onwards. The Palestinian cause is an example of an instant and tactical factor (as a foreign policy choice) rather than an alliance of strategic importance which can be deduced from the fact that it has not continued to gather momentum, but started to recede in importance in the same vein as the importance of the water issue for Turkey, Syria and Iran, which, while critical, has not yet caused major repercussions in the broader region. Finally, current Russian predominance in the broader Caucasus leaves little room for Iranian and Turkish policies to have as much influence as they would like.

In addition to the different empirical approaches pursued throughout the study, this chapter will finally conclude and conceptualise the book's objective, which has been built, on my previous extensive work based on a critique of IR theories. My intention is to make a further test of the applicability of my theoretical approach by examining international politics using an alternative IR outlook which combines 'multi-dimensional', 'interactional' and 'interrelational' aspects to address important areas that have hitherto been given insufficient attention in the discipline. It therefore embraces the interrelation among politics, IR and foreign policy on the one hand, and, on the other, the interaction between state and non-state actors other than structures and policies. The premise results in an informative model of 'multi-dimensional inter-relations'[8] that attempts to bridge the gap between agent and structure, time and space, epistemology and ontology and objectivity and subjectivity.[9]

In studying Turkish–Iranian interactions the book demonstrated how the direction of their foreign policies have been stimulated by critical factors that transcend traditional structures resulting in the enhanced role of non-state actors who now increasingly act as a catalyst in foreign policy formulation. The analysis examined the impact of non-state actors on Turkish and Iranian foreign policies, but also shows that the foreign policy of a state can be affected by, and interacts with, non-state entities, thus disproving the premise that interstate interactions are the only forces driving the international relations system. The argument for the interactive role of material and ideational structures and agents to shape foreign policy is thus vindicated through detailed examination of the way Iranian and Turkish foreign policies are formulated as another interesting multi-dimensional interactive set of dynamics.

## EMPIRICAL AND CONCEPTUAL IMPLICATIONS

The book focuses on the determinants that played a decisive role in Middle Eastern foreign policy making through their influence on Turkish and Iranian foreign policies. I therefore traced the evolution of such factors from their earlier history to the Iranian Revolution (1979) and examined their impact on relations between Iran and Turkey after Iran broke away from its former secular tradition to become an Islamic theocratic state. The book's chronological order provides a useful trajectory for observing how these factors have steadily unfolded.

In analysing the present day situation, this study first considers the structural differences between Iran and Turkey and how these formulated their foreign policies, and clearly demonstrates that this has been an historical factor in the development of these two powers. Since the Ottoman and Safavid empires it is quite evident that the roles of the controlled *ulama* of the Ottoman bureaucracy versus the independent religious clergy in Iran formed their structures which then had an impact on their foreign policy orientation and policy making. In the post-World War period these religious institutions developed even further in their capacity to act as agents of change. In Turkey the clergy became more submissive and were controlled by the army, which acted as a guarantor for the preservation of the Turkish state. In Iran the influence of the religious societal stratum steadily increased, and, along with economic independent elites, evolved into a domestic agent whose revolutionary attitude towards state structures reached its peak with the Iranian Revolution and the establishment of the Revolutionary Guards which, in turn, ultimately achieved control over the state's rule and its army.

It was thus shown how domestic structural parameters were able to shape Turkey and Iran throughout this historical period. Within this context and counter to the literature, I claimed that analysing the Turko-Persian tradition should be perceived more as a factor of unity rather than a determinant responsible for formulating their foreign policy practice per se. This also explains why Turkish–Iranian relations, despite being diametrically different, have managed to continue to avoid severe conflicts in their relations even when their interests have not converged.

The role of religion and religious ideology does not appear to dictate the foreign policy of either power. However, it does stand out as a considerable ideational structural factor that on occasion has evolved to become an instrument of legitimacy, especially in the case of the Safavid empire's structure when it diverted from mainstream Sunni orthodoxy circles with the introduction of the Twelver Shi'a Islam as the empire's official dogma of faith.

In the Ottoman case, and later on in the Turkish state following the formation of the nation-states, the role of the army was a major institution and structural material factor that determined the fate of the Turks and their foreign policy making to a great extent. In contrast, the Safavid empire based its formation upon the ideational factor of its religious identity so that it became a structure of ideational nature, which in turn acted as a foundation for the formation of the Iranian state following the Iranian Revolution. This is also reflected in the contemporary Iranian discourse's reliance on norms such as Shi'a religious identity and the state's Islamic character, and also influences the way most Iranian scholars will interpret and analyse contemporary Iranian foreign policy.[10]

This continuity of the normative approach traces its roots right back to the very beginning of the construction of Iran's society when powerful religious tribal and economically independent elites questioned the state's survival under the rule of the Shah leading to a clash between the interests of a secular ruling elite and the traditional stance held by advocates of Shi'ism. The elite faction composed of followers of the Shi'a doctrine ultimately prevailed, and the same inherently revolutionary, as opposed to traditional Islam and secular authority, attitude which they possessed is still a major influence today, and explains the nature of the religious beliefs that form Iranian foreign policy principles as well as the Iranian political system's decentralisation of power.

Indeed, Iranian ideas which support dominance versus hegemony and Islamic values versus a non-divine legitimate authority have been a considerable ideational factor in the formulation of foreign policy making. Although the impact of the *ayatollah* on Iranian foreign policy principles runs in parallel to the formative role that the army has played in Turkey's foreign policy paradigm, the role of the leadership as another ideational factor appears particularly influential, as can be seen in charismatic leaders such as Mustafa Kemal and Ayatollah Khomeini who have both left a remarkable legacy to their states. Therefore, this book highlights the role of the leadership as critical in the formulation of political policies, and also capable of strongly influencing events, although this is not to imply that it will necessarily therefore supersede the power of the institutions.

Iranian and, to a lesser extent, Turkish reaction in favour of a more independent foreign policy practice has strong links to the effect external interference, an external structure, has had on the formation of Middle Eastern politics. Whereas Republicanism aimed at liberating Iran from Western control, in Turkey European influence targeted preservation of the unity of the state. The escalation of external involvement, first witnessed in the actions of European powers and later in those of the US, was perpetuated by the collapse of the Safavid and Ottoman empires and the formation of the Iranian and Turkish states, finally reaching a climax during the Cold War. While adoption of European reforms could be regarded as contributing to the disintegration of both empires, the role of the US and

Soviet involvement in determining regional politics today also appears to be steadily increasing. Indeed, it seems that international interference and its attempts to impose European democratic values and rights on the Middle East has been largely responsible for the vast changes the region is currently experiencing as the following section will further elaborate.

Turkey's absorption in its domestic (structural) problems throughout the Cold War rather than reacting to or interacting with regional and national political affairs had a tremendous impact on Iranian foreign policy making. In Iran aversion to international meddling into regional affairs found expression in the Islamic Revolution of 1979, while the creation of the Islamic Republic of Iran represented an attempt to dispel its past dependent relations on the West and follow independent foreign policies. Somewhat ironically, this has also been echoed in the Turkish case in the 21st century under another Islamist government and is reflected in its attempts to develop a multi-dimensional foreign policy.

As far as Turkish–Iranian relations are concerned, the literature seems to have exaggerated the role of the Iranian Revolution as a factor shaping the formulation of mutual policies and affecting the course of Turkish politics. I rather argue that the impact of the revolution only had short-term repercussions on Iran's relations with Turkey as Islamist parties were already involved in power (i.e., the National Order Party, Millî Nizam Partisi, MNP – followed by the National Salvation Party, Millî Selâmet Partisi, MSP) prior to the outbreak of the Iranian revolution. Moreover, Turkey's foreign policy followed a combined approach of Islamism coupled with a Kemalist/ secular foreign policy orientation. Besides, Iran was not strong enough to export the revolution, especially given the fact that Iran is Shi'ite-oriented while the majority of the Middle East is Sunni and that its resources were severely depleted in the aftermath of Gulf War I. Thus, the Iranian Revolution, as a form of internal structural change influenced by external developments and, to some extent, by the stalemate of the secular modernising mode of governance in the region, demarcated the camps of alliances even more clearly. In particular, one result of the revolution was to transmit the message to the masses that a dictatorial regime could be overthrown and

Islamists take over as would later be the case in the first period of the Arab Uprisings. This realisation had the effect of swiftly bringing Turkey back to the American bandwagon, despite recent efforts toward the pursuit of an indepedent foreign policy.

Similarly, I have argued that the role of Iraq (a regional structure) as the undisputed arbiter and trader of the Persian Gulf oil supply together with the economic benefits it has been able to offer the United States seems to have affected the course of Iranian–Turkish relations much more than Gulf War I. The war posed a security dilemma for Turkey as the possibility of Iraq losing raised the issue of the power vacuum that could then result which Iran would be keen to exploit. Throughout Gulf War I and its aftermath, the economic dimensions of relations between Turkey and Iran remained intact, due mainly to the war which reinforced their need for each other. Turkish ports and goods along with Iranian gas facilitated further interdependence. However, to some extent, this mutual reliance can also be attributed to Özal's liberalisation policies and Europeanisation aspirations which dictated extrovert policies.

Undoubtedly, the post-Cold War context marked the end of the bipolar system and heralded the rise of a multipolar international relations system which proved to be an external structural determinant of great impact on the formulation of Turkish and Iranian politics. This period signalled the beginning of the role that Iraq, Syria and the Kurds (in both Iraq and Turkey and particularly the PKK) would play in the formulation of Iranian and Turkish foreign policies vis-à-vis Iranian–PKK tactical on/off interactions as players able to exert pressure on Turkey and vice-versa. Iran and its Axis of Resistance policy were also found at the epicentre of change in contrast to the pro-Western Turkish foreign policy outlook adopted by Ankara, a situation that still continues today. The 1990s marked a season of dramatic global change as Turkish and Iranian foreign policies were largely formed on the basis of developments in Iraq and the Kurdish issue as well as the dissolution of the former Soviet Union which impacted on Turkey's relations with the TransCaucasus. The creation of the first Kurdish de facto state entity in the North of Iraq (KRG, May 1992) and the activities of PKK that monopolised regional interest revealed the role of the Kurds of Iraq as an influential non-state entity. US–Kurdish interactions and the gradual formulation of a US Kurdish policy toward the KRG together with the PKK leadership's capture in February 1999 and a series of regional inter-state security meetings which aimed to confront the Kurds as a rising threat on their borders, highlighted the Kurdish issue as one of the main determinants for the 1990s changes in the formulation of Turkish and Iranian foreign and regional policies. This can be explained by the fact that the Kurds constitute a geopolitical barrier between Iran and Turkey and the Arabs, while PKK has become a significant factor because of its presence in four parts of Kurdistan since 2003.

In spite of the rise of moderates and, specifically, Khatami's election to the Iranian Presidency, the post-Cold War setting appears to have had more benefits for the pro-Western camp. The US administration under Clinton and Albright and, later on, George W. Bush's US Middle East Partnership Initiative (11 December 2002) placed Turkey at the centre of US foreign policy as a democratic and moderate Middle Eastern model on which new examples of governance could be created throughout the MENA.

This contrasted with US policy towards Syria and Iraq with the State Department listing them as nations supporting terrorism in its annual report on terrorism (30 April 1990), which was followed by a series of legislation known as the Iran–Libya Sanctions Act of 1996 (ILSA) and the Iraq Liberation Act (1998). However, these had the opposite effect to that desired by the US administration, as they reinforced Russia–Iran's economic cooperation in the fields of energy, oil, gas and transportation sealed by MoU throughout the 1990s. Through actions like this and, in particular, the pressure exerted on Iran concerning its nuclear issue, it is evident that institutions, such as the US bureaucracy and international organisations like the EU play an important role, while also revealing the contribution of non-state determinants as dynamics of influence on foreign policy practices.

This period also demonstrates the extent to which external structures along with the role of leadership are able to influence the pattern of regional relations and impact on the formulation of foreign policies as demonstrated when Turkish foreign policy was favoured over that of Iran (especially during Mahmoud Ahmadinejad's tenure of office). Surprising events like 9/11 and the outbreak of the Arab Uprisings along with their consequences such as the rise of the IS have also played a major part.

The rise in the US presidency of George W. Bush (2001–2009), in Turkey of Recep Tayyip Erdoğan's AK Parti, Mahmoud Ahmadinejad (2005–2013) in Iran and Hafez Al Assad's succession by Bashar Al Assad to the Syrian Presidency (20 June 2000) initiated a radical period leading to regional turmoil, which reached its peak with the eruption of the Syrian crisis and its culmination into civil war with regional and international repercussions. The devastating impact of such surprising events as external or internal structures has been largely ignored by the dominant schools in IR, while they have also failed to take into account the role of economic pressures such as those exerted on Iran by international organisations like the EU.

The book also revealed the increasing domination of international foreign policy agenda by non-state entities and the steady growth of Iranian and Turkish interdependence. One example of this was the mediating role of the PKK between Iran and PJAK vis-à-vis the 2011 Agreement and the subsequent cease-fire, which demonstrated how a non-state entity can exert its own tactical foreign policies. PJAK had also influenced Kurdish Iranian policies by exerting pressure through its tactical support of Tehran, with the aim of reducing its open fronts in exchange for concessions to diminish Iranian tensions with Turkey.

Therefore, the book deduces that Turkish–Iranian relations and their resultant courses of action have not really produced any significant effect in the formulation of their shared policies. Instead, it has been clearly demonstrated how other factors have impacted on their foreign policy making. This has been evidenced by the fact that, despite their conflictual relations, the two states have always tried to avoid an escalation of their rivalry. Therefore, they have now been forced to adopt a more proactive stance in order to maintain their position and maximise their influence and status in the resettled regional balance of power. This has been evident even in the economic sphere. Despite controversies over their role in Syria and a decline in the volume of their bilateral trade in spite of the lifting of sanctions against Iran, still there is mutual commitment for economic cooperation. Although the Turkish–Iranian volume of trade was $9.65 billion in 2016, compared to $13.71 billion in 2014 or $14.57 billion in 2013 (amid the war in Syria),[11] mutual determination to strengthen economic ties as according to the Iranian President, Hassan Rouhani, 'the situation is ripe for cooperation between Turkey and Iran in the post-sanctions era' has been expressed through bilateral meetings (April 2016).[12] In the same context, Turkey and Iran signed (9 April 2016) a banking protocol and a Joint Economic Commission protocol to improve economic and trade ties.[13] A decline thus of the bilateral trade volume can be related more to the escalation of the war in Syria and its effects on the trade routes rather than to their political differences over the Syrian crisis as pragmatism prevails.

The conditions that the Syrian crisis created and its role in Turkish and Iranian politics along with the important geopolitical and economic role of the Kurds cleared the ground for a new Middle Eastern order to emerge within a totally different political setting. The repercussions of this have been widespread and have also affected the former relatively steady interrelations between Iran and Turkey by transforming them into a much more intense interaction directly influenced by the competition for survival and maximisation of control over regional developments together with a much greater dependence on alliances with powerful non-state actors.

In the same vein, the book's observation of events from a regional and international perspective has led to the conclusion that, whereas in the period after 1970 there was a sense of Iran's containment in favour of Turkey, the Iraq war and, even more significantly, the Syrian crisis, has changed the balance of power to such an extent that today there is a dual containment of both Iran and Turkey. However, Middle Eastern politics should also be viewed within the bigger framework of the role played by external interference, and particularly the dictation of politics in the region by the two traditional superpowers of Russia and the US which was clearly demonstrated in the Syrian and Iraqi cases respectively. For example, the 14 July 2015 nuclear deal between the US and Iran followed straight afterwards by the US–Turkish agreement on a no-fly zone north of Syria (16 August 2015) with the aim of strengthening the Free Syrian Army, a key element in the Syrian Arab opposition, was cancelled out by the US–Moscow agreement and the subsequent creation of a Russo-Syrian Military Commission (August 2015). This was an indicative example of the play for power and influence within the region between these two powerful international actors to become the prime architect of the new Middle Eastern order.

## A NEW PATTERN OF ALLIANCES:
## THE INTERNATIONAL DIMENSION

### The Kurds: A determinant in regional restructuring

The Syrian crisis was a landmark in Middle Eastern politics that also affected Iranian and Turkish policies and generated new developments that were intensified by the deeper involvement of the international factor. The current course of events was analysed within the wider context of international politics, and viewed through the lens of the national interest of both the US and Russian administrations as well as the latter's revival of its foreign policy objectives toward the Middle East with Syria and the Kurdish issue at the epicentre.

The sectarianism instigated after the Iraq War and the advent of IS as another surprising event not only intensified external intervention vis-à-vis Russia's gradual re-entry into Middle Eastern politics after 2003, but also consolidated the Kurdish status in Iraq, resulting in the establishment of a second Kurdish de facto state-entity in North East Syria in 2013. Kurdish status in Syria was also boosted by the formation of the Council of Democratic Syria (CDS), which set aims for change, free elections and the establishment of a democratic constitution in Syria in the post-war period without Bashar al Assad at a meeting held in Derik (8–9 December 2015). Subsequently, the Constituent Assembly of the Democratic Federal System of Rojava in Northern Syria made a unilateral declaration for the formation of a democratic federal system within the Syrian borders on 17 March 2016.

The rise of non-state actors and, in particular, IS created regional disorder and strengthened the Resistance Axis camp and its policies, especially in the case of the Iranian foreign policy owing to its structural and inherently revolutionary nature. The Islamic

Republic's tradition of forming alliances with non-state actors to promote its regional policies has been evident in a number of cases ranging from its strong ties with the Lebanese Shi'a group Hizbullah, which fought shoulder to shoulder with Assad, to Iran's role as a major partner in the Syrian war in support of the Palestinian Islamist movement Hamas, and its economic and political ties with the KRG. As was the case in the years following the Shah's era, today's Iran has once again risen to become one of the most significant players at the epicentre of developments in the Middle East. Assisted by the transformation of the Middle Eastern region, Tehran, along with the Resistance Axis, appears to have consolidated its position as a tactical winner for the time being since, in its attempts to assert power in the broader Gulf region and the Strait of Hormuz – a major outlet for Iran's oil and gas exports – its policies have thrived on the rapid changes experienced by the region. Yet the repercussions of these policies on the existing chaotic disorder brings the threat of further divisions while Iran's ability to sustain 'the 'Shi'ite crescent' from Baghdad and Damascus to Lebanon and Sana'a has also been called into question, especially as Iran itself represents a synthesis of so many different ethnicities including Kurds, Azeris, Arabs, Turkmens, Baluchis and Lurs. There is no doubt that the perception of Iran as a staunch ally supporting al Assad's regime facilitated its direct role in the regional restructuring of the Middle East. However, such non-state entities should by no means be considered just proxies because their choice to build these alliances is driven by the convergence of their own foreign policy interests happening to lie in the same direction as those of a stronger power, rather than being led by them.

The KRG's growing economic independence from Baghdad achieved through its direct exports of petroleum and gas together with the growing energy interdependence between Turkey and Iran, despite their regional competition for control over Kurdish resources, elevated the Kurds of Iraq into a strategic regional player, especially in their important role as the frontline standing against the IS and terrorism. Despite the current crisis caused by regional and domestic reactions to the 25 September Referendum in the KR, KRG's EU-turn normalised again its federal status, which could prove effective and sustain previous developments. Economic interdependence between Turkey and the KRG has been illustrated in a statement made by Tony Hayward, the chairman of Genel Energy: 'The first batch of Kurdistan Regional Government (KRG) gas is planned to flow into Turkey in the next two or three years, and 20 billion cubic meters of it is expected to pour into the Turkish market in early 2020.'[14]

The Kurds have also formed an important front against IS and terrorism and this has granted them international support and greater prominence as they are now strategically significant in an increasingly critical situation. The fight against terrorism and its connection to the rise and expansion of radical Islam, a US strategic priority, explains the US administration's support for the PYD in creating a Kurdish front in Syria against IS discussed at the Salahaddin meeting (15 September 2015) when the US 'having realised their loss of control as far as Iraq is concerned asked for the cooperation of both YPG and peshmerga forces'.[15] This important meeting united the KR's President, the Co-chair of PYD and TEVDEM and State Department representatives in a united front against IS and led to an agreement between the Kurds of Syria, the KRG and the Ministry of peshmerga for the establishment of a Joint Cooperation Committee. On 20 September 2015 the PYD Conference in Qamishli, supported by the KRG and an international community of 300 participants and 274 delegates, constituted a positive step towards the unification of the Kurdish movement in Syria and Iraq.[16] US–KRG institutionalised relations and interactions along with the US initiative aimed at bringing the Kurds of Syria and Iraq together further demonstrates the steady emergence of the Kurds as a main determinant and critical element in the implementation of the US Middle Eastern policy of fragmentation and regional reformation through the Kurdish issue in Iraq and Syria. This has enhanced the role of the Kurds, despite their non-state status, so that they are now a formative and interactional actor of considerable impact.

However, it is interesting to note that long before the US–Kurdish interactive relations, the Soviets played a major role in protecting the Kurds in Iran by creating the Republic of Mahabad (1946–1947) alongside the Azerbaijan People's Government to act as a counter-balance to the West. Khider Marassana explained the role Russian intervention played at an early stage in Kurdish politics: 'In 1964

Mullah Mustafa sent me to Tehran to the Embassy of the USSR with a letter saying that Iran, Turkey, Iraq, and Syria were trying to destroy the only Kurdish party (KDP) but Moscow warned them not to fight the Kurds.'[17] More recently, the KR received anti-aircraft guns from the Russian Federation in its fight to defeat IS, an action that has caused considerable comment among Russian analysts who believe that this represents a change in Moscow's Middle Eastern foreign policy and underlines the importance of the Kurds in the region.[18] The KR has also enjoyed regional and international recognition from states like Germany along with their long-term supporter France. Interestingly, France has recently embarked on amicable relations with Russia as expressed through their alliance and the former's will 'to enlist the latter into a 'grand coalition' alongside the US to combat Islamic State', in spite of some disagreement over the future role of Syrian leader Bashar al-Assad.[19]

In this context Moscow continues to balance between Iran and Turkey despite incidents with severe impact on their bilateral relations such as the Russian–Turkish hostility over the latter's shooting down of a Russian Sukhoi Su-24M bomber aircraft (24 November 2015). Given Moscow's re-entry in regional politics from March 2011 onward, Russia appears determined to maintain a dominant role in the Middle East through its traditional ally Syria. Moscow's reinforcement of its anti-aircraft capacities in Syria when it installed S-400 ground-air missiles at its military airport in Hmaymime (close to Lattakia) with a range of 600 kilometres, capable of detecting and destroying up to 160 targets at once[20] together with its increased deployment of missile defences based on the New Russian Defence Plan (2016–2020) drawn up on 13 November 2015 (partly in response to US plans for deployment of a missile defence shield in Europe)[21] also led to further complications for the region and its political systems, and thereby created even more problems for Turkish foreign policy.

These multi-dimensional and interactive interrelations have become intrinsic in the analysis of the foreign policy making, impact the IR discipline and challenge the adequacy of current IR perspectives to consider and evaluate newly rising phenomena; for example, the meetings between the Kurds (of both Syria and Iraq) and

Turkish Foreign Ministry officials demonstrate the active participation in the formulation of foreign policy of stronger state powers
by other actors as well as state entities.[22]

## A changing balance of power: Instruments of transformation

The Syrian crisis and the creation of IS radicalised the Iranian foreign
policy's objective of resistance and maximisation of power against the
West in a continuation of the 1970s Iranian revolutionary practice.
At the same time, the effect of the crisis – which subsequently evolved
into a multi-faceted war – was to refocus international attention on
the regional level and result in changed perceptions. In consequence,
alliances with regional powers appeared as essential as those with
strong international states, while the role of non-state actors proved
indispensable in the implementation of foreign policy goals.

In spite of Obama's efforts to apply a pacifist policy vis-à-vis the US
policy of disengagement including Iraq, and his inaction in Syria for
fear of making a second mistake, the US President's failure to act
promptly, i.e., to gather the international community together and
start a dialogue concerning possible actions, has had severe
repercussions. Although the US Presidency attempted to change the
hard-core policy of Washington with regard to MENA, he could not
form an effective parallel policy, thus seeming to confirm the
rectilinear nature of US foreign policy and its apparent reluctance to
disappoint Ankara. US disengagement policy from the Middle East
was interrupted by the increasing and critical role that Russia plays in
Syria and was further reconsidered under the new Presidency of
Donald Trump. However, a total and probably abrupt, rather than
gradual, US withdrawal from the Middle Eastern region might have
also created further problems, given its dominant role. This concern
over US withdrawal and its possible consequences is also shared by
Henry Kissinger who wonders 'how can we [the US] get out, without,
and maintain the capability of contributing to shaping the kind of
world that needs to be shaped'.[23] Another consideration affecting US
decisions is that Russia, in spite of its previous policies of partial
withdrawal of Russian forces from Syria, continues to persist in its
support of the Assad regime, viewing it as the only way it can
continue to exert regional influence and preserve its naval bases in

Syria, which further complicates the situation. The course of events has changed so that it now includes policies of eliminating or restraining Russian influence in the region; inter-state conflict within the GCC itself; and a shift in the regional balance of power probably for the first time since the onset of the post-Cold War era with repercussions on Turkey and Iran.[24] The 26 August 2015 Russian–Syrian Military Pact aiming at the free passage of Russian military personnel and shipments in and out of Syria without being subject to controls by Syrian authorities in their pursuit of rebel groups opposing Assad[25] is also indicative of such alliances.

Henry Kissinger believes we are standing at a political crossroads:

> We're at a moment when the international system is in a period of change like we haven't seen for several hundred years. In some parts of the world, the nation state, on which the existing international system was based, is either giving up its traditional aspects, like in Europe, or as in the Middle East, where it was never really fully established, it is no longer the defining element.[26]

In this context, it was inevitable that the continuous role of the international factor reflected in policies that facilitated the goal of penetration that aimed to change the current status quo would increase Turkey's importance, especially as its role as a crucial link between the East and Europe had become more and more significant in the post-Cold War period, particularly from the Syrian crisis onward. Turkey is important for many reasons – for the absorption of the rising refugee wave travelling from the Middle East to Europe, as a country offering accommodation for the refugees, as a NATO ally, as a gateway to Europe, and also in terms of its Europeanisation process, which could be completed if Turkey were willing to show flexibility in addressing the Kurdish issue and instigate a constitutional change to guarantee Kurdish status. In contrast, the trajectory of Turkish–Iranian relations is being altered by their separate interests, although this seems something of a contradiction given that Islamist governments are in power in both states. However, it is not clear whether Turkey would be ready at this stage to accept the effects its Syrian policy could have on its own Kurdish issue even though it is actively supporting the Syrian Arab opposition, especially the FSA. Yet there are Islamist circles in Turkey that would prefer to follow the US Kurdish policy in favour of a solution to the Kurdish issue in Syria, although probably with the *proviso* that Turkey is involved in controlling its implementation.

One result of the Syrian war has been Syria's nuclear deterrence with the complete destruction of its nuclear facility (31 October 2013).[27] This was announced by the Organisation for the Prohibition of Chemical Weapons, thereby eliminating a very immediate threat to Israeli security, although the Syrian state and its security apparatus are increasingly infiltrated by different actors as Iranians, Russians and others are now operating within its territory.

The Syrian case also demonstrated the high importance that the role of the (Iranian Islamic) army structure continues to hold as a driving force and the main tool for the application and facilitation of Iranian policies through leading figures such as the Revolutionary Guards' leader, General Qasem Soleimani.

## Sunni–Shia conflict: A clash of interests

The Sunni–Shi'a competition does not seem to have been the main element of Turkish foreign policy compared to its much more dominant role in Iranian foreign policy objectives, but it is an on-going issue that has been causing repercussions since 2003. In this respect it clearly supports the book's argument concerning the role of religion, not just in the sense of ideology, but as a means of legitimisation for the exercise of certain policies. It seems that this determinant that has historically shaped Turkish and Iranian foreign policies has come into play again today as a continuing ideational structural factor with the same impetus, *mutatis mutandis*.

Even though Turkish and Iranian foreign policies have not necessarily consciously formed their policies on the basis of their religion, the fact that groups in the Middle East dispersed throughout different states developed their own distinctive traits based on religion, ethnicity or culture meant that the course of events divided the region into different factions according to these variations. This resulted in Russia, Iran and Syria (also supported by Hasan Nasrallah's Hizbullah) on the one hand, and a US–Gulf–Turkish block supported by powerful European powers on the other. In the middle between these two was another division that consisted of Baghdad and the Kurds with some degree of relations to both sides, and also important to both in their role as a first defence against IS.

The consensus between Turkey and the US agreeing shared participation in the implementation of the US initiative for transformation of the region was achieved, as asserted by a high-level Iranian political figure, by using political Islam via the Muslim Brotherhood in Tunisia, Egypt and Syria.[28] However, Turkey's later attempts to position the Free Syrian Army on the Turkish/Syrian border between Mare and Jarablus to block the emergence of a Kurdish state in the North seemingly indicates a divergence of the two NATO allies' interests regarding the Kurdish issue. The same person also claimed that a confrontation between Iran and Turkey is very unlikely as 'only if Turkey wanted to establish a Neo-Ottoman Empire, would it then be in conflict with Iran'.[29]

Thus the main concern is not whether these two regional powers will be led into any serious conflict, as this has already happened indirectly with the Syrian crisis and its ongoing war, where Iran and Turkey support and are in reality placed in different camps. Deep divisions have also been seen in the Syrian Opposition and it seems a clear strategic vision is not in place yet, as far as post-war Syria is concerned vis-à-vis the dissolution of FSA in September 2014.[30] Its members have returned to Jabhat Al Nushra (known as *Jabhat Fateh Al Sham* after July 2016), which, together with organisations such as Ahrar al Sham (the Islamic Movement of the Free Men of the Levant, حركة أحرار الشام الإسلامية), wants to opt for a free, democratic Syria outside the control of the Alawite regime, but this is opposed by many dissenting voices within the Syrian National Council, another issue which makes the Syrian political scenario even more confusing.

These developments, boosted by the war in Syria and turmoil in Iraq, unrest in different states such as Turkey and Egypt, and the increase in fundamentalism and growing external interference, have seen the deployment of Iranian foreign policy's 'Shi'a Crescent' card, in other words the joining of Shi'a powers united in their aim of expansion, as a means of exerting pressure to contain US Middle Eastern policies.

## Economic parameters

> *Despite some differences of opinion on Syria, there is a mutual understanding between Turkey and Iran on three basic points; namely taking precautions concerning the humanitarian situation, meeting the democratic demands of the Syrian people and achieving political transition peacefully.*[31]
>
> Ahmet Davutoğlu

A steady economic partnership between Iran and Turkey has survived thus far, unscathed by any external or internal structural factors or any non-state actor's involvement.[32] However, repercussions from the Syrian crisis and the dichotomy between their different foreign policy interests as to what kind of post-war Syria Iran and Turkey want and what format the new Middle Eastern political framework should take could place their economic interactions on a different footing and instigate change. Yet, as this book has analysed, Turkey's and Iran's interdependence in relation to energy and goods[33] does not appear to play a formative role in the formulation of their foreign policy. Nevertheless, it is clearly a connecting factor – similar to the argument concerning Turko-Islamic tradition – and this seemingly ensures the perpetuation of their relations.

Indeed, the security dimension that has hitherto united Turkey and Iran; namely, the Kurdish factor, is still reinforcing their economic parameters, particularly in the field of energy, although it is possible that this may eventually become the sole bond between the two players in the imminent regional order. New figures talk about 150 billion cubic metres of gas found which could satisfy Turkey's gas requirements for the next 50 years.[34] These economic factors are responsible for the Kurds high profile as Khider Marassana explains: 'The Kurds are important given that Bashur [that is the KR in Iraq] and Kirkuk are oil rich zones, and [regional and international] states want stability for the KR to transfer this oil.'[35] Likewise, the Kurdish Region in Syria is also important due to its proximity to the Mediterranean Sea while a potential alliance with either a future Alawi region or with Turkey could provide another major energy corridor to replace the damaged Kirkuk–Baniyas pipeline. This is now vital as the Kurdish pipeline to the Ceyhan export terminal on Turkey's Mediterranean coast was the only route transferring oil from

Northern Iraq to the world market after Islamic State prevented access to the former route near Mosul. The pipeline transports around 450,000 barrels a day of Kurdish oil and a further 150,000 barrels per day from the Baghdad-controlled North Oil Company (NOC) oilfields. Such oil supply routes have become important tools, allowing regional states to be stabilised and acting as a bargaining tool in regional actors' foreign policies to establish long-term security for their territories.[36] For Iran, relations with the Kurds could also establish a secure route to the Mediterranean Sea, bypassing Turkey to deliver oil and gas to the EU.

## THEORETICAL FRAMEWORK: A MODEL OF MULTI-DIMENSIONAL INTERRELATIONS

*A single article that advances a new theory or makes sense of a body of disparate findings will be more valuable than dozens of empirical studies with short shelf lives.[37]*

John J. Mearsheimer, Stephen M. Walt

This book attempted to analyse and make clear how ideas, interests and other ideational factors such as the role of the leadership along with state entities can shape domestic structures while non-state actors and structures demonstrate a similar ability to influence and shape foreign policy practices. Whereas in the Safavid empire – the precursor of the Iranian state – the legitimisation of the (power) structure and therefore its survival was based on clearly ideological premises founded on religion, the subsequent process of formation and change in Iranian and Turkish foreign policies has clearly revealed that the role of structures, either internal or external, appears more powerful than ideas, just as the interactions between state and non-state entities have been. Indeed, structural changes have affected and influenced Iran's foreign policies more than its actual (diplomatic) relations with Turkey. The impact of state foreign policies upon non-state entities and vice-versa, and, equally, the interactions between state and non-state actors as the facilitators of regional (and international) politics would therefore appear to play a steadily growing role with theoretical implications.

Based on my previous work suggesting a coherent and more nuanced and holistic approach to IR, this case study complements my perception of IR as a complex field of multi-dimensional interrelations between and among actors within local, sub-state, trans-state, state, regional and global spheres. In particular, it draws attention to the role – both direct and indirect – played in IR by non-state actors, though without *a priori* favouring either type of actor. The interactive importance of the material and the ideational was also recognised in the mutual shaping of structures and agents through this multi-dimensional interactive set of dynamics.

Studying Iranian and Turkish foreign policy is of great value today because of its interesting role as both an intrinsic component of the future formation of the Middle Eastern region, and a means through which this transformation is in the process of being achieved. This makes it a fascinating case study for IR, not least because it explicitly shows, especially from the Syrian crisis onward, how a set of major players with different orientations both at the regional and international level have interacted to such an extent that the boundaries of the sphere of interactions are now in the process of being replaced by a new international relations system that is much more homogenised.

It has become increasingly evident today that domestic developments of state and non-state actors do affect international affairs, while, in turn, the impact of international relations influences domestic politics and thus affects the shape of foreign policies. In addition, the fragile political environment that is now emerging has stimulated further cooperation and alliances so that, even though in one sense all the participants on the various levels are acting to promote their own interests and satisfy their individual intentions with the aim of maximising their influence and control over arising developments, it has created a situation where every player matters. Therefore, the context of time and space regarding the multiple factors affecting international relations has also been taken into account. The aim was not just to consider the role of structures and agents in the formulation of foreign policy decisions, but also to analyse the relations formed by assessing the level of interactions between state and non-state actors in international relations as an alternative to the existing paradigms which had formerly been largely confined to the study of inter-state relations.

In order to be able to comprehend each case in terms of its unique qualities, given that no phenomenon is exactly the same; a valid study should explore each particular characteristic and test whether certain conditions are satisfied. This means that any analysis within IR needs to consider the interplay between structures and agents, and the role of non-state actors (other than economic NGOs) as well as the impact of ideas and beliefs. It will also take into account the role of time, the emergent domestic conditions of the state, the interaction between state and non-state actors (with the latter not merely functioning as an input for foreign policies of states), and the impact of surprising internal and external events such as 9/11 or the rise of IS and other terrorist acts. This does not mean that all these criteria will necessarily be justified and in any case it does not presuppose any outcomes, but allows the scholar to reach various conclusions for phenomena by careful analysis of the constituents of specific case studies according to the circumstances existing at the time and other relevant factors for the period under scrutiny.

Using these criteria, the focus of this case study on the factors influencing Turkish–Iranian relations and the formulation of their foreign policies is unique because for the first time this subject matter has been placed within a theoretical frame. This different approach also justifies theoretical claims that 'no single theory of IR' so far 'can fully explain the behaviour of states and the intricacies of their foreign policies', especially when referring to Iran or Turkey.[38]

In the course of this complex and interesting case study, I have developed an alternative outlook, a theoretical framework that provides a set of principles on which any independent analysis can be based in its consideration of different cases that may occur in different eras and thereby attempt 'to bring theory and the world together'.[39] This agrees strongly with Dunne, Hansen and Wight's statement that: 'theory can be considered a simplifying device that abstracts from the world in order to locate and identify key factors of interest'.[40] The difference between this and previous approaches in IR is its assumption that change is inherent in the international relations system and will inevitably occur through the surprising events that direct the flow of history. It thus gives scholars the advantage of an approach that addresses the ontological problems that have arisen within IR and which important theorists like Colin Wight have emphasised, while it also goes some way towards solving the dilemma experienced by Mearsheimer and Walt who claim that IR scholars face discouragement in their attempts to perform theory-guided empirical tests 'and we are not optimistic that this situation will change'.[41] Moreover, the topic of the 'resolution of the agent-structure problem',[42] i.e., the theoretical dilemma of which constituent is the real influence behind the factors involved in the rising phenomena, a long-standing debate among academics, and how we can overcome it, has been addressed, at least to some extent, through the carefully structured arguments presented in the study.

The case of the Kurds has been a key example illuminating the changing issues that IR must now address. Their role has undergone massive transformation so that they currently occupy a position at the epicentre of the alliances between major international and regional powers in the fight against IS and terrorism, while they also have economic importance through their ability to provide an alternative energy corridor. Consequently, they are increasingly viewed as strategic players in international and regional foreign policies. Jülide Karakoç[43] has highlighted the role of the Kurds (in Turkey) as a critical factor in the foreign policy formulation process and a determinant in Turkey's relations with Iran, while the major role of the Kurds in Syria is expected to have a significant impact on Syria's political future. Thus, the emergence of the Kurds as a de facto state entity exerting an independent foreign policy is a shining example that exemplifies theoretical claims for more consideration of the ontology vis-à-vis the IR discipline's fixation 'on epistemological or methodological matters at the expense of ontology' and the 'importation of the agent-structure problem from social theory to IR'.[44]

Therefore, by steering clear of attempts to import theories from other fields of natural sciences or humanities and social sciences, and in an attempt to bridge the gap between methodology and epistemology – expressed through different positions of rationalism, empiricism or pragmatism[45] depending on the perspective of the scholar – the study has chosen to consider all the factors required by the analysis. Thus the book taking into account scholarly claims that the ontology outweighs the epistemology, and therefore there is need for empirical cases showing state/non-state interaction, as well as extensive reference to non-state actors per se, has focused on their implementation both theoretically and empirically.[46]

Empirical observation has been extensively used throughout the chapters of this book in an attempt to explain and understand the theme under examination by shedding light on the interrelations of agents and structures. However, at the same time, I have also tried to show how this works in practice through a comprehensive overview of the ontological differences between different agents of state and non-state status along with the nature of their foreign policy objectives both at a regional and international level in concurrence with Colin Wight's assertion that: 'Understanding the ontological differences ... should be the aim of any conceived critical discipline of IR.'[47] The book has sought to preserve awareness of the ontological differences involved in this case study by being careful to carry out analysis according to the definitions outlined in Chapter 1. Indeed, the book itself constitutes an illustration of this dilemma per se as different constituents have shaped these state's foreign policies, and therefore the analysis attempts to follow their processes by adopting its own thematic approach. It is interesting that in IR theorists originally began from a general approach which then evolved into the development of specific schools of thought, whereas nowadays IR is turning once again towards a more general and inclusive approach. From Sayer's viewpoint, 'abstraction is a necessary component of all theorising'[48] and 'the role of theory is to provide an organisational device that allows us to identify what is important and what is not, and specify what the relations are between the factors we deem to be important since the empirical realm is infinite; and therefore [all] theory is abstraction'.[49]

This research has thus shown how regional forces have evolved into central powers able to play an equal role as important partners in the emerging developments that are transforming the broader MENA and use their influence to reconfigure the new post-war political setting within the region. By carrying out a thorough examination of

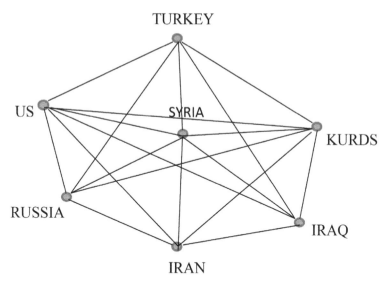

FIGURE 7.1 Polygonal interrelations.

their interrelations the case study has been able to draw the conclusion that 'Agents and structures are independent entities.'[50]

Since the focus of the international agenda has become increasingly preoccupied with the transformation of the Syrian crisis into a prolonged war, the circular relations presented in the previous chapter have shifted due to: the increasing number of agents involved; the constant diffusion of power and the change of supremacy in the power dynamics of the pyramid to become a polygonal structure with much greater levels of interaction.

CONCLUSION

> We support the Kurds in Syria and Americans also support the Kurds in Syria.
>
> Simakov Victor Victorovich[51]

The changes that have taken place in the Middle Eastern region seem to have revived the importance of the Turkish and Iranian foreign policies for different reasons. The opposing positions taken by Iran as part of the Alliance of the Axis of Resistance on the one hand and Turkey as EU partner and NATO ally along with its pro-Western stance on the other have resulted in the two powers forming different patterns of tactical and strategic alliances in their attempts to establish control over the broader MENA. Yet, as far as the Middle East is concerned, this control primarily concerns the triptych of Iraq, Syria, and the Kurdish territories.

In contrast to Iran which has been attempting to abandon its long-standing position of isolation and revive its role since the onset of the Syrian crisis, Ankara is enmeshed in political contradictions. The geostrategic value of Turkey has raised its status as a significant partner so that international powers like the US in pursuit of successful implementation of its Middle Eastern policies, and the EU in its desire to maintain political balance within the region seek good relations with Ankara in order to implement their strategies. The Turkish–Russian rapprochement, despite the downing of the Russian warplane as explained before, could be viewed within the same context. What has been demonstrated further is that the prioritisation of the national interest, in the forms that each time arise, is predominant in both the Iranian and Turkish foreign policies. Beliefs in an Iranian response to help IS against Turkish support of Syrian opposition at the start of the crisis[52] are instrumental in the formation of a clear understanding of this context, while others assign blame to the West in line with Henry Kissinger's assertion that the US will sometimes create the problem in order to solve it.[53] In contrast, Ankara's own foreign policy does not seem to have resulted in any particular benefits for Turkey so far.

The Iranian case seemingly occupies a more favourable position, but it is still very doubtful that Russia will allow Tehran to play any role that has real influence in the post-war political settlement. The continued lack of any dedicated pursuit aimed at establishing an independent foreign policy for both Turkey and Iran also puts them at risk of potential instrumentalisation by higher powers. Indeed, this seems an increasingly probable outcome in view of the deepening of international interference in regional affairs. The Iranian ability to sustain its rise in power and influence will be mainly determined by external and domestic determinants which are, in turn, dependent on Iranian domestic dynamics set by the Iranian structures and their tolerance to pressures. At the same time, Iran is also strongly influenced by the need to preserve its relations with Ankara. This is because the rise of Iran as a major power in the region is subject to the changing scenario, which to a great extent is dictated by the orientation of Iran's relations with Turkey. Moreover, Iran itself is undergoing a major shift in its constitutional framework. The Iranian internal struggle between competing centrist/reformist and conservative/hard-line factions, as per the example of Ali Akbar Hashemi Rafsanjani's provision for a 'Council' of leadership appointed by the Assembly of Experts, as opposed to a single supreme leader (which has been the norm since 1979), is effectively challenging the very foundation of the Iranian political system. There are certainly signs of greater openness, especially since the US–Iran nuclear deal, which reflected a new moderation in Iran's approach. These developments seem to be sowing the seeds of future changes to come (unless Trump's administration adopts the US–Iranian policy in place since the Shah's fall.[54]

The transformation of the region involves stakes that none of the powers involved are willing to lose. Although there has been no public expression, military cooperation between Syria's Kurds and both Washington and Moscow in the context of the fight against IS in Syria perhaps hints at the possibility of closer relations, especially between Russia and Syria's Kurds in a post-war political setting. Thus, the role of the US or Russia (while the UN and EU also possess influence, given Turkey's Europeanisation attempts) has the ability to determine the direction of the foreign policies which could swing one way or the other unless an unconditional relation between the two is formed.

The power that has somewhat surprisingly emerged from the current turmoil is that of the Kurds who appear to be deepening their relations with other regional actors at the same time as developing stronger links with Europe and the powers of the international relations system. The threat of IS and Europe's response together with the deepening of the Kurds' strategic relations with the US, and increasing international support, have all played a decisive role in elevating the Kurds – especially the KRG – to a stronger power status. The Kurds' ascendancy has been accelerated further by developments like the US–Russia anti-terrorism and military cooperation to bring the crisis into peaceful agreement between the warring parties through the successive Geneva conferences, and incidents such as the alleged

'Euphrates Agreement' through which Russia has agreed to provide weaponry for the Kurds of YPG on the west bank of the Euphrates, in the same way as it did with the peshmerga in the KR, with the US following suit on the east bank. In mere contrast at the same time, Turkey's open war in Afrin followed by incidents such as the three vetoes submitted by Russia and China opposing the adoption of previous resolutions condemning the Syrian regime by the UN Security Council, and the vetoed UNSC resolution for the ninth time by Russia (25 October 2017) that would ensure accountability for war crimes committed against the Syrian people can also be seen as attempts to jeopardise the strengthening of the Kurdish position in Syria in a political theatre determined by the Russians and the US.

The phenomenon of IS per se clearly indicates that non-state entities have already been a high priority on the foreign policy agenda of the regional powers as they seek to facilitate their objectives and strategies and as Iran demonstrated by taking advantage of non-state interactions to achieve its aim of creating a regional order in line with its preferences.

It was thus argued that the increasing role of both Iran and Turkey as regional players could be seen in their meddling in Iraqi affairs.[55] More importantly, their influence in determining political outcomes in Syria appears to be pivotal in dictating the future of the regional transformation, at least so far as the Middle Eastern region is concerned. In this period of deepening crisis, Turkey and Iran appear to have settled on a pragmatic approach in spite of their differences where their contradictory positions do not harm the stability of their relations such as the sphere of economy. However, a closer Turkish–Iranian alliance appears unlikely in view of these contradictory structures unless the emergence of a Kurdish autonomous entity in both states alters the traditional pattern of their alliance. At the time of writing, although it seems that the effect of their policies has so far had some benefits relating to the consolidation of the status of non-state entities, first and foremost of which are the Kurds, this development does not appear to have had any particular consequences for the regional balance of power. Yet there are strong grounds for believing that it is the transformation of the region itself, in combination with the ability of regional and international powers to agree on a division of the region into spheres of influence, that will eventually determine the regional balance of power within it. There is certainly a historic precedent for this, given that the creation of the region was established by similar policies following the Sykes–Picot Agreement, a landmark event that celebrated its centenary in 2016.

Moreover, the extent to which the US foreign policy agenda safeguards the security of Israel, and promotes different interests in the Middle East through supporting the transformation of the region could mean that it finds itself in agreement with Russia as they appear to be more in consensus (than in the past), albeit Russia's intention originally appeared determined to counterbalance US Middle Eastern foreign policies. It is thus interesting to observe how the determinant of foreign interference analysed throughout the book, particularly in the context of the extent to which their foreign policy interests converge, clearly demonstrates that this is where the power not only to determine Turkish–Iranian relations but also regional change lies, instead of mistakenly assigning such changes to non-state actors whose capacity is limited despite their ability to exert influence on the region's foreign policies.

In the turbulent context of the Middle Eastern political arena, especially at a regional level, the stance of both Iranian and Turkish foreign policies toward the course of events is extremely critical. The policy path they decide to ally with or against could act as a determinant to drastically change the region, their own position within it, and even their inter relation. Therefore, an important role for Iran and Turkey could be to act as a stabilising influence, not just to create a balance within their own relations and strengthen their cooperation in the event of further crises, but also to act as mediators within the wider region, which could, in turn, elevate their status. It seems that now, more than ever, Iran and Turkey are the pivotal point that can bring the Middle East out of crisis or plunge it deeper into turmoil.

# APPENDIX

# KCK Structure[1]

THE KURDISTAN COMMUNITES UNION
ORGANISATIONAL CHART

*A) LEGISLATION/CHAMBERS*
1. President
2. Vice Presidents (constituted by four members)
3. Members of Presidency Council
4. General Assembly

*B) EXECUTIVE:* Committee of Leadership
1. President of Executive Council
2. Vice Presidents (Four members)
3. Executive Council
4. Related Areas
    4.1 Centre of Study of Ideology
    4.1.1 Science Enlightenment Committee
    4.1.2 Committee of Culture
    4.1.3 Media and Publishing Committee
    4.1.4 Social Construction Committee
    4.1.5 AJK Committee
    4.2 Centre of the People Defence
    4.2.1 HPG General Command Headquarter
    4.2.2 HPG Assembly (41 persons)
    4.2.3 Commandership of Main Headquarter (five persons)
    4.2.4 HPG Commanding Council

4.2.5 Commanders of Law Enforcement Officer

    a) Academia of Command

    b) The Powers of the Self Defence

    c) Special Powers

4.2.6 Related Areas

A) Northern Side

    a) Dersim Zone

      - Province of Dersim

      - Kocgiri Field

      - Black Sea Province

    b) Botan Zone

      - Botan Province

      - Mardin Province

      - Haftanin Province

    c) Amed Zone

      - Amed Province

      - Erzurum Province

      - Garzan Province

    d) Serhat Province

    e) Zagros Province

    f) Kandil Zone

    g) Asos Zone

B) Southern Side

    a) Province of Hakurk

    b) Zone of the Main Headquarter

    c) Province of Gare

    d) (HRK) The Field of Kandil

    e) Province of Metina

4.3 Centre of Women Forces

4.3.1 High Women Group (KJB)

4.3.2 Kurdistan Women's Freedom Party

4.3.3 Union of Free Women

4.3.4 Organization of Young Women

4.3.4 YJA Star

4.4 Centre of Social Relations

4.4.1 Social Committee

4.4.2 Public Health Committee

4.4.3 Language and Education Committee

4.4.4 Coordination of Free Citizenship

4.4.5 Committee of Economics and Finance

4.4.6 Youth Community Coordination

  a) YDGH (Turkey)

  b) TCM (Iraq)

  c) TCA (Syria)

  d) TCD (Iran)

  e) YXK (Europe)

4.5 Centre of Political Relations

4.5.1 Committee of Minorities and Religion

4.5.2 Committee of Law

4.5.3 Committee of Foreign Relations

  a) CDK

  b) Union of Kurdish Yazidis

  c) Union of Kurdish Alevis

  d) Association of Kurdistan Lawyers

  e) Association of Kurdish Artists

  f) Association of Kurdistan Imams

  g) Associations of Kurdistan Workers

  h) Associations of Kurdistan Writers

  i) Association of Kurdistan Women

  j) Kon – Kurd

  FEY-KOM / YEK-KOM

  FEY-KURD / FEK-BEL

  FED-KOM / FEY-KA

  FKKS / FED-BIR

  FEKAR

  KURDISTAN NATIONAL CONGRESS (KNK)

4.5.4 Committee Ecology and Local Administration

  a) DKB (Turkey)

  b) PJAK (Iran)

  c) PYD (Syria)

  d) PCDK (Iraq)

*C) JURISDICTION*

# Notes

CHAPTER 1   INTRODUCTION

1. Reza Qelichkhan (Iran's Consul General in Erzurum), *Islamic Republic News Agency* (12/02/2014), http://www.irna.ir/en/News/2638066/Politic/ Iranian_diplomat__Minor_differences_not_to_affect__Iran-Turkey_long-standing_ties (last accessed March 2014).
2. In this book, I refer to the Iran–Iraq War (1980–1988) as Gulf War I; Saddam's invasion of Kuwait (1990–1991) is called Gulf War II, while the US invasion of Iraq (2003) is referred to as Gulf War III.
3. The Arab Uprisings, as I prefer to call it, more commonly identified as the 'Arab Spring', consisted of a series of revolts that broke out in different countries simultaneously and spread throughout the MENA (Middle East and North Africa) region. These were both civilian (Egypt, Tunisia and Yemen) and militarised (Libya and Syria) but were united in their demand for a fair and just order, an end to authoritarianism, and the guarantee of civil rights. Yet, they suffered from the insurgents' lack of a clear strategic vision – especially with the fragmentation between Islamic and fundamentalist groups and the more nationalistically oriented segments of each society. The term 'Arab Spring' was used to designate 'regime change' *en route* to regional democratisation, but the Arab uprisings were not a recent phenomenon, dating back to the Iraqi War (2003) and the US policy of 'regime change'.
4. The bibliography is limited to some academic articles – not that contemporary – such as John Calabrese's writings and a few books written by Robert Olson, Suleyman Elik and Elliot Hentov. Works by Iranian and Turkish scholars on this subject *per se* are absent and this reveals that there is further room for research. Stephen Kinzer's book, *Reset: Iran, Turkey and America's Future*, is not examined critically in the main body of the text as it revolves around the idea of 'how Iran should

change' and raises the necessity of 'a new power triangle the US, Iran and Turkey' can mutually create.

5. Ali Akbar Salehi, 'Ιράν: Άγκυρα και Τεχεράνη έχουν κρίσιμο ρόλο να παίξουν στη Συρία' ('Iran: Ankara and Tehran have critical role to play in Syria'] in *Kathimerini* (Greek Newspaper) (07/08/2012) in http://www.kathimerini.com.cy/index.php?pageaction=kat&modid= 1&artid=100883&show=Y (last accessed April 2014).

6. Interview by author with Reza Altun, co-founder of PKK, executive member of KCK (Qandil, 20/03/2014).

7. Turgut Tülümen, 'The Future of Turkish–Iranian relations', *Turkish Review of Middle East Studies* (Istanbul: Isis, 1998), p. 135.

8. Interview with Reza Altun, op. cit.

9. Elik claims that 'middle powers are not able to entrench a coalition … characterized by an absence of institutional engagement [as] they only make political alliance relationships with less threatening parties.' First of all, this is no longer the case considering the transforming nature of the Middle Eastern region, especially in the aftermath of the Arab uprisings (17/12/2010), but also historically, starting with the Baghdad Pact (1955), a defensive organisation for promoting shared political, military and economic goals, among others, between Turkey and Iran. Secondly, this statement can be applicable for middle or minor powers; in Suleyman Elik, *Iran–Turkey Relations, 1979–2011*, p. 25.

10. According to Turgut Tülümen, it is the 'the differences in religious understanding that create problems between Turkey and Iran again today' in: 'The Future of Turkish–Iranian Relations', op. cit, p. 135.

11. See Marianna Charountaki, *The Kurds and US Foreign Policy: International Relations in the Middle East since 1945* (Routledge, 2010).

12. See Marianna Charountaki, Chapter 7, *The Kurds and US Foreign Policy: International Relations in the Middle East since 1945* (Routledge, 2010).

13. Robert Olson, *Turkey–Iran Relations, 1979–2004*, op. cit., p. 26 and Robert Olson, *The Kurdish Question and Turkish–Iranian Relations: From World War I to 1998*, Kurdish Studies Series, No. 1 (California, Mazda Publishers, 1998), p. 11.

14. Robert Olson, *Turkey–Iran Relations, 1979–2004*, op. cit., p. 25.

15. The absence from the analysis of the contemporary role of the Kurds in both Iraq and Syria, but especially those in Syria within the context of the Syrian crisis in addition to the current developments in Iraq as determining factor can be also observed in the contemporary short-length article by Mansoureh Ebrahimi, and Kamaruzaman Yusoff, and Mir Mohamadali Seyed Jalili, 'Economic, Political, and Strategic Issues in Iran–Turkey Relations, 2002–2015', *Contemporary Review of the Middle East*, Vol. 4, Issue 1 (2017): 67–83.

16. Ibid., p. 85.

17. Ibid., p. 18.

18. I explain why the Kurds are considered as non-state entities rather than proxies in Chapter 1: 'Terminological definitions in the literature: a critique', Marianna Charountaki, *The Kurds and US Foreign Policy: International Relations in the Middle East since 1945* (Routledge, October, 2010), p. 11.

19. Robert Olson, *Turkey–Iran Relations, 1979–2004*, op. cit., p. 37. For the author's argument, see Marianna Charountaki, *The Kurds and US Foreign Policy*, op. cit., pp. 5, 7.

20. Robert Olson, *The Kurdish Question and Turkish-Iranian Relations: From World War I to 1998*, op. cit., p. 12.

21. Robert Olson's 'omni-balancing theory' concentrates on internal threats to the regime(s) in ibid.

22. Ibid., p. 85.

23. Suleyman Elik, *Iran–Turkey Relations, 1979–2011 Conceptualizing the Dynamics of Politics, Religion and Security in Middle-Power States* (Routledge, 2012), p. 66.

24. Ibid., p. 64.

25. Ibid., p. 6.

26. Ibid., pp. 22–23.

27. Marianna Charountaki, 'The Increasing Importance of Iran', *Your Middle East*, online newspaper (12/12/2013), http://www.yourmiddleeast.com/opinion/the-increasing-importance-of-iran_20133 (last accessed, April 2014).

28. Suleyman Elik, *Iran–Turkey Relations, 1979–2011*, pp. 198–199.

29. References to Iran as 'negative balance' and Turkey as a 'facilitator' are indicative as both are part of the same conflicts. Also in Gokhan Cetinsaya, Review: 'Turkey–Iran Relations 1979–2004: Revolution, Ideology, War, Coups and Geopolitics", *International Journal of Middle East Studies*, Vol. 39, No. 2, May, 2007.

30. The examination of the Syrian factor and consequently the post-Arab Uprisings context is missing from Wang Bo, 'Turkey–Iran Reconciliatory Relations: Internal and External Factors', *Journal of Middle Eastern and Islamic Studies* (in Asia) Vol. 5, No. 1 (2011) in http://mideast.shisu.edu.cn/_upload/article/86/f1/a2903ac544dab4e4aba6c9bfcce9/8f07916c-765e-4523-996e-28ae286974c6.pdf (last accessed August 2017). An identical article where contemporary evens also missing from the analysis Nihat Ali Özcan and Özgür Özdamar, 'Uneasy Neighbours: Turkish–Iranian Relations Since the 1979 Islamic Revolution', *Middle East Policy*, Vol. XVII, No. 3 (Fall 2010) in http://ozgur.bilkent.edu.tr/download/10Uneasy%20 Neigbors%20Turkish-Iranian%20Relations%20since%20the%201979 %20I.pdf (last accessed August 2017).

31. Elliot Hentov, *Asymmetry of Interest: Turkish Iranian Relations since 1979* (Lambert Academic Publishing House, 2012), p. 7.

32. Ibid., p. 208. Hentov 'attributes the 'asymmetry' reference to the fact that Tehran did not view Ankara as a 'primary actor' in the Middle East or the

wider Islamic world, despite the fact that Turkey was acutely cognizant of Iranian actions' (p. 4), in Michael B. Bishku, Book Review, 'Asymmetry of Interest: Turkish–Iranian Relations since 1979' by Elliot Hentov, *The Middle East Journal*, Vol. 67, No. 3 (Summer 2013), p. 489.

33. Since 2002 the author notices a 'suspended asymmetry of interest' generating 'parity of interest between Turkish and Iranian leaders' in ibid., p. 6.

34. The basic argument of Hentov's book consists of the notion of 'Iran's centrality in the minds of Turkish policy makers in contrast to Turkey's absence in Iranian politics; [that is] Turkish secularist elites viewed Iran as a major security threat and source of regional instability whereas Tehran saw Ankara as a marginal player' in Elliot Hentov, *Asymmetry of Interest: Turkish Iranian Relations since 1979* (Lambert Academic Publishing House, 2012), pp. 197, 208, 264.

35. Interview by the researcher with Dr. Ata'ollah Mohajerani, former Iranian Minister (London, 23/10/2013).

36. See Marianna Charountaki, Chapter 7, *The Kurds and US Foreign Policy*, op. cit.

37. With minor adjustments, I apply my own perception and thus terminology of the notion of foreign policy here in ibid., p. 74.

38. Recep Tayyip Erdoğan, 'We are not rooted in religion', *Yeni Şafak* (Turkish newspaper) (4 May 2008).

39. Talk by Dr. Ata'ollah Mohajerani, former Iranian Minister (Reading University, ReadiMUN, 28/11/2014).

40. Interview by the researcher with Dr. Ata'ollah Mohajerani, former Iranian Minister (London, 23/10/2013).

41. According to *Bugün* newspaper, the Governor of Hatay, Celalettin Lekesiz, has reported to the Interior Ministry how Islamic State of Iraq and Syria (ISIS) members from Syria use Turkey like a backyard with the help of smugglers. In his report, the Governor complains about increasing ISIS activity and requests that preventive measures be taken in 'ISIS activities in Turkey confirmed by Governor's report', *Firat News* (5/05/2014) in http://en.firatnews.com/news/news/isis-activities-in-turkey-confirmed-by-governor-s-report.htm (last accessed June 2014).

42. Claims made during interview by author with a high level political figure in Iranian politics (London, 17/06/2013).

43. Ahmet Davutoğlu, 'Turkey's zero problems foreign policy', *Foreign Policy* (20/05/2010).

44. Interview by the researcher with Dr. Ata'ollah Mohajerani, former Iranian Minister (London, 23/10/2013).

45. Hentov struggles with their relation, which he characterizes as an 'indefinable relationship because it is discordant' in Elliot Hentov, *Asymmetry of Interest*, op. cit., pp. 3, 263.

46. Marianna Charountaki, *The Kurds and US Foreign Policy*, op. cit., pp. 251–252.

47. For further analysis, ibid., p. 71.

48. Interview by the author with a high level political figure in Iranian politics (London, 17/06/2013).

49. Rouhollah K. Ramazani,'Iran's Foreign Policy: Contending Orientations', *Middle East Journal*, Vol. 43, Issue 2 (Spring 1989), p. 211.

50. Suleyman Elik, *Iran–Turkey Relations, 1979–2011 Conceptualizing the Dynamics of Politics*, op. cit., pp. 35, 64–65.

51. Interview by the author with a high level political figure in Iranian politics (London, 17/06/2013).

52. For further information, see John Vidal, 'Water supply key to outcome of conflicts in Iraq and Syria, experts warn', *The Guardian* (2/07/2014) in http://www.theguardian.com/environment/2014/jul/02/water-key-conflict-iraq-syria-isis (last accessed March 2015).

53. Islamist foreign policy is recognized by two elements. It is against Israel and NATO and is supportive of the Palestinian cause in ibid.

54. *New York Times* (19/02/1979), in 'Chronology', *Middle East Journal*, Vol. 33, No. 3 (Summer 1979), p. 349.

55. *Reuters*, 'Turkey: Yasser Arafat visits Ankara for Official Opening of PLO office' (08/10/1979) cited in http://www.itnsource.com/shotlist//RTV/1979/10/08/BGY511140091/?v=0 (last accessed December 2015).

56. Ervand Abrahamian, 'Mass Protests in the Islamic Revolution, 1977–79', in Adam Roberts and Timothy Garton Ash, *Civil Resistance and Power Politics: The Experience of Non-Violent Action from Gandhi to the Present* (Oxford University Press, 2009), pp. 162–178.

57. Interview by the author with a high level political figure in Iranian politics (London, 17/06/2013).

58. Interview by the researcher with Dr. Ata'ollah Mohajerani, former Iranian Minister (London, 23/10/2013).

59. Famil Şamiloğlu, Kafkasya'da *Dengeler Değişiyor Mu?* (*Have the balances been changing in Caucasus?*) (USAK: International Strategic Research Organization, 15/02/2010), http://www.usak.org.tr/print.php?id=365366349&z=2 (last accessed December 2014).

60. Alvin Z. Rubinstein, and Oles M. Smolansky, *Regional Power Rivalries in the New Eurasia: Russia, Turkey and Iran* (New York: Armonk, 1995), pp. 45, 22.

61. Gareth M. Winrow, 'Azerbaijan and Iran' in ibid., p. 106.

62. According to Şamiloğlu, 'Now Russia has been increasing its control over the whole region [given] the Russian military bases in Armenia, the main threat for Turkey. The Russian effectiveness in Caucasia has been a barrier between Turkey and the Turkish population in CA' in ibid. This conflicts with Elik's theorisation that 'competition and hegemonic ambition of great powers will maintain domestic and regional instability in the wider region of CA and the Caucasus' which is rather abstract when examining its impact on the Turkish–Iranian relations in Suleyman

Elik, *Iran–Turkey Relations, 1979–2011 Conceptualizing the Dynamics of Politics*, op. cit., p. 128.

63. Gareth M.Winrow, 'Azerbaijan and Iran' in Alvin Z. Rubinstein and Oles M. Smolansky, *Regional Power Rivalries in the New Eurasia: Russia, Turkey and Iran* (New York: Armonk, 1995), p. 106.
64. In April 1918 the first Democratic Federal Republic of the Trans Caucasus was created and a month after split into the Democratic Republics of Armenia, Azerbaijan, and Georgia. In 1922 the new union established among Armenia, Azerbaijan and Georgia was called Trans Caucasian Soviet Federal Socialist Republic. After the 1990s, Trans Caucasus was renamed South Caucasus in Eldar Ismailov and Vldimer Papava, 'A New Concept for the Caucasus', *Southeast European and Black Sea Studies*, Vol. 8, No. 3 (September 2008), pp. 284–285.
65. Ibid., pp. 283, 292.
66. Alvin Z. Rubinstein, and Oles M. Smolansky, *Regional Power Rivalries in the New Eurasia: Russia, Turkey and Iran* (New York: Armonk, 1995), p. 26
67. Ibid., pp. 283, 291–293.
68. Hooman Peimani, *Regional Security and the Future of Central Asia: the Competition of Iran, Turkey and Russia* (Praeger, 1998), p. 27.
69. Touraj Daryaee, *The Oxford Handbook of Iranian History* (Oxford University Press, 2012), p. 325.
70. Sergey Markedonov, 'Debating Eurasia: the Search for New Paradigms', *Caucasus International*, Vol. 2, No. 3 (Autumn 2012), pp. 66, 70.
71. Alex Vatanka, 'Tangle in the Caucasus: Iran and Israel Fight for Influence in Azerbaijan', *Foreign Affairs* (15/01/2013) in http://www.foreignaffairs.com/articles/138753/alex-vatanka/tangle-in-the-caucasus (last accessed December 2014).
72. 'Το Ισραήλ προετοιμάζει το Αζερμπαϊτζάν για ένα «Μεγάλο Πόλεμο» με την Τουρκία' ('Israel prepares Azerbaijan for a "Great War" with Turkey'), Πενταπόσταγμα (pentapostagma.gr) (10/01/2015) in http://www.pentapostagma.gr/2015 (last accessed October 2015).
73. Alla Mirzoyan, *Armenia, the Regional Powers and the West between History and Geopolitics* (Palgrave Macmillan, 2010), p. 61.
74. Hasan Kanbolat, 'A New Railway Line in the Southern Caucasus: Kars-Iğdır-Nakhchivan', *Today's Zaman* (8/07/2008), in http://www.todayszaman.com/columnist/hasan-kanbolat/a-new-railway-line-in-the-southern-caucasus-kars-igdir-nakhchivan_146857.html (last accessed December 2014).
75. Sergey Markedonov, 'Debating Eurasia: the Search for New Paradigms', op. cit. p. 73.
76. Gennady Chufrin, *The Security of the Caspian Sea Region* (Oxford University Press, 2001), p. 18.
77. Lyda Filippaki, 'The Azeri of Iran Seek Independence', *The Theme* (Το Θέμα, Greek newspaper) (15/05/2012) in http://www.protothema.gr/

world/article/197495/oi-azeroi-toy-iran-theloyn-aneksarthsia/ (last accessed June 2014).

78. Turgut Tülümen, 'The Future of Turkish–Iranian Relations', *Turkish Review of Middle East Studies* (Istanbul: Isis, 1998), p. 39.

79. The name بازاری is the one given to the merchants' class and workers of bazaars, the traditional marketplaces in Iran.

80. Robert Olson, *Turkey–Iran Relations, 1979–2004*, op. cit., p. 5.

81. Shahin Abbasov, 'Azerbaijan: WikiLeaks Cable Compares Ilham Aliyev to Movie Mafia Bosses', *Eurasianet.org* (2/10/2010) in http://www.eurasi anet.org/node/62487 (last accessed January 2015).

82. *Radio Free Europe*, 'Baku Minister Says Azerbaijan Wouldn't Be Used For Attack On Iran' (12 March 2012) in http://www.rferl.org/content/ azerbaijan_minister_says_territory_wont_be_used_for_attack_on_iran/ 24513361.html (last accessed October 2015).

83. Lamiya Adilgizi, 'Iranian–Armenia Ties being Boosted to Counter Turkey', *Sunday's Zaman* (31/03/2013), p. 6.

84. Alex Vatanka, 'Μπλέξιμο στον Καύκασο: Το Ιράν και το Ισραήλ ανταγωνίζονται για επιρροή στο Αζερμπαϊτζάν' ('Tangling in the Caucasus: Iran and Israel are Competing for Influence in Azerbaijan'), *Foreign Affairs: the Hellenic edition* (16/01/2013).

85. Interview by the author with Reza Altun, co-founder of PKK, executive member of KCK (Qandil, 20/03/2014).

86. 'Israel's Water Challenge', *Stratfort* (25/12/2013) in https://www.stratfor. com/analysis/israels-water-challenge (last accessed December 2015).

87. Yvette Talhamy, 'The Syrian Muslim Brothers and the Syrian–Iranian Relationship', *Middle East Journal*, Vol. 63, No. 4 (Autumn, 2009), pp. 561–580.

88. 'It includes 13 irrigation and hydropower schemes, involving the construction of 22 dams and 19 hydroelectric power plants on both the Tigris and the Euphrates. The GAP is expected to bring two million new hectares of land under irrigation, potentially making Turkey an exporter of agricultural goods' in Tsakalidou, Ilektra, 'The Great Anatolian Project: Is Water Management a Panacea or Crisis Multiplier for Turkey's Kurds?', *New Security Beat* (5/08/2013), htp://www.newsecuritybeat.org/2013/08/ great-anatolian-project-water-management-panacea-crisis-multiplier- turkeys-kurds/ (last accessed February 2015).

89. Tulay Karadeniz and Ibon Villelabeitia, 'U.S. presses Turkey to enforce sanctions on Iran', *Reuters*, http://www.reuters.com/article/idUSTRE69K4 6920101021 (last accessed October 2015).

90. John Calabrese, 'Turkey and Iran: Limits of a Stable Relationship', *British Journal of Middle Eastern Studies*, Vol. 25, No. 1 (May 1998).

91. Robert Olson, *Turkey–Iran Relations, 1979–2004: Revolution, Ideology, War, Coups and Geopolitics* (Costa Mesa, CA: Mazda Publishers, 2004); 'Turkey's Relations with Iran, Syria, Israel, and Russia, 1991–2000', *Kurdish Studies Series* (Costa Mesa, Calif.: Mazda, 2001); 'The Kurdish Question and

Turkish–Iranian Relations: From World War I to 1998', *Kurdish Studies Series*, No. 1 (California, Mazda Publishers, 1998).

92. Suleyman Elik, *Iran–Turkey Relations, 1979–2011*, op. cit.

93. In these respects, Hunter argues that 'foreign policy is determined by systemic factors [whereas] smaller states play a minimal role in shaping the international system', which is no longer the case as far as international politics is concerned, especially from 9/11 onwards, Shireen T. Hunter, *Iran's Foreign Policy in the Post-Soviet Era: Resisting the New International Order* (Praeger, 2010), p. 9.

94. Ibid., p. 10.

95. Louise Fawcett, *International Relations of the Middle East* (Oxford University Press, 2009), pp. 2, 192.

## CHAPTER 2   DETERMINANTS OF IRANIAN–TURKISH RELATIONS: A HISTORICAL REVIEW

1. The same argument with regard to the origins of the Kurdish nation has been argued in Marianna Charountaki, *The Kurds and US Foreign Policy: International Relations in the Middle East since 1945* (Routledge, 2010), p. 35.

2. 'Massive Turkish-speaking populations (culminating with the rank and file of the Mongol armies) settled in large areas of Iran (particularly in Azerbaijan and the northwest)' in John Perry, 'The Historical Role of Turkish in Relation to Persian of Iran', *Iran and the Caucasus*, Vol. 5 (2001), p. 193.

3. As opposed to Hentov's argument that one of the four determinants of Turkish–Iranian relations since 1979 is historical legacy issues – besides bilateral exchanges, regional dynamics and international systemic effects on middle power states, which are very general – I support in contrast that such connections only prove their cooperative relations since very early historical stages rather than their foreign policy attitudes in Elliott Hentov, *Asymmetry of Interest: Turkish–Iranian Relations since 1979*, op. cit., p. 10.

4. Former Turkish Foreign Minister Ahmet Davutoğlu, 'Foreign Minister Zarif of Iran pays a visit to Turkey' (1/11/2013), Turkish Ministry of Foreign Affairs, in http://www.mfa.gov.tr/foreign-minister-zarif-of-iran-pays-a-visit-to-turkey.en.mfa (last accessed April 2014).

5. 'The basis of the tradition is the development of an 'ethnically composite Islamicate society' defined in the context of its Turko-Persian variant as a Persian lettered tradition, rulership and patronage by Turkic rulers (or rulers of Turkic ancestry), and adherence to an Islamic ethic defined by Islamic law and the growing influence of Muslim scholars' in John R. Perry, 'Review: Turko-Persia in Historical Perspective', edited by Robert L. Canfield, *Iranian Studies*, Vol. 26, No. 1/2 (Winter – Spring, 1993), pp. 195–196.

6. Robert L., Canfield, Chapter 1 'Introduction: The Turko-Persian tradition', *Turko-Persia in Historical Perspective* (Cambridge University Press, 1991), p. 9. 'We should distinguish two complementary ways in which the advent of the Turks affected the language map of Iran. First, since the Turkish-speaking rulers of most Iranian polities from the Ghaznavids and Seljuks onward were already Iranized and patronized Persian literature in their domains, the expansion of Turk-ruled empires served to expand the territorial domain of written Persian into the conquered areas, notably Anatolia and Central and South Asia. Secondly, the influx of massive Turkish-speaking populations (culminating with the rank and file of the Mongol armies) and their settlement in large areas of Iran (particularly in Azerbaijan and the northwest), progressively Turkicized local speakers of Persian, Kurdish and other Iranian languages' in John Perry, 'The Historical Role of Turkish in Relation to Persian of Iran', *Iran and the Caucasus*, Vol. 5 (2001), p. 193.

7. Robert L., Canfield, *Turko-Persia in Historical Perspective*, p. 20.

8. Thomas R. Mattair, *Global Security Watch: Iran a Reference Handbook* (Praeger Security International, 2008), p. 3.

9. Güneş Murat Tezcür, *Muslim Reformers in Iran and Turkey: The Paradox of Moderation* (Austin: University of Texas Press, 2010), p. 90.

10. Ibid., p. 99.

11. Foreign Broadcast Information Service (FBIS) (10/01/1989) 'Chronology', *Middle East Journal*, Vol. 43, No. 1 (Winter 1989), p. 288.

12. Claims made during interview by the author with a high level political figure in Iranian politics (London, 17/06/2013).

13. It seems that indeed in agreement with Elik today: 'There are no tendencies by the Turkish state to use Sunnism as a foreign policy tool in politics' in Elik, *Iran–Turkey Relations, 1979–2011*, op. cit, p. 48, yet the current ongoing sectarianism in the Middle East makes a future scenario of Ankara slipping into this situation seem unavoidable.

14. The Bektashi Order is an Islamic Sufi order founded by the Persian Wali Haji Bektash Veli in the 13th century and combines elements of both Shi'ism and Sufism. Alevism is also a cultural, political identity centred on humanism.

15. This rebellion, supported by Ismail Shah, was a short lived (9 April to 7 July 1511) and pro-Shia uprising in Anatolia against the Ottoman Empire.

16. A very good distinction and thus explanation of these two different terms is provided by Güneş Murat Tezcür: '"Islamic" is a religious identity where commitment is priority whereas "Islamist" is a set of beliefs aiming to restructure societal relationships by means of state power' in Güneş Murat Tezcür, *Muslim Reformers in Iran and Turkey: The Paradox of Moderation* (Austin: University of Texas Press, 2010), p. 221.

17. Shapour Ghasemi, *History of Iran: Safavid Empire 1502–1736*, Iran Chamber Society in http://www.iranchamber.com/history/safavids/safavids.php# sthash.aiSGZhpy.dpuf (27/04/2014) (last accessed April 2014).

18. In contrast, though, at this point the author is trying to explain Islamic revivalism in Sena Karasipahi, 'Comparing Islamic Resurgence Movements in Turkey and Iran', *Middle East Journal*, Vol. 63, No. 1 (Winter 2009), p. 106.

19. Interview by the author with a high level political figure in Iranian politics (London, 17/06/2013).

20. Tolga Gürakar, *Türkiye ve İran Gelenek, Çağdaşlaşma, Devrim (Turkey and Iran: Tradition, Modernization, Revolution)* (Kaynak Yayınları: Tarih Dizisi, 2012), p. 349.

21. Karasipahi, 'Comparing Islamic Resurgence Movements in Turkey and Iran', op. cit, p. 92.

22. Interview by the researcher with the Turkish politician, Mr. Akif Çagatay Kiliç, AKP MP (Ankara, 28/03/2013).

23. Interview by the researcher with Dr. Ata'ollah Mohajerani, former Iranian Minister (London, 12/03/2014).

24. Claims made during an interview by the author with a high level political figure in Iranian politics (London, 17/06/2013).

25. Interview by the researcher with Dr. Aykan Erdemir, Former MP CHP (Cumhuriyet Halk Partisi) in Bursa (Ankara, 2/04/2013).

26. Tolga Gürakar, 'Bölüm 1: tarihsel arkaplan: Yüzyıl öncesi dönemde Osmanlı ve İran'a genel bir bakiş' (Chapter 1: Ottoman and Safavid sociological structure and state system, relations between religion and state – historical perspective) in *Türkiye ve İran Gelenek, Çağdaşlaşma, Devrim (Turkey and Iran: Tradition, Modernization, Revolution)* (Kaynak Yayınları: Tarih Dizisi, 2012), pp. 64−68.

27. Shapour Ghasemi, *History of Iran: Safavid Empire 1502−1736*, Iran Chamber Society in http://www.iranchamber.com/history/safavids/safavids.php#sthash.aiSGZhpy.dpuf (27/04/2014) (last accessed April 2014).

28. Karasipahi, 'Comparing Islamic Resurgence Movements in Turkey and Iran', op. cit, p. 92.

29. During the 1909 Revolution, 'it was the Bahktiari tribemen who supported the constitutionalists against the Shah' in Richard N. Frye, *The US and Turkey and Iran* (Archon Books, 1971), p. 190.

30. Gürakar, *Türkiye ve İran*, op. cit. pp. 64−68.

31. Interview by the researcher with Dr. Ata'ollah Mohajerani, former Iranian Minister (London, 12/03/2014).

32. Ahmet Davutoğlu, 'Turkey's zero problems foreign policy', *Foreign Policy* (20/05/2010).

33. Ervand Abrahamian, *A History of Modern Iran* (Cambridge University Press, 2008), p. 66.

34. For further information see Tolga Gürakar, *Türkiye ve İran*, op. cit, pp. 349−350 and Karasipahi, 'Comparing Islamic Resurgence Movements in Turkey and Iran', op.cit, p. 92.

35. Mohammad Fazlhashemi, *Turkey: Iran's Window on Europe*, Vol. 98, No. 6 (Boundaries of Europe: Swedish Council for Planning and Coordination of Research, 1998), p. 72.

36. See Marianna Charountaki, *The Kurds and US Foreign Policy*, op. cit., p. 86.

37. Touraj Daryaee (ed.), *The Oxford Handbook of Iranian History*, (Oxford University Press, 2012), p. 347.

38. Ervand Abrahamian, *A History of Modern Iran* (Cambridge University Press, 2008), p. 92.

39. Maryam Panah, *The Islamic Republic and the World: Global Dimensions of the Iranian Revolution* (Pluto Press, 2007), p. 20.

40. Shireen T. Hunter, *Iran's Foreign Policy in the Post-Soviet Era: Resisting the New International Order*, (Praeger, 2010), p. 29.

41. Interview by the author with a high level political figure in Iranian politics (London, 17/06/2013).

42. Dr. Ata'ollah Mohajerani, *Public Talk*, 'Discussing Iran after Ahmadinejad: A New Leaf?' (London, Reading University, 12/03/2014).

43. *Washington Post* (27/11/1987) in 'Chronology', *Middle East Journal*, Vol. 41, No. 2 (Spring 1987), p. 266.

44. See Ahmet Davutoğlu, 'Turkey's zero problems foreign policy', op. cit.

45. Former Turkish FM, Ahmet Davutoğlu, Principles of Turkish Foreign Policy and Regional Political Structuring, Paper No. 3 (SAM, April 2012) in http://sam.gov.tr/wp-content/uploads/2012/04/vision_paper_TFP2.pdf (last accessed May 2014).

46. Ibid.

47. These principles are: firstly, Nationalism (Milliyetcilik) which aimed to restore a homogenous societal order based on the Turkish identity. Secondly, according to Secularism (*Laiklik*), religion was separated from politics as a private matter. Thirdly, Republicanism (*Cumhuriyetcilik*) recognised the identity of the state as one of constitutional democracy with the acceptance of the first Turkish Constitution in 1921. Hence, the Ottoman dominance of the Sultan was abolished. Later on came Populism (*Halkcilik*), which concerned the equity of Turkish citizens, while Revolutionarism (*Inkilapcilik*) implied the process of reforms in the domestic agenda of the state, regardless of the means – the use, or not, of force. Finally, there is the principle of Etatism (*Devletcilik*) which is linked to the state's control over the economy. See Marianna Charountaki, *The Kurds and US Foreign Policy*, op. cit., p. 46.

48. Karasipahi, 'Comparing Islamic Resurgence Movements in Turkey and Iran', op. cit, p. 101.

49. It is distinguished into three phases; the fighting between Maronite and Palestinian forces in 1974–1975; between Maronite Lebanese Forces (LF) militia and the Syrian troops of the Arab Deterrent Force between 1977 – 1982; and the Israeli invasion of Lebanon in 1982–1983.

50. Karayılan, Murat, *Η Ανατομία του Πολέμου στο Κουρδιστάν* (*Bir Savaşın Anatomisi, Anatomy of a War*) (Infognomon, 2012), pp. 40, 42, 64.

51. See Marianna Charountaki, *The Kurds and US Foreign Policy*, op. cit., pp. 5, 86.
52. Ibid., p. 140 and Marianna Charountaki, 'The US policy of 'containment': Iraq versus Iran', *Today's Zaman*, Turkish Newspaper in English (23/01/2012) in http://www.todayszaman.com/news-269392-the-us-policy-of-containment-iraq-versus-iranby-marianna-charountaki.html (last accessed May 2014).
53. See Marianna Charountaki, *The Kurds and US Foreign Policy*, op. cit., p. 137.
54. Turkish Daily News (30/11/1978), in 'Chronology', *Middle East Journal*, Vol. 33, No. 3, p. 204.
55. For further information see Karasipahi, 'Comparing Islamic Resurgence Movements in Turkey and Iran', op. cit, pp. 93–95.
56. See Marianna Charountaki, *The Kurds and US Foreign Policy*, op. cit., p. 136.
57. According to Güneş Murat Tezcür, 'the Assembly of Experts consists of 86 clerics elected every 8 years according to article 107 of the Constitution; the Guardians Council is 12 members, 6 of them appointed by the *faqih* and other 6 jurists selected by the parliament' in Güneş Murat Tezcür, *Muslim Reformers in Iran and Turkey: the Paradox of Moderation* (Austin: University of Texas Press, 2010), pp. 90, 92.
58. Saideh Lotfian in Homa Katouzian and Hossein Shahidi, *Iran in the 21st Century: Politics, Economics and Conflict* (Routledge, 2008), p. 118.
59. Interview by the author with Ibrahim Kalin, Ambassador, Spokesman for the Presidency, and Chief Advisor in Middle East Affairs to the Turkish President, Recep Tayip Erdoğan (Ankara, 1/04/2013).
60. In the elections of 1950 they gathered 52.7 per cent of the national vote, in the 1954 elections won with a 57. 5 per cent majority and in 1957 in the midst of an economic crisis received 47.9 per cent of the popular vote.
61. 'First priority in Iran's foreign policy is the national security and the preservation of the balance of power', interview by the author with a high level political figure in Iranian politics (London, 17/06/2013).
62. Thomas R. Mattair, *Global Security Watch Iran: a Reference Handbook*, op. cit., pp. 13, 14, 20.
63. Ibid.
64. Interview by the researcher with Osman Korutürk, former Deputy Chairman at CHP (Cumhuriyet Halk Partisi, Republican People's Party) (Ankara, 1/04/2013).
65. Ibid.
66. Interview by the researcher with Osman Aşkın Bak, Co-Chairman of Turkey–Iran Parliamentary Friendship Group (Ankara, 28/03/2013).
67. Interview by the researcher with Osman Korutürk, op. cit. (Ankara, 1/04/2013).

68. Interview with a high level political figure in Iranian politics, op. cit (London, 17/06/2013).
69. Interview by the researcher with Osman Korutürk, op. cit. (Ankara, 1/04/2013).

CHAPTER 3   TURKEY–IRAN RELATIONS DURING THE COLD WAR

1. Leader of the Palestine Liberation Organization (PLO), *New York Times* (18/02/1979) in 'Chronology', *Middle East Journal*, Vol. 33, No. 4, p. 349.
2. Murat Karayılan, *H Ανατομία του Πολέμου στο Κουρδιστάν* (*Anatomy of a War, Bir Savaşın Anatomisi*) (Infognomon, 2012), p. 36.
3. *New York Times* (16/08/1979) in 'Chronology', *Middle East Journal*, Vol. 33, No. 1, p. 43.
4. 'Khomeini said that anyone whose direction is separate from Islam was an enemy of the revolution ...' in *New York Times* (24/05/1979), 'Chronology', *Middle East Journal*, Vol. 33, No. 4, p. 485.
5. Marianna Charountaki, *The Kurds and US Foreign Policy: International Relations in the Middle East since 1945* (Routledge, 2010), p. 137.
6. See US Department of State, Directorate of Plans, 'Israeli aid to Kurdish Rebels', IN-039040 (9 April 1970), http://www.state.gov/r/pa/ho/frus/nixon/e4/69591.htm (last accessed April 2014).
7. Interview by the researcher with Mahmoud Othman, former President of the Kurdistan Socialist Party, former member of the Iraq Interim Governing Council, member of the Iraqi Parliament and member of the Iraqi delegation during the 1970s Manifesto negotiations (Erbil, 15 April 2007).
8. Interview by the researcher with Mohsin Dizayee, Massoud Barzani's special envoy (Salahaddin, 13 June 2007).
9. The first phase (1975–1977) involved fighting between the Lebanese National Movement (الحركة الوطنية اللبنانية) headed by Kamal Jumblatt, a Druze, and the Lebanese Phalange Party (حزب الكتائب اللبنانية) supported by Maronites. The second phase (1977–1982) was fought between the Maronite Lebanese Forces (LF) militia and the Syrian troops of the Arab Deterrent Force (ADF), while the third phase (1985–1989), known as the War of the Camps, was fought between Amal and Hezbollah.
10. *Washington Post* (27/11/1986), in 'Chronology', *Middle East Journal*, Vol. 41, No. 2, p. 266.
11. Howard Teicher, and Gayle Radley Teicher, *Twin Pillars to Desert Storm: America's Flawed Vision in the Middle East from Nixon to Bush* (New York: Morrow, 1993), p. 62.
12. Interview by the author with Seyid Azim Hosseini, former Iranian Consul General in Erbil (Erbil, 6/04/2013).
13. Abbas William Samii, 'A Stable Structure on Shifting Sands: Assessing the Hizbullah–Iran–Syria Relationship', Middle East Journal, Vol. 62, No. 1 (Winter 2008), p. 37.

14. 'Syrian, Libyan and Iranian Ministers met in Damascus [and] pledged support for efforts to overthrow Iraqi President Hussein and to support Iran against hostile forces', *New York Times* (24/01/1983), in 'Chronology', *Middle East Journal*, Vol. 37, No. 3, p. 455.

15. *New York Times* (16/10/1979) in 'Chronology', *Middle East Journal*, Vol. 33, No.1, p. 47.

16. *Washington Post* (8/06/1986) in 'Chronology', *Middle East Journal*, Vol. 40, No. 4, p. 699.

17. Hizbullah's Open Letter to the World of 16 February, 1985, which notably assigned the leadership role to Iran, cited Khomeini's view that 'America is the reason for all our catastrophes . . .' in Abbas William Samii, 'A Stable Structure on Shifting Sands: Assessing the Hizbullah-Iran-Syria Relationship', *Middle East Journal*, Vol. 62, No. 1 (Winter, 2008), p. 37.

18. 'Turkey–Iran gold trade wiped out by US sanctions', *World Bulletin* (16/02/2013) in http://www.worldbulletin.net/?aType=haber&Article ID=103420 (accessed December 2014).

19. Marianna Charountaki, *The Kurds and US Foreign Policy*, op. cit., pp. 88–89.

20. Ibid., p. 87.

21. Dilip Hiro, *Iran Under the Ayatollahs* (London: Routledge and Kegan Paul, 1985), p. 329.

22. Henry Kissinger, *Diplomacy* (New York, 1994), p. 774.

23. *Washington Post* (03/02/1983), in 'Chronology', *Middle East Journal*, Vol. 37, No. 3, p. 455.

24. The no-win goal in the Gulf', *New York Times* (22/05/1984); and 'US goal was to keep either side from winning the Persian Gulf War', *New York Times* (12 January 1987), p. A1.

25. Ömer Karasapan, 'Turkey and US Strategy in the Age of Glasnost', *MERIP*, No. 160 in http://www.merip. org/mer/mer160/turkey-us-strategy-age-glasNo.st (last accessed April 2015).

26. Jimmy Carter, State of the Union Message to the 96th Congress (23 January 1980), http://www.presidency.ucsb.edu/ws/index.php? pid=33079 (accessed January 2015).

27. Larry Everest, *Oil, Power, & Empire: Iraq and the U.S. Global Agenda* (Common Courage Press, 2004), p. 34.

28. Henry A. Kissinger, 'Continuity and Change in American Foreign Policy', The Arthur K. Solomon Lecture (New York University, 19 September 1977) in Henry A. Kissinger, *For the Record: Selected Statements, 1977–1980* (Boston: Little Brown & Co, 1981), pp. 299–300.

29. Interview by the researcher with Dr. Ata'ollah Mohajerani, former Iranian Minister (London, 11/03/2015).

30. *New York Times* (14/11/1979) in 'Chronology', *Middle East Journal*, Vol. 33, No. 1, p. 53.

31. *New York Times* (07/04/1980) in 'Chronology', *Middle East Journal*, Vol. 34, No. 3 (Summer, 1980), p. 330.

32. *Washington Post* (11/03/1982) in 'Chronology', *Middle East Journal*, Vol. 36, No. 3, p. 401.

33. *New York Times* (11/09/1982) in 'Chronology', *Middle East Journal*, Vol. 37, No. 1 (Winter 1983), p. 81.

34. Arab News CSM (6/12/1986) in 'Chronology', *Middle East Journal*, Vol. 41, No. 2, p. 279.

35. According to Hentov, with the Revolution 'the dynamic of Turkish-Iranian relations [was] one of Turkey responding to events unfolding in Iran' which was not true considering their economic interdependence and the fact that in Middle Eastern politics, one entity is being highly affected by another. Turkey and Iran were primarily exposed to both the Russian and Western spheres of influence who understood them as security buffer zones. The reference to the term 'asymmetric relations' in the sense that 'Turkey has not been the central focus of Iranian geopolitical strategy [because] Turkey is absent from Iran's foreign policy conceptualization [in contrast to] Iran that is a major player in Turkey's national security discourse' again does not appear accurate *vis-à-vis* the more recent unfolding of events that the Syrian crisis has brought about and its repercussion on the foreign policy of both states, in addition to the role the Kurdish issue has played so far which has again made the Iranian and Turkish détente imperative. Turkish and Iranian competition for influence in the case of Iraq is another rationale. See Elliot Hentov, *Asymmetry of Interest: Turkish–Iranian Relations since 1979* (Lambert Academic Publishing House, 2012), pp. 39, 181.

36. According to Yücel Bozdağlıoğlu, 'polarization between Islamists and secularists [constitutes] important determinant on Turkey's domestic and foreign policy' in Yücel Bozdağlıoğlu, *Turkish Foreign Policy and Turkish Identity: A Constructivist Approach* (Routledge, 2003), p. 89.

37. Interview by author with Massoud Barzani, former President of the KR in Iraq (Erbil, 25/09/2013).

38. Interview by the author with Ibrahim Kalin, Ambassador, Spokesman for the Presidency, and Chief Advisor in Middle East Affairs to the Turkish President, Recep Tayip Erdoğan (Ankara, 1/04/2013).

39. Bozdağlıoğlu, *Turkish Foreign Policy and Turkish Identity*, op. cit., p. 123.

40. 'The Johnson letter made it clear that the US did not have any intention to call in the NATO mechanism in favour of Turkey even though the most vital Turkish interests were at stake' in Yücel Bozdağlıoğlu, *Turkish Foreign Policy and Turkish Identity: A Constructivist Approach* (Routledge, 2003), p. 63.

41. George S. Harris, 'Chapter 1: the Russian Federation and Turkey' in Alvin Z. Rubinstein and Oles M. Smolansky, *Regional Power Rivalries in the New Eurasia: Russia, Turkey and Iran* (New York, Armonk, 1995), pp. 8, 10.

42. Ömer Karasapan, 'Turkey and US Strategy in the Age of Glasnost', op. cit.

43. Meltem Müftüler-Bac, *Turkey's Relations with a Changing Europe* (Manchester University Press, 1997), pp. 32–33 and Galia Golan, *Soviet*

*Policies in the Middle East From World War Two to Gorbachev* (Cambridge Russian Paperbacks, 1991), p. 251.

44. Bozdağlıoğlu, *Turkish Foreign Policy and Turkish Identity*, op. cit., pp. 64, 121.

45. Ibid., p. 126.

46. *Washington Post* (25/02/1983) in 'Chronology', *Middle East Journal*, Vol. 37, No. 3, p. 464.

47. Rouhullah K. Ramazani, *Revolutionary Iran; Challenge and Response in the Middle East* (4th edn) (Johns Hopkins University Press: 1988), pp. 24–25.

48. Turgut Tülümen, 'The Future of Turkish–Iranian Relations', *Turkish Review of Middle East Studies* (Istanbul: Isis, 1998), pp. 136–137.

49. Mahan Abedin, 'Khamenei throws the gauntlet at the West', *Asia Times* (21/09/2011).

50. David Menashri, 'Khomeini's Vision: Nationalism or World Order?' in David Menashri (ed.), *The Iranian Revolution and the Muslim World* (Boulder, San Francisco, Oxford: Westview Press, 1990), p. 49.

51. F. Stephen Larrabee and Alireza Nader, *Turkish–Iranian Relations in a Changing Middle East*, Report, Issue 258 (RAND, 2013), http://www.rand.org/content/dam/rand/pubs/research_reports/RR200/RR258/RAND_RR258.pdf, p. 2 (last accessed May 2015).

52. The movement was created in 1969 from the merging of Bağımsızlar Hareketi (Aligned Movement) and Millî Nizam Partisi (the National Order Party) under Erkaban.

53. Trita Parsi, *Treacherous Alliance: The Secret Dealings of Israel, Iran and the US* (Yale University Press, 2007), pp. 58, 71.

54. 'Members of Fethullah Gülen's Islamic sect have infiltrated the police force among other public institutions with the aim of complete control of Turkish affairs ... Fethullahism was enriched by the same leaders of the 12th September, 1980 coup, a system later renamed "the Turkish-Islamic synthesis". Before the 1980s, anarchists and Marxists posed a danger. Afterwards we had religious fanatics. Therefore it was necessary (for the deep state) to establish relations with these religious groups and to work together with them. The goal was to make peace between them and the state. Thus, members of the intelligence services approached Fethullah Gülen's group. There were other components of the Turkish-Islamic synthesis and other movements. These circles are now in conflict with the military in order to develop to a level where they can fight for themselves. They are all nationalists. Fethullah Gülen is a nationalist. They grew up and were politicized in the anti-Communist movement. Gülen himself founded an anti-Communist group in the 1960s. The deep state allows them to continue, as long as it is under its regulation. Gülen was arrested and sentenced to 3 years in prison under the 163rd article of Turkish Criminal Law in 1972. In 1974 an amnesty was issued and after 7 months imprisonment Gülen was freed. Gülen, whose attachment to the military was unshaken by this period in captivity, wrote these words

of the 12th March, 1971 coup: 'The 27th May was a leftist-led manoeuvre. They wanted the 12th March to be too. But five minutes before the insurrection it came into the hands of Memduh Tağmaç and his friends who removed some of the leaders of the memorandum adventure. The leftists, who hadn't predicted this audacity, were unsure how to act. They had foreseen that the opposition on the 12th March would be unready and insufficient. If those who had wished to act on the 9th March had not been obstructed, the subversion carried out would have been very different; the draft "Revolutionary Constitution" would have been put into force and Turkey would have become, bar the name, a complete Communist country. This was the common hope of these leftist powers and the civilian vanguard they had mentored. Thus, during the Ziverbey interrogations their true colours were revealed and one by one their atrocious ideas came to light. The 12th of March was not an insurrection and coup. It was a warning to the government in clear terms' in Ahmet Şık, *The Imam's Army* (*İmamın Ordusu*) (Postacı Publishing House, 2011).

55. Dilip Hiro, *Inside Central Asia: A Political and Cultural History of Uzbekistan, Turkmenistan, Kazakjstan, Kyrgyzstan, Tajikistan, Turkey and Iran* (New York: Overlook Duckworth, 2009), p. 91; see also Hasan Kösebalaban, *Turkish Foreign Policy: Islam, Nationalism and Globalization* (Palgrave Macmillan: 2011), p. 110.

56. *New York Times* (29/03/1980) in 'Chronology', *Middle East Journal*, Vol. 34, No. 3, p. 339.

57. Arshin Adib-Moghaddam, Report: 'Turkey & Iran: Islamic Brotherhood or Regional Rivalry?' (Al Jazeera Center for Studies, 4 June, 2013). Indeed 'Erbakan signed agreement with Iran to import $20billion worth of natural gas' stating that 'Turkey will not allow any third country to interfere in the growing trend of cooperation between Iran and Turkey' *vis-à-vis* the US legislation that prescribes penalties for companies trading above a low limit with Iran and Libya (D'Amato Law) in Yücel Bozdağlıoğlu, op. cit., p. 134.

58. *New York Times* (11/11/1983) in 'Chronology', *Middle East Journal*, Vol. 38, No. 2, p. 305.

59. Foreign Broadcast Information Service (15/12/1986) in 'Chronology', *Middle East Journal*, Vol. 41, No. 2, p. 266. Similarly in '1926 the Soviets aided in the installation of the first radio station in Tehran' in Basil Dmytryshyn and Frederick Cox, *The Soviet Union and the Middle East: a documentary record of Afghanistan, Iran and Turkey 1917–1985* (The Kingston Press: 1987, p. 237).

60. Hasan Kösebalaban, 'Preface' in *Turkish Foreign Policy: Islam, Nationalism and Globalization* (Palgrave Macmillan: 2011).

61. Interview by the researcher with Dr. Ata'ollah Mohajerani, former Iranian Minister (London, 11/03/2015).

62. Ibid.

63. Touraj Daryaee (ed.), *The Oxford Handbook of Iranian History* (Oxford University Press, 2012), p. 370.

64. Mahan Abedin, 'Khamenei throws the gauntlet at the West', *Asia Times* (21/09/2011).

65. Arash Karami, 'The tumbling turban: Who is behind attacks on Reformists in Iran?', *Al Monitor* (30/11/2015) in http://www.al-monitor.com/pulse/originals/2015/11/iran-reformists-attacked-parliament-elections-2016.html (last accessed December, 2015).

66. Amanat Abbas argues that such divisions can also be witnessed today within Principalism, especially between hardline Neo-Principalists versus moderate conservative Traditional Principalists for different debates such as the issue over the nature of the Guardianship of the Jurist have created an increasingly profound conflict between Neo- and Traditional Principalists and the lack of Principalist unity overall, in *Iran Politik: The Iran Political Analysis Project* (24/06/2013) in http://www.iranpolitik.com/2013/06/24/analysis/principalists-divided-neo-principalists-attack-traditional-principalists/ (last accessed October 2015).

67. Mahan Abedin, 'Hardliners manoeuvre as Iran nuclear talks enter extra time', *Middle East Eye* (21 July 2014) in http://www.middleeasteye.net/columns/iran-hardliners-manoeuvre-nuclear-talks-enter-extra-time-1241138768 (last accessed December 2015).

68. Tolga Gürakar, *Türkiye ve İran Gelenek, Çağdaşlaşma, Devrim* (*Turkey and Iran: Tradition, Modernization, Revolution*), Kaynak Yayınları: Tarih Dizisi, 2012), p. 352.

69. Hootan Shambayati, 'The Rentier State, Interest Groups, and the Paradox of Autonomy: State and Business in Turkey and Iran', *Comparative Politics*, Vol. 26, No. 3 (April 1994), pp. 320–327.

70. Interview by the researcher with Dr. Ata'ollah Mohajerani, former Iranian Minister (London, 11/03/2015).

71. Touraj Daryaee (ed.), *The Oxford Handbook of Iranian History* (Oxford University Press, 2012), p. 372.

72. Interview by the researcher with Dr. Ata'ollah Mohajerani, former Iranian Minister (London, 11/03/2015).

73. Ibid.

74. Güneş Murat Tezcür, *Muslim Reformers in Iran and Turkey: the Paradox of Moderation* (University of Texas Press, Austin, 2010), p. 93.

75. Dividing Turkish–Iranian relations into set periods constitutes a methodological subjectivity, since the division is always subjected to the hypothesis under examination. For instance, Ehteshami and Elik divide Turkish–Iranian relations into four specific periods: the revolt crisis in the late 1920s followed by the Friendship Agreement (1962) and the Turkish–Iranian border agreement (1932); the Anglo-Russian occupation of Iran when Turkey and Iran viewed each other as security buffer zones against Russia's demand for passage through the Strait of Hormuz and the Straits of Istanbul; the Cold War period; and 'the 1979

period onwards along with the Gulf War' in Anoushiravan Ehteshami and Süleyman Elik, 'Turkey's Growing Relations with Iran and Arab Middle East', *Turkish Studies*, Vol. 12, No. 4 (December 2011), pp. 647–649.

76. Ansari separates the Iranian political fractions into: the hardline Conservative Populists, the Moderate Conservatives, the Neo-Conservatives and the Principalists. See Ali M. Ansari, 'Iran under Ahmadinejad: the Politics of Confrontation', *Adelphi Paper* 393 (International Institute for Strategic Studies, 2007), pp. 7–14, 20–21, 69. Ehteshami and Zweiri refer to the traditional Conservatives, Liberal Reformists, and Neo-Conservatives: see Anoushiravan Ehteshami and Mahjoob Zweiri, *Iran and the Rise of its Neoconservatives: The Politics of Tehran's Silent Revolution New Right Faction in Iran* (I.B.Tauris, 2007), p. 16.

77. This division is found in David Menashri, *Post-Revolutionary Politics in Iran: Religion, Society, and Power* (Frank Cass Publishers, 2001), p. 50.

78. M. R. Dehshiri and M. R. Majidi, 'Iran's Foreign Policy in Post-Revolution Era: a Holistic Approach', *The Iranian Journal of International Affairs*, Vol. XXI, No. 1–2: 101–114 (Winter Spring 2008–2009), p. 104.

79. 'Iran had provided some 60,000 new weapons to Shi'i rebels in central Afghanistan', *Washington Post* (28/05 1989), in 'Chronology', *Middle East Journal*, Vol. 43, No. 4, p. 669.

80. Foreign Broadcast Information Service Daily Report (12/11/1982) in 'Chronology', *Middle East Journal*, Vol. 36, No. 2, p. 223.

81. *New York Times* (4/02/1980), in 'Chronology', *Middle East Journal*, Vol. 34, No. 2 (Spring 1980), p. 165.

82. *Turkish Daily News* (10/01/1980), in ibid., p. 179.

83. Maryam Panah, *The Islamic Republic and the World: Global Dimensions of the Iranian Revolution* (Pluto Press, 2007), p. 80.

84. Interview by the author with Mahmoud Othman, former President of the Kurdistan Socialist Party, former member of the Iraq Interim Governing Council, member of Iraqi Parliament and member of the Iraqi delegation during the 1970s Manifesto negotiations (Erbil, 4/04/2013).

85. Ali Akbar Velayati, 'Velayati: US unable to attack Iran', *Mehr News Agency* (26/01/2013).

86. Robert Baer, *The Devil We Know: Dealing with the New Iranian Superpower* (Crown Publishers, 2008), p. 53.

87. Augustus Richard Norton, 'Hizballah and the Israeli Withdrawal from Southern Lebanon', *Journal of Palestine Studies*, Vol. 30, No. 1 (Autumn, 2000), pp. 22–35.

88. Thomas R. Mattair, *Global Security Watch – Iran: a Reference Handbook* (Praeger Security International, 2008), pp. 35–36.

89. Foreign Broadcast Information Service (03/12/1987), in 'Chronology', *Middle East Journal*, Vol. 42, No. 2, p. 290.

90. Claims made during interview between author and a high level political figure in Iranian politics (London, 17/06/2013).

91. Robert Baer, *The Devil We Know: Dealing with the New Iranian Superpower*, op. cit., pp. 114–115.
92. Robert Olson, 'Turkey–Iran Relations, 1997 to 2000: the Kurdish and Islamist Questions', *Third World Quarterly*, Vol. 21, No. 5 (October 2000), pp. 49, 876.
93. Interview by author with Reza Altun, co-founder of PKK, executive member of KCK (Qandil, 20/03/2014).
94. Interview by author with Massoud Barzani, former President of the KR in Iraq (Erbil, 25/09/2013).
95. Interview by the author with Mahmoud Othman, former President of the Kurdistan Socialist Party, former member of the Iraq Interim Governing Council, member of Iraqi Parliament and member of the Iraqi delegation during the 1970s Manifesto negotiations (Erbil, 4/04/2013).
96. *New York Times* (12 January 1987), p. A1.
97. Turgut Tülümen, *'The Future of Turkish–Iranian Relations'*, op. cit., p. 127.
98. Ibid., pp. 137–138.
99. *Pike Report* (19 January 1976), republished in *The Village Voice* (New York: 23 February, 1976).
100. Marianna Charountaki, 'Turkish Foreign Policy and the Kurdistan Regional Government', *Perceptions*, Vol. XVII, No. 4 (Winter 2012), pp. 185–208 in http://sam.gov.tr/wp-content/uploads/2013/03/8-Marianna_Charountaki.pdf (accessed February 2015).
101. Claims made during interview between author and a high level political figure in Iranian politics (London, 17/06/2013).
102. Murat Karayılan, *H Αvατομία τov Πoλέμov στo Koυρδιστάv* (*Anatomy of a War, Bir Savaşın Anatomisi*) (Infognomon, 2012), p. 190.
103. Frederick W. Axelgard, 'US–Iraqi Relations: a Status Report' in *American-Arab Affairs*, No. 13 (Summer, 1985), pp. 1, 6.
104. Larry Everest, *Oil, Power and Empire: Iraq and the US Global Agenda* (Canada: Common Courage Press, 2004) (4th edn), p. 72.
105. *New York Times* (2/12/1980) in 'Chronology', *Middle East Journal*, Vol. 35, No. 2, p. 209.
106. *Washington Post* (30/05/1982), in 'Chronology', *Middle East Journal*, Vol. 36, No. 4, p. 572.
107. Touraj Daryaee (ed.), *The Oxford Handbook of Iranian History* (Oxford University Press, 2012), p. 375.
108. Trita Parsi, *Treacherous Alliance: The Secret Dealings of Israel, Iran and the US* (Yale University Press, 2007), p. 94.
109. *Washington Post* (13–14/11/1987) in 'Chronology', *Middle East Journal*, Vol. 41, No. 2, p. 261.
110. Larry Everest, *Oil, Power and Empire: Iraq and the US Global Agenda* (4th edn) (Canada: Common Courage Press, 2004), p. 104.
111. William R. Polk, *The Arab World Today* (London: Harvard University Press, 1991), pp. 339–340.

112. National Security Archive, Document 17: 'Department of State, Office of the Secretary Delegation Cable from George P. Shultz to the Department of State: Secretary's May 10 Meeting with Iraqi Foreign Minister Tariq Aziz', No. 04218 (11 May 1983), George Washington University, in http://www.gwu.edu/~nsarchiv/NSAEBB/NSAEBB82/index.htm

113. *Washington Street Journal* (13/01/1984), in 'Chronology', *Middle East Journal*, Vol. 38, No. 2, p. 306.

114. 'Iranians agreed on 28 November 1984 to the 1983 October Security Agreement between Turkey and Baghdad. For Turkey the threat was the PKK, [and] for Iran the oppositional movements such as the Mojahedin-e Khalq' in Robert Olson, *Turkey−Iran Relations, 1979−2004: Revolution, Ideology, War, Coups and Geopolitics* (Mazda Publishers, 2004), p. 4. Similarly, Elliot argues that in December, 1986 President Khamenei warned against any intervention in Iraq; see Elliot Hentov, *Asymmetry of Interest: Turkish Iranian Relations since 1979* (Lambert Academic Publishing House, 2012), p. 103.

115. *Washington Post* (7/02/1979), 'Chronology' in the *Middle East Journal*, Vol. 41, No. 3, p. 440.

116. *New York Times* (23/09/1980) in 'Chronology', *Middle East Journal*, Vol. 35, No. 1, p. 48.

117. Suha Bolukbasi, 'Chapter 3: From the Islamic Revolution to the Persian Gulf War: 1979−1991' in Robert Olson, *The Kurdish Question and Turkish-Iranian Relations: from World War I to 1998* (Mazda Publishers, 1998), p. 28.

118. George S. Harris, 'The Russian Federation and Turkey' in *Regional Power Rivalries in the New Eurasia: Russia, Turkey and Iran*, ed. Alvin Z. Rubenstein and Oles M. Smolansky (New York: Armonk, 1995), p. 10.

119. Elliot Hentov, *Asymmetry of Interest:* op. cit., pp. 16−18.

120. Arzu Celalifer Ekinci, *İran Türkiye Enerji İşbirliği (Iran Turkey Energy Cooperation)* (Uluslararası Stratejik Araştırmalar Kurumu Kasım, 2008).

121. 'In 1980 Iran provided to Turkey 2.6 mil tons of oil whereas after the war Turkey exported to Iran 400,000 tons of wheat in exchange for 560,000 tons of oil' in Alon Liel, *Turkey in the Middle East: Oil, Islam and Politics* (Lynne Rienner Publishers, 2001), pp. 92−94.

122. *New York Times* (11/09/1982) in 'Chronology', *Middle East Journal*, Vol. 36, No. 3, p. 81.

123. Evren Altinkaş, 'The Iran-Iraq War And its Effects On Turkey', *Uluslararasr Hukuk ve Politika (International Law and Policy)*, Vol. 1, No. 4 (2005), p. 142.

124. Nihat Ali Özcan and Özgür Özdamar, 'Uneasy Neighbors: Turkish−Iranian Relations since the 1979 Islamic Revolution', *Middle East Policy*, Volume XVII, No. 3 (Fall 2010) (22/09/2010).

125. Hasan Kösebalaban, *Turkish Foreign Policy*, op. cit., p. 109.

126. Foreign Broadcast Information Service (18/10/1988), in 'Chronology', *Middle East Journal*, Vol. 43, No. 1, p. 287.

127. Arab News CSM (3/07/1985) in ibid., Vol. 39, No. 4, p. 827.

128. *New York Times* (07/12/1980), in 'Chronology', *Middle East Journal*, Vol. 34, No. 2 (Spring, 1980), p. 168.

129. *New York Times* (14/11/1979), in 'Chronology', *Middle East Journal*, Vol. 33, No. 1, p. 53.

130. *New York Times* (16/02/1980), in 'Chronology', *Middle East Journal*, Vol. 34, No. 3, p. 329.

131. According to Sick, 'in the summer of 1980, Khomeini had agreed with Reagan not to release the 52 American hostages in the US Embassy in Tehran until after the November elections, so that Carter would not be credited with any political success. In exchange, the US would lift economic sanctions and provide Iran with weaponry via Israel' in Gary Sick, *October Surprise: America's Hostages in Iran and the Election of Ronald Reagan* (New York: Times Books, 1992), pp. 10–12; also Donald Neff, 'US: the ghost of 1980', *Middle East International*, No. 400 (Washington DC, 17 May 1991), p. 11.

132. Neil A. Lewis, 'House Inquiry Finds No Evidence of Deal on Hostages in 1980', *New York Times* (13/01/1993), http://www.nytimes.com/1993/01/13/us/house-inquiry-finds-No.-evidence-of-deal-on-hostages-in-1980.html (last accessed March 2015).

133. David P. Houghton, *US Foreign Policy and the Iran Hostage Crisis* (Cambridge University Press, 2001), p. 143.

134. Interview by the author with Fadhil Merani, Secretary of Political Bureau, Kurdistan Democratic Party (Erbil, 27 August 2015).

135. Interview by the researcher with Dr. Ata'ollah Mohajerani, former Iranian Minister (London, 11/03/2015).

136. M. R. Dehshiri, and M. R Majidi, 'Iran's Foreign Policy in Post-Revolution Era: a Holistic Approach', *The Iranian Journal of International Affairs*, Vol. XXI No. 1–2: 101–114 (Winter Spring 2008–2009), p. 107.

137. *Middle East Economic Survey* (5/10/1979) in 'Chronology', *Middle East Journal*, Vol. 33, No. 1, p. 50; 'Iran signed contract with Kraftwerk Union' in Saideh Lotfian, *Iran in the 21st Century: Politics, Economics and Conflict* edited by Homa Katouzian and Hossein Shahidi (Routledge, 2008), p. 159.

138. *New York Times* (11/11/1979), in 'Chronology', *Middle East Journal*, Vol. 33, No. 1, p. 52.

139. *New York Times* (12/09/1980) in 'Chronology', *Middle East Journal*, Vol. 35, No. 1, p. 46.

140. Turgut Tülümen, 'The Future of Turkish–Iranian Relations', op. cit., p. 137.

141. Maryam Panah, *The Islamic Republic and the World*, op. cit, p. 53.

142. Marianna Charountaki, *The US policy of 'containment': Iraq versus Iran* (23/01/2012) in http://www.todayszaman.com/op-ed_the-us-policy-of-

containment-iraq-versus-iranby-marianna-charountaki-_269392.html (accessed December 2014).

143. *Washington Post* (29/12/1983), in 'Chronology', *Middle East Journal*, Vol. 38, No. 2, p. 294.

144. Marianna Charountaki, *The Kurds and US Foreign Policy*, op. cit., p. 126.

145. Maryam Panah, *The Islamic Republic and the World:* op. cit., p. 89.

146. *Washington Post* (28/09/1987), (30/09/1987), in 'Chronology', *Middle East Journal*, Vol. 42, No. 1, p. 95.

147. *New York Times* (5/01/1988) and Foreign Broadcast Information Service (15/01/1988), in 'Chronology', *Middle East Journal*, Vol. 42, No. 2, p. 279.

148. Shahram Chubin and Charles Tripp, *Iran–Saudi Arabia Relations and Regional Order*, Adelphi Paper 304 (Oxford University Press, 1996), p. 14.

149. Homayoun Mafi, 'The Dilemma of US Economic Sanctions on Iran: an Iranian Perspective', *The Iranian Journal of International Affairs*, Vol. XIX, No. 4 (Fall, 2007), p. 100.

150. *Christian Science Monitor* (11/06/1985), in 'Chronology', *Middle East Journal*, Vol. 39, No. 4 (Autumn, 1985), p. 804.

151. From the viewpoint of Bozdağlıoğlu, 'In order to exert pressure on Turkey via the Kurds and persuade Ankara not to support the Chechens in their war against Russia (October–November 1992), the members of the Russian Duma agreed to host the 3rd international conference of the Kurdish Parliament in Exile' in Bozdağlıoğlu, *Turkish Foreign Policy and Turkish Identity*, op. cit., p. 101.

152. Foreign Broadcast Information Service (23/08/1989), in 'Chronology', *Middle East Journal*, Vol. 44, No. 1 (Winter 1990) p. 112.

CHAPTER 4    TURKISH–IRANIAN RELATIONS IN THE 1990S: THE IMPACT OF GULF WAR II AND THE CONSOLIDATION OF THE KURDISH STATUS

1. Interview by the researcher with Osman Aşkın Bak, former Co-chairman of Turkey–Iran Parliamentary Friendship Group (Ankara, 28 March 2013).

2. According to Brzezinski, National Security Advisor (March 1980), the hostage crisis and the Afghanistan problem made forging relations with Iraq imperative, cited in Maryam Panah, *The Islamic Republic and the World: Global Dimensions of the Iranian Revolution* (Pluto Press, 2007), p. 80.

3. Marianna Charountaki, *The Kurds and US Foreign Policy: International Relations in the Middle East since 1945* (Routledge, 2010), p. 89.

4. Dilip Hiro, *Iran under the Ayatollahs* (London: Routledge and Kegan Paul, 1985), p. 329.

5. National Security Archive, 'Ronald Reagan's letter to Saddam Hussein', Document 30, 'United States Embassy in Italy Cable from Maxwell M. Rabb to the Department of State: Rumsfeld's Larger Meeting with Iraqi

Deputy PM [Prime Minister] and FM [Foreign Minister] Tariz [Tariq] Aziz, December 19' (20 December 1983), George Washington University, in http://www.gwu.edu/~nsarchiv/NSAEBB/NSAEBB82/index.htm (last accessed 2008).

6. The no-win goal in the Gulf', *New York Times* (22/05/1984); and 'US goal was to keep either side from winning the Persian Gulf War', *New York Times* (12 January 1987), p. A1.

7. More information on the reasons as to why Saddam intervened Kuwait in Charountaki, *The Kurds and US Foreign Policy*, op. cit., p. 92.

8. The 'Anfal' (The Spoils) campaign was significant for the Iraqi regime's use of poison gas against the Kurdish population in the North.

9. Martin J. Rochester, US Foreign Policy in the 21st century (Boulder CO: Westview Press, 2008), p. 40.

10. Thomas C. Hayes, 'Confrontation in the Gulf: the oil-field lying below the Iraq–Kuwait dispute', *New York Times* (3 September 1990).

11. *New York Times* (2 September 1990) reported that 'Kuwait's overall production in 1989 had averaged 1.8 million barrels/day, exceeding thus its OPEC quota by 700,000 barrels'.

12. The first change saw a shift in the emphasis of US foreign policy (following a long absence from world affairs) towards indirect political involvement with a particular focus on the Middle Eastern region. The second change (from the 1970s until 1990) is distinguished by the gradual militarisation of US foreign policy. This is indicated by the use of specific regional states as US regional proxies; thus 'Saudi Arabia, Iran in the beginning and then Iraq (in place of Iran)' were praised as 'protectors of the US vital interests in the Gulf'. The third change in US foreign policy was marked by the collapse of the USSR. Direct political intervention by the US in the Middle East *vis-a-vis* Gulf War II, and US use of force alongside its interactions with such non-state actors as the Iraqi Kurds, signalled a new era on the stage of international politics linked to the impressive impact of such developments on US foreign policy. Clinton's era, the fourth shift in US foreign policy, focused on US containment of both state actors *vis-a-vis* the Iraq Liberation Act and non-state ones – namely terrorist groups – a policy continued with great zeal by George W. Bush who was responsible for the last change in US foreign policy. This direct interventionist policy of the US rather than a limited use of force, along with Bush's National Security Directive for implementing the nationalistic objectives of US foreign policy in the Middle East, has overtaken the humanitarian foreign policy discourse of the United States, cited in Charountaki, *The Kurds and US Foreign Policy*, op. cit., pp. 102–103.

13. Secretary of Defense Dick Cheney, House of Foreign Affairs Committee, *Hearing*, 'President's FY '92 Security Assistance Request' (19 March 1991), Nathan K. Miller, *Report* (August 2008), published in Charountaki, *The Kurds and US Foreign Policy*, op. cit.

14. *Baghdad Domestic Service* (18 June 1990), Reuters (2 April 1990) in Mitchell Bard, 'The Gulf War', http://www.jewishvirtuallibrary.org/ jsource/History/Gulf_War.html (last accessed 2008).

15. Former Secretary of State, James Baker, expressed US concerns: 'The administration was alarmed by Saddam's rhetoric about fire eating up Israel, and by the development of binary chemical weapons (1 April 1990) by Iraqi scientists that were matched only by those of the United States and the Soviet Union and would be used against anyone who threatens Iraq, including Israel if it attempted to do anything against Iraq. The US administration had concluded that Saddam's behavior was becoming abhorrent and therefore began to have internal debates about modulating our policy of trying to moderate Iraq ... At that point we got tougher with him ... and embarked on a policy of trying to moderate his behaviour. The intention was to engage him politically and economically and, in effect, bring Iraq into the community of responsible nations' in James Baker, 'Interview with James Baker: Oral History', *PBS* http://www.pbs.org/wgbh/ pages/frontline/gulf/oral/baker/4.html (last accessed September 2017).

16. Charountaki, *The Kurds and US Foreign Policy*, op. cit., p. 151.

17. John Calabrese, 'Turkey and Iran: Limits of a Stable Relationship', *British Journal of Middle Eastern Studies*, Vol. 25, No. 1 (May 1998), p. 88.

18. Ali Khedery, 'Iran's Shia militias are running amok in Iraq' (19/02/2015) in *Foreign Policy*, http://foreignpolicy.com/2015/02/19/irans-shiite-militias- are-running-amok-in-iraq/ (last accessed June 2015).

19. *Washington Post* (29/11/1992), in 'Chronology', *Middle East Journal*, Vol. 47, No. 2, p. 316.

20. Hossein S. Seifzadeh, 'The Landscape of Factional Politics and Its Future in Iran', *Middle East Journal*, Vol. 57, No. 1 (Winter 2003), p. 58.

21. Jahangir Amuzegar, 'Iran's Economy and the US Sanctions', *Middle East Journal* Vol. 51, No. 2 (Spring 1997), pp. 185, 188.

22. *New York Times* (27/12/1992), in 'Chronology', *Middle East Journal*, Vol. 47, No. 2, p. 317.

23. In the 1990s there is a turn from Khomeini's discourse replaced by new slogans of economic prosperity and privatization programs announced for over 400 companies, cited in Maryam, Panah, *The Islamic Republic and the World*, op. cit., p. 133.

24. Interview by the researcher with Dr. Ata'ollah Mohajerani, former Iranian Minister (London, 11/03/2015).

25. Hossein S. Seifzadeh, 'The Landscape of Factional Politics and Its Future in Iran', *Middle East Journal*, op. cit., p. 61.

26. Shahram Chubin, 'Whiter Iran? Reform, Domestic Politics and National Security', *Adelphi Paper* (The International Institute for Strategic Studies, 2002), p. 91.

27. Ruhi K. Ramazani, 'The Shifting Premise of Iran's Foreign Policy: towards a Democratic Peace?' *Middle East Journal*, Vol. 52, No. 2 (Spring 1998), pp. 177, 184.

28. Stephen F. Larrabee, 'Turkey Rediscovers the Middle East', *Foreign Affairs*, Vol. 86, No. 4 (July/August 2007), p. 103.

29. *Washington Post* (12/02/1992), in 'Chronology', *Middle East Journal*, Vol. 46, No. 3, p. 498.

30. *Financial Times* (4/12/1992), in 'Chronology', *Middle East Journal*, Vol. 47, No. 2, p. 316.

31. *Financial Times* (6/03/1992), in 'Chronology', *Middle East Journal*, Vol. 46, No. 3, p. 498.

32. Gareth M. Winrow, Chapter 4: 'Azerbaijan and Iran', in *Regional Power Rivalries in the New Eurasia: Russia, Turkey and Iran* (Armonk, New York, 1995), p. 97.

33. Foreign Broadcast Information Service (3/05/1989), in 'Chronology', *Middle East Journal*, Vol. 45, No. 4, p. 653.

34. Foreign Broadcast Information Service in (27/02/1990), 'Chronology', *Middle East Journal*, Vol. 44, No. 3, p. 474.

35. *Financial Times* (15/09/1992), in 'Chronology', *Middle East Journal*, Vol. 47, No. 1, p. 111.

36. Foreign Broadcast Information Service (19/10/1992), in 'Chronology', *Middle East Journal*, Vol. 47, No. 2, p. 322.

37. National Security Archive, Document 17: 'Department of State, Office of the Secretary Delegation Cable from George P. Shultz to the Department of State: Secretary's May 10 Meeting with Iraqi Foreign Minister Tariq Aziz', No: 04218 (11 May 1983), George Washington University, in http://www.gwu.edu/~nsarchiv/NSAEBB/NSAEBB82/index.htm (last accessed April, 2015).

38. *Washington Post* (01/05/1990), in 'Chronology', *Middle East Journal*, Vol. 44, No. 4, p. 679.

39. Foreign Broadcast Information Service (11/02/1992) and 'Velayati would mediate between Armenia and Azerbaijan cause of Nagorno Karabakh' (24/02/1992), in 'Chronology', *Middle East Journal*, Vol. 46, No. 3, p. 488.

40. Foreign Broadcast Information Service (18/02/1992), in 'Chronology', *Middle East Journal*, Vol. 46, No. 3, p. 482.

41. 'The Jerusalem Post reported that Turkey's *charge d'affaires*, Ekrem Guvendiren, met with Israeli foreign minister Moshe Arens in Jerusalem. It was the first public meeting between Israeli and Turkish officials in 10 years', cited in Foreign Broadcast Information Service (09/05/1990) in 'Chronology', *Middle East Journal*, Vol. 44, No. 4, p. 679,

42. *Washington Post* (7/02/1992), in 'Chronology', *Middle East Journal*, Vol. 46, No. 3, p. 488.

43. *New York Times* (13/02/1992), in 'Chronology', *Middle East Journal*, Vol. 46, No. 3, p. 488.

44. Trita Parsi, *Treacherous Alliance: the Secret Dealings of Israel, Iran and the US* (Yale University Press, 2007), p. 230.

45. Roya Hakakian, 'The Verdict on Mykonos – and the Future of Iran', Foreign Policy Research Institute (December 2012) in http://www.fpri.

org/articles/2012/12/verdict-mykonos-and-future-iran (last accessed June 2015).

46. 'The Damascus Declaration was a plan signed on the 6th March in Damascus calling for the formation of an Arab security force to replace allied forces in Kuwait. The force was to include Egyptian and Syrian forces', *Financial Times* (18/06/1991) cited in 'Chronology', *Middle East Journal*, Vol. 45, No. 4, p. 659.

47. Interview by the researcher with Nechirvan Barzani, Prime Minister of KRG (Erbil, 23 April 2007).

48. Daniel Pipes, "Iraq's weapons and the road to war", *New York Post* (3 June 2003).

49. Interview by the researcher with Massoud Barzani, former President of KRG and KDP Iraq (Salahaddin, 23 June 2007).

50. President George H. W. Bush, White House Briefing, Press Conference, *Untitled Document*, No 28/4/2549 (16 April 1991), http://bushlibrary. tamu.edu/research/public_papers.php?year=1991&month=4 (last accessed March 2009), pp. 378–385.

51. Secretary of Defense Dick Cheney, House of Foreign Affairs Committee, *Hearing*, 'President's FY '92 Security Assistance Request' (19 March 1991); Nathan K. Miller, *Report* (August 2008), Unpublished.

52. George H. W. Bush, White House Briefing, Press Conference (16 April 1991) in http://bushlibrary.tamu.edu/research/public_papers.php? year=1991&month=4 (last accessed March 2009).

53. *PBS*, 'Interview with James Baker' in http://www.pbs.org/wgbh/pages/ frontline/gulf/oral/baker/4.html (last accessed December 2015).

54. Gulf War II has been extensively analysed in Charountaki, *The Kurds and US Foreign Policy*, op. cit., pp. 93, 95.

55. Yüksel Taşkın, 'Turkey's Search for Regional Power', *MERIP* (21/08/2010) http://www.merip.org/mero/mero082110.html#_edn7 (last accessed January 2016).

56. Robert Olson, *Turkish–Iran Relations 1979–2004 Revolution, Ideology, War, Coups and Geopolitics* (California: Mazda Publishers, 2004), p. 14.

57. Calabrese, 'Turkey and Iran: Limits of a Stable Relationship', op. cit., p. 84.

58. *Financial Times* (24/09/1996), in 'Chronology', *Middle East Journal*, Vol. 51, No. 1 (Winter 1997), p. 102.

59. Hasan Kösebalaban, *Turkish foreign policy: Islam, nationalism, and globalization* (Palgrave Macmillan, 2011), p. 134.

60. Murat Karayılan, op. cit., p. 313.

61. Ibid., p. 223.

62. Murat Karayılan, *Η Ανατομία του Πολέμου στο Κουρδιστάν* (*Bir Savaşın Anatomisi, Anatomy of a War*) (Infognomon, 2012), p. 314. In 1993 for instance 'Turkey received close to $500 million in military assistance from the US' in Maryam, Elahi, 'Washington Watch: Clinton, Ankara

and Kurdish Human Rights', *Middle East Report*, No. 189 (July–August 1994), pp. 22–23.

63. Interview by the researcher with Osman Aşkın Bak, former Co-Chairman of Turkey–Iran Parliamentary Friendship Group (Ankara, 28/03/2013).

64. Jerry Gray, 'Foreigners Investing In Libya or in Iran Face US Sanctions', *New York Times* (24/07/1996) in http://www.nytimes.com/1996/07/24/world/foreigners-investing-in-libya-or-in-iran-face-us-sanctions.html (last accessed June 2015).

65. Javad Moeinaddini and Mahin Rezapour, 'Iran's Regional Power and Prominence in the Context of International System', *The Iranian Journal of International Affairs*, Vol. 20, No. 3 (Summer 2008), p. 102.

66. Shireen T. Hunter, *Iran's Foreign Policy in the Post-Soviet Era: Resisting the New International Order* (Praeger, 2010), p. 53.

67. Kenneth Katzman, 'Iran Current Developments and US Policy', *Congressional Research Service Report* (25 April 2003), in http://fpc.state.gov/documents/organization/20242.pdf (last accessed April 2015), p. 10.

68. More information on US foreign policy toward the Middle East in Marianna Charountaki, *The Kurds and US Foreign Policy*, op. cit., p. 96.

69. *New York Times* (13/02/1992), in 'Chronology', *Middle East Journal*, Vol. 46, No. 3, p. 488.

70. *Washington Post* (11/03/1992), in ibid.

71. Daphne McCurdy, 'Turkish–Iranian Relations: When Opposites Attract', *Turkish Policy Quarterly*, Vol. 7, No. 2 (Summer 2008), p. 89. Anthony H. Cordesman, Bryan H. Gold, Shelala Robert and Michael Gibbs, 'US and Iranian Strategic Competition: Turkey and the South Caucasus' (6 February 2013), CIS, p. 37. Also Kaya, Karen, *Turkey–Iran Relations after the Arab Spring* (FMSO, Department of the Army, Department of Defense) in http://fmso.leavenworth.army.mil/documents/Turkey-Iran.pdf (last accessed April 2015), p. 3.

72. *New York Times* (13/08/1996), in 'Chronology', *Middle East Journal*, Vol. 51, No. 1 (Winter 1997), p. 101.

73. Alvon Z. Rubinstein and Oles M. Smolansky, *Regional Power Rivalries in the New Eurasia: Russia, Turkey and Iran* (Armonk, New York, 1995), pp. 37, 38.

74. From 1989 to 1992 64 per cent of Iran's arms imports were from Russia (40 MiG-29s, Su-24s, 3 submarines, armor, artillery, sea mines and others), cited in Gareth, M. Winrow, Chapter 4 'Azerbaijan and Iran', *Regional Power Rivalries in the New Eurasia*, op. cit., p. 106.

75. Stephen J. Flanagan, 'The Turkey–Russia–Iran Nexus: Eurasian Power Dynamics', *The Washington Quarterly* (Winter 2013) in http://csis.org/files/publication/TWQ_13Winter_Flanagan.pdf (last accessed December 2015).

76. In June 1995 the Speaker of the Majlis in Iran told the Deputy Chairman of the Duma, Alexander Vengerovsky, in an official visit that the 'two strategic states of Iran and Russia can limit the expansion of US

hegemony in the region'. Russia could be hoping to use the Iranian card for access to the Persian Gulf and for curbing the possibility of anti-Russian action from extremist forces not only in Iran but also in Central Asia and the Caucasus, cited in Jahangir, Amuzegar, 'Iran's Economy and the US Sanctions', *Middle East Journal*, op. cit., p. 208.

77. Alvin Z. Rubinstein, *Regional Power Rivalries in the New Eurasia*, op. cit., p. 20.

78. Lena Jonson, Chapter 2: 'The New Geopolitical Situation in the Caspian Region', *The Security of the Caspian Sea Region* (Oxford University Press, 2001), p. 19.

79. 'Israel signed agreement with Turkey (December, 5th) to modernize 54 of Turkey's F-4 warplanes for $600 million', Foreign Broadcast Information Service (09/12/1996) in 'Chronology', *Middle East Journal*, Vol. 51, No. 2 (Spring 1997), p. 264.

80. Foreign Broadcast Information Service (06/12/1996) in ibid., p. 269.

81. Foreign Broadcast Information Service (07/10/1997), in 'Chronology', *Middle East Journal*, Vol. 52, No. 1 (Winter 1998), p. 101.

82. Gedalyah Reback, 'Activist Urges Israel to Raise Kurdistan as Ally against Iran', Israel National News (20/04/2015), in http://www.israelnational news.com/News/News.aspx/194319#.VXnLTfmqqkq (last accessed June 2015).

83. Marianna Charountaki, 'Kurdish policies in Syria under the Arab Uprisings: A Revisiting of IR in the New Middle Eastern Order', *Third World Quarterly*, Vol. 36, No. 2 (27 March 2015), p. 348.

84. Murat Karayılan, op. cit., p. 190.

85. Marianna Charountaki, 'Turkish Foreign Policy and the Kurdistan Regional Government', *Perceptions: Journal of International Affairs*, Volume XVII, No. 4, Center for Strategic Research (Winter 2012), pp. 187–188.

86. Marianna Charountaki, *The Kurds and US Foreign Policy*, op. cit., p. 152.

87. Foreign Broadcast Information Service (29/10/1993) in 'Chronology', *Middle East Journal*, Vol. 28, No. 2, p. 352.

88. *Financial Times* (18/07/1991), in 'Chronology', *Middle East Journal*, Vol. 45, No. 1, p. 123.

89. *Financial Times* (18/09/1991) in 'Chronology', *Middle East Journal*, Vol. 46, No. 1, p. 95.

90. Foreign Broadcast Information Service (7/04/1992), in 'Chronology', *Middle East Journal*, Vol. 46, No. 3, p. 499.

91. *New York Times* (19/09/1996) in 'Chronology', *Middle East Journal*, Vol. 51, No. 1 (Winter 1997), p. 111.

92. Murat, Karayılan, op. cit., p. 187.

93. Foreign Broadcast Information Service (13/10/1995), in 'Chronology', *Middle East Journal*, Vol. 50, No. 1 (Winter 1996), p. 103.

94. 'Kurdish leaders, Talabani and Barzani, accuse Iran, Turkey and Syria of aiding Kurdish rebels of Turkey in North Iraq', *Washington Post* (2/11/1992) in 'Chronology', *Middle East Journal*, Vol. 47, No. 2, p. 323.

95. Murat Karayılan, op. cit., p. 313.
96. *New York Times* (20/01/1993), in 'Chronology', *Middle East Journal*, Vol. 47, No. 3, p. 488.
97. Foreign Broadcast Information Service (10/02/ 1993) in 'Chronology', *Middle East Journal*, Vol. 46, No. 3, p. 489.
98. David Menashri, *Post-revolutionary Politics in Iran: Religion, Society and Power* (Frank Cass Publishers, 2001), p. 113.
99. Foreign Broadcast Information Service (21/12/1994), in 'Chronology', *Middle East Journal*, Vol. 48, No. 2, p. 338.
100. Foreign Broadcast Information Service (29/10/1996), in 'Chronology', *Middle East Journal*, Vol. 51, No. 2 (Spring 1997), p. 262.
101. Marianna Charountaki, *The Kurds and US Foreign Policy*, op. cit., 173.
102. 'In July/August 1997 PKK–PUK was against KDP and Iran–Syria Cooperation Agreement', Foreign Broadcast Information Service (25/2/1997), in 'Chronology', *Middle East Journal*, Vol. 51, No. 3 (Summer 1997), p. 423.
103. Interview by the author with Reza Altun, Co-founder of PKK, Executive member of KCK (Qandil, 20/03/2014).
104. Interview by the author with a high level political figure in Iranian politics (London, 17/06/2013).
105. 'Kurdish Identity Determining Factor in Turkey's Relations with Iran', cited in Jülide, Karakoç, 'The Impact of the Kurdish Identity on Turkey's Foreign Policy from the 1980s to 2008', *Middle Eastern Studies*, Vol. 46, No. 6 (November 2010), p. 922.
106. Karen Kaya, *Turkey–Iran Relations after the Arab Spring*, op. cit., p. 4.
107. Kösebalaban, *Turkish Foreign Policy*, op. cit., p. 22.
108. Murat Karayılan, op. cit., pp. 285, 359, 360.
109. 'PM of Syria and Turkey agreed (20/01/1993) to renegotiate 1987 convention regulating the control of the Euphrates River waters and produce a more satisfactory agreement. Syria claimed it was not receiving enough water to meet its basic needs. Turkey dismissed Syrian concerns [and] planned to launch a large irrigation project in May 1993 that would reduce the Euphrates River waters downstream', Foreign Broadcast Information Service (21/1/1993), Vol. 47, No. 3, p. 488.
110. Madeleine K. Albright, 'Remarks before the American-Iranian Council', US State Department (17 March 2000) in http://1997-2001.state.gov/www/statements/2000/000317a.html (last accessed April 2015).
111. *New York Times* (18/061998), in 'Chronology', *Middle East Journal*, Vol. 52, No. 4 (Autumn 1998), p. 593.
112. Foreign Broadcast Information Service (15/09/1998), in 'Chronology', *Middle East Journal*, Vol. 53 No. 1 (Winter 1999), p. 103.
113. *Financial Times* (10/08/1998), in ibid., p. 101.
114. *Financial Times* (22/1/1999), in 'Chronology', *Middle East Journal*, Vol. 53, No. 3 (Summer 1999), p. 453.
115. Tom Lansford, *Political Handbook of the World 2014* (Sage, 2014), p. 675.

116. Alan Makovsky, 'The New Activism in Turkish Foreign Policy', *SAIS Review*, Vol. 19, No. 1 (Washington DC: The Johns Hopkins University Press for the School of Advanced International Studies, 1999), p. 109.

117. Dana Bauer (Deputy Director of the Office of Southern Europe), 'US officials speak on Turkey and the Kurdish Question', US Information Service (ed.), Dr. Karl Renner Institute (Austria, 6 July 1998), 'On the Way to Europe: the Future of the Kurdish Question for Turkey and its Neighbours', http://www.mtholyoke.edu/acad/intrel/kurdtur.htm (last accessed April 2016), p. 5.

118. Ibid., p. 108.

119. 'In 1995 US military aid to Turkey was said to be up to US$350 million'; see James Ciment, 'Issues, Tactics and Negotiations', *The Kurds: State and Minority in Turkey, Iraq and Iran* (New York: Barnes and Noble, 1996), p. 156.

120. *New York Times* (8/04/1999), in 'Chronology', *Middle East Journal*, Vol. 53, No. 3 (Summer 1999), p. 465.

121. *New York Times* (14/08/2000) in 'Chronology', *Middle East Journal*, Vol. 54, No. 1 (Winter 2000), p. 103.

122. According to State Department spokesman Tom Casey, 'We certainly do not think that unilateral military action from Turkey or any place else in Iraq would solve anything'; see Ümit Enginsoy, 'US once again warns against Turkish military action inside Iraq', *Turkish Daily News* (26 May 2007), http://www.turkishdailynews.com.tr/article.php?enewsid=74230 (last accessed April 2015); Condoleezza Rice reportedly said that 'the Turks should not engage in over the border intervention. We have warned that responding in this way will affect the stability of the region.' see article: 'Rice warns: Turkey should not intervene in Northern Iraq', in *Hurriyet* (25 October 2007). For further information see Marianna Charountaki, *The Kurds and US Foreign Policy*, op. cit., pp. 177, 191.

123. According to Hasan Celal Güzel, a minister serving in Prime Minister Turgut Özal's government, speaking in the 74th hearing at the Ankara 5th High Criminal Court, it was an illegal junta group that aimed to overthrow the government with the active participation of former Prime Minister and President Süleyman Demirel in http://www.todayszaman.com/anasayfa_feb-28-a-clear-military-coup-with-former-president-demirel-complicit-says-guzel_372881.html (last accessed April, 2015).

124. *Financial Times* (08/09/1998), in 'Chronology', *Middle East Journal*, Vol. 53, No. 1 (Winter 1999), p. 103.

125. 'After 40 Years, First Visit by an Israeli PM, Barak Visits Turkey' in *Washington Post* (26/10/2000), 'Chronology', *Middle East Journal*, Vol. 54, No. 2 (Spring 2000), p. 279.

126. Interview by the researcher with Massoud Barzani, former President of the KR and KDP in Iraq (Salahaddin, 23 June 2007).

127. 'The US Congress directed covert funds to the INC of US$40 million in the 1990s' stated in an interview conducted by the author with

Dr. Najmaldine O. Karim, former Governor of Kirkuk Governorate in Iraq, and Mullah Mustafa Barzani's private doctor (Washington, 8 March 2008). 'A further US$3 million was donated in 1999, and US$12 million in 2001', cited in Kenneth Katzman, 'Iraq: US Efforts to Change the Regime', *Report for Congress*, Order Code RL31339 (The Library of Congress, 16 August 2002), p. 13.

128. Charountaki, *The Kurds and US Foreign Policy*, op. cit., p. 260.

129. Savvas, Kalederidis, 'Πώς έγινε η παράδοση του Άπο', *Παράδοση Οτζαλάν: η ώρα της αλήθειας* (*'How Apo was captured'*, *The Capture of Ocalan: the Time of the Truth*) (Athens: Infognomon, 2007), p. 212.

130. Ocalan's Diary, Imrali, *Φωνή του Κουρδιστάν* (*Voice of Kurdistan*, Magazine of the National Liberation Front of Kurdistan) (Athens, 25 November 1999), pp. 26–27.

131. *Φωνή του Κουρδιστάν* (*Voice of Kurdistan*, Magazine of the National Liberation Front of Kurdistan) (Athens, March–May 2000), pp. 8–11.

132. Douran Kalkan, member of the PKK Presidential Council, quoted by DEM News Agency, in *Φωνή του Κουρδιστάν* (*Voice of Kurdistan*, Magazine of the National Liberation Front of Kurdistan) (Athens, 5 August 1999), p. 6.

133. 'United States would continue to support human rights and democratic principles in the region. America and Islam are not exclusive, and need not be in competition. Instead, they overlap and share common principles – principles of justice and progress; tolerance and the dignity of all human beings.' President Barack Obama's Middle East Speech, 'A New Beginning' (Cairo, 4/06/2009). http://www.huffingtonpost.com/2009/06/04/obamas-middle-east-speech_n_211217.html (last accessed December 2015).

134. For further information, see Marianna Charountaki Chapter 14: 'The Kurdish Factor in Turkish Politics: Impediment or Facilitator to Turkey's European Prospects?' Part Five: Politics and International Relations in *Perspectives on Kurdistan's Economy and Society in Transition* (Nova Science Publishers: New York, 2012), pp. 163–192. Translated into Kurdish (Sorani), *Wata Journal*, No. 29 (April 2013).

## CHAPTER 5   THE IRAQ WAR AND THE RISE OF NON-STATE ACTORS (2001–2010)

1. Based on the promotion of the US 'national interests' and 'sovereignty', this new doctrine targets the battle against the 'New Threats' arising within the international system. As depicted in the 'National Security Strategy' of 20 September 2002, the doctrine appeared to support the claim that the United States was 'inherently entitled to establish the conditions within which international relations should operate'. Therefore, the United States, in its traditional role, stepped up its special

mission 'to defend justice and advance freedom around the world'. The United States had thus to defeat those who helped or harboured the terrorists and therefore had to be punished. In Marianna Charountaki, *The Kurds and US Foreign Policy: International Relations in the Middle East since 1945* (Routledge, 2010), pp. 95–98.

2. 107th Congress Public Law 243, US Government Printing Office in http://www.gpo.gov/fdsys/pkg/PLAW-107publ243/html/PLAW-107publ243.htm (last accessed July 2015).

3. 'The New Containment Policy', *American Foreign Policy*, Vol. 3, No. 4 (6 November 2003).

4. National Commission on Terrorist Attacks upon the United States, 'Chapter 6: From threat to threat', *The 9/11 Commission Report*, http://www.9-11commission.gov/report/911Report.pdf (last accessed March 2009), p. 199.

5. George W. Bush Administration, National Security Presidential Directives [NSPD]-9: *Combating Terrorism* (25/10/2001), in http://www.fas.org/irp/offdocs/nspd/nspd-9.htm (last accessed July 2015).

6. George W. Bush, 'Text of Bush's act of war statement', *BBC News* (12/09/2001) in http://news.bbc.co.uk/1/hi/world/americas/1540544.stm and in http://www.whitehouse.gov/news/releases/2001/09/20010912–14.html (last accessed February 2016).

7. See Charountaki, Chapter 7, *The Kurds and US Foreign Policy*, op. cit., pp. 187, 199.

8. From the President's Deputy Assistant for National Security Affairs (Al Haig) to the President's Assistant for National Security Affairs (Henry Kissinger), Memorandum, 'Kurdish Problem' (28/07/1972), http://www.state.gov/r/pa/ho/frus/nixon/e4/71903.htm (last accessed March 2009).

9. Interview by the researcher with Mohsin Dizayee, Massoud Barzani's Special Envoy (Salahaddin, 13 June 2007).

10. US State Department, '*Foreign Relations*, 1969–1972, Volume E-4, Iran and Iraq' in http://2001-2009.state.gov/r/pa/ho/frus/nixon/e4/72108.htm (last accessed July 2015).

11. Murat, Karayılan, *Η Ανατομία του Πολέμου στο Κουρδιστάν* (*Bir Savaşın Anatomisi, Anatomy of a War*) (Infognomon, 2012), p. 375.

12. Charountaki, *The Kurds and US Foreign Policy*, op. cit.

13. 'Prevailing in 12 of the country's 16 metropolitan municipalities, 46 of 65 provincial municipalities, 425 of 789 county municipalities and 1,216 of 2,250 district municipalities, the AK Parti achieved a landslide victory in the local elections' available at: http://eng.akparti.org.tr/english/index.html (last accessed October 2009).

14. It is said that Erdoğan was the choice of the US foreign policy makers in Washington as he represented a promising leadership that appeared capable of facilitating the resolution of the Kurdish issue in Turkey, hitherto opposed by the dominant Kemalist/militarist – influenced leading political elite. Analysis on Turkish reforms can be further found

in Marianna Charountaki 'The Kurdish factor in Turkish politics: impediment or facilitator to Turkey's European prospects?' Chapter 14, Part Five: Politics and International Relations in *Perspectives on Kurdistan's Economy and Society in Transition* (Nova Science Publishers: New York, September 2012), pp. 163–192. Translated in Kurdish (Sorani), *Wata Journal*, No. 29 (April 2013).

15. 'Turkey will not go down in history as a country of *coup d' états*, be assured of that', 'Erdoğan: era of *coup d'états* closed in Turkey', *Today's Zaman* (1/10/2007).

16. Keynote Address by H.E. İbrahim Kalın, Annual Conference on Turkey 2015 in SETA DC (01/06/2015) https://www.youtube.com/watch?v=vOSfMdjyja8&list=PLFsiqhkioRXqhFBDrINRtvUqzZ2sQ2ea4 (last accessed January 2016).

17. 'Los principios fundadores de nuestro Partido de Justicia y Desarrollo es que no se basa en la religión. Tiene una identidad conservadora y demócrata', in Recep Tayyip Erdoğan, Interview: 'Si Turquía entra en la UE, el mundo musulmán cambiará su visión de Europa', *El País* (19/10/2003), p. 6.

18. Recep Tayyip Erdoğan, 'Keynote Speech at International Symposium on Conservatism and Democracy' (AK Parti 2004) cited in Ahmet Kuru, 'From Islamism to Conservative Democracy: the Justice and Development Party in Turkey', paper presentation at the Annual Meeting of the American Political Science Association, http://www.allacademic.com/meta/p151181_index.html (31/08/2006) (last accessed January 2016).

19. 'The most dominant Islamic groups involved in the formation of political parties acting as lobbies within the Turkish society since the late 1960s have been the Naksibendis and Nurcus orders. From the latter, the Yeni Asya (New Asia) group supportive of democracy and the Fethullahcis headed by Fethullah Giilen have also emerged. There also exist the Moderate Islamists, intellectuals who are in favour of an Islamic order via political struggle. On the other hand, Moderate Secularists do recognize the significance of religion for the people, whilst the radical ones are proponents of the supremacy of the state over the citizenship.' See Heper, *Islam and Democracy in Turkey*, op. cit., pp. 39–41. Cizre adds to Turkey's Islamist groups, "business associations, trade unions, human rights associations and independent small organizations such as journals and foundations". Cf. Cizre, *Secular and Islamic politics in Turkey*, p. 25.

20. Emin Yaşar Demirci, *Modernisation Religion and Politics in Turkey: the case of the İskenderpaşa Community* (Istanbul: Insan publications 2008), p. 14.

21. Recep Tayyip Erdoğan, 'We are not rooted in religion: PM', op. cit.

22. Angel Rabasa, and F. Stephen Larrabee, *The rise of political Islam in Turkey* (RAND, National Defense Research Institute, 2008), p. 13.

23. Iran's Reformist President stated that he would not negotiate with the US and asked his supporters to abide by the Ayatollah Ali Khamenei's policies in BBC (30 May 2001) cited in 'Chronology', *Middle East Journal*,

Vol. 56, No. 4 (Autumn 2002), p. 690. On 17 September 2002 the conflict between Khatami and other Reformists as well as the conservative Islamic element in Iran was incited by the President's announcement that hard-liners were aimed to stymie his reform program in RU (Reuters), in 'Chronology', *Middle East Journal*, Vol. 57, No. 1 (Winter 2003), p. 139.

24. Bob Woodward, *State of Denial* (Simon & Schuster: 2006), pp. 84–85 in Joyce Battle, 'THE IRAQ WAR – PART I: The US Prepares for Conflict', 2001 *National Security Archive* Electronic Briefing Book No. 326, Timeline, p. 17 in http://nsarchive.gwu.edu/NSAEBB/NSAEBB326/IraqWarPart1-Timeline.pdf (last accessed February 2016).
25. For more info on the US foreign policy towards Iraq see Charountaki, *The Kurds and US Foreign Policy*, op. cit.
26. The National Security Archive, 'Declassified Studies from Cheney Pentagon Show Push for U.S. Military Predominance and a Strategy to "Prevent the Re-emergence of a New Rival"' (26/02/2008) in http://nsarchive.gwu.edu/nukevault/ebb245/ (last accessed July 2015). Further info, see Charountaki, *The Kurds and US Foreign Policy*, op. cit., p. 151.
27. Its key points are: 'to prevent the emergence of a rival superpower, safeguard US interests and promote American values, address sources of regional conflict and instability in such a way as to promote increasing respect for international law, limit international violence, and encourage the spread of democratic forms of government and open economic systems' in 'The number one objective of U.S. post-Cold War political and military strategy should be preventing the emergence of a rival superpower', http://www.pbs.org/wgbh/pages/frontline/shows/iraq/etc/wolf.html (last accessed July 2015).
28. Wesley Clark, former NATO Supreme Allied Commander, Europe 1997–2000, http://fora.tv/2007/10/03/Wesley_Clark_A_Time_to_Lead/Wesley_Clark_on_America_s_Foreign_Policy__Coup_ (last accessed July 2015).
29. Joyce Battle, 'THE IRAQ WAR – PART I: The US Prepares for Conflict, 2001', *National Security Archive Electronic Briefing Book*, No. 326, p. 12 in http://nsarchive.gwu.edu/NSAEBB/NSAEBB326/IraqWarPart1-Timeline.pdf (last accessed February 2016).
30. 'Pentagon wants more money for war' in the online version of *Al-Jazeera* (September 2011) at http://english.aljazeera.net/News/aspx/print.htm (last accessed January 2016).
31. Ron Suskind, *The Price of Loyalty* (New York: Simon and Schuster, 2004), pp. 85–86.
32. Nicholas Lemann, 'How it came to War', *The New Yorker* (31 March 2003), p. 39.
33. Paul T. McCartney, 'American nationalism and US foreign policy from Sept 11 to the Iraq War', *Political Science Quarterly*, 119(3) (2004), p. 418.
34. *Washington Post* (26/12/2002), in 'Chronology', *Middle East Journal*, Vol. 57, No. 2 (Spring 2003), p. 302.

35. 'In Moscow President Khatami and Vladimir Putin signed a cooperation and security agreement that would enable Russia to sell conventional weapons to Iran' in Robin Wright, *The Iran Primer: Power, Politics and the US policy* (The US Institute of Peace, November 2010), p. 235. The Presidents of Iran and China (Jiang Zemin) signed six cooperation agreements marking the first time a Chinese leader visited Iran since the 1979 revolution in BBC (20/04/2001), cited in *Middle East Journal*, Vol. 56, No. 4 (Autumn 2002), p. 689.
36. 'Iran's Judiciary Chief Ayatollah Mahmoud Hashemi Shahroudi visit to Syria' (14/07/2002) in, *Middle East Journal*, Vol. 56, No. 4 (Autumn 2002), pp. 690–691.
37. Joshua W. Walker, 'Re-examining the US–Turkish alliance', *The Washington Quarterly* (Winter 2007–2008), p. 96.
38. 'Iran: Regional Perspectives and US Policy', Congressional Research Service, Order No. R40849 (13 January 2010), p. 30.
39. 'Iran is an important reason for the success of the Bonn Conference that was convened in 2001 to decide Afghanistan's future' in Vali Nasr, *The dispensable nation: American foreign policy in retreat*, First Anchor Books Edition (2013), p. 100.
40. Kenneth Katzman and James Nichol, 'Iran: Relations with key central Asian states', CRS Report for Congress (23/07/1998), p. 123.
41. BBC (04/09/2002), 'Chronology', *Middle East Journal*, Vol. 57, No. 1 (Winter 2003), p. 146.
42. *New York Times* (25 December 2002), 'Chronology', *Middle East Journal*, Vol. 57, No. 2 (Spring 2003), p. 306.
43. *Washington Post* (10/01/2003), 'Chronology', *Middle East Journal*, Vol. 57, No. 2 (Spring 2003), p. 307.
44. 'IAEA found nothing serious at Iran site: ElBaradei', *Reuters* (5/11/2009) in http://www.reuters.com/article/2009/11/05/us-iran-nuclear-elbaradei-idUSTRE5A13KW20091105 (last accessed July 2015).
45. *Washington Post* (28-29/12/2002), 'Chronology', *Middle East Journal*, Vol. 57, No. 2 (Spring 2003), p. 316.
46. *New York Times* (19/02/2003), 'Chronology', *Middle East Journal*, Vol. 57, No. 3 (Summer 2003), p. 488.
47. *Financial Times* (11/04/2003), ibid., p. 483.
48. Arabic News (13/08/2004), 'Chronology', *Middle East Journal*, Vol. 58, No. 1 (Winter 2004), p. 121.
49. Interview by the researcher with Dr. Aykan Erdemir, CHP Cumhuriyet Halk Partisi – Member of the Turkish Parliament (representing Bursa) (Ankara, 2 April 2013).
50. The branches of the military, such as 'Security Forces, Intelligence, Paramilitary and Military groups –all representatives of Ataturk's nationalistic ideology' are known in Ankara as the 'deep state', and have been particularly powerful in Turkish politics as the guardians of the six principles of Mustafa Kemal on which the state is founded;

see John Tirman, 'The trouble with Turkey', *The Boston Globe* (30 November 2005).

51. Interview with Dr. Aykan Erdemir, op. cit.
52. 'Bashar submitted a list of six proposals to Israel through Turkey which set the basis for direct talks between the two' in *BBC* (04/09/2008).
53. 'Israel ready to return Golan', *BBC* (23/04/2008) in http://news.bbc.co.uk/1/hi/world/middle_east/7362937.stm (last accessed July 2015).
54. Fred H. Lawson, *Syria's Relations with Iran: Managing the Dilemmas of Alliance, Middle East Journal*, Vol. 61, No. 1 (Winter 2007), p. 35.
55. Republic of Turkey, Ministry of Foreign Affairs, 'Turkey–Syria Economic and Trade Relations', in http://www.mfa.gov.tr/turkey_s-commercial-and-economic-relations-with-syria.en.mfa (last accessed January 2016).
56. Bilal Y. Saab, 'Syria and Turkey Deepen Bilateral Relations', Brookings (06/052009) in http://www.brookings.edu/research/articles/2009/05/06-syria-turkey-saab (last accessed July 2015).
57. 'Turkey, Syria renew diplomatic pledges', *Hürriyet Daily News* (12/21/2010).
58. 'Iran and Syria sign pact against "common threats"', The *Daily Star* (16/06/2006) in http://www.dailystar.com.lb/News/Middle-East/2006/Jun-16/72583-iran-and-syria-sign-pact-againstcommon-threats.ashx (last accessed July 2015).
59. See Charountaki, *The Kurds and US Foreign Policy*, op. cit., p. 232.
60. 'Iran sanctions 'depend on proof'', *BBC* (21/04/2006) in http://news.bbc.co.uk/1/hi/world/middle_east/4929450.stm (last accessed July 2015).
61. The Iranian ambassador in Ankara stated that Turkey, Iran and Syria should follow a joint policy on the Kurdish issue: in Gordon H. Philip and Taşpınar Ömer, *Winning Turkey, How America, Europe, and Turkey Can Revive a Fading Partnership* (Washington: Brooking Institution Press, 2008), pp. 55–56.
62. Charountaki, *The Kurds and US Foreign Policy*, op. cit., pp. 201–202.
63. Interview by researcher with Massoud Barzani, former President of the Kurdistan Region in Iraq. (Salahaddin, 23 June 2007).
64. 'President Barzani meets Turkey's Prime Minister and Foreign Minister in Ankara', KRG.org (4/06/2010), http://www.krg.org/articles/detail.asp?rnr=223&lngnr=12&smap=02010100&anr=35401 (last accessed June, 2010).
65. The meeting was with Ilnur Cevik the Chief of MIT (Turkish National Intelligence Organization), in Salahaddin; see 'MIT boss secretly visited Barzani in Erbil', *The New Anatolian* (23 November 2005).
66. Marianna Charountaki, 'Turkish foreign policy and the Kurdistan Regional Government', *Perceptions: Journal of International* Affairs, Volume XVII, No. 4 (Center for Strategic Research, Winter 2012), p. 191.
67. This involved a nationalist terrorist organisation determined to overthrow the established political structure. The current and retired members of the Turkish military were detained for suspected connections to the 'Balyoz'

(Sledgehammer) Operation, an alleged military coup plan against the ruling Justice and Development Party, written in 2003 and brought to light by the daily Taraf in January.

68. Charountaki, 'Turkish foreign policy and the Kurdistan Regional Government', op. cit., p. 192.
69. Ibid., p. 193.
70. Ibid.
71. *New York Times* (12/03/2008), 'Chronology', *Middle East Journal*, Vol. 62, No. 3 (Summer 2008), p. 512.
72. *New York Times* (09/06/2008), 'Chronology', *Middle East Journal*, Vol. 62, No. 4 (Autumn 2008), p. 680.
73. *Washington Post* (15/08//2007), 'Chronology', *Middle East Journal*, Vol. 61, No. 4 (Autumn 2007), p. 692.
74. 'Syria signed a multi-billion dollar agreement with Tehran that would guarantee 105 billion cubic feet of oil to Syria annually, starting in 2009' in Middle East Online (10/10/2007), 'Chronology', *Middle East Journal*, Vol. 62, No. 1 (Winter 2008), p. 124.
75. Radio Free Europe –Radio Liberty (17/02/2009), 'Chronology', *Middle East Journal*, Vol. 63, No. 3 (Summer 2009), pp. 473–474.
76. The People's Labour Party (Halkin Emek Partisi, HEP) formed in 1989 which won the October 1991 elections was outlawed by the State Security Court as a separatist party (15 July 1993) and its members were charged for crimes against the state (Article 125). Its successor, the Democracy Party (DEP, 05/1993–16/06/1994), which was formed by members of HEP, supported political and cultural rights for the Kurds, but because the MPs in the People's Democracy Party (HADEP), which replaced DEP in 1994, took the parliamentary oath in Kurdish. HADEP met the same fate as the PKK extension. Finally, another Kurdish party, the Democracy People's Party (DEHAP, 24 October 1997) merged with the Democratic Society Party (DTP, 17 August 2005) founded by Leyla Zana; the case against its ban by the country's Constitutional court, since it was also accused of affiliation with the PKK, resulted in its closure (11 December 2009) and its replacement by BDP (Baris ve Demokrasi Partisi). In 2012 the Peoples' Democratic Party (Halkların Demokratik Partisi, HDP), was formed in Turkey acting as the fraternal party to pro-Kurdish Democratic Regions Party (BDP).
77. The seventh PKK congress (20 January 2000), which decided to politicise the struggle, has been of major importance given that most of its recommendations were reflected in Turkey's 2004 reforms. The PKK's political transformation into KADEK (Kongreya Azadi u Demokrasiya Kurdistan–Kurdistan Freedom and Democracy Congress in April 2002), and a year later into KGK (2003), in connection with replacing the committee as a decision-making body with an assembly, not only signifies the movement's shift towards a legal means of struggle but also stands out as a major adjustment in the PKK's ideological discourse and

practice. Instead, Ankara perceived this transformation merely as a change prompted by the need to continue the movement despite its classification as a terrorist organisation by both the European Union (May 2002) and the United States (January 2004).

78. Interview by the author with Reza Altun, co-founder of PKK, executive member of KCK (Qandil, 20 March 2014).

79. 'The Obama administration declared the PJAK on 4 February 2009 as a terrorist organization' in Ertuğrul Mavioğlu, *Radikal* (31/10/2010) 'Interview with Murat Karayılan', http://www.reuters.com/article/2009/02/04/idUSN04297671 (last accessed July 2011).

80. Interview by the author with Reza Altun, co-founder of PKK, executive member of KCK (Qandil, 20 March 2014).

81. Ibid.

82. Stephen J. Flanagan, 'Drivers and Strategy in Turkey, Russia, Iran Economic and Energy Relations' (Center for Strategic and International Studies, 29/03/2012) in http://csis.org/files/attachments/120529_Flanagan_TRI_Economic_EnergyDimensions.pdf, pp. 2, 7 (last accessed January 2016).

83. Republic of Turkey, Ministry of Foreign Affairs, 'Turkey–Iran Economic and Trade Relations' in http://www.mfa.gov.tr/turkey_s-commercial-and-economic-relations-with-iran.en.mfa (last accessed July 2015).

84. Stephen J. Flanagan, *Drivers and Strategy in Turkey, Russia, Iran*, op. cit, p. 6.

85. Ibid., p. 5.

86. Ibid.

87. 'Marmara University and the Iranian Consulate in Istanbul arranged an Iran-Turkey Cultural Relations Conference in 2009 (IRNA, January 19, 2009) and on March 1 2009 Turkish Minister of Transportation Binali Yildirim visited Tehran and signed a memorandum of understanding to improve the transportation routes between the two countries (CNNTurk)' in Emrullah Uslu, 'Turkey–Iran Relations: A Trade Partnership or a Gateway for Iran to Escape International Sanctions?', *Eurasia Daily Monitor*, Vol. 6, No. 41 (3 March 2009).

88. 'Iran, Turkish firm in EUR1b gas link deal', *Khaleej Times* (24 July 2010) in http://imra.org.il/story.php3?id=48830 (last accessed July 2015).

89. David Pupkin, 'Iran–Turkey Economic Relations: What Their Rapid Growth Means for Iran's Nuclear Program', *Iran Tracker* (24/06/2010) in http://www.irantracker.org/analysis/iran-turkey-economic-relations-what-their-rapid-growth-means-iran%E2%80%99s-nuclear-program (last accessed July 2015).

90. Stephen J. Flanagan, *Drivers and Strategy in Turkey, Russia, Iran*, op. cit.

91. *NewsBlaze* 'Turkish–Iran Relations: Old Rivals or New Best Friends?' (7/07/2010)in http://www.alahwaz.info/en/?p=953 (last accessed January 2016).

92. BBC, 'Turkey agrees to plans for Arab 'free trade zone'' (6/10/2010) in http://www.bbc.co.uk/news/10290025 (last accessed April 2016).

93. Interview by the author with Reza Altun, co-founder of PKK, executive member of KCK (Qandil, 20/03/2014).
94. Ahmet Davutoğlu, 'The Restoration of Turkey: Strong Democracy, Dynamic Economy, and Active Diplomacy' in Center for Strategic Research (SAM), No. 7 (August 2014).
95. Ahmet Davutoğlu, 'Seminar' (George Washington University, 09/02/2012) in https://www.youtube.com/watch?v=Se6ynRCqlb4 (last accessed July 2015).
96. Akcali Emel and Mehmet Perincek, 'Kemalist Eurasianism: An Emerging Geopolitical Discourse in Turkey', *Geopolitics*, Vol. 14, No. 3 (July 2009), pp. 551, 560.
97. *International Herald Tribune* (06/06/2008), 'Chronology', *Middle East Journal*, Vol. 62, No. 4 (Autumn 2008), p. 695.
98. Younkyoo Kim and Stephen Blank, 'Turkey and Russia on Edge: Russo-Turkish Divergence: the Security Dimension', GLORIA Center (27/04/2012) in http://www.thecuttingedgenews.com/index.php?article=73149&pageid=13&pagename=Analysis (last accessed January 2016).
99. *Washington Post* (06/06//2009), 'Chronology', *Middle East Journal*, Vol. 63, No. 4 (Autumn 2009), p. 656.
100. *Washington Post* (18/09/2009), 'Chronology', *Middle East Journal*, Vol. 64, No. 1 (Winter 2010), p. 113.
101. 'Lieberman trip to South America aimed at curbing Iran influence' (20/07/2009) in http://www.haaretz.com/news/lieberman-trip-to-south-america-aimed-at-curbing-iran-influence-1.280380 (last accessed July 2015).
102. Eric Walberg, 'Turkey vs the US: A kinder Middle East hegemon', *Global Research* (21 July 2011) in http://www.globalresearch.ca/turkey-vs-the-us-a-kinder-middle-east-hegemon/25718 (last accessed January 2016).
103. Yüksel Taşkın, *Turkey's Search for Regional Power* (21 August 2010), http://www.merip. org/mero/mero082110 (last accessed January 2016).
104. 'Putin seals new Turkey gas deal', BBC (06/08/2009) in http://news.bbc.co.uk/1/hi/business/8186946.stm (last accessed July 2015).
105. Saul B. Cohen, 'Turkey's Emergence as a Geopolitical Power Broker' in *Eurasian Geography and Economics*, Vol. 52, No. 2 (2011), p. 224.
106. Stephen, J. Flanagan, 'Drivers and Strategy in Turkey, Russia, Iran economic and energy relations', CSIS (29 March 2012) in http://csis.org/files/attachments/120529_Flanagan_TRI_Economic_EnergyDimensions.pdf, pp. 2, 7 (last accessed January 2016).
107. Murat Karayılan, Interview (15/01/2013) in *Κυριακάτικη Δημοκρατία* (*Sunday Democracy* newspaper) in http://infognomonpolitics.blogspot.co.uk/2013/01/blogpost_6796.html?utm_source=feedburner&utm_medium=email&utm_campaign=Feed:+InfognomonPolitics + (Infognomon Politics)&utm_content = Yahoo!+Mail#.UP1alW82lu5 (last accessed January 2016).

108. Zaman (9/07/2010), 'Chronology', *Middle East Journal*, Vol. 64, No. 4 (Autumn 2010), p. 641.

109. 'According to this Plan, the transformation of the Arab and Muslim World for promoting American political and economic national interests in the Middle East by way of the countries in need of change became the core of US foreign policy strategy' in *Policy Perspectives*. http://www.ips. org.pk/the-muslimworld/1004-the-us-greater-middle-east-initiative.html (last accessed July 2015).

110. Extensive analysis on Obama's tenure of office in Marianna Charountaki, 'US foreign policy in theory and practice: from Soviet-era containment to the era of the Arab Uprising(s)', *American Foreign Policy Interests: The Journal of the National Committee on American Foreign Policy*, Vol. 36, Issue 4 (2014), pp. 255–267.

111. Trita Parsi, *A single roll of the dice: Obama's diplomacy with Iran* (Yale Uni Press, 2012), p. 99.

112. Ibid., pp. 58, 68, 71.

113. Ibid., p. 215.

114. Fawaz A.Gerges, *Obama and the Middle East: The End of America's Moment?* (Palgrave Macmillan, 2012), p. 91.

115. Trita Parsi, *A single roll of the dice*, op. cit., p. 65.

116. Ibid., p. 224.

117. On 27 March 2009 Obama revived America policy in defeating Al- Qaeda through his 'New Strategy for Afghanistan and Pakistan'. The so-called new strategy provisioned the deployment of another 17,000 troops and included more aid for Pakistan: in *Washington Post* (27/03/2009), 'Chronology', *Middle East Journal*, Vol. 63, No. 3 (Summer 2009), p. 468.

118. Trita Parsi, *A single roll of the dice*, op. cit., pp. 58, 68, 71.

119. Al Jazeera (4/5/2010), 'Chronology', *Middle East Journal*, Vol. 64, No. 4 (Autumn 2010), p. 638.

120. Alfred B. Prados, 'Syria: U.S. Relations and Bilateral Issues', *CRS Brief for Congress* (13 March 2006).

121. Ibid.

122. For further information, see Council on Foreign Relations, 'What Are the Sanctions Against Iran?', *PBS* (13/06/2013) in http://www.pbs.org/news hour/rundown/the-lengthening-list-of-iran-sanctions/ (last accessed January 2016).

123. 'Turkey can help world understand Iran: Mottaki', *GEO Business* (16/02/2010), http://www.geo.tv/2-16-2010/59408.htm (last accessed July 2015).

124. Reza Moghadam, *Turkey at the Crossroads: From Crisis Resolution to EU Accession* (Washington DC: International Monetary Fund, 29/09/2005), p. 3.

125. 'Turkish–Iranian trade grew by 500 percent between 2002 and 2009, Reuters, 'Turkey Says Iran Sanctions "Mistake" Deepens Ties' (10 June

2010), http://uk.reuters.com/article/2010/06/10/idINIndia-491943201
00610 (last accessed July 2015).

126. Interview by the researcher with Osman Korutürk, former Deputy
     Chairman at CHP (Ankara, 1 April 2013).

127. Interview by the researcher with Osman Aşkın Bak, former Co-Chairman
     of Turkey–Iran Parliamentary Friendship Group (Ankara, 28 March
     2013).

128. Arshin Adib-Moghaddam, Report, 'Turkey and Iran: Islamic Brotherhood
     or Regional Rivalry?' (Al Jazeera Center for Studies, 4 June 2013), p. 2.

129. Turkey is seeking to reduce its heavy dependency on Russian natural gas
     (55 percent of total in 2011) and oil (12 percent in 2011 but higher in
     previous years) imports through diversification. Russian efforts to
     control the flow of energy from the Black Sea and Caspian Basin regions
     threaten Turkey's ambition to play a key role in expanding the East–
     West energy transit corridor – even as it further develops the North–
     South energy axis with Russia: in Stephen, J. Flanagan, 'Drivers and
     Strategy in Turkey, Russia, Iran economic and energy relations', CSIS (29
     March 2012) in http://csis.org/files/attachments/120529_Flanagan_TRI_
     Economic_EnergyDimensions.pdf, p. 3 (last accessed January 2016).

130. Middle East Online (26/08/2009), 'Chronology', *Middle East Journal*,
     Vol. 63, No. 1 (Winter 2009), p. 120.

131. 'The White House said today that the only way to prevent war in Iraq
     would be to disarm the country and depose Saddam Hussein … Later,
     asked whether Mr. Bush's standard for war goes beyond that of the
     United Nations, Mr. Fleischer said, "It's disarmament and regime
     change"' in Felicity Barringer and David E. Sanger, 'US Says Hussein Must
     Cede Power to Head Off War', *New York Times*, in http://www.nytimes.
     com/2003/03/01/international/middleeast/01IRAQ.html (last accessed
     July 2015).

132. See Charountaki, *The Kurds and US Foreign* Policy, op. cit., pp. 80, 251.

CHAPTER 6   TURKISH–IRANIAN RELATIONS UNDER THE LENS OF
THE SYRIAN CRISIS: A NEW ERA FOR MIDDLE EASTERN POLITICS

1. Interview by the author with Reza Altun, Co-founder of PKK, Executive
   member of KCK (Qandil, 20 March 2014).

2. Interview by the author with Osman Aşkın Bak, former Co Chairman of
   Turkey–Iran Parliamentary Friendship Group (Ankara, 28 March 2013).

3. Interview by the author with Ibrahim Kalin, Ambassador, Spokesman for
   the Presidency, and Chief Advisor in Middle East Affairs to the Turkish
   President, Recep Tayip Erdoğan (Ankara, 1 April 2013).

4. 'Erdogan puts hopes for peace with Kurds in hands of Barzani', *Middle
   East Online* (16/11/2013) in http://www.middle-east-online.com/english/
   ?id=62642 (last accessed February 2016).

5. 'Syria has real friends in the region and the world that will not let Syria fall in the hands of America, Israel or Takfiri (extreme jihadi) groups' Nasrallah said in a broadcast on Hizbullah's Al-Manar TV channel, cited in *The Guardian* (30/04/2013), http://www.theguardian.com/world/2013/apr/30/hezbollah-syria-uprising-nasrallah (last accessed February 2016).

6. The Iranians and Hizbullah are also said to have trained members of the Alawi paramilitary groups, known as the Shabiha, which were re-formed into a group called the National Defence Forces (NDF). The Badr Organization, along with the militias of the Asa'ib Ahl al-Haq (عصائب أهل الحق, League of the Righteous) which has close ties with the former Iraqi Prime Minister Nouri al-Maliki, and the Saraya al-Difa' ash-Sha'abi, have deployed in Syria to assist the Assad regime, and the three also participated in the military efforts of the Iraqi government in Anbar when Fallujah and parts of Ramadi fell out of government control. The best-known of these groups is Saraya al-Salam (The Peace Brigades), the reconstituted Mahdi Army of the Islamist political leader Muqtada al-Sadr. Sadrist-leaning militia groups (Liwa al-Shabab al-Risali or Liwa Dhu al-Fiqar) which first emerged in Syria and were later withdrawn to Iraq are also interesting cases in Jonathan Spyer, and Jawad Aymenn Al-Tamimi, 'How Iraq Became a Proxy of the Islamic Republic of Iran', *The Tower*, Issue 21 (December 2014) in http://www.thetower.org/article/how-iraq-became-a-wholly-owned-subsidiary-of-the-islamic-republic-of-iran/ (accessed February 2015).

7. 'Assad defends presence of Hezbollah fighters in Syria', *Al Jazeera* (25/08/2015) in http://www.aljazeera.com/news/2015/08/assad-defends-presence-hezbollah-fighters-syria-150825203254106.htm (last accessed September 2015).

8. 'Nasr is a member of the State Department's Foreign Affairs Policy Board and served as senior advisor to the US special representative for Afghanistan and Pakistan, Ambassador Richard Holbrooke, between 2009 and 2011' in Vali Nasr, *The dispensable nation: American foreign policy in retreat* (Doubleday Books, 2013), p. 157.

9. Interview by the author with Fadhil Merani, Secretary of Political Bureau, Kurdistan Democratic Party (Erbil, 27 August 2015).

10. Interview by the researcher with Dr. Aykan Erdemir, CHP Cumhuriyet Halk Partisi – former Member of the Turkish Parliament (representing Bursa) (Ankara, 2 April 2013).

11. 'Iran's Basij lash out at nuclear deal', *Al Monitor* (30/07/2015) in http://www.al-monitor.com/pulse/originals/2015/07/basij-reaction-iran-deal.html, and http://farsi.khamenei.ir/speech-content?id=30331 (last accessed September 2015).

12. Mahan Abedin, 'Going ballistic: The defiant Iranian message in Deir Ezzor', *Middle East Eye* (26 June 2017) in http://www.middleeasteye.net/columns/going-ballistic-defiant-iranian-message-deir-ezzor-650430774 (last accessed August 2017).

13. The peshmerga forces are recognised by the Iraqi Constitution of October 2005 as 'security forces and guards of the region' in implementing the foreign policy of the Kurdistan Regional Government (KRG), as well as in preserving and providing the conditions necessary for the stability and security of the KR in Article 121 section 5 of the Iraqi constitution provisions the establishment of the internal security forces for the region, such as policy, security forces and regional guards; in Ben Smith, Jon Lunn and Rob Page, House of Commons, British Library, Standard Note SNIA 6963: 'UK arms transfers to the Peshmerga in Iraqi Kurdistan' (18/08/2014).

14. Haider al-Abadi (Iraqi Prime Minister), 'Iraqi PM praises Peshmerga–Iraqi army cooperation in fight against ISIS', *Ara News* (9 March 2017) in http://aranews.net/2017/03/iraqi-pm-praises-peshmerga-iraqi-army-cooperation-in-fight-against-isis/ (last accessed August 2017).

15. 'The ruler of the Gulf state of Qatar has said Arab countries should send troops into Syria to stop government forces killing civilians there' Sheikh Hamad bin Khalifa Al Thani, US television channel CBS in *BBC News* (14/01/2012) cited in http://www.bbc.co.uk/news/world-middle-east-16561493 (last accessed February 2016).

16. It has been recorded that 'Saudi Arabia supported FSA with anti-tank weapons costing $5,000 each' in Fehim Tastekin, 'Radical groups operate on Turkey's border', *Al Monitor* (17/10/2013).

17. Elena Sergienko, 'Οι προτεραιότητες της Ρωσίας στην εξωτερική πολιτική', ('The Priorities of the Russian Foreign Policy'), *Η Ρωσία Τώρα* (*Russia Today*) (08/01/2013) in http://gr.rbth.com/politics/2013/01/27/oi_proteraiotite_ti_rosia_stin_eksoteriki_politiki_19577 (last accessed September 2015).

18. 'CSTO member-states begin Unbreakable Brotherhood 2014 war games in Kyrgyzstan', *Kazinform* (29/07/2014) in http://www.inform.kz/eng/article/2682365 (last accessed September 2015).

19. Matthew Jones, 'The Preferred Plan: The Anglo-American Working Group Report on Covert Action in Syria, 1957', *Intelligence and National Security*, Vol. 19, No. 3 (Autumn 2004), pp. 401–402, 406–408, 413.

20. Marios Evriviadis, 'Συρία 1957 και 2012' ('Syria 1957 and 2012'), *Infognomon* (16/09/2012) in http://infognomonpolitics.blogspot.co.uk/2012/09/1957-2012.html (last accessed September 2015).

21. 'Until 2011 the EU imported €17billion in Iranian goods and exported €10.05billion according to the EU Directorate General for Trade. For the Europeans the agreement can open a potential market of 77million people. Yet, nuclear deal oil diplomacy does not mean we have an immediate breakthrough' in Alissa J. Rubin, 'With risks Europeans rush back to Iran', *International New York Times* (1–2 August 2015), p. 6.

22. Moshe Ma'oz, 'The "Arab Spring" and the New Geo-strategic Environment in the Middle East', *Insight Turkey*, Vol. 14, No. 4 (2012), p. 22.

23. *New York Times* (1/08/2010).

24. Ahmed Davutoğlu, *Hürriyet* (23/07/2014), p. 9 and Haaretz, 'Turkey Denies Defense, Energy Ties With Israel Amid Gaza Fighting' (23/07/2014) in http://www.haaretz.com/israel-news/1.606786 (last accessed February 2016).

25. 'Turkey's Erdogan Urges Assad to 'Finally Step Down' for Sake of Mideast Peace', Haaretz (22/10/ 2011) in http://www.haaretz.com/middle-east-news/turkey-s-erdogan-urges-assad-to-finally-step-down-for-sake-of-mideast-peace-1.397058 (last accessed February 2016).

26. Fareed Zakaria, 'Interview with Erdoğan', *CNN* (26/09/2011) and Younkyoo Kim and Stephen Blank, 'Turkey and Russia on Edge: Russo-Turkish Divergence: the Security Dimension', *GLORIA Center* (27/04/2012),http://www.thecuttingedgenews.com/index.php?article=73149&pageid=13&pagename=Analysis (last accessed September 2015).

27. 'Turkey has decided to become a strong agent of the containment of Iran. Clear evidence for this is Turkey's decision to host radar installations for NATO's missile defense cooperation' in Omer Taspinar, Robert Malley, Sadjadpour Karim, 'Symposium: Israel, Turkey and Iran in the changing Arab World', *Middle East policy*, Vol. 19, No. 1 (Spring 2012), p. 10.

28. Daren Butler, 'Turkey's Erdoğan moots three-way regional talks on Syria', *The Daily Star* (16/10/2012).

29. Tulay Karadeniz and Simon Cameron-Moore, 'Turkey's saves ire for Israel, concern for Syria', *Reuters* (30/05/2011) in http://www.reuters.com/article/2011/05/30/us-turkey-mideast-interview-idUSTRE74T3SE20110530 (last accessed September, 2015).

30. Fehim Tastekin, 'Radical groups operate on Turkey's border', *Al Monitor* (17/10/2013).

31. 'In 2012 the rial dropped by 10 per cent, the inflation increased by 40 per cent whereas unemployment reached 33 per cent' in *Επίκαιρα* (*NewsReel*, Greek newspaper) (14/08/2013).

32. 'Turkish Leader Volunteers to be US–Iran Mediator', *New York Times* (12/11/2008), http://www.nytimes.com/2008/11/12/world/europe/12turkey.html?_r=1&sq=TURKEY (last accessed September 2015).

33. Alireza Bigdeli (Iran's Ambassador to Ankara), 'Iran ready to arbitrate between Turkey, Syria', *Iranian Student's News Agency* (30/11/2013).

34. Marianna Charountaki, 'US foreign policy in theory and practice: from Soviet-era containment to the era of the Arab Uprisings(s)', *Journal of American Foreign Policy Interests: the Journal of the National Committee on American Foreign Policy*, Vol.36, Issue 4 (Routledge, 2014), p. 261.

35. Barack Obama, *National Security Strategy of the US* (May 2010) in https://www.whitehouse.gov/sites/default/files/rss_viewer/national_security_strategy.pdf (last accessed September 2015).

36. George H.W. Bush, 'US Policy Towards the Persian Gulf', National Security Directive 26 (Washington, DC: The White House, 2 October

1989), http://www.fas.org/irp/offdocs/nsd/nsd26.pdf; and George H. W. Bush, 'US Policy in Response to the Iraqi Invasion of Kuwait', National Security Directive 45 (Washington, DC: The White House, 20 August 1990). http://www.fas.org/irp/offdocs/nsd/nsd45.pdf (last accessed February 2016).

37. James Mann, *The Obamians: The Struggle Inside the White House to Redefine American Power* (New York: Viking Adult: 2012), p. 258.

38. Ibid., pp. 266–267.

39. Amy L. Beam, Ed D, 'Appeal to secretary of state John Kerry on his visit to Ankara' (02/02/2013) cited in http://www.infognomonpolitics.blogspot.gr/2013/03/appeal-to-secretary-of-state-john-kerry.html?m=1 (last accessed September 2015).

40. Barack Obama, US president, 'The future of Syria must be determined by its people, but President Bashar al-Assad is standing in their way. His calls for dialogue and reform have rung hollow while he is imprisoning, torturing and slaughtering his own people. We have consistently said that President Assad must lead a democratic transition or get out of the way. He has not led. For the sake of the Syrian people, the time has come for President Assad to step aside' in 'Syria: Assad must resign, says Obama', *The Guardian* (19 August 2011) in https://www.theguardian.com/world/2011/aug/18/syria-assad-must-resign-obama (last accessed August 2017).

41. Aram Nerguizian, 'US and Iranian strategic competition: the proxy cold war in the Levant, Egypt and Jordan', *CSIS* (12 March 2012) in http://csis.org/files/publication/120312_Iran_VIII_Levant.pdf, p. 79 (last accessed September 2015).

42. Thierry Meyssan, 'An Empire Without a Military Strategy for a Military Strategy Without an Empire', Voltairenet.org (2/06/2014) in http://www.voltairenet.org/article184056.html (last accessed November 2015).

43. Walter Russell Mead, 'The Return of Geopolitics: The Revenge of the Revisionist Powers', *Foreign Affairs* (May/June 2014).

44. Vali Nasr, *The dispensable nation: American foreign policy in retreat* (Random House, 2013), pp. 186, 220, 221, 255.

45. Ibid., p. 199.

46. Ibid., pp. 100, 200–201.

47. Alfred B. Prados, 'Syria: US Relations and Bilateral Issues', *CRS Brief for Congress* (13 March 2006).

48. Ibid.

49. Aram Nerguizian, CSIS, 'US and Iranian strategic competition: the proxy cold war in the Levant, Egypt and Jordan' (12 March 2012), p. 81 in http://csis.org/files/publication/120312_Iran_VIII_Levant.pdf (last accessed September, 2015).

50. Jess Staufenberg, 'Vladmir Putin admits supporting President Assad in Syrian civil war', *Independent* (05/09/2015) in http://www.independent.

co.uk/news/world/europe/vladmir-putin-admits-supporting-president-assad-in-syrian-civil-war-10488165.html (last accessed September 2015).

51. 'Russia confirms weapons on flights to Syria', *Al Jazeera* (11/09/2015) in http://www.aljazeera.com/news/2015/09/aid-flights-syria-carry-military-equipment-150910110117672.html (last accessed September 2015).

52. Omar Sanadiki, *Reuters* cited in 'Russian Troops Join Combat in Syria – Sources', *The Moscow Times* (09/09/2015) in http://www.themoscowtimes.com/news/article/russian-troops-join-combat-in-syria/529831.html (last accessed September 2015).

53. 'Assad defends presence of Hezbollah fighters in Syria', *Al Jazeera* (25/08/2015) in http://www.aljazeera.com/news/2015/08/assad-defends-presence-hezbollah-fighters-syria-150825203254106.html (last accessed September 2015).

54. 'Algeria to Purchase 14 Russian-Made Sukhoi Fighter Jets', *The Moscow Times* (11/09/2015) in http://www.themoscowtimes.com/business/article/algeria-to-purchase-14-russian-made-sukhoi-fighter-jets/530046.html (last accessed September 2015).

55. Younkyoo Kim and Stephen Blank, 'Turkey and Russia on Edge: Russo-Turkish Divergence: the Security Dimension', *GLORIA Center* (27 April 2012) in http://www.thecuttingedgenews.com/index.php?article=73149&pageid=13&pagename=Analysis (last accessed September 2015).

56. Volker Perthes, 'The Syrian Solution', *Foreign Affairs*, Vol. 85, No. 6 (November/December 2006), p. 38.

57. Murat Yetkin, 'Russia accesses warm waters through Turkey', *Hürriyet* (4/12/2012) in http://www.hurriyetdailynews.com/russia-accesses-warm-waters-through-turkey.aspx?pageID=449&nID = 36060&NewsCatID = 409 (last accessed September 2015).

58. Murat Yetkin, 'Turkey, Russia work on new plan for Syria', *Hürriyet* (07/12/2012) in http://www.hurriyetdailynews.com/turkey-russia-work-on-new-plan-for-syria.aspx?pageID=449&nID=36301&NewsCatID=409 (last accessed September 2015).

59. 'Cable: Turkey more dependent on Russia with nuclear plant', *Today's Zaman* (02/09/2011) in http://www.todayszaman.com/diplomacy_cable-turkey-more-dependent-on-russia-with-nuclear-plant_255546.html (last accessed September 2015).

60. *Russia Beyond the Headlines*, 'Russia delivers Night Hunter helicopters to Iraq' (02/02/2015) in http://rbth.com/news/2015/02/02/russia_delivers_night_hunter_helicopters_to_iraq_43334.html (last accessed September 2015).

61. Simon Tisdall, 'Syrian safe zone: US relents to Turkish demands after border crisis grows', *The Guardian* (27/07/2015) in http://www.theguardian.com/world/2015/jul/27/syrian-safe-zone-us-relents-to-turkish-demands-border-crisis-kurd-uk-military (last accessed September 2015).

62. Gordon Duff, 'NEO: US, Turkey Ignore Russian Warning, Move into Syria' in (17/08/2015), http://www.veteranstoday.com/2015/08/21/us-turkey-ignore-russian-warning-move-into-syria-new-eastern-outlook/ (last accessed September 2015).

63. Duff believes that IS has been aided only by Israel, Turkey and the United States in ibid.

64. Jack Moore, 'Turkey YouTube Ban: Full Transcript of Leaked Syria 'War' Conversation Between Erdoğan Officials', *International Business Times* (27/04/2014) in http://www.ibtimes.co.uk/turkey-youtube-ban-full-transcript-leaked-syria-war-conversation-between-erdogan-officials-1442161 and Nick Tattersall, 'Turkey calls Syria security leak 'villainous' blocks YouTube', *Reuters* (27/04/2014) in http://www.reuters.com/article/2014/03/27/us-syria-crisis-turkey-idUSBREA2Q17420140327 (last accessed September 2015).

65. Thierry Meyssan, 'Clinton, Juppé, Erdoğan, Daesh and the PKK' (03/08/2015) in http://www.voltairenet.org/article188337.html (last accessed September 2015).

66. Umit Enginsoy and Burak Ege Bekdil, 'Arab uprising undermines Turkey–Iran–Syria alliance', *Defense News*, Vol. 26, No. 30 (15/08/2011), p. 4.

67. The Iranian concern was such that in November 2011, 'General Amir Ali Hajizadeh, a senior commander in Iran's RG declared that if Iran were attacked by the US or Israel its first response would be to target elements of the NATO missile shield in Turkey' in Gareth H. Jenkins, 'Tactical Allies and Strategic Rivals: Turkey's Changing Relations With Iran', *The Turkey Analyst*, Vol. 4, No. 23 (05/12/2011) in http://www.turkeyanalyst.org/publications/turkey-analyst-articles/item/285-tactical-allies-and-strategic-rivals-turkeys-changing-relations-with-iran.html (last accessed September 2015).

68. Thierry Meyssan, 'The Russian army is beginning to engage in Syria' (24/08/2015) in http://www.voltairenet.org/article188522.html (last accessed September 2015).

69. 'The agreement includes a plan to drive the Islamic State out of a 68-mile-long area west of the Euphrates River and reaching into the province of Aleppo that would then come under the control of the Syrian opposition' in Karen DeYoung and Liz Sly, 'US–Turkey deal aims to create de facto 'safe zone' in northwest Syria', *Washington Post* (26/07/2015) https://www.washingtonpost.com/world/new-us-turkey-plan-amounts-to-a-safe-zone-in-northwest-syria/2015/07/26/0a533345-ff2e-4b40-858a-c1b36541e156_story.html (last accessed September 2015).

70. Julian Pecquet, 'Congress rethinks anti-Assad stance', *Al Monitor* (16/09/2015) in http://www.al-monitor.com/pulse/originals/2015/09/congress-democrats-assad-regime-change-isis.html?utm_source=Al-Monitor+Newsletter+%5BEnglish%5D&utm_campaign=96c4f7b649-September_17_2015&utm_medium=email&utm_term=0_28264b27a0-96c4f7b649-93109129 (last accessed September 2015).

71. *Press Tv*, 'Iran, Turkey to set up ties committee' (30/01/2014) in http://www.presstv.ir/detail/2014/01/30/348416/iran-turkey-to-set-up-ties-committee/ (last accessed September 2015).

72. Al Monitor, 'Zarif presses diplomacy on Syria' (16/08/2015) in http://www.al-monitor.com/pulse/originals/2015/08/zarif-syria-lapid-peace-syria-netanyahu-turkey-temple.html (last accessed September 2015).

73. Mariam Karouny, 'Will Syria's Nusra Front split from al-Qaeda?', *Al Arabiya News* (04/03/2015) in http://english.alarabiya.net/en/perspective/features/2015/03/04/Will-Syria-s-al-Nusra-Front-split-from-al-Qaeda-.html (last accessed September 2015).

74. 'Vladimir Putin has signalled "mission semi-accomplished" in Syria as Russia announced the start of a withdrawal of forces, beginning with the departure from the Mediterranean of a naval group led by the Admiral Kuznetsov aircraft carrier' in Patrick Wintour, 'Russia begins military withdrawal from Syria', *The Guardian* (6 January 2017) in https://www.theguardian.com/world/2017/jan/06/russia-aircraft-carrier-mediterranean-syria-admiral-kuznetsov (last accessed August 2017).

75. Hürriyet, 'US denies plans to change strategy in Syria' (14/11/2014) in http://www.hurriyetdailynews.com/us-denies-plans-to-change-strategy-in-syria-.aspx?pageID=238&nID=74343&NewsCatID=359 (last accessed September 2015).

76. Burak Bekdil, 'ISIS Going Rogue in Turkey, or Is It?', *Middle East Forum* (04/08/2015) in http://www.meforum.org/5422/turkey-isis (last accessed September 2015).

77. *Debka File*, 'First Iranian marines land in Syria, link up with newly-arrived Russian troops' (11/09/2015) in http://www.debka.com/article/24883/First-Iranian-marines-land-in-Syria-link-up-with-newly-arrived-Russian-troops (last accessed September 2015).

78. TABID is a Gülenist business and trade association with branches in several states. According to their website, TABID held a fundraising event in December 2007 at which 'Turkish Americans raised $250,000 for Hillary Clinton' in Why Bill Clinton mentioned Gulen at the Turkish Cultural Center's Dinner in September 2008 'Gulenists' campaign contributions to Hillary Clinton likely played a role' in http://turkishinvitations.weebly.com/why-bill-clinton-mentioned-gulen-at-the-tccny-dinner.html (last accessed September 2015).

79. Daron Acemoglu, 'The Failed Autocrat', *Foreign Affairs* (22/05/2014) in http://www.foreignaffairs.com/print/138488 (last accessed September 2015).

80. Murat, Karayılan, *Η Ανατομία του Πολέμου στο Κουρδιστάν* (*Bir Savaşın Anatomisi, Anatomy of a War*) (Infognomon, 2012), p. 40.

81. 'Already since 1982 it is said that an Israeli strategy is being formed that provisions the division of the majority of the Arab states including Iran and Turkey on a national, ethnic and religious basis' in Oded Yinon, 'A Strategy for Israel in the 1980's', *Kivunim* (*Directions*), No. 14, Issue

5742 (February 1982), http://www.informationclearinghouse.info/pdf/ The%20Zionist%20Plan%20for%20the%20Middle%20East.pdf (last accessed February 2016).

82. *TV Interview* cited in 'Iraq, Refugees and Oil', *BBC Newsnight* (12/08/2014).

83. Interview by the author with Fadhil Merani, Secretary of Political Bureau, Kurdistan Democratic Party (Erbil, 27 August 2015).

84. General Qasim Suleimany, head of the elite Iranian Al-Quds forces, himself has visited Erbil and held many hours discussion in Interview by the author with Fadhil Merani, Secretary of Political Bureau, Kurdistan Democratic Party (Erbil, 27 August 2015).

85. Namik Durukan, 'Davutoğlu, Kuzey Irak için "Kürdistan" dedi', ('Davutoğlu, called Northern Iraq, "Kürdistan"'], *Milliyet* (22/07/2016) in, www.milliyet.com.tr/davutoglu-kuzey-irak-icin-kurdistan-dedi/siyaset/ haberdetay/22.07.2010/1266720/default.htm (last accessed April 2016).

86. In terms of clarification, the difference between 'Özerklik' and 'Otonomi' is here distinguished. The DTP's programme suggests *yerel özerklik* (local sufficiency) as a broader term to describe a system of local self-governments. *Özerklik* (öz=auto + erk = power) then is a situation of *self-sufficiency* which does not imply an entirely autonomous Kurdish internal organization separate from the state. Rather, it proposes a restrained Otonomi-autonomy into the field of cultural and economic rights that will enable the Kurds to have control over their education, culture and media at a local level. On the other hand, *Otonomi* as defined in political sciences is a concept necessitates the existence of a separate legislative assembly at a local level. However, the concept of the creation of local governments depicted in 'Demokratik Özerklik' does not involve any kind of legislative authority. Therefore, the idea behind the Kurdish model is not *Otonomi*. In this sense, this model talks about the self-governance of local authorities at the level of the municipalities, villages and so on, as sub-central administrations – term used by authors such as Bekir Parlak, Zahid Sobaci and Mustafa Ökmen in 'The evaluation of restructured local governments in Turkey within the context of the European charter on local self-government', *Ankara Law Review*, Vol. 5 No. 1 (Summer 2008), p. 27.

87. Former Turkish Minister of Interior, Idris Naim Sahin, has also spoken about an Iran–Kurdistan Workers Party (PKK) linkage. *Zaman* headlined on 24 December 2012 the minister's statement under the title 'Logistics support to PKK from Iran'. Minister Sahin said, 'The terror organization is using Iran for accommodation, transit, training, medical care, recruiting, financing and propaganda. Moreover, some weapon transfers are conducted from there. Iran is not paying much attention to security measures in border regions' in Cengiz Candar, *Al Monitor*, 'Turkey Claims Iran Providing Logistical Support for PKK' (30/12/2012).

88. Emre Uslu, 'PKK–Iran axis', *Today's Zaman* (05/10/2011) in https:// wikileaks.org/gifiles/docs/13/135269_-os-turkey-iran-iraq-turkish-op-ed-pkk-iran-axis-.html (last accessed September 2015).

89. 'Iran captured but later released PKK leader Karayılan, report claims', *Today's Zaman* (11/10/2011) in http://www.todayszaman.com/news-259497-iran-captured-but-later-released-pkk-leader-karayilan-report-claims.html (last accessed September 2015).

90. Interview by the author with Reza Altun, co-founder of PKK, executive member of KCK (Qandil, 20/03/2014).

91. Interview by the author with Fadhil Merani, Secretary of Political Bureau, Kurdistan Democratic Party (Erbil, 27 August 2015).

92. Turkey's Erdogan Urges Assad to 'Finally Step Down' for Sake of Mideast Peace', *Haaretz* (22/10/2011) in http://www.haaretz.com/middle-east-news/turkey-s-erdogan-urges-assad-to-finally-step-down-for-sake-of-mideast-peace-1.397058 (last accessed February 2016).

93. Former Rector of Turkey's Çanakkale University in Vitaly Naumkin, 'Russia's Kurdish dilemma', *Al Monitor* (26/01/2014).

94. Interview by the author with Ibrahim Kalin, Ambassador, Spokesman for the Presidency, and Chief Advisor in Middle East Affairs to the Turkish President, Recep Tayip Erdoğan (Ankara, 1 April 2013).

95. 'Turkey warns against Kurdish autonomy in Syria', *Ya Libnan* (15/11/2013).

96. According to a survey of Kadir University (January 2012) 51, 8 per cent of the Turkish public opinion in 26 provinces, considers that the government should not negotiation neither with any representative of the Kurdish parties and its affiliations nor with Abdullah Öcalan himself.

97. Savvas Kalederidis, 'Developments in Turkey and geopolitical repercussions', Κυριακάτικη Δημοκρατία (*Sunday Democracy*) (05/01/2014) in http://infognomonpolitics.blogspot.co.uk/2014/01/blog-post_6108.html (last accessed September 2015).

98. Karim Abed Zayer, 'Maliki Deploys 'Tigris Force' to Kirkuk', Al Monitor (13/12/2012) in http://www.almonitor.com/pulse/politics/2012/11/kirkuk-paramilitary-tigrispeshmerga.html?utm_source=&utm_medium=email&utm_campaign=5167#ixzz2CDvXmmZz (last accessed September 2015).

99. Steve Dobransky, 'Why the US Failed in Iraq: Baghdad at the Crossroads', *Middle East Quarterly*, Vol. 21. No. 1 (Winter 2014).

100. *Today's Zaman*, 'Iraq bars minister's plane from landing in Arbil amid tensions' (04/12/2012) in http://www.todayszaman.com/latest-news_iraq-bars-ministers-plane-from-landing-in-arbil-amid-tensions_300121.html (last accessed September 2015).

101. Jake Hess, Interview with Selahattin Demirtaş, 'The AKP's 'New Kurdish Strategy' Is Nothing of the Sort', *MERIP*, No. 275 (2/05/2012) in http://www.merip. org/mero/mero050212 (last accessed September 2015).

102. Marianna Charountaki, 'Kurdish policies in Syria under the Arab Uprisings: A revisiting of IR in the New Middle Eastern Order', *Third World Quarterly*, Vol. 36, Issue 2, pp. 337–356 (27 March 2015).

103. 'The more recent negotiations were closer to achieving results. As Mr. Öcalan stated in notes from conferences with his lawyers, these meetings have been characterized as the most important ever carried out in the hundred-year history of the Kurdish issue. Unfortunately, however, the meetings became deadlocked due to the government's incorrect approach and attempt to use them as a policy to liquidate the Kurdish movement. They came to an end without realizing concrete results. We can't be certain, but what emerged is that the government wanted to carry out these negotiations up until the 2011 elections' in ibid.

104. The 'Dolmabahçe Agreement' referring to the reconciliation declaration consisting of ten points, which was shared with the public following the meeting between pro-Kurdish Peoples' Democratic Party (HDP) deputies and Deputy Prime Minister Yalçın Akdoğan at Istanbul's Dolmabahçe Palace on February 28. The ten points were declared as a roadmap for a final solution of Turkey's Kurdish issue and 30-year-old PKK armed insurgency.

105. In this same context, we find a change in Turkey's dogma, reorientating its reference from 'international' to 'external threats' which allows Ankara to operate against neighbouring states under the pretext of the threat of the national security and possibly with less attention to the internal security issues such as Islam and the Kurds than previously.

106. 'Iran says it will be Turkey's turn if it goes ahead with Syria policies', *Today's Zaman* (07/08/2012) in http://www.todayszaman.com/latest-news _iran-says-it-will-be-turkeys-turn-if-it-goes-ahead-with-syria-policies_ 288818.html (last accessed September 2015).

107. More information in Mac Thornberry, 'H.R. 1735 Passes: House Armed Services Committee' 60–2, http://armedservices.house.gov/index. cfm/press-releases?ContentRecord_id=F0AC8FF7-C044-40CA-97AA-7562A4C7E5FD (last accessed February 2016).

108. Hevidar Ahmed, 'Kurdish role: Kurdistan Region announces plans for second oil pipeline to Turkey', *Rudaw* (21/05/2013).

109. 'Northern Iraq begins international oil exports, defying Baghdad', *Trend News Agency* (23/10/2012) in http://en.trend.az/world/arab/2079726. html (lastaccessed September 2015).

110. Raziye Akkoc, 'How Turkey's economy went from flying to flagging – and could get worse', *The Telegraph* (30/05/2015) in http://www. telegraph.co.uk/finance/economics/11640135/How-Turkeys-economy-went-from-flying-to-flagging-and-could-get-worse.html (last accessed September 2015).

111. According to EUROSTAT 'Iran's most important partner in 2010 was the EU par 19 per cent, China par 15.4 per cent in 2012 and Asia

par 51.4 per cent in 2011' in Charalambos Tsardanidis and Vivi Kefala, *Ιράν: Πολιτική Οικονομία, Διεθνείς και Περιφερειακές Σχέσεις* (*Iran: Political Economy and International and Regional Relations*) (Εκδόσεις Παπαζήση, 2014), pp. 101–102.

112. 'KRG oil exports in December more than 18 million barrels', *Rudaw* (12/1/2016) in http://rudaw.net/english/kurdistan/110120162 (last accessed February 2016).

113. *KRG cabinet*, 'Border crossing points between Iran and Kurdistan Region to be reinforced' (23/04/2015) in http://cabinet.gov.krd/a/d.aspx?s=040000&l=12&a=53213 (last accessed September 2015).

114. *Hürriyet Daily News*, 'KRG slams Maliki, calls for dialogue' (04/12/2012) in http://www.hurriyetdailynews.com/krg-slams-maliki-calls-for-dialogue.aspx?pageID=238&nID=36057&NewsCatID=352 (last accessed September 2015).

115. Rudaw, 'Erbil, Ankara Finalize 'Historic' Oil Pipeline Agreement' (11/07/2013) in http://rudaw.net/english/business/06112013 (last accessed September 2015).

116. *Reuters*, 'Iraqi Kurdistan plans 10 bcm natural gas exports to Turkey in two years' (20/11/2015) in https://en-maktoob.news.yahoo.com/iraqi-kurdistan-plans-10-bcm-natural-gas-exports-094406617–business.html (last accessed February 2016).

117. Ministry of Natural Resources, 'Monthly Export Report for October 2015' (10/11/2015) in http://mnr.krg.org/index.php/en/press-releases/501-mnr-publishes-monthly-export-report-for-october-2015 (last accessed November 2015).

118. Humeyra Pamuk and Orhan Coskun, 'Iraqi Kurdistan's oil pipeline capacity to double after upgrade – sources', *Reuters* (27/10/2014) in http://www.dailymail.co.uk/wires/reuters/article-2809518/Iraqi-Kurdistans-oil-pipeline-capacity-double-upgrade-sources.html (last accessed September 2015).

119. Hawar Abdulrazaq, 'Iraq and Iran to Increase Trade to $20 Billion', *BasNews* (06/09/2015) in http://www.basnews.com/index.php/en/economy/217660 (last accessed September 2015).

120. *Rudaw*, 'Iran–Erbil Agree on Energy Deals and Boosting Trade' (29/04/2014) in http://rudaw.net/english/kurdistan/29042014 (last accessed September 2015).

121. *Rudaw*, 'KRG says delayed salaries to be paid this month' (20/10/2015) in http://rudaw.net/mobile/english/kurdistan/201020151 (last accessed November 2015).

122. *Rudaw*, 'Kurdistan says UN can supervise oil exports' (29/07/2015) in http://rudaw.net/english/kurdistan/290720152 (last accessed September 2015).

123. Marina and David Ottaway, 'How the Kurds got their way', *Foreign Affairs* (May/June 2014), p. 5.

124. *Press TV*, 'Iran–Turkey ties eradicate terrorism in Middle East: Rouhani' (29/01/2014) in http://www.presstv.ir/detail/2014/01/29/348352/iranturkey-ties-destroy-terrorism-in-me/ (last accessed September 2015).

125. Ambassador W.R. Pearson, 'The Turkish General Staff: a fractious and sullen political coalition', *Telegram* (18/04/2003) in https://wikileaks.org/plusd/cables/03ANKARA2521_a.html (last accessed September 2015).

126. 'Turkey would send Turkish liras to Iran, which would then convert the liras to gold to accept as payment for the natural gas' in Şaban Gündüz, 'Iran proposes joint barter company to evade US sanctions', *Today's Zaman* (28/12/2012).

127. Eskandar Sadeghi-Boroujerdi, 'Former IRGC chief says US working to turn Turkey into Iran's strategic rival', *Iran Pulse* (08/02/2013) in http://iranpulse.al-monitor.com/index.php/2013/02/1316/former-irgc-chief-says-us-working-to-turn-turkey-into-irans-strategic-rival/ (last accessed September 2015).

128. Barbara Slavin, 'Former US diplomat warns of possible 'grave mistake' in Syria', *Al Monitor* (01/05/2014) in http://www.al-monitor.com/pulse/originals/2014/05/syria-ryan-crocker-grave-mistake.html?utm_source=Al-Monitor+Newsletter+%5BEnglish%5D&utm_campaign=0813e812a6-January_9_20141_8_2014&utm_medium=email&utm_term=0_28264b27a0-0813e812a6-93128913#English%5D&utm_campaign=0813e812a6-January_9_20141_8_2014&utm_medium=email&utm_term=0_28264b27a0-0813e812a6-93128913# (last accessed February 2016).

129. Fehim Tastekin, 'Radical groups operate on Turkey's border', *Al Monitor* (17/10/2013).

130. Salih Muslim Mohammed, *Keynote speech*, Kurdish conference in London (18/11/2012).

131. Nesie Diouzel, 'Interview' in *Taraf* (8/10/2012).

132. The fall of the Russian aircraft Sukhoi Su-24M attack aircraft near the Syria–Turkey border on 24 November 2015 which was shot down by a Turkish Air Force F-16 fighter jet is a key example.

133. Phil Stewart, 'Iraq's Kurdish forces 'model' for fighting Islamic State – Pentagon chief', *Reuters* (24/07/2015) in http://uk.reuters.com/article/2015/07/24/uk-mideast-crisis-usa-iraq-idUKKCN0PY0R120150724 (last accessed September 2015).

134. 'The US and Turkey are increasingly divided over Kurds', *Reuters* (09/07/2015) in http://uk.businessinsider.com/the-us-and-turkey-are-increasingly-divided-over-kurds-2015-7?r=US#ixzz3fVOoPoDW (last accessed September 2015).

135. 'Quds Force Commander Qassem Soleimani visited Iraqi Kurdistan in late September to request Iranian weapons transfer to Syria. Barzani also reacted coolly to Soleimani's proposal of a détente with Maliki. Barzani's uncooperative position led Iran to reach out to other Kurdish parties, in an attempt to isolate and pressure the Kurdish president. Tehran is

reportedly also fostering a rapprochement Kurdistan Workers' Party (PKK)' in Tony Badran, 'Obama runs from Iran', *Now Lebanon* (1/11/2012). Similar requests are said to date back to 1995 and have also occurred more recently when the request was repeated first from the Iranian side to the KR's President and later to President Talabani.

136. 'Israel purchased 77 per cent of KR's oil supplies' in *The Kurdish Globe*, No504 (31/08/2015), p. 6.

137. 'EU Continues its support for Kurdistan Region', KRG cabinet (28/07/2015) in http://cabinet.gov.krd/a/d.aspx?s=040000&l=12& a=53572 (last accessed September 2015).

138. According to PYD's co-chairman Salim Muslim, 'these two Councils [Kurdish Supreme Committee and KNC] wanted to join the Syrian Coalition. We refused to become part of the Syrian Coalition' in interview by the researcher with Salih Muslim, Co-leader of the Democratic Union Party (PYD) (London, 24/05/2014).

139. 'President Barzani Slams PYD in Syria, Rejects Autonomy Declaration', *Rudaw* (15/11/2013) in http://rudaw.net/english/kurdistan/14112013 (last accessed September 2015) and 'PKK must 'absolutely lay down arms against Turkey': HDP co-chair', *Hürriyet* (15/07/2015) in http://www.hurriyetdailynews.com/pkk-must-absolutely-lay-down-arms-against-turkey-hdp-co-chair.aspx?pageID=238&nID=85469&NewsCatID=338 (last accessed September 2015).

140. This is impossible with refusal from the Kurdish side for cooperation or escalation and prioritisation of power politics over the Kurdish movement foreign policy agenda at a time of turmoil and regional transformation in Selahattin Demirtaş, 'HDP's Demirtaş rules out coalition with AK Party after elections', *Today's Zaman* (27/05/2015) in http://www.todayszaman.com/anasayfa_hdps-demirtas-rules-out-coalition-with-ak-party-after-elections_381910.html (last accessed September 2015).

141. Salih Muslim Mohammed, *Keynote speech*, Kurdish conference in London (18/11/2012).

142. Kurdistan Region Statistics Office, Ministry of Planning in http://www.krso.net/Default.aspx?page=article&id=899&l=1&#krso2 (last accessed September 2015).

143. Mahan Abedin, 'Shiite militias deepen Iraq's sectarian conflict', *Middle East Eye* (10/12/2014), http://www.middleeasteye.net/columns/shiite-militias-deepen-iraq-s-sectarian-conflict-216999860 (accessed December 2014).

144. Interview by the author with Reza Altun, Co-founder of PKK, Executive member of KCK (Qandil, 20 March 2014).

## CHAPTER 7   CONCLUSIONS AND CONCEPTUALISATIONS

1. Donald Trump, 'Transcript: Donald Trump's Foreign Policy Speech', *New York Times* (27 April 2016) in https://www.nytimes.com/2016/04/28/us/

politics/transcript-trump-foreign-policy.html (last accessed August 2017).

2. Mahan Abedin, 'The results of Iranian parliamentary and Assembly elections will set the tone and pace for domestic and foreign policy in the next decade', *Middle East Eye* (26 February 2016) in http://www. middleeasteye.net/essays/irans-historic-elections-2045716001 (last accessed August 2017).

   According to Abedin "Neither Ahmadinejad nor Rafsanjani presidency was either principalist (appear to be taking the defeat) or conservative in the strictest meaning of the terms" in Mahan Abedin, 'Rouhani landslide redraws Iranian political map', *Middle East Eye* (21 May 2017) in http://www. middleeasteye.net/news/analysis-rouhani-landslide-redraws-iranian-political-map-833237805 (last accessed December, 2017).

3. The Aftermath of the Kurdish Referendum and Its Historic Connotations, *Harvard International Review*, (25 December 2017) in http://hir.harvard. edu/article/?a=14567

4. 'UN Syria envoy Staffan de Mistura praised the Russian-brokered Syria talks in Astana, Kazakhstan, which ended Jan. 24, as a "concrete step" toward implementation of United Nations Security Council resolutions dealing with Syria, commending Russia, Turkey and Iran for setting up a mechanism to ensure compliance with the cease-fire announced last month' in 'Why did Russia offer autonomy for Syria's Kurds?' *Al Monitor* (29 January 2017) in http://www.al-monitor.com/pulse/originals/ 2017/01/russia-offer-kurds-syria-autonomy-turkey-islamic-state.html #ixzz4XFA47rrf (last accessed, April 2017).

5. Ibid.

6. According to the spokesperson of the SDF-led Euphrates Wrath Operation, Jihan Sheikh Ahmad, they have liberated 45 per cent of Raqqa city in 'SDF says 45 per cent of Raqqa city liberated, operations ongoing', *Ara News* (25 July, 2017) http://aranews.net/2017/07/sdf-says-45-raqqa-city-liberated-operations-ongoing/ (last accessed August 2017).

7. Interview by author with Reza Altun, co-founder of PKK, executive member of KCK (Qandil, 20/03/2014).

8. See Marianna Charountaki, Chapter 7, *The Kurds and US Foreign Policy: International Relations in the Middle East since 1945* (Routledge, 2010).

9. 'We need models of science able to incorporate the chaotic complexity of the international system [rather than] a view of science that takes science itself as the primary good and then attempts to force the international system into it' in Colin Wight, *Agents, Structures and International Relations: politics as ontology* (New York: Cambridge University Press, 2006), pp. 294–295.

10. 'The aims of the [Iranian] foreign policy are development, [preservation] of Islam, struggle against hegemony and injustice. The Iran foreign policy principles focus on soft power, Islamic order, opposing tyranny, pacifism, autonomy, and the supremacy of Islam.' According to Dehshiri and

Majidi 'foreign policy is been shaped by two factors, namely, the values and conceptions of policy-makers as well as the objective environment' in M.R. Dehshiri, M.R. Majidi, 'Iran's Foreign policy in post-revolutionary era: a holistic approach', *The Iranian Journal of International Affairs*, Vol. XXI No. 1–2, 101–114 (Winter Spring 2008–2009), pp. 106–107, 109.

11. Ministry of Foreign Affairs, Republic of Turkey, 'Turkey-Iran Economic and Commercial Relations' in http://www.mfa.gov.tr/economic-and-commercial-relations-with-iran.en.mfa (last accessed August 2017).

12. 'Turkey and Iran agree to strengthen economic ties', *Al Jazeera* (16 April 2016) in http://www.aljazeera.com/news/2016/04/turkey-iran-agree-strengthen-economic-ties-160416155434319.html (last accessed August, 2017).

13. 'Turkey, Iran ink two key protocols to boost economic, trade ties', *Hürriyet Daily News* (10 April 2016) in http://www.hurriyetdailynews.com/turkey-iran-ink-two-key-protocols-to-boost-economic-trade-ties.aspx?pageID=238&nID=97575&NewsCatID=345 (last accessed August 2017).

14. Barış Sabah, 'First KRG gas to flow to Turkey in two years', *Daily Sabah* (20/11/2015) in http://www.dailysabah.com/energy/2015/11/21/first-krg-gas-to-flow-to-turkey-in-two-years (last accessed November 2015).

15. Interview by author with Alan Semo, PYD representative of foreign relations at the UK (London, 29/09/2015).

16. Ibid.

17. Interview by author with Khider Marassana, former member of Leading Committee KDPI (1991–1996) (Stockholm, 16/06/2014).

18. Nikolai Litovkin, *Russia Beyond the Headlines*, 'Russia delivers first weapons supplies to Iraqi Kurds' (18/03/2016) in http://rbth.com/defence/2016/03/18/russia-delivers-first-weapons-supplies-to-iraqi-kurds_576809 (last accessed March 2016).

19. Yaroslav Trofimov, 'France Wants Alliance With Russia, but Divisions Over Assad's Future a Hurdle', *The Wall Street Journal* (17/11/2015) in http://www.wsj.com/articles/assads-future-may-be-stumbling-block-in-plan-to-fight-isis-1447791663 (last accessed April 2016).

20. Thierry Meyssan, 'Why did Turkey shoot down the Russian Soukhoï 24?', *Voltairenet.org* (30/11/2015) in http://www.voltairenet.org/article 189474.html (last accessed December 2015).

21. 'Putin: US missile defense aimed at neutralizing Russia nukes, N. Korea and Iran just a cover', *Russia Today* (10/11/2015) in https://www.rt.com/news/321434-us-missile-shield-putin/ (last accessed December 2015).

22. Salih Muslim, head of a delegation from the Kurdish Supreme Council (composed of Syrian Kurdish parties), met on 8 October 2013 with Turkish officials from the Turkish Ministry of Foreign Affairs in Ankara. About this meeting Ahmet Davutoğlu said that the visit was 'routine, with no special agenda' in Amberin Zaman, 'Syrian Kurdish Leader Urges Turkey To End Support for Salafists', *Al Monitor* (9/10/2013).

23. Charlie Rose, 'Interviews with Zbigniew Brzezinski, Henry Kissinger and Brent Scowcroft', *New York Times* (18/06/2007) in http://www.nytim es.com/2007/06/18/world/americas/18iht-web-rose.html?page wanted=all (last accessed, December 2015).

24. This policy could possibly target at the control of regional resources so that Qatar for instance can transmit their gas and oil pipelines to Europe *via* Turkey in Savvas Kalederidis, 'Ξύπνα Ευρώπη-Ξύπνα Ελλάδα' ('Wake up Europe-Wake up Greece'), *Δημοκρατία* (*Democracy*, Greek newspaper) (21/11/2015) in http://infognomonpolitics.blogspot.co.uk/2015/11/ blog-post_412.html (last accessed December 2015).

25. Michael Birnbaum, 'The secret pact between Russia and Syria that gives Moscow carte blanche', *Washington Post* (15/01/2016) in https://www. washingtonpost.com/news/worldviews/wp/2016/01/15/the-secret-pact- between-russia-and-syria-that-gives-moscow-carte-blanche/　　　(last accessed February 2016).

26. Charlie Rose, 'Interviews with Zbigniew Brzezinski, Henry Kissinger and Brent Scowcroft', *New York Times* (18/06/2007) in http://www.nytimes. com/2007/06/18/world/americas/18iht-web-rose.html?pagewanted=all (last accessed March 2016).

27. Daryl Kimball and Kelsey Davenport, 'Timeline of Syrian Chemical Weapons Activity, 2012–2015', *Arms Control Association*, in https://www. armscontrol.org/factsheets/Timeline-of-Syrian-Chemical-Weapons- Activity (last accessed March 2016).

28. Claims made during interview by author with a high level political figure in Iranian politics (London, 17/06/2013).

29. Ibid.

30. 'Syrian opposition coalition dissolves military council after withdrawal threats', *Middle East Eye* (22/09/2014), in http://www.middleeasteye. net/news/syrian-opposition-coalition-dissolves-military-council-after- withdrawal-threats-1647588004 (last accessed March 2016).

31. Ministry of Foreign Affairs, Republic of Turkey, Foreign 'Minister Zarif of Iran pays a visit to Turkey' in http://www.mfa.gov.tr/foreign-minister- zarif-of-iran-pays-a-visit-to-turkey.en.mfa (last accessed December 2015).

32. 'The corruption scandal involving the head of the state-owned *Halk Bankasi* (People's Bank), or *Halkbank* for short, that emerged on December 17, 2013, is an interesting case and a reflection of the continuation of business and trade between Turkey and Iran. Sales from Iran were silently facilitated by the Turkish bank through the purchasing of gold that was given to Tehran as payment, instead of a currency, after Tehran was blocked from using the SWIFT international money-transfer system in March 2012. Halkbank maintains that the transactions were legal and that no rules prevented trading precious metals with Iran until July 2013 and that it ceased doing so on June 10, 2013' in Mahdi Darius Nazemroaya, 'Turkey and Iran: More than meets the eye', *RT*

(20/01/2014), https://www.rt.com/op-edge/turkey-iran-sanctions-cor-ruption-scandal-883/ (last accessed March 2016).

33. Turkish–Iranian trade volume in 2014 reached $13.7 billion whereas Iran is Turkey's second biggest gas supplier after Russia and provides Turkey with a significant portion of its imported Iranian natural gas to generate electricity. According to former Turkish Foreign Affairs Minister, Ahmet Davutoğlu: 'We should work together to increase our annual trade volume to $100 billion by the next five years. The volume of Iran–Turkey annual trade exchanges reached roughly USD16 billion in 2011, and soared past USD22 billion by the end of 2012' in *Tasnim News Agency*, 'Iranian, Turkish FMs Discuss Regional, International Issues in Pakistan' (19/12/2013) in http://www.tasnimnews.com/English/Home/ Single/225835 (last accessed March 2016).

34. Bariş Ergin, 'First KRG gas to flow to Turkey in two years', *Sabah* newspaper (20/11/2015) in http://www.dailysabah.com/energy/2015/11/ 21/first-krg-gas-to-flow-to-turkey-in-two-years (last accessed December 2015).

35. Interview with Khider Marassana, op. cit.

36. Julian Lee, 'Oil Output Freeze Hope Gets Help From an Unlikely Source: Gadfly', *Washington Post* (29/03/2016) in http://washpost.bloomberg. com/Story?docId=1376-O4QM456KLVRV01-2FL2KA8AOEMK78L1UGV5 D5S3RE (last accessed March 2016).

37. John J. Mearsheimer and Stephen M. Walt, 'Leaving theory behind: Why simplistic hypothesis testing is bad for International Relations', *European Journal of International Relations*, Vol. 19, No. 3 (2013), p. 448.

38. Shireen T. Hunter, *Iran's foreign policy in the post-Soviet era: resisting the new international order* (Santa Barbara, CA: Praeger, 2010), p. 14.

39. Tim Dunne, Lene Hansen, Colin Wight, 'The end of IR theory?', *European Journal of International Relations*, Vol. 19, No. 3 (2013), p. 408.

40. Ibid., p. 409.

41. John J. Mearsheimer and Stephen M. Walt, 'Leaving theory behind … ', op., cit., p. 449.

42. Colin Wight, *Agents, Structures and International Relations*, op. cit., p. 88.

43. Jülide Karakoç, 'The Impact of the Kurdish identity on Turkey's foreign policy from the 1980s to 2008', *Middle Eastern Studies*, Vol. 46, No. 6 (November 2010), p. 922.

44. Ibid., p. 290.

45. Colin Wight, *Agents, Structures and International Relations*, op. cit, p. 232.

46. Ibid., pp. 7, 293–294.

47. Ibid., p. 2.

48. Cited in Colin Wight, *Agents, Structures and International Relations*, op. cit, p. 121.

49. Tim Dunne, Lene Hansen, Colin Wight, 'The end of IR theory?', op. cit., p. 410.

50. Colin Wight, *Agents, Structures and International Relations*, op. cit, p. 295.

51. Interview by the author with Simakov Victor Victorovich General Consul, Consulate General of the Russian Federation in Erbil (Erbil, 30 April 2017).

52. Interview with Khider Marassana, op. cit.

53. 'The challenge that we face is rooted much more in the immediate problem, which we have partially created' in Charlie Rose, 'Interviews with Zbigniew Brzezinski, Henry Kissinger and Brent Scowcroft', *New York Times* (18/06/2007) in http://www.nytimes.com/2007/06/18/world/americas/18iht-web-rose.html?pagewanted=all (last accessed March 2016).

54. Mahan Abedin, 'Iran's Rafsanjani pushes for new role in power', *Middle East Eye* (31/12/2015) in http://www.middleeasteye.net/columns/irans-rafsanjani-pushes-new-role-power-799271826 (last accessed February 2016).

55. Iraqi Prime Minister, Haider Jawad Kadhim Al-Abadi, gave *ultimatum* (December 2015) calling for the withdrawal from the Iraqi territory within 48 hours of 400 Turkish troops and 24 tanks that stationed at a military Turkish training camp, 40 km North-East of Mosul, called Bashiqa, against Baghdad's consent.

## APPENDIX   KCK STRUCTURE

1. This structure is important as it clearly demonstrates the degree of organisation – in the form of a state – that a non-state entity can be identified by.

# Bibliography

BOOKS

Abrahamian, Ervand, *A History of Modern Iran* (New York: Cambridge University Press, 2008).

———, *Mass Protests in the Islamic Revolution, 1977–79* in Roberts, Adam and Timothy Garton Ash, eds, *Civil Resistance and Power Politics: The Experience of Non-violent Action from Gandhi to the Present* (Oxford: Oxford University Press, 2009).

Baer, Robert, *The Devil We Know: Dealing with the New Iranian Superpower* (New York: Crown, 2008).

Bolukbasi, Suha, 'Chapter 3: From the Islamic Revolution to the Persian Gulf War: 1979–1991' in Olson, Robert, *The Kurdish Question and Turkish–Iranian Relations: from World War I to 1998* (Mazda Publishers, Kurdish Studies Series, No. 1. Costa Mesa, CA: 1998).

Bozdağlioğlu, Yücel, *Turkish Foreign Policy and Turkish Identity: A Constructivist Approach* (New York: Routledge, 2003).

Canfield, Robert L., ed., *Turko-Persia in Historical Perspective* (Cambridge: Cambridge University Press, 1991).

Charountaki, Marianna, *The Kurds and US Foreign Policy: International Relations in the Middle East since 1945* (London: Routledge, 2010).

———, 'Chapter 14: The Kurdish Factor in Turkish Politics: Impediment or Facilitator to Turkey's European Prospects?' in *Part Five: Politics and International Relations: Perspectives on Kurdistan's Economy and Society in Transition* (New York: Nova Science Publishers, 2012).

Chubin, Shahram, '*Whither Iran? Reform, Domestic Politics and National Security*', Adelphi Paper 342 (New York: The International Institute for Strategic Studies, Oxford University Press, 2002).

Chubin, Shahram and Charles Tripp, '*Iran–Saudi Arabia Relations and Regional Order*', Adelphi Paper 304 (New York: The International Institute for Strategic Studies, Oxford University Press, 1996).

Chufrin, Gennady, ed., *The Security of the Caspian Sea Region* (Oxford: Oxford University Press, 2001).

Ciment, James, *The Kurds: State and Minority in Turkey, Iraq and Iran* (New York: Barnes and Noble, 1996).

Cizre, Ümit, *Secular and Islamic Politics in Turkey: The Making of the Justice and Development Party* (Routledge Studies in Middle Eastern Politics, London: Routledge, 2008).

Daryaee, Touraj, ed., *The Oxford Handbook of Iranian History* (New York: Oxford University Press, 2012).

Demirci, Emin Yaşar, *Modernisation Religion and Politics in Turkey: the Case of The İskenderpaşa Community* (Istanbul: Insan, 2008).

Dmytryshyn, Basil and Frederick Cox, *The Soviet Union and the Middle East: A Documentary Record of Afghanistan, Iran and Turkey 1917–1985* (NJ: Kingston, 1987).

Ehteshami, Anoushiravan and Mahjoob Zweiri, *Iran and the Rise of its Neoconservatives: The Politics of Tehran's Silent Revolution* (London: I.B.Tauris, 2007).

Elik, Suleyman, *Iran–Turkey Relations, 1979–2011: Conceptualizing the Dynamics of Politics, Religion and Security in Middle-Power States* (London: Routledge, 2012).

Everest, Larry, *Oil, Power & Empire: Iraq and the U.S. Global Agenda* (4th edn) (Canada: Common Courage Press, 2004).

Fawcett, Louise, ed., *International Relations of the Middle East* (Oxford: Oxford University Press, 2009).

Frye, Richard N., *The United States and Turkey and Iran* (USA: Archon Books, 1971).

Gerges, Fawaz A., *Obama and the Middle East: The End of America's Moment?* (New York: Palgrave Macmillan, 2012).

Golan, Galia, *Soviet Policies in the Middle East From World War Two to Gorbachev:* (Cambridge Russian Paperbacks. Cambridge, Cambridge University Press, 1991).

Gürakar, Tolga, *Türkiye ve İran Gelenek, Çağdaşlaşma, Devrim [Turkey and Iran: Tradition, Modernization, Revolution]* (Istanbul: Kaynak Yayınları: Tarih Dizisi, 2012).

Harris, George S., 'Chapter 1: the Russian Federation and Turkey' in Rubinstein, Alvin Z. and Oles M. Smolansky, eds, *Regional Power Rivalries in the New Eurasia: Russia, Turkey and Iran* (New York, Armonk, 1995).

Hentov, Elliot, *Asymmetry of Interest: Turkish–Iranian Relations since 1979* (Lambert Academic Publishing, 21 December 2012).

Hiro, Dilip, *Iran Under the Ayatollahs* (London: Routledge and Kegan Paul, 1985).
———, *Inside Central Asia: A Political and Cultural History of Uzbekistan, Turkmenistan, Kazakjstan, Kyrgyzstan, Tajikistan, Turkey and Iran* (New York: Overlook Duckworth, 2009).

Houghton, David P., *US Foreign Policy and the Iran Hostage Crisis* (New York: Cambridge University Press, 2001).

Hunter, Shireen T., *Iran's Foreign Policy in the Post-Soviet Era: Resisting the New International Order* (Santa Barbara, CA: Praeger, 2010).

Jonson, Lena, 'Chapter 2: The New Geopolitical Situation in the Caspian Region' in Chufrin, Gennady, ed., *The Security of the Caspian Sea Region* (Oxford University Press, 2001).

Karayılan, Murat, *Η Ανατομία του Πολέμου στο Κουρδιστάν [Bir Savaşın Anatomisi, Anatomy of a War, Mezopotamya Yayinlari, 2011]* (Athens: Infognomon, 2012).

Kalenteridis, Savvas, 'Πώς έγινε η παράδοση του Άπο', *Παράδοση Οτζαλάν: η ώρα της αλήθειας [How Apo was captured: The Capture of Öcalan: the Time of the Truth]* (Athens: Infognomon, 2007).

Kinzer, Stephen, *Reset: Iran, Turkey and America's Future* (New York: Times Books, 2010).

Kissinger, Henry A., 'Continuity and Change in American Foreign Policy': The Arthur K. Solomon Lecture (New York University: 19 September 1977) in Kissinger, Henry A., *For the Record: Selected Statements, 1977–1980* (Boston: Little Brown & Co, 1981).

———, *Diplomacy* (New York, Simon & Schuster, 1994).

Kösebalaban, Hasan, *Turkish Foreign Policy: Islam, Nationalism and Globalization* (New York: Palgrave Macmillan, 2011).

Lansford, Tom, *Political Handbook of the World 2014* (Thousand Oaks, CA: Sage/ CQ Press, 2014).

Liel, Alon, *Turkey in the Middle East: Oil, Islam and Politics* (Boulder, CO: Lynne Rienner Publishers, 2001).

Lotfian, Saideh in Katouzian, Homa and Hossein Shahidi, eds, *Iran in the 21st Century: Politics, Economics and Conflict* (London: Routledge, 2008).

Mann, James, *The Obamians: The Struggle Inside the White House to Redefine American Power* (New York: Viking Adult: 2012).

Mattair, R. Thomas, *Global Security Watch – Iran: A Reference Handbook* (Westport, CT: Praeger, 2008).

Menashri, David, *Post-Revolutionary Politics in Iran: Religion, Society, and Power* (London and Portland, Ore: Frank Cass, 2001).

———, 'Khomeini's Vision: Nationalism or World Order?' in Menashri, David, ed., *The Iranian Revolution and the Muslim World* (Boulder, San Francisco: Westview, 1990).

Mirzoyan, Alla, *Armenia, the Regional Powers and the West. Between History and Geopolitics* (New York: Palgrave Macmillan, 2010).

Müftüler-Bac, Meltem, *Turkey's Relations with a Changing Europe* (Manchester University Press, 1997).

Nasr, Vali, *The Dispensable Nation: American Foreign Policy in Retreat* (New York: Anchor Books, 2013).

Olson, Robert, *The Kurdish Question and Turkish–Iranian Relations: From World War I to 1998*, Kurdish Studies Series, No. 1 (Costa Mesa, CA: Mazda Publishers, 1998).

———, *Turkey's Relations with Iran, Syria, Israel, and Russia, 1991–2000: The Kurdish and Islamist Questions*, Kurdish Studies Series (Costa Mesa, CA: Mazda Publishers, 2001).

———, *Turkey–Iran Relations, 1979–2004: Revolution, Ideology, War, Coups and Geopolitics* (Costa Mesa, CA: Mazda Publishers, 2004).

Panah, Maryam, *The Islamic Republic and the World: Global Dimensions of the Iranian Revolution* (London: Pluto, 2007).

Parsi, Trita, *Treacherous Alliance: The Secret Dealings of Israel, Iran and the United States* (New York: Yale University Press, 2007).

———, *A Single Roll of the Dice: Obama's Diplomacy with Iran* (New York: Yale University Press, 2012).

Peimani, Hooman, *Regional Security and the Future of Central Asia: The Competition of Iran, Turkey, and Russia* (Westport: Praeger, 1998).

Philip, Gordon H. and Taşpınar Ömer, *Winning Turkey: How America, Europe and Turkey Can Revive a Fading Partnership* (Washington: Brookings Institution, 2008).

Polk, William R., *The Arab World Today* (Cambridge, Mass: Harvard University Press, 1991).

Ramazani, Rouhullah K., *Revolutionary Iran: Challenge and Response in the Middle East* (4th ed.) (Baltimore, London: Johns Hopkins University Press: 1988).

Rochester, Martin J., *US Foreign Policy in the Twenty-First Century* (Boulder CO: Westview: 2008).

Rubinstein, Alvin Z. and Oles M. Smolansky, eds, *Regional Power Rivalries in the New Eurasia: Russia, Turkey and Iran* (New York: Armonk, 1995).

Sick, Gary, *October Surprise: America's Hostages in Iran and the Election of Ronald Reagan* (New York: Times Books, 1991).

Şık, Ahmet, *The Imam's Army [Imamın Ordusu]* (Turkey: Postacı, 2011).

Suskind, Ron, *The Price of Loyalty* (New York: Simon and Schuster, 2004).

Teicher, Howard and Gayle Radley Teicher, *Twin Pillars to Desert Storm: America's Flawed Vision in the Middle East from Nixon to Bush* (New York: William Morrow and Co, 1993).

Tezcür, Güneş Murat, *Muslim Reformers in Iran and Turkey: The Paradox of Moderation* (Austin: University of Texas Press, 2010).

Tsardanidis, Charalambos and Vivi Kefala, Ιράν: Πολιτική Οικονομία, Διεθνείς και Περιφερειακές Σχέσεις, [*Iran: Political Economy and International and Regional Relations*] (Athens: Εκδόσεις Παπαζήση, 2014).

Wight, Colin, *Agents, Structures and International Relations: Politics as Ontology* (New York: Cambridge University Press, 2006).

Winrow, Gareth M., 'Azerbaijan and Iran' in Rubinstein, Alvin Z. and Oles M. Smolansky, eds, *Regional Power Rivalries in the New Eurasia: Russia, Turkey and Iran* (New York: Armonk, 1995).

Woodward, Bob, *State of Denial* (New York, Simon & Schuster: 2006).

## ARTICLES

Akcali, Emel and Mehmet Perincek, 'Kemalist Eurasianism: An Emerging Geopolitical Discourse in Turkey', *Geopolitics*, Vol. 14, No. 3 (July 2009).

Altinkaş, Evren, 'The Iran–Iraq War and its Effects on Turkey', *International Law and Policy [Uluslararasr Hukuk ve Politika]*, Vol. 1, No. 4 (2005).

Amuzegar, Jahangir, 'Iran's Economy and the US Sanctions', *Middle East Journal* Vol. 51, No. 2 (Spring 1997).

Ansari, Ali M., 'Iran under Ahmadinejad: the Politics of Confrontation', *Adelphi Paper* 393 (International Institute for Strategic Studies, 2007).

Axelgard, Frederick W., 'US–Iraqi Relations: a Status Report', *American–Arab Affairs*, No. 13 (Summer, 1985).

Bishku, Michael B., Review: 'Asymmetry of Interest: Turkish–Iranian Relations since 1979' by Elliot Hentov in *The Middle East Journal*, Vol. 67, No. 3 (Summer 2013).

Calabrese, John, 'Turkey and Iran: Limits of a Stable Relationship', *British Journal of Middle Eastern Studies*, Vol. 25, No. 1 (May 1998).

Canfield, Robert L., *Iranian Studies*, Vol. 26, No. 1/2 (Winter–Spring: 1993).

Cetinsaya, Gokhan, Review: 'Turkey–Iran Relations 1979–2004: Revolution, Ideology, War, Coups and Geopolitics' by Robert Olson in *International Journal of Middle East Studies*, Vol. 39, No. 2 (May 2007).

Charountaki, Marianna, 'Turkish Foreign Policy and the Kurdistan Regional Government', *Perceptions: Journal of International Affairs*, XVII, No. 4 (Center for Strategic Research: Winter 2012): 185–208 in http://sam.gov.tr/wp-content/uploads/2013/03/8-Marianna_Charountaki.pdf (last accessed February 2015).

———, 'US Foreign Policy in Theory and Practice: from Soviet-era Containment to the Era of the Arab Uprisings', *Journal of American Foreign Policy Interests: the Journal of the National Committee on American Foreign Policy*, Vol. 36, Issue 4 (2014): 255–267.

———, 'Kurdish Policies in Syria under the Arab Uprisings: A Revisiting of IR in the New Middle Eastern Order', *Third World Quarterly*, Vol. 36, Issue 2 (27 March 2015).

Cohen, Saul B., 'Turkey's Emergence as a Geopolitical Power Broker', *Eurasian Geography and Economics*, Vol. 52, No. 2 (2011).

Cordesman, Anthony H., Bryan H. Gold, Robert Shelala and Michael Gibbs, 'US and Iranian Strategic Competition: Turkey and the South Caucasus', *CIS* (6 February 2013).

Davutoğlu, Ahmet, 'Turkey's Zero Problems Foreign Policy', *Foreign Policy* (20/05/2010).

———, 'Principles of Turkish Foreign Policy and Regional Political Structuring', Paper No. 3 (SAM, April 2012) in http://sam.gov.tr/wp-content/uploads/2012/04/vision_paper_TFP2.pdf (last accessed May 2014).

————, 'The Restoration of Turkey: Strong Democracy, Dynamic Economy, and Active Diplomacy' in Center for Strategic Research (SAM), No. 7 (August 2014).

Dehshiri, M.R. and M.R. Majidi, 'Iran's Foreign Policy in Post-Revolution Era: A Holistic Approach', *The Iranian Journal of International Affairs*. Vol. XXI, No. 1–2: (Winter–Spring 2008–2009): 101–114.

Dobransky, Steve, 'Why the US Failed in Iraq: Baghdad at the Crossroads', *The Middle East Quarterly*, Vol. 21, No. 1 (Winter 2014) in http://www.meforum.org/3680/iraq-us-failure (last accessed April 2016).

Dunne, Tim, Lene Hansen and Colin Wight, 'The End of IR Theory?' *European Journal of International Relations*, Vol. 19, No. 3 (2013).

Ebrahimi, Mansoureh and Yusoff, Kamaruzaman and Seyed Jalili, Mir Mohamadali 'Economic, Political, and Strategic Issues in Iran–Turkey Relations, 2002–2015', *Contemporary Review of the Middle East*, Vol. 4, Issue 1 (2017): 67–83.

Ehteshami, Anoushiravan and Süleyman Elik, 'Turkey's Growing Relations with Iran and Arab Middle East', *Turkish Studies*. Vol. 12, No. 4 (December 2011): 647–649.

Ekinci, Arzu Celalifer, *İran Türkiye Enerji İşbirliği [Iran–Turkey Energy Cooperation]* (Kasım: Uluslararası Stratejik Araştırmalar Kurumu, 2008).

Elahi, Maryam, 'Washington Watch: Clinton, Ankara and Kurdish Human Rights' *Middle East Report*, No. 189 (July–August 1994).

Enginsoy, Umit and Bekdil, Burak Ege, 'Arab uprising undermines Turkey–Iran–Syria alliance', *Defense News*, Vol. 26, No. 30 (15 August 2011).

Fazlhashemi, Mohammad, 'Turkey: Iran's Window on Europe' in Larsson, Rickard, ed., *Boundaries of Europe?* (Swedish Council for Planning and Coordination of Research) FRN Report 98: 6 (1998): 71–84.

Flanagan, Stephen J., Drivers and Strategy in Turkey, Russia, Iran Economic and Energy Relations (Center for Strategic and International Studies, 29/03/2012) in http://csis.org/files/attachments/120529_Flanagan_TRI_Economic_Energy_Dimensions.pdf (last accessed April 2016).

————, 'The Turkey–Russia–Iran Nexus: Eurasian Power Dynamics', *Washington Quarterly* (Winter 2013) in http://csis.org/files/publication/TWQ_13Winter_Flanagan.pdf (last accessed December 2015).

Heper, Metin, 'Islam and Democracy in Turkey: Toward a Reconciliation', *Middle East Journal*. Vol. 1, No. 1 (1997): 39–41.

Ismailov, Eldar and Vldimer Papava, 'A New Concept for the Caucasus', *Southeast European and Black Sea Studies*, Vol. 8, No. 3 (September 2008): 283–298.

Jenkins, Gareth H., 'Tactical Allies and Strategic Rivals: Turkey's Changing Relations With Iran', *Turkey Analyst*, Vol. 4, No. 23 (5 December 2011) in http://www.turkeyanalyst.org/publications/turkey-analyst-articles/item/285-tactical-allies-and-strategic-rivals-turkeys-changing-relations-with-iran.html (last accessed September 2015).

Jones, Matthew, 'The Preferred Plan: The Anglo-American Working Group Report on Covert Action in Syria, 1957', *Intelligence and National Security*, Vol. 19, No. 3 (Autumn 2004).

Karakoç, Jülide, 'The Impact of the Kurdish Identity on Turkey's Foreign Policy from the 1980s to 2008', *Middle Eastern Studies*, Vol. 46, No. 6 (November 2010).

Karasipahi, Sena, 'Comparing Islamic Resurgence Movements in Turkey and Iran', *Middle East Journal*, Vol. 63, No. 1 (Winter, 2009): 87–108.

Kim, Younkyoo and Stephen Blank, 'Turkey and Russia on Edge: Russo-Turkish Divergence: the Security Dimension', GLORIA Center (27 April 2012) in http://www.thecuttingedgenews.com/index.php?article=73149&pageid =13&pagename=Analysis (last accessed April 2016).

Larrabee, Stephen F., 'Turkey Rediscovers the Middle East', *Foreign Affairs*, Vol. 86, No. 4 (July/August 2007).

Lawson, Fred H., 'Syria's Relations with Iran: Managing the Dilemmas of Alliance', *Middle East Journal*, Vol. 61, No. 1 (Winter, 2007).

Mafi, Homayoun, 'The Dilemma of US Economic Sanctions on Iran: an Iranian Perspective', *The Iranian Journal of International Affairs*, Vol. XIX, No. 4 (Fall, 2007).

Makovsky, Alan, 'The New Activism in Turkish Foreign Policy', *SAIS Review*, Vol. 19, No. 1 (Washington DC: The Johns Hopkins University Press for the School of Advanced International Studies, 1999).

Ma'oz, Moshe, 'The 'Arab Spring' and the New Geo-strategic Environment in the Middle East', *Insight Turkey*, Vol. 14, No. 4 (2012).

Markedonov, Sergey, 'Debating Eurasia: The Search for New Paradigms', *Caucasus International*, Vol. 2, No. 3 (Autumn 2012): 66–70.

McCartney, Paul T., 'American nationalism and US foreign policy from Sept 11 to the Iraq War', *Political Science Quarterly*, 119(3) (2004).

McCurdy, Daphne, 'Turkish–Iranian Relations: When Opposites Attract', *Turkish Policy Quarterly*, Vol. 7, No. 2 (Summer 2008).

Mearsheimer, John J. and Stephen M. Walt, 'Leaving Theory Behind: Why Simplistic Hypothesis Testing is Bad for International Relations', *European Journal of International Relations*, Vol. 19, No. 3 (2013).

Moeinaddini, Javad and Mahin Rezapour, 'Iran's Regional Power and Prominence in the Context of International System', *The Iranian Journal of International Affairs*, Vol. 20, No. 3 (Summer 2008).

Moghadam, Reza, 'Turkey at the Crossroads: From Crisis Resolution to EU Accession' (Washington DC: International Monetary Fund, 2005).

Neff, Donald, 'US: the ghost of 1980', *Middle East International*, No. 400 (Washington DC, 17 May 1991).

Nerguizian, Aram, 'US and Iranian Strategic Competition: the Proxy Cold War in the Levant, Egypt and Jordan', *CSIS* (12/03/2012) in http://csis.org/ files/publication/120312_Iran_VIII_Levant.pdf (last accessed September 2015).

Norton, Augustus Richard, 'Hizballah and the Israeli Withdrawal from Southern Lebanon', *Journal of Palestine Studies*, Vol. 30, No. 1 (Autumn 2000): 22–35.

Olson, Robert, 'Turkey–Iran Relations, 1997 to 2000: The Kurdish and Islamist Questions', *Third World Quarterly*, Vol. 21, No. 5 (October 2000).

Özcan, Ali Nihat and Özgür Özdamar, 'Uneasy Neighbors: Turkish–Iranian Relations since the 1979 Islamic Revolution', *Middle East Policy*, Vol. 17, No. 3 (Fall 2010).

Parlak, Bekir, Zahid Sobaci and Mustafa Ökmen, 'The evaluation of restructured local governments in Turkey within the context of the European charter on local self-government', *Ankara Law Review*, Vol. 5, No. 1 (Summer 2008).

Perry, John, Review: 'Turko-Persia in Historical Perspective' in *Iranian Studies*, ed. Canfield, Robert L., Vol. 26, No. 1/2 (Winter–Spring 1993).

———, 'The Historical Role of Turkish in Relation to Persian of Iran' in *Iran and the Caucasus*, Vol. 5 (2001), ed. Asatrian, Garnik (Tehran: International Publications of Iranian Studies): 193–200.

Pupkin, David, 'Iran–Turkey Economic Relations: What Their Rapid Growth Means for Iran's Nuclear Program', *Iran Tracker* (24/06/2010) in http://www.irantracker.org/analysis/Iran–Turkey-economic-relations-what-their-rapid-growth-means-iran%E2%80%99s-nuclear-program (last accessed July 2015).

Rabasa, Angel and F. Stephen Larrabee, 'The Rise of Political Islam in Turkey', RAND, National Defense Research Institute (USA 2008).

Ramazani, Ruhi K., 'Iran's Foreign Policy: Contending Orientations', *Middle East Journal*, Vol. 43, No. 2 (Spring 1989).

———, 'The Shifting Premise of Iran's Foreign Policy: Towards a Democratic Peace?', *Middle East Journal*, Vol. 52, No. 2 (Spring 1998).

Saab, Bilal Y., 'Syria and Turkey Deepen Bilateral Relations', *Brookings* (06/05/2009) in http://www.brookings.edu/research/articles/2009/05/06-syria-turkey-saab (last accessed July 2015).

Samii, Abbas William, 'The Nation and its Minorities: Ethnicity, Unity and State Policy in Iran', *Comparative Studies of South Asia, Africa and the Middle East*, Vol. 20, No. 1–2 (2000): 128–137.

———, 'A Stable Structure on Shifting Sands: Assessing the Hizbullah–Iran–Syria Relationship', *Middle East Journal*, Vol. 62, No. 1 (Winter 2008).

Şamiloğlu, Famil, 'Kafkasya'da Dengeler Değişiyor Mu? [*Have the balances been changing in Caucasus?*] (USAK: International Strategic Research Organization, 15/02/2010).

Seifzadeh, Hossein S., 'The Landscape of Factional Politics and its Future in Iran', *Middle East Journal*, Vol. 57, No. 1 (Winter, 2003).

Shambayati, Hootan, 'The Rentier State, Interest Groups, and the Paradox of Autonomy: State and Business in Turkey and Iran', *Comparative Politics*, Vol. 26, No. 3 (April 1994): 320–327.

Spyer, Jonathan and Jawad Aymenn Al-Tamimi, 'How Iraq Became a Proxy of the Islamic Republic of Iran', *The Tower*, Issue 21 (December 2014) in http://www.thetower.org/article/how-iraq-became-a-wholly-owned-subsidiary-of-the-islamic-republic-of-iran/ (last accessed February 2015).

Talhamy, Yvette, 'The Syrian Muslim Brothers and the Syrian–Iranian Relationship', *Middle East Journal*, Vol. 63, No. 4 (Autumn 2009), 561–580.

Taşkın, Yüksel, 'Turkey's Search for Regional Power', *Middle East Report Online* (21/08/ 2010) in http://www.merip.org/mero/mero082110 (last accessed April 2016).

Taspinar, Omer, Robert Malley and Sadjadpour Karim, 'Symposium: Israel, Turkey and Iran in the changing Arab World', *Middle East Policy*, Vol. 19, No. 1 (Spring 2012).

Tülümen, Turgut, 'The Future of Turkish–Iranian Relations', *Turkish Review of Middle East Studies*, Vol. 10 (1999): 135–142.

Walberg, Eric, 'Turkey vs the US: A kinder Middle East hegemon', *Global Research* (21/07/2011) in http://www.globalresearch.ca/turkey-vs-the-us-a-kinder-middle-east-hegemon/25718 (last accessed April 2016).

Wang Bo, 'Turkey–Iran Reconciliatory Relations: Internal and External Factors', *Journal of Middle Eastern and Islamic Studies* (in Asia) Vol. 5, No. 1 (2011) in http://mideast.shisu.edu.cn/_upload/article/86/f1/a2903ac544d ab4e4aba6c9bfcce9/8f07916c-765e-4523–996e-28ae286974c6.pdf (last accessed August 2017).

Wright, Robin, *The Iran Primer: Power, Politics and the US Policy* (The US Institute of Peace, November 2010).

## PUBLIC TALKS

Al-Abadi, Haider (Iraqi Prime Minister), 'Iraqi PM praises Peshmerga–Iraqi army cooperation in fight against ISIS', *Ara News* (9 March 2017) in http://aranews.net/2017/03/iraqi-pm-praises-peshmerga-iraqi-army-cooperation-in-fight-against-isis/ (last accessed August 2017).

Barack, Obama, 'A New Beginning', Middle East Speech (4 June 2009) in http://www.huffingtonpost.com/2009/06/04/obamas-middle-east-speech_n_211217.html (last accessed December 2015).

———, 'Syria: Assad must resign, says Obama', *The Guardian* (19 August 2011) in https://www.theguardian.com/world/2011/aug/18/syria-assad-must-resign-obama (last accessed August 2017).

Bauer, Dana (Deputy Director of the Office of Southern Europe), 'On the Way to Europe: the Future of the Kurdish Question for Turkey and its Neighbours', Dr. Karl Renner Institute, Austria (6 July 1998). Speech reported in: 'US officials speak on Turkey and the Kurdish Question' in US Information Service, http://www.mtholyoke.edu/acad/intrel/kurdtur.htm (last accessed April 2016).

Clark, Wesley (former NATO Supreme Allied Commander, Europe 1997–2000), 'A Time to Lead' (Lisbon, 5 May 2000) in http://fora.tv/2007/10/03/

Wesley_Clark_A_Time_to_Lead/Wesley_Clark_on_America_s_Foreign_Policy__Coup_ (last accessed July 2015).

Davutoğlu, Ahmet, Seminar at George Washington University (9 February 2012) in https://www.youtube.com/watch?v=Se6ynRCqlb4 (last accessed July 2015).

Erdoğan, Recep Tayyip, 'Keynote Speech at International Symposium on Conservatism and Democracy' (AK Parti, 2004) cited in Kuru, Ahmet, 'From Islamism to Conservative Democracy: the Justice and Development Party in Turkey', Paper presentation at the Annual Meeting of the American Political Science Association in http://www.allacademic. com/meta/p151181_index.html (31 August 2006) (last accessed October 2009).

Kalın, İbrahim, 'Keynote Address', Annual Conference on Turkey 2015, Foundation for Political, Economic and Social Research, SETA DC (Washington, 1 June 2015). https://www.youtube.com/watch?v=vOSfMdjyja8&list=PLFsiqhkioRXqhFBDrINRtvUqzZ2sQ2ea4 (last accessed April 2016).

Kuru, Ahmet, 'From Islamism to Conservative Democracy: the Justice and Development Party in Turkey', Paper presentation at the Annual Meeting of the American Political Science Association (Chicago: 31 August 2006) http://www.allacademic.com/meta/p151181_index.html (last accessed October 2009).

Mohajerani, Dr. Ata'ollah (former Iranian Minister), 'Discussing Iran after Ahmadinejad: A New Leaf?', Reading University (12 March 2014).

———, 'Public Talk' at ReadiMUN. Reading University (28 November 2014).

Mohammed, Salih Muslim, 'Keynote speech', Kurdish conference in London (London, 18 November 2012).

Trump, Donald, 'Transcript: Donald Trump's Foreign Policy Speech', *New York Times* (27 April 2016) in https://www.nytimes.com/2016/04/28/us/politics/transcript-trump-foreign-policy.html (last accessed August 2017).

## REPORTS

Adib-Moghaddam, Arshin, 'Turkey & Iran: Islamic Brotherhood or Regional Rivalry?', *Al Jazeera Center for Studies* (4 June 2013).

Larrabee, F. Stephen and Alireza Nader, 'Turkish–Iranian Relations in a Changing Middle East', *RAND* Report: Issue 258 (2013) in http://www.rand.org/content/dam/rand/pubs/research_reports/RR200/RR258/RAND_RR258.pdf: 2 (last accessed May 2015).

Miller, Nathan K, 'Report' (August 2008) published in Charountaki Marianna, *The Kurds and US Foreign Policy: International Relations in the Middle East since 1945* (London: Routledge, October 2010).

*Stratfor*, 'Israel's Water Challenge' (25 December 2013) in http://www.stratfor.com/analysis/israels-water-challenge (last accessed April 2016).

'Why Bill Clinton mentioned Gülen at the Turkish Cultural Center's Dinner: Gülenists' campaign contributions to Hillary Clinton likely played a role' (September 2008) in http://turkishinvitations.weebly.com/why-bill-clinton-mentioned-gulen-at-the-tccny-dinner.html (last accessed September 2015).

OFFICIAL DOCUMENTS

Albright, Madeleine K., 'Remarks before the American-Iranian Council', US State Department (17 March 2000) in http://1997–2001.state.gov/www/statements/2000/000317a.html (last accessed April 2015).

Armed Services Committee Press Releases in http://armedservices.house.gov/index.cfm/press-releases?ContentRecord_id=F0AC8FF7-C044–40CA-97AA-7562A4C7E5FD (last accessed May 2015).

Barack Obama, 'National Security Strategy of the US' (26 May 2010) in https://www.whitehouse.gov/sites/default/files/rss_viewer/national_security_strategy.pdf (last accessed September 2015).

Bush, George H.W., 'US Policy Towards the Persian Gulf', National Security Directive 26 (Washington, DC: The White House, 2 October 1989), http://www.fas.org/irp/offdocs/nsd/nsd26.pdf (last accessed April 2016).

———, 'US Policy in Response to the Iraqi Invasion of Kuwait', National Security Directive 45 (Washington, DC: The White House, 20 August 1990). http://www.fas.org/irp/offdocs/nsd/nsd45.pdf (last accessed February 2016).

———, White House Briefing, Press Conference, *Untitled Document*, No. 28/4/2549 (16 April 1991), http://bushlibrary.tamu.edu/research/public_papers.php?year=1991&month=4 (last accessed March 2009).

———, National Security Presidential Directives [NSPD]-9: *Combating Terrorism* (25 October 2001) in http://www.fas.org/irp/offdocs/nspd/nspd-9.htm (last accessed July 2015).

Carter, Jimmy, State of the Union Message to the 96th Congress (23 January 1980), http://www.presidency.ucsb.edu/ws/index.php?pid=33079 (last accessed January 2015) (last accessed April 2016).

Cheney, Dick, Secretary of Defense, House of Foreign Affairs Committee Hearing, 'President's FY '92 Security Assistance Request' (19 March 1991).

Congressional Research Service, 'Iran: Regional Perspectives and US Policy', Order No: R40849 (13 January 2010).

Davutoğlu, Ahmet, 'Foreign Minister Zarif of Iran pays a visit to Turkey' (1 November 2013), Turkish Ministry of Foreign Affairs in http://www.mfa.gov.tr/foreign-minister-zarif-of-iran-pays-a-visit-to-turkey.en.mfa (last accessed April 2014).

Katzman, Kenneth, 'Iraq: US Efforts to Change the Regime', *Report for Congress*, Order Code RL31339 (The Library of Congress, 16 August 2002).

———, 'Iran Current Developments and US Policy', *Congressional* Research Service Report (25 April 2003) in http://fpc.state.gov/documents/organization/20242.pdf (last accessed April 2015).

Katzman, Kenneth and James Nichol, 'Iran: Relations with Key Central Asian States', *CRS Report for Congress* (23 July 1998).

Kaya, Karen, 'Turkey–Iran Relations after the Arab Spring' (FMSO, Department of the Army, Department of Defense) in http://fmso.leavenworth.army.mil/documents/Turkey–Iran.pdf (last accessed April 2015).

Kimball, Daryl and Kelsey Davenport, 'Timeline of Syrian Chemical Weapons Activity, 2012–2015', Arms Control Association, in https://www.arms-control.org/factsheets/Timeline-of-Syrian-Chemical-Weapons-Activity (last accessed March 2016).

KRG Cabinet, 'Border crossing points between Iran and Kurdistan Region to be reinforced' (23 April 2015) in http://cabinet.gov.krd/a/d.aspx?s=040000&l=12&a=53213 (last accessed September 2015).

———, 'EU continues its support for Kurdistan Region' (28 July 2015) in http://cabinet.gov.krd/a/d.aspx?s=040000&l=12&a=53572 (last accessed September 2015).

'Kurdish Problem Memorandum' (28 July 1972) from the President's Deputy Assistant for National Security Affairs (Al Haig) to the President's Assistant for National Security Affairs (Henry Kissinger), http://www.state.gov/r/pa/ho/frus/nixon/e4/71903.htm (last accessed March 2009).

Ministry of Foreign Affairs, Republic of Turkey, 'Foreign Minister Zarif of Iran pays a visit to Turkey' (1 November 2013) in http://www.mfa.gov.tr/foreign-minister-zarif-of-iran-pays-a-visit-to-turkey.en.mfa (last accessed December 2015).

Ministry of Foreign Affairs, Republic of Turkey, 'Turkey–Iran Economic and Commercial Relations' in http://www.mfa.gov.tr/economic-and-commercial-relations-with-iran.en.mfa (last accessed August 2017).

Ministry of Natural Resources, 'Monthly Export Report for October 2015' (10 November 2015) in http://mnr.krg.org/index.php/en/press-releases/501-mnr-publishes-monthly-export-report-for-october-2015 (last accessed November 2015).

Ministry of Planning, Kurdistan Region Statistics Office in http://www.krso.net/Default.aspx?page=article&id=899&l=1Chapter 6: From threat to threat', The 9/11 Commission Report, http://www.9–11commission.gov/report/ (last accessed March 2009).

National Security Archive, Document 17: 'Department of State, Office of the Secretary Delegation Cable from George P. Shultz to the Department of State: Secretary's May 10 Meeting with Iraqi Foreign Minister Tariq Aziz', No. 04218 (11 May 1983), George Washington University, in http://www.gwu.edu/~nsarchiv/NSAEBB/NSAEBB82/index.htm (last accessed April 2015).

———, 'Ronald Reagan's letter to Saddam Hussein', Document 30, United States Embassy in Italy cable from Maxwell M. Rabb to the Department of State: Rumsfeld's larger meeting with Iraqi Deputy PM [Prime Minister] and FM [Foreign Minister] Tariz [Tariq] Aziz, December 19 (20 December 1983), George Washington University, in http://www.gwu.edu/~nsarchiv/NSAEBB/NSAEBB82/index.htm (last accessed 2008).

———, Battle, Joyce, 'The Iraq War – PART I: The US Prepares for Conflict' (2001) Electronic Briefing Book No. 326, Timeline: 17 in http://nsarchive. gwu.edu/NSAEBB/NSAEBB326/IraqWarPart1-Timeline.pdf (last accessed February 2016).

———, 'Declassified Studies from Cheney Pentagon Show Push for US Military Predominance and a Strategy to 'Prevent the Re-emergence of a New Rival' (26 February 2008) in http://nsarchive.gwu.edu/nukevault/ebb245/ (last accessed July 2015).

Pearson, Ambassador W.R., Telegram: 'The Turkish General Staff: a Fractious and Sullen Political Coalition' (18 April 2003) in https://wikileaks.org/plusd/cables/03ANKARA2521_a.html (last accessed September 2015).

Prados, Alfred B., 'Syria: U.S. Relations and Bilateral Issues', *CRS Brief for Congress* (13 March 2006).

Republic of Turkey, Ministry of Foreign Affairs, 'Turkey–Iran Economic and Trade Relations' in http://www.mfa.gov.tr/turkey_s-commercial-and-economic-relations-with-iran.en.mfa (last accessed April 2016).

Smith, Ben and Lunn, Jon and Page, Rob in Standard Note SNIA 6963: 'UK arms transfers to the Peshmerga in Iraqi Kurdistan', House of Commons, British Library (18 August 2014).

Thornberry, Mac, 'H.R. 1735 Passes: House Armed Services Committee' 60–2, http://armedservices.house.gov/index.cfm/press-releases?ContentRecord_ id=F0AC8FF7-C044-40CA-97AA-7562A4C7E5FD (last accessed February 2016).

US State Department, 'Foreign Relations, 1969–1972, Volume E-4, Iran and Iraq', in http://2001-2009.state.gov/r/pa/ho/frus/nixon/e4/72108.htm (last accessed July 2015).

———, Directorate of Plans, 'Israeli aid to Kurdish Rebels', IN-039040 (9 April 1970) in http://www.state.gov/r/pa/ho/frus/nixon/e4/69591.htm (last accessed April 2016).

White House Government News Release in http://www.whitehouse.gov/news/ releases/2001/09/20010912-14.html (last accessed April 2016).

107th Congress Public Law 243, US Government Printing Office, http://www. gpo.gov/fdsys/pkg/PLAW-107publ243/html/PLAW-107publ243.htm (last accessed July 2015).

## PERIODICALS, NEWSPAPERS, OTHER MEDIA

### *Al Arabiya News*

Karouny, Mariam, 'Will Syria's Nusra Front split from al-Qaeda?' (4 March 2015) http://english.alarabiya.net/en/perspective/features/2015/03/04/ Will-Syria-s-al-Nusra-Front-split-from-al-Qaeda-.html.

## Al Jazeera

Cited in 'Chronology', *Middle East Journal*, Vol. 64, No. 4 (4 May 2010).

'Pentagon wants more money for war', online version (September 2011), http://english.aljazeera.net/News/aspx/print.htm (last accessed January 2016).

'Russia confirms weapons on flights to Syria' (11 September 2015) in http://www.aljazeera.com/news/2015/09/aid-flights-syria-carry-military-equipment-150910110117672.html (last accessed September 2015).

'Assad defends presence of Hezbollah fighters in Syria' (25 August 2015) in http://www.aljazeera.com/news/2015/08/assad-defends-presence-hezbollah-fighters-syria-150825203254106.htm (last accessed September 2015).

'Turkey and Iran agree to strengthen economic ties', *Al Jazeera* (16 April 2016) in http://www.aljazeera.com/news/2016/04/Turkey–Iran-agree-strengthen-economic-ties-160416155434319.html (last accessed August 2017).

## Al Monitor

Candar, Cengiz, 'Turkey Claims Iran Providing Logistical Support for PKK' (30 December 2012).

Karami, Arash, 'The tumbling turban: Who is behind attacks on Reformists in Iran?' (30/11/2015) in http://www.al-monitor.com/pulse/originals/2015/11/iran-reformists-attacked-parliament-elections-2016.html (last accessed December 2015).

Naumkin, Vitaly, 'Russia's Kurdish dilemma' (26 January 2014).

Pecquet, Julian, 'Congress rethinks anti-Assad stance' (16 September 2015) in http://www.al-monitor.com/pulse/originals/2015/09/congress-democrats-assad-regime-change-isis.html# (last accessed April 2016).

Slavin, Barbara, 'Former US diplomat warns of possible 'grave mistake' in Syria' (1 May 2014), http://www.al-monitor.com/pulse/originals/2014/05/syria-ryan-crocker-grave-mistake.html (last accessed April 2016).

Tastekin, Fehim, 'Radical groups operate on Turkey's border' (17 October 2013).

Zaman, Amberin, 'Syrian Kurdish Leader Urges Turkey To End Support for Salafists' (9 October 2013).

Zayer, Karim Abed., 'Maliki Deploys 'Tigris Force' to Kirkuk' (13 December 2012) http://www.almonitor.com/pulse/politics/2012/11/kirkuk-paramilitarytigrispeshmerga.html?utm_source=&utm_medium=email&utm_campaign=5167#ixzz2CDvXmmZz (last accessed September 2015).

'Iran's Basij lash out at nuclear deal' (30 July 2015) in http://www.al-monitor.com/pulse/originals/2015/07/basij-reaction-iran-deal.html&http://farsi.khamenei.ir/speech-content?id=30331 (last accessed September 2015).

'Why did Russia offer autonomy for Syria's Kurds?' *Al Monitor* (29 January 2017) in http://www.al-monitor.com/pulse/originals/2017/01/russia-offer-kurds-syria-autonomy-turkey-islamic-state.html#ixzz4XFA47rrf (last accessed April 2017).

'Zarif presses diplomacy on Syria' (16 August 2015) in http://www.al-monitor.com/pulse/originals/2015/08/zarif-syria-lapid-peace-syria-netanyahu-turkey-temple.html (last accessed September 2015).

## American Foreign Policy
'The New Containment Policy', Vol. 3, No. 4 (6 November 2003).

## Ara News
'SDF says 45% of Raqqa city liberated., operations ongoing', *Ara News* (25 July 2017) in http://aranews.net/2017/07/sdf-says-45-raqqa-city-liberated-operations-ongoing/ (last accessed August 2017).

## Arab News CSM
Cited in 'Chronology', *Middle East Journal*, Vol. 39, No. 4 (3 July 1985); Vol. 41, No. 2 (6 December 1986).

## Arabic News
Cited in 'Chronology', *Middle East Journal*, Vol. 58, No. 1 (13 August 2004).

## Asia Times
Abedin, Mahan, 'Khamenei throws the gauntlet at the West', *Asia Times* (21 September 2011).

## Baghdad Domestic Service
*Baghdad Domestic Service* (18 June 1990).

## BasNews
Abdulrazaq, Hawar, 'Iraq and Iran to Increase Trade to $20 Billion' (6 September 2015) in http://www.basnews.com/index.php/en/economy/217660 (last accessed September 2015).

## BBC
Bush, George W., 'Text of Bush's act of war statement' (12 September 2001) in http://news.bbc.co.uk/1/hi/world/americas/1540544.stm and in http://www.whitehouse.gov/news/releases/2001/09/20010912–14.html (last accessed February 2016).

Sheikh Hamad bin Khalifa Al Thani, US television channel CBS cited in *BBC News* (14 January 2012) http://www.bbc.co.uk/news/world-middle-east-16561493 (last accessed February 2016).

BBC cited in 'Chronology', *Middle East Journal*, Vol. 56, No. 4: 20 April 2001, 30 May 2001, 14 July 2002; Vol. 57, No. 1: 4 September 2002.

'Iran sanctions 'depend on proof'' (21 April 2006) in http://news.bbc.co.uk/1/
    hi/world/middle_east/4929450.stm (last accessed July 2015).
'Israel 'ready to return Golan'' (23 April 2008), http://news.bbc.co.uk/1/hi/
    world/middle_east/7362937.stm (last accessed July 2015).
'Putin seals new Turkey gas deal' (6 August 2009) in http://news.bbc.co.uk/1/
    hi/business/8186946.stm (last accessed July 2015).
'Turkey agrees to plans for Arab 'free trade zone'' (6 October 2010) in http://
    www.bbc.co.uk/news/10290025 (last accessed April 2016).

## BBC Newsnight
'Iraq, Refugees and Oil' (12 August 2014).

## Boston Globe
Tirman, John, 'The trouble with Turkey' (30 November 2005).

## CBS (US television channel)
CBS interview with Sheikh Hamad bin Khalifa Al Thani cited in *BBC News*
    (14 January 2012) http://www.bbc.co.uk/news/world-middle-east-
    16561493 (last accessed February 2016).

## Christian Science Monitor
Cited in 'Chronology', *Middle East Journal*, Vol. 39, No. 4 (11 June 1985).

## CNN
Zakaria, Fareed., 'Interview with Erdoğan' (26 September 2011).

## Daily Sabah
Ergin, Bariş, 'First KRG gas to flow to Turkey in two years' (20 November 2015),
    http://www.dailysabah.com/energy/2015/11/21/first-krg-gas-to-flow-to-
    turkey-in-two-years (last accessed November 2015).

## Daily Star
Butler, Daren, 'Turkey's Erdoğan moots three-way regional talks on Syria'
    (16 October 2012).
'Iran and Syria sign pact against 'common threats' (16 June 2006), http://www.
    dailystar.com.lb/News/Middle-East/2006/Jun-16/72583-iran-and-syria-
    sign-pact-againstcommon-threats.ashx (last accessed July 2015).

## Debka File
'First Iranian marines land in Syria, link up with newly-arrived Russian troops'
    (11 September 2015), http://www.debka.com/article/24883/First-Iranian-
    marines-land-in-Syria-link-up-with-newly-arrived-Russian-troops (last
    accessed September 2015).

*Sunday Democracy* (Greek Newspaper – Κυριακάτικη Δημοκρατία)
Kalederidis, Savvas, 'Developments in Turkey and geopolitical repercussions', ['Εξελίξεις στην Τουρκία και γεωπολιτικές επιπτώσεις'] (5 January 2014), http://infognomonpolitics.blogspot.co.uk/2014/01/blog-post_6108.html (last accessed September 2015).

———, 'Ξύπνα Ευρώπη – Ξύπνα Ελλάδα', ['Wake up, Europe – Wake up, Greece'] (21 November 2015) in http://infognomonpolitics.blogspot.co.uk/2015/11/blog-post_412.html (last accessed December 2015).

Murat Karayılan, Interview (15 January 2013) in http://infognomonpolitics.blogs pot.co.uk/2013/01/blogpost_6796.html?utm_source=feedburner&utm_medium=email&utm_campaign=Feed:+InfognomonPolitics+(Infognom onPolitics)&utm_content=Yahoo!+Mail#.UP1alW82lu5 (last accessed January 2016).

*El País* (Spanish Newspaper)
Erdoğan, Recep Tayyip. Interview, 'Si Turquía entra en la UE, el mundo musulmán cambiará su visión de Europa' (19 October 2003).

*Επίκαιρα* [NewsReel, Greek newspaper], (14 August 2013).

*Eurasia Daily Monitor*
Uslu, Emrullah, 'Turkey–Iran Relations: A Trade Partnership or a Gateway for Iran to Escape International Sanctions?' (3 March 2009), Vol. 6, No. 41.

*Financial Times*
Cited in 'Chronology', *Middle East Journal*: Vol. 45, No. 1 (18 July 1991); Vol. 45, No. 4 (18 June 2001); Vol. 46, No. 1 (18 September 1991) (10 August 1998); Vol. 46, No. 3 (6 March 1992); Vol. 47, No. 1 (15 September 1992); Vol. 47, No. 2 (4 December 1992); Vol. 51, No. 1 (24 September 1996); Vol. 53, No. 1 (8 September 1998); Vol. 53, No. 3 (22 January 1999); Vol. 57, No. 3 (11 April 2003).

*Foreign Affairs*
Acemoglu, Daron, 'The Failed Autocrat' (22 May 2014) in http://www.forei gnaffairs.com/print/138488 (last accessed September 2015).

Mead, Walter Russell, 'The Return of Geopolitics: The Revenge of the Revisionist Powers' (May/June 2014).

Ottaway, Marina, and David Ottaway, 'How the Kurds Got Their Way' (May/June 2014).

Perthes, Volker, 'The Syrian Solution', Vol. 85, No. 6 (November/December 2006).

Vatanka, Alex, 'Μπλέξιμο στον Καύκασο: Το Ιράν και το Ισραήλ ανταγωνίζονται για επιρροή στο Αζερμπαϊτζάν' ['Tangling in the Caucasus: Iran and Israel are Competing for Influence in Azerbaijan'], *the Hellenic edition* (16 January 2013) in http://www.foreignaffairs.com/articles/138753/alex-vatanka/ tangle-in-the-caucasus (last accessed December 2014).

## Foreign Broadcast Information Service (FBIS)

Foreign Broadcast Information Service cited in 'Chronology', *Middle East Journal*,
Vol. 28, No. 2 (29 October 1993); Vol. 36, No. 2 (12 November 1982);
Vol. 41, No. 2 (15 December 1986); Vol. 42, No. 2 (15 January 1988)
(3 December 1987); Vol. 43, No. 1 (18 October 1988) (10 January 1989);
Vol. 44, No. 1 (23 August 1989); Vol. 44, No. 3 (27 February 1990); Vol. 44,
No. 4 (9 May 1990); Vol. 45, No. 4 (3 May 1989); Vol. 46, No. 3
(18 February 1992) (11 February 1992) (24 February 1992) (10 February
1993) (7 April 1992); Vol. 47, No. 2 (19 October 1992); Vol. 47, No. 3
(21 January 1993); Vol. 48, No. 2 (21 December 1994); Vol. 50, No.1
(13 October 1995); Vol. 51, No. 2 (29 October 1996) (9 December 1996)
(6 December 1996); Vol. 51, No. 3 (25 February 1997); Vol. 52, No. 1
(7 October 1997); Vol. 53, No. 1 (8 September 1998) (15 September 1998).

## Foreign Policy

Davutoğlu, Ahmet, 'Turkey's Zero Problems Foreign Policy' (20 May 2010).
Khedery, Ali, 'Iran's Shiite militias are running amok in Iraq' (19 February
2015) in http://foreignpolicy.com/2015/02/19/irans-shiite-militias-are-
running-amok-in-iraq/ (last accessed June 2015).

## GEO Business

'Turkey can help world understand Iran: Mottaki' (16 February 2010) in http://
www.geo.tv/2–16–2010/59408.htm (last accessed July 2015).

## Guardian

Nasrallah, Hassan, Al-Manar TV channel, cited in *The Guardian* (30 April 2013)
in http://www.theguardian.com/world/2013/apr/30/hezbollah-syria-
uprising-nasrallah (last accessed February 2016).
Tisdall, Simon, 'Syrian safe zone: US relents to Turkish demands after border
crisis grows' (27 July 2015) in http://www.theguardian.com/world/2015/
jul/27/syrian-safe-zone-us-relents-to-turkish-demands-border-crisis-kurd-
uk-military (last accessed September 2015).
Vidal, John, 'Water supply key to outcome of conflicts in Iraq and Syria,
experts warn' (2 July 2014) in http://www.theguardian.com/environment/
2014/jul/02/water-key-conflict-iraq-syria-isis (last accessed March 2015).
Wintour, Patrick, 'Russia begins military withdrawal from Syria' (6 January
2017) in https://www.theguardian.com/world/2017/jan/06/russia-aircraft-
carrier-mediterranean-syria-admiral-kuznetsov (last accessed August
2017).

## Haaretz.com (Israeli News source)

Davutoğlu, Ahmed., 'Turkey Denies Defense, Energy Ties With Israel Amid
Gaza Fighting' (23 July 2014) in http://www.haaretz.com/israel-news/
1.606786 (last accessed February 2016).

'Lieberman trip to South America aimed at curbing Iran influence' (20 July 2009) in http://www.haaretz.com/news/lieberman-trip-to-south-america-aimed-at-curbing-iran-influence-1.280380 (last accessed July 2015).

'Turkey's Erdogan urges Assad to "finally step down" for sake of Mideast peace' (22 October 2011) in http://www.haaretz.com/middle-east-news/turkey-s-erdogan-urges-assad-to-finally-step-down-for-sake-of-mideast-peace-1.397058 (last accessed February 2016).

## Harvard International Review

Charountaki Marianna, The Aftermath of the Kurdish Referendum and Its Historic Connotations, (25 December 2017) in http://hir.harvard.edu/article/?a=14567 (last accessed February, 2018).

## Hürriyet (Daily News)

HDP co-chair, 'PKK must 'absolutely lay down arms against Turkey' (15 July 2015) in http://www.hurriyetdailynews.com/pkk-must-absolutely-lay-down-arms-against-turkey-hdp-co-chair.aspx?pageID=238&nID=85469&NewsCatID=338 (last accessed September 2015).

Yetkin, Murat, 'Russia accesses warm waters through Turkey' (4 December 2012) in http://www.hurriyetdailynews.com/russia-accesses-warm-waters-through-turkey.aspx?pageID=449&nID=36060&NewsCatID=409 (last accessed September 2015).

———, 'Turkey, Russia work on new plan for Syria' (7 December 2012) in http://www.hurriyetdailynews.com/turkey-russia-work-on-new-plan-for-syria.aspx?pageID=449&nID=36301&NewsCatID=409 (last accessed September 2015).

'Rice warns: Turkey should not intervene in Northern Iraq' (25 October 2007) in http://www.hurriyet.com.tr/rice-warns-turkey-should-not-intervene-in-northern-iraq-7556700 (last accessed April 2016).

'Turkey and Syria renew diplomatic pledges' (21 December 2010) in http://www.hurriyetdailynews.com/default.aspx?pageid=438&n=turkey-and-syria-gathered-8220intergovernmental-cabinet8221-in-ankara-2010–12–21 (last accessed April 2016).

'KRG slams Maliki, calls for dialogue' (4 December 2012) in http://www.hurriyetdailynews.com/krg-slams-maliki-calls-for-dialogue.aspx?pageID=238&nID=36057&NewsCatID=352 (last accessed September 2015).

'US denies plans to change strategy in Syria' (14 November 2014) in http://www.hurriyetdailynews.com/us-denies-plans-to-change-strategy-in-syria-.aspx?pageID=238&nID=74343&NewsCatID=359 (last accessed September 2015).

'Turkey, Iran ink two key protocols to boost economic, trade ties' (10 April 2016) in http://www.hurriyetdailynews.com/Turkey–Iran-ink-two-key-protocols-to-boost-economic-trade-ties.aspx?pageID=238&nID=97575&NewsCatID=345 (last accessed August 2017).

### Independent

Staufenberg, Jess, 'Vladmir Putin admits supporting President Assad in Syrian civil war' (5 September 2015) in http://www.independent.co.uk/news/world/europe/vladmir-putin-admits-supporting-president-assad-in-syrian-civil-war-10488165.html (last accessed September 2015).

### Infognomon

Beam, Amy L., Ed. D., 'Appeal to Secretary of State John Kerry on his Visit to Ankara' (2 February 2013) cited in http://www.infognomonpolitics.blogs pot.gr/2013/03/appeal-to-secretary-of-state-john-kerry.html?m=1 (last accessed September 2015).

Evriviadis, Marios, 'Συρία 1957 και 2012' ['Syria 1957 and 2012'] (16 September 2012) in http://infognomonpolitics.blogspot.co.uk/2012/09/1957–2012. html (last accessed September 2015).

### International Business Times

Moore, Jack, 'Turkey YouTube Ban: Full Transcript of Leaked Syria 'War' Conversation Between Erdoğan Officials' (27 April 2014) in http://www.ibtimes.co.uk/turkey-youtube-ban-full-transcript-leaked-syria-war-conversation-between-erdogan-officials-1442161 (last accessed April 2016).

### International Herald Tribune

Cited in 'Chronology', *Middle East Journal*, Vol. 62, No. 4 (6 June 2008).

### International New York Times

Rubin, Alissa J., 'With risks, Europeans rush back to Iran' (1–2 August 2015).

### Iranian Student's News Agency

Bigdeli, Alireza (Iran's Ambassador to Ankara), 'Iran ready to arbitrate between Turkey, Syria' (30 November 2013).

### Iran Pulse

Sadeghi-Boroujerdi, Eskandar, 'Former IRGC chief says US working to turn Turkey into Iran's strategic rival' (8 February 2013) in http://iranpulse.al-monitor.com/index.php/2013/02/1316/former-irgc-chief-says-us-working-to-turn-turkey-into-irans-strategic-rival/ (last accessed September 2015).

### Islamic Republic News Agency

Qelichkhan, Reza, 'Iranian Diplomat: minor differences not to affect Iran–Turkey long-standing ties' (12 February 2014) in http://www.irna.ir/en/News/2638066/Politic/Iranian_diplomat__Minor_differences_not_to_affect__Iran–Turkey_long-standing_ties (last accessed December 2014).

## Israel National News

Reback, Gedalyah, 'Activist Urges Israel to Raise Kurdistan as Ally against Iran' (20 April 2015) in http://www.israelnationalnews.com/News/News.aspx/194319#.VXnLTfmqqkq (last accessed June 2015).

## Kathimerini (Greek Newspaper)

Salehi, Ali Akbar, 'Ιράν: Άγκυρα και Τεχεράνη έχουν κρίσιμο ρόλο να παίξουν στη Συρία', ['Iran: Ankara and Tehran have critical role to play in Syria'] (7 August 2012),http://www.kathimerini.com.cy/index.php?pageaction=kat&modid=1&artid=100883&show=Y (last accessed April 2014).

## Kazinform

'CSTO member-states begin Unbreakable Brotherhood 2014 war games in Kyrgyzstan' (29 July 2014) in http://www.inform.kz/eng/article/2682365 (last accessed September 2015).

## Khaleej Times

'Iran, Turkish firm in EUR1b gas link deal' (24 July 2010) in http://imra.org.il/story.php3?id=48830 (last accessed July 2015).

## Kivunim (Directions)

Yinon, Oded., 'A Strategy for Israel in the 1980s', No. 14, Issue 5742 (February 1982),http://www.informationclearinghouse.info/pdf/The%20Zionist%20Plan%20for%20the%20Middle%20East.pdf (last accessed April 2016).

## Kurdish Globe

'Israel purchased 77% of KR's oil supplies' (31 August 2015) No. 504.

## Mehr News Agency

Velayati, Ali Akbar, 'Velayati: US unable to attack Iran' (26 January 2013).

## Middle East Economic Survey

Cited in 'Chronology', *Middle East Journal*, Vol. 33, No. 1 (5 October 1979).

## Middle East Eye

Abedin, Mahan, 'Rouhani landslide redraws Iranian political map' (21 May 2017) in http://www.middleeasteye.net/news/analysis-rouhani-landslide-redraws-iranian-political-map-833237805 (last accessed December, 2017).

———, 'Hardliners manoeuvre as Iran nuclear talks enter extra time' (21 July 2014) in http://www.middleeasteye.net/columns/iran-hardliners-manoeuvre-nuclear-talks-enter-extra-time-1241138768 (last accessed April 2016).

———, 'Syrian opposition coalition dissolves military council after withdrawal threats' (22 September 2014) in http://www.middleeasteye.net/news/

syrian-opposition-coalition-dissolves-military-council-after-withdrawal-threats-1647588004 (last accessed April 2016).

———, 'Shiite militias deepen Iraq's sectarian conflict' (10 December 2014) in http://www.middleeasteye.net/columns/shiite-militias-deepen-iraq-s-sectarian-conflict-216999860 (accessed December 2014).

———, 'Iran's Rafsanjani pushes for new role in power' (31 December 2015) in http://www.middleeasteye.net/columns/irans-rafsanjani-pushes-new-role-power-799271826 (last accessed February 2016).

———, 'The results of Iranian parliamentary and Assembly elections will set the tone and pace for domestic and foreign policy in the next decade', *Middle East Eye* (26 February 2016) in http://www.middleeasteye.net/essays/irans-historic-elections-2045716001 (last accessed August 2017).

———, 'Going ballistic: The defiant Iranian message in Deir Ezzor' (26 June 2017) in http://www.middleeasteye.net/columns/going-ballistic-defiant-iranian-message-deir-ezzor-650430774 (last accessed August 2017).

## Middle East Forum
Bekdil, Burak, 'ISIS Going Rogue in Turkey, or Is It?' (4 August 2015) in http://www.meforum.org/5422/turkey-isis (last accessed September 2015).

## Middle East Online
'Erdogan puts hopes for peace with Kurds in hands of Barzani' (16 November 2013) in http://www.middle-east-online.com/english/?id=62642 (last accessed February 2016).

Cited in'Chronology', *Middle East Journal*, Vol. 62, No. 1 (10 October 2008); Vol. 63, No. 1 (26 August 2009).

## Milliyet
Durukan, Namik, 'Davutoğlu, Kuzey Irak için 'Kürdistan' dedi' ['Davutoğlu, called Northern Iraq, 'Kürdistan'], *Milliyet* (22/07/2016), www.milliyet.com.tr/davutoglu-kuzey-irak-icin-kurdistan-dedi/siyaset/haberdetay/22.07.2010/1266720/default.htm (last accessed April 2016).

## Moscow Times
Sanadiki, Omar/*Reuters*, 'Russian Troops Join Combat in Syria – Sources' (9 September 2015) cited in http://www.themoscowtimes.com/news/article/russian-troops-join-combat-in-syria/529831.html (last accessed September 2015).

'Algeria to Purchase 14 Russian-Made Sukhoi Fighter Jets' (11 September 2015) in http://www.themoscowtimes.com/business/article/algeria-to-purchase-14-russian-made-sukhoi-fighter-jets/530046.html (last accessed September 2015).

### New Anatolian

'MIT boss secretly visited Barzani in Erbil' (23 November 2005).

### NewsBlaze

'Turkish–Iran Relations: Old Rivals or New Best Friends?' (7 July 2010) in http://www.alahwaz.info/en/?p=953 (last accessed April 2016).

### New York Post

Pipes, Daniel, 'Iraq's Weapons and the Road to War' (3 June 2003).

### New York Times

Barringer, Felicity and David E. Sanger, 'US Says Hussein Must Cede Power to Head Off War' (1 March 2003), http://www.nytimes.com/2003/03/01/international/middleeast/01IRAQ.html (last accessed July 2015).

Gray, Jerry, 'Foreigners Investing in Libya or Iran Face US Sanctions' (24 July 1996) in http://www.nytimes.com/1996/07/24/world/foreigners-investing-in-libya-or-in-iran-face-us-sanctions.html (last accessed June 2015).

Hayes, Thomas C., 'Confrontation in the Gulf: The Oilfield Lying Below the Iraq-Kuwait Dispute' (3 September 1990).

Lewis, Neil A., 'House Inquiry Finds No Evidence of Deal on Hostages in 1980' (13 January 1993) in http://www.nytimes.com/1993/01/13/us/house-inquiry-finds-No.-evidence-of-deal-on-hostages-in-1980.html (last accessed March 2015).

Rose, Charlie, 'Interviews with Zbigniew Brzezinski, Henry Kissinger and Brent Scowcroft' (18 June 2007),http://www.nytimes.com/2007/06/18/world/americas/18iht-web-rose.html?pagewanted=all (last accessed March 2016).

'The no-win goal in the Gulf' (22 May 1984).

'Turkish Leader Volunteers to be US–Iran Mediator' (12 November 2008) in http://www.nytimes.com/2008/11/12/world/europe/12turkey.html?_r=1&sq=TURKEY (last accessed September 2015).

'US goal was to keep either side from winning the Persian Gulf War' (12 January 1987).

Cited in 'Chronology', *Middle East Journal*: Vol. 33, No. 1 (16 August 1979) (16 October 1979) (11 November 1979) (14 November 1979); Vol. 33, No. 3 (19 February 1979); Vol. 33, No. 4 (18 February 1979) (24 May 1979); Vol. 34, No. 2 (4 February 1980) (7 December 1980); Vol. 34, No. 3 (16 February 1980) (29 March 1980) (7 April 1980); Vol. 35, No. 1 (12 September 1980) (23 September 1980); Vol. 35, No. 2 (2 December 1980); Vol. 36, No. 3 (11 September 1982); Vol. 37, No. 1 (11 September 1982); Vol. 37, No. 3 (24 January 1983); Vol. 38, No. 2 (11 November 1983); Vol. 42, No. 2 (5 January 1988); Vol. 44, No. 3 (13 February 1992); Vol. 46, No. 3 (13 February 1992); Vol. 47, No. 2 (27 December 1992); Vol. 47, No. 3 (20 January 1993); Vol. 51, No. 1 (13 August 1996) (19 September 1996); Vol. 52, No. 4 (18 June 1998); Vol. 53, No. 3 (8 April

1999); Vol. 54, No.1 (14 August 2000); Vol. 57, No. 2 (25 December 2002);
Vol. 57, No. 3 (19 February 2003); Vol. 62, No. 3 (12 March 2008); Vol. 62,
No. 4 (9 June 2008).

## New Yorker
Lemann, Nicholas, 'How it came to War' (31 March 2003).

## Now Lebanon
Badran, Tony, 'Obama runs from Iran' (1 November 2012).

## Press TV
'Iran, Turkey to set up ties committee' (30 January 2014) in http://www.press
   tv.ir/detail/2014/01/30/348416/Iran–Turkey-to-set-up-ties-committee/
   (last accessed September 2015).
'Iran–Turkey ties eradicate terrorism in Middle East: Rouhani' (29 January
   2014) in http://www.presstv.ir/detail/2014/01/29/348352/iranturkey-ties-
   destroy-terrorism-in-me/ (last accessed September 2015).

## Radikal
Mavioğlu, Ertuğrul, 'The Obama administration declared PJAK as a terrorist
   organization on 4 February 2009' (31 October 2010).

## Radio Free Europe–Radio Liberty
'Baku Minister Says Azerbaijan Wouldn't Be Used For Attack On Iran'
   (12 March 2012) in http://www.rferl.org/content/azerbaijan_minister_
   says_territory_wont_be_used_for_attack_on_iran/24513361.html (last
   accessed October 2015)
Cited in 'Chronology', *Middle East Journal*, Vol. 63, No. 3 (17 February 2009).

## Reuters
Karadeniz, Tulay and Ibon Villelabeitia, 'US presses Turkey to enforce
   sanctions on Iran' (21 October 2010),http://www.reuters.com/article/
   idUSTRE69K46920101021 (last accessed October 2015).
Karadeniz, Tulay and Simon Cameron-Moore, 'Turkey's saves ire for Israel,
   concern for Syria' (30 May 2011), http://www.reuters.com/article/2011/
   05/30/us-turkey-mideast-interview-idUSTRE74T3SE20110530 (last accessed
   September 2015).
Pamuk, Humeyra and Orhan Coskun, 'Iraqi Kurdistan's oil pipeline capacity to
   double after upgrade – sources' (27 October 2014) in http://www.dailymail.
   co.uk/wires/reuters/article-2809518/Iraqi-Kurdistans-oil-pipeline-capacity-
   double-upgrade-sources.html (last accessed September 2015).
Stewart, Phil, 'Iraq's Kurdish forces 'model' for fighting Islamic State –
   Pentagon chief' (24 July 2015) in http://uk.reuters.com/article/2015/07/

24/uk-mideast-crisis-usa-iraq-idUKKCN0PY0R120150724 (last accessed September 2015).

Tattersall, Nick, 'Turkey calls Syria security leak "villainous" blocks YouTube' (27 March 2014), http://www.reuters.com/article/2014/03/27/us-syria-crisis-turkey-idUSBREA2Q17420140327 (last accessed September 2015).

'IAEA found nothing serious at Iran site: ElBaradei' (5 November 2009) in http://www.reuters.com/article/2009/11/05/us-iran-nuclear-elbaradei-idUSTRE5A13KW20091105 (last accessed July 2015).

'Interview with Murat Karayılan' (2 April 2009) in http://www.reuters.com/article/2009/02/04/idUSN04297671 (last accessed April 2016).

'Iraqi Kurdistan plans 10 bcm natural gas exports to Turkey in two years' (20 November 2015), https://en-maktoob.news.yahoo.com/iraqi-kurdistan-plans-10-bcm-natural-gas-exports-094406617–business.html (last accessed February 2016).

'The US and Turkey are increasingly divided over Kurds' (9 July 2015) in http://uk.businessinsider.com/the-us-and-turkey-are-increasingly-divided-over-kurds-2015–7?r=US#ixzz3fVOoPoDW (last accessed September 2015).

'Turkey Says Iran Sanctions 'Mistake' Deepens Ties',(10 June 2010) in http://uk.reuters.com/article/2010/06/10/idINIndia-49194320100610 (last accessed July 2015).

'Turkey: Yasser Arafat visits Ankara for Official Opening of PLO Office' (8 October 1979) cited in http://www.itnsource.com/shotlist//RTV/1979/10/08/BGY511140091/?v=0 (last accessed December 2015).

Cited in 'Chronology', *Middle East Journal*, Vol. 57, No. 1 (17 September 2002).

### *RT.com (Russia television network)*

'Turkey/Iran sanctions corruption scandal' (20 January 2014) in http://rt.com/op-edge/Turkey–Iran-sanctions-corruption-scandal-883/ (last accessed April 2016).

### *Rudaw*

Ahmed., Hevidar, 'Kurdish role: Kurdistan Region announces plans for second oil pipeline to Turkey' (21 May 2013).

'Erbil, Ankara Finalize "Historic" Oil Pipeline Agreement' (11 July 2013) in http://rudaw.net/english/business/06112013 (last accessed September 2015).

'Iran–Erbil Agree on Energy Deals and Boosting Trade' (29 April 2014) in http://rudaw.net/english/kurdistan/29042014 (last accessed September 2015).

'KRG oil exports more than 18 million barrels in December' (12 January 2016) in http://rudaw.net/english/kurdistan/110120162 (last accessed February 2016).

'KRG says delayed salaries to be paid this month' (20 October 2015) in http://rudaw.net/mobile/english/kurdistan/201020151 (last accessed November 2015).

'Kurdistan says UN can supervise oil exports' (29 July 2015) in http://rudaw.net/english/kurdistan/290720152 (last accessed September 2015).

'President Barzani Slams PYD in Syria, Rejects Autonomy Declaration' (15 November 2013) in http://rudaw.net/english/kurdistan/14112013 (last accessed September 2015).

### Russia Beyond the Headlines

Litovkin, Nikolai, 'Russia delivers first weapons supplies to Iraqi Kurds' (18 March 2016) in http://rbth.com/defence/2016/03/18/russia-delivers-first-weapons-supplies-to-iraqi-kurds_576809 (last accessed March 2016).

'Russia delivers Night Hunter helicopters to Iraq' (2 February 2015) http://rbth.com/news/2015/02/02/russia_delivers_night_hunter_helicopters_to_iraq_43334.html (last accessed September 2015).

### Russia Today (Η Ρωσία Τώρα/Russian Newspaper in English)

Nazemroaya, Mahdi Darius, 'Turkey and Iran: More than meets the eye' (20 January 2014) in https://www.rt.com/op-edge/Turkey-Iran-sanctions-corruption-scandal-883/ (last accessed March 2016).

Sergienko, Elena, 'Οι προτεραιότητες της Ρωσίας στην εξωτερική πολιτική', [The Priorities of the Russian Foreign Policy] (8 January 2013), http://gr.rbth.com/politics/2013/01/27/oi_proteraiotite_ti_rosia_stin_eksoteriki_politiki_19577 (last accessed September 2015).

'Putin: US missile defense aimed at neutralizing Russia nukes, N. Korea and Iran just a cover' (10 November 2015) in https://www.rt.com/news/321434-us-missile-shield-putin/ (last accessed December 2015).

### Sunday's Zaman

Adilgizi, Lamiya, 'Iranian–Armenia Ties being Boosted to Counter Turkey' (31 March 2013).

### Taraf

Diouzel, Nesie, 'Interview' (8 October 2012).

### Tasnim News Agency

Davutoğlu, Ahmet, 'Iranian, Turkish FMs Discuss Regional, International Issues in Pakistan' (19/12/2013), http://www.tasnimnews.com/English/Home/Single/225835 (last accessed March 2016).

## Telegraph

Akkoc, Raziye, 'How Turkey's economy went from flying to flagging – and could get worse' (30 May 2015), http://www.telegraph.co.uk/finance/economics/11640135/How-Turkeys-economy-went-from-flying-to-flagging-and-could-get-worse.html (last accessed September 2015).

## The Theme (To Θέμα, Greek Newspaper)

Filippaki, Lyda, 'The Azeri of Iran seek independence' (15 May 2012) in http://www.protothema.gr/world/article/197495/oi-azeroi-toy-iran-theloyn-aneksarthsia/ (last accessed June 2014).

## Today's Zaman (Turkish Newspaper in English)

Charountaki, Marianna, 'The US policy of 'containment': Iraq versus Iran' (24 January 2012) in http://www.todayszaman.com/news-269392-the-us-policy-of-containment-iraq-versus-iranby-marianna-charountaki.html (last accessed May 2014).

Demirtaş, Selahattin, 'HDP's Demirtaş rules out coalition with AK Party after elections' (27 May 2015) in http://www.todayszaman.com/anasayfa_hdps-demirtas-rules-out-coalition-with-ak-party-after-elections_381910.html (last accessed September 2015).

Gündüz, Şaban, 'Iran proposes joint barter company to evade US sanctions' (28 December 2012).

Güzel, Hasan Celal (8 July 2008) in http://www.todayszaman.com/anasayfa_feb-28-a-clear-military-coup-with-former-president-demirel-complicit-says-guzel_372881.html (last accessed April 2015).

Kanbolat, Hasan, 'A New Railway Line in the Southern Caucasus: Kars-Iğdır-Nakhchivan' (8 July 2008), http://www.todayszaman.com/columnist/hasan-kanbolat/a-new-railway-line-in-the-southern-caucasus-kars-igdir-nakhchivan_146857.html (last accessed December 2014).

Uslu, Emre, 'PKK-Iran axis' (5 October 2011) in https://wikileaks.org/gifiles/docs/13/135269_-os-Turkey–Iran–Iraq-turkish-op-ed-pkk-iran-axis-.html (last accessed September 2015).

'Cable: Turkey more dependent on Russia with nuclear plant' (2 September 2011) in http://www.todayszaman.com/diplomacy_cable-turkey-more-dependent-on-russia-with-nuclear-plant_255546.html (last accessed September 2015).

'Erdoğan: era of *coup d'états* closed in Turkey' (1 October 2007).

'Iran captured but later released PKK leader Karayılan, report claims' (11 October 2011) in http://www.todayszaman.com/news-259497-iran-captured-but-later-released-pkk-leader-karayilan-report-claims.html (last accessed September 2015).

'Iran says it will be 'Turkey's turn' if it goes ahead with Syria policies' (7 August 2012) in http://www.todayszaman.com/latest-news_iran-says-it-will-be-turkeys-turn-if-it-goes-ahead-with-syria-policies_288818.html (last accessed September 2015).

'Iraq bars minister's plane from landing in Arbil amid tensions' (4 December 2012) in http://www.todayszaman.com/latest-news_iraq-bars-ministers-plane-from-landing-in-arbil-amid-tensions_300121.html (last accessed September 2015).

## Trend News Agency

'Northern Iraq begins international oil exports, defying Baghdad' (23 October 2012) in http://en.trend.az/world/arab/2079726.html (last accessed September 2015).

## Turkish Daily News

Enginsoy, Ümit, 'US once again warns against Turkish military action inside Iraq' (26 May 2007) in http://www.turkishdailynews.com.tr/article.php?enewsid=74230 (last accessed April 2015).

Cited in 'Chronology', *Middle East Journal*, Vol. 33, No. 3 (30 November 1978); Vol. 34, No. 2 (10 January 1980).

*Turkish Daily News* (7 October 1978).

## Veterans Today

Duff, Gordon, 'NEO: US, Turkey Ignore Russian Warning, Move into Syria' (17 August 2015) in http://www.veteranstoday.com/2015/08/21/us-turkey-ignore-russian-warning-move-into-syria-new-eastern-outlook/ (last accessed September 2015).

## Village Voice

'Republished Pike Report' (19 January 1976) (New York: 23 February 1976).

## Voice of Kurdistan [Φωνή του Κουρδιστάν] [Magazine of the National Liberation Front of Kurdistan]

Douran Kalkan, member of the PKK Presidential Council quoted by DEM News Agency (Athens, 5 August 1999).

'Öcalan's Diary: Imrali' (Athens, 25 November 1999).

*Voice of Kurdistan: [Φωνή του Κουρδιστάν]* (Athens, March–May 2000): 8–11.

## Voltaire Network (Réseau Voltaire/French NetWork)

Meyssan, Thierry, 'An Empire Without a Military Strategy for a Military Strategy Without an Empire' (2 June 2014) in http://www.voltairenet.org/article184056.html (last accessed November 2015).

———, 'Clinton, Juppé, Erdoğan, Daesh and the PKK' (3 August 2015) in http://www.voltairenet.org/article188337.html (last accessed September 2015).

———, 'The Russian army is beginning to engage in Syria' (24 August 2015), http://www.voltairenet.org/article188522.html (last accessed September 2015).

———, 'Why did Turkey shoot down the Russian Soukhoï 24?' (30 November 2015), http://www.voltairenet.org/article189474.html (last accessed December 2015).

## Washington Post

Birnbaum, Michael, 'The secret pact between Russia and Syria that gives Moscow carte blanche' (15 January 2016), https://www.washingtonpost.com/news/worldviews/wp/2016/01/15/the-secret-pact-between-russia-and-syria-that-gives-moscow-carte-blanche/ (last accessed February 2016).

De Young, Karen and Liz Sly, 'US-Turkey deal aims to create de facto 'safe zone' in northwest Syria' (26 July 2015) in https://www.washingtonpost.com/world/new-us-turkey-plan-amounts-to-a-safe-zone-in-northwest-syria/2015/07/26/0a533345-ff2e-4b40–858a-c1b36541e156_story.html (last accessed September 2015).

Lee, Julian, 'Oil Output Freeze Hope Gets Help From an Unlikely Source: Gadfly' (29 March 2016), http://washpost.bloomberg.com/Story?docId=1376-O4QM456KLVRV01–2FL2KA8AOEMK78L1UGV5D5S3RE (last accessed March 2016).

Cited in 'Chronology', *Middle East Journal*: Vol. 36, No. 3 (11 March 1982); Vol. 36, No. 4 (30 May 1982); Vol. 37, No. 3 (3 February 1983) (25 February 1983); Vol. 38, No. 2 (29 December 1983); Vol. 40, No. 4 (8 June 1986); Vol. 41, No. 2 (13–14 November 1987) (27 November 1986) (27 November 1987); Vol. 41, No. 3 (7 February 1979); Vol. 42, No. 1 (28–30 September 1987); Vol. 43, No. 4 (28 May 1989); Vol. 44, No. 4 (1 May 1990); Vol. 46, No. 3 (7 February 1992) (12 February 1992) (11 March 1992); Vol. 47, No. 2 (2 November 1992) (29 November 1992); Vol. 54, No. 2 (26 October 2000); Vol. 57, No. 2 (26 December 2002) (28–29 December 2002) (10 January 2003); Vol. 61, No. 4 (15 August 2007); Vol. 63, No. 3 (27 March 2009); Vol. 63, No. 4 (6 June 2009); Vol. 64, No. 1 (18 September 2009).

## Wall Street Journal

Trofimov, Yaroslav 'France Wants Alliance With Russia, but Divisions Over Assad's Future a Hurdle' (17 November 2015) in http://www.wsj.com/articles/assads-future-may-be-stumbling-block-in-plan-to-fight-isis-1447791663 (last accessed April 2016).

## Washington Quarterly

Walker, Joshua W., 'Re-examining the US–Turkish alliance' (Winter 2007–2008).

## The Washington Street Journal
Cited (13 January 1984) in 'Chronology', *Middle East Journal*, Vol. 38, No. 2.

## World Bulletin
'Turkey–Iran gold trade' (16 February 2013) in http://www.worldbulletin.
net/?aType=haber&ArticleID=103420 (last accessed December 2014).

## Ya Libnan
'Turkey warns against Kurdish autonomy in Syria' (15 November 2013).
## Yeni Şafak (Turkish newspaper)
Erdoğan, Recep Tayyip, 'We are not rooted in religion' (4 May 2008).

## Your Middle East (online newspaper)
Charountaki, Marianna, 'The increasing importance of Iran' (12 December
2013) in http://www.yourmiddleeast.com/opinion/the-increasing-
importance-of-iran_2013 (last accessed April 2014).

## Zaman
'Logistics support to PKK from Iran (24 December 2012).
Cited in 'Chronology', *Middle East Journal*, Vol. 64, No. 4 (9 July 2010).

## INTERVIEWS

Altun, Reza, co-founder of PKK, executive member of KCK. Author interview.
Qandil, 20 March 2014.
Bak, Osman Aşkın, former Co-Chairman of Turkey–Iran Parliamentary
Friendship Group. Author interview. Ankara, 28 March 2013.
Barzani, Massoud, former President of the KR in Iraq. Author interview.
Salahaddin, 23 June 2007 & Erbil, 25 September 2013.
Barzani, Nechirvan, Prime Minister of KRG. Author interview. Erbil, 23 April
2007.
Dizayee, Mohsin, Massoud Barzani's Special Envoy. Author interview.
Salahaddin, 13 June 2007.
Erdemir, Dr. Aykan, former MP CHP (Cumhuriyet Halk Partisi) in Bursa.
Author interview. Ankara, 2 April 2013.
Hess, Jake: Interview with Selahattin Demirtaş, 'The AKP's 'New Kurdish
Strategy' is Nothing of the Sort' in *MERIP*, No. 275 (2 May 2012) in http://
www.merip.org/mero/mero050212 (last accessed September 2015).
High Level Political Figure in Iranian politics (anonymous). Author interview.
London, 17 June 2013.
Hosseini, Seyid Azim, former Iranian Consular in Erbil. Author interview.
Erbil, 6 April 2013).

Kalin, Ibrahim, Recep Tayip Erdoğan's Chief Foreign Policy Advisor in Middle East Affairs. Author interview. Ankara, 1 April 2013.

Karim, Dr. Najmaldine O., former Governor of Kirkuk Governorate in Iraq and Mullah Mustafa Barzani's private doctor. Author interview. Washington, 8 March 2008.

Kiliç, Akif Çagatay, AKP MP. Author interview. Ankara, 28 March 2013.

Korutürk, Osman, former Deputy Chairman at CHP (Cumhuriyet Halk Partisi, Republican People's Party). Author interview. Ankara, 1 April 2013.

Marassana, Khider, former member of Leading Committee KDPI (1991–1996). Author interview. Stockholm, 16 June 2014.

Merani, Fadhil, Secretary of Political Bureau, Kurdistan Democratic Party. Author interview. Erbil, 27 August 2015.

Mohajerani, Dr. Ata'ollah, former Iranian Minister. Author interview. London, 23 October 2013. London, 12 March 2014, London, 11 March 2015.

Muslim, Salih, former co-leader of the Democratic Union Party (PYD). Author interview. London, 24 May 2014.

Othman, Mahmoud, former President of the Kurdistan Socialist Party, former member of the Iraq Interim Governing Council, Member of Iraqi Parliament and Member of the Iraqi delegation during the 1970s (Manifesto) negotiations. Author interview. Erbil, 15 April 2007. Erbil, 4 April 2013.

Semo, Alan, PYD representative of foreign relations in the UK. Author interview. London, 29 September 2015.

Victorovich, Simakov Victor, General Consul, Consulate General of the Russian Federation in Erbil. Author interview. Erbil, 30 April 2017.

OTHER INTERNET SOURCES

Abbas, Amanat, 'The Iran Political Analysis Project, *Iran Politik* (24 June 2013) in http://www.iranpolitik.com/2013/06/24/analysis/principalists-divided-neo-principalists-attack-traditional-principalists/ (last accessed October 2015).

Abbasov, Shahin, 'Azerbaijan: WikiLeaks Cable Compares Ilham Aliyev to Movie Mafia Bosses', *Eurasianet.org* (2 December 2010) in http://www.eurasianet.org/node/62487 (last accessed January 2015).

*AK Parti* in http://eng.akparti.org.tr/english/index.html (last accessed October 2009).

Bard, Mitchell, 'The Gulf War', in http://www.jewishvirtuallibrary.org/jsource/History/Gulf_War.html (last accessed 2008).

Ghasemi,Shapour, 'Safavid Empire 1502- 1736: History of Iran', *Iran Chamber Society* (27 April 2014) in http://www.iranchamber.com/history/safavids/safavids.php#sthash.aiSGZhpy.dpuf (last accessed April 2014).

Hakakian, Roya, 'The Verdict on Mykonos – and the Future of Iran', _Foreign Policy Research Institute_ (December 2012) in http://www.fpri.org/articles/2012/12/verdict-mykonos-and-future-iran (last accessed June 2015).

Karasapan, Ömer, 'Turkey and US Strategy in the Age of Glasnost', _MERIP_: No. 160 in http://www.merip.org/mer/mer160/turkey-us-strategy-age-glasNo.st (last accessed April 2015).

_Kurdistan Regional Government_, 'President Barzani meets Turkey's Prime Minister and Foreign Minister in Ankara' (4 June 2010) in http://www.krg.org/articles/detail.asp?rnr=223&lngnr=12&smap=02010100&anr=35401 (last accessed June 2010).

Lekesiz, Celalettin, 'ISIS activities in Turkey confirmed by Governor's report', _Firat News_ (5 May 2014) in http://en.firatnews.com/news/news/isis-activities-in-turkey-confirmed-by-governor-s-report.htm (last accessed June 2014).

Nasrallah, General Sayyed Hasan, Hezbollah Secretary, _Al-Manar TV_ (Hizbullah channel broadcast) (30 April 2013), cited in _The Guardian_. http://www.theguardian.com/world/2013/apr/30/hezbollah-syria-uprising-nasrallah (last accessed February 2016).

### PBS

Baker, James, 'Interview with James Baker: Oral History', _PBS_ http://www.pbs.org/wgbh/pages/frontline/gulf/oral/baker/4.html (last accessed September 2017).

———, 'The number one objective of US post-Cold War political and military strategy should be preventing the emergence of a rival superpower', http://www.pbs.org/wgbh/pages/frontline/shows/iraq/etc/wolf.html (last accessed July 2015).

———, 'What Are the Sanctions Against Iran?', Council on Foreign Relations (13 June 2013) in http://www.pbs.org/newshour/rundown/the-lengthening-list-of-iran-sanctions/ (last accessed April 2016).

_Pentapostagma_ (10 January 2015), Πενταπόσταγμα (pentapostagma.gr), 'Το Ισραήλ προετοιμάζει το Αζερμπαϊτζάν για ένα «Μεγάλο Πόλεμο» με την Τουρκία', [Israel prepares Azerbaijan for a 'Great War' with Turkey] (10 January 2015) in http://www.pentapostagma.gr/2015 (last accessed October 2015).

_Policy Perspectives_ (June 2006) in http://www.ips.org.pk/the-muslimworld/1004-the-us-greater-middle-east-initiative.html (last accessed July 2015).

Tsakalidou, Ilektra, 'The Great Anatolian Project: Is Water Management a Panacea or Crisis Multiplier for Turkey's Kurds?', _New Security Beat_ (blog) (5 August 2013), htp://www.newsecuritybeat.org/2013/08/great-anatolian-project-water-management-panacea-crisis-multiplier-turkeys-kurds/ (last accessed February 2015).

# Index

9/11 attacks, 15, 20, 121, 128–9, 138, 222–3
1953 coup d'état, 11, 41, 86

Abbas Mirzad, 39
Abbasid Empire, 32
Abdoli, Fattah, 105
Abdullah bin Abdulaziz, King, 143
Abiev, Saraf, 24
Abu Musa, 101
Adib-Moghaddam, Arshin, 159
Afghanistan, 13, 42, 121, 135, 136, 137
  and Soviet Union, 60, 61, 73–4, 84–5
Ahmadinejad, Mahmoud, 11, 12–13, 70, 133, 153–4, 223
  and Khamenei, 141
  and radicalisation, 162
Ahrar Al Sham, 190, 232
AIPAC (American Israel Public Affairs Committee), 110, 156
Akbulut, Yıldırım, 104
AKP see Justice and Development Party
Akreyi, Abdulla, 203
Alawis, 25, 289n.6
Albright, Madeleine K., 120, 222
Alevi massacre, 35
Algeria, 183

Algiers Accords, 60, 62, 77
Aliyev, Ilham, 24
Alizadeh, Ebrahim, 69
Allen, John, 187
Alp Arslan, 192
Altun, Reza, 3–4, 25, 75–6, 148, 196
Amasya, Peace of, 35
Anatolia, 45, 192
'Anfal' (The Spoils) campaign, 96–7
Anglo-Iranian Oil Company, 41
Anglo-Russian Convention (1907), 40, 41
AP see Justice Party
Arab League, 25
Arab Uprisings, 1, 9, 15, 18, 120, 168
  and cause, 247n.3
  and influence, 3, 8, 223
  and Kurds, 208
  and Obama, 179–80
  and regional politics, 212
Arafat, Yasser, 67
Ardalan, Homayoun, 105
Arınç, Bülent, 154
armed forces, 37, 47, 53–4, 91, 190–2, 218; see also Islamic Revolutionary Guards Corps
Armenia, 21–3, 24, 104

arms supplies, 21, 41, 56, 115
  and Iran, 80, 137
  and Russia, 112, 182, 183, 185
Al Assad, Bashar, 20, 74, 141, 154,
    174, 223
  and Iran, 168–70, 226
  and Russia, 182–3, 189
  and Turkey, 176
  and USA, 180, 188
Al Assad, Hafez, 59, 92
Al Qaeda, 18, 129, 141, 157–8, 163
Astana Summits, 214
asymmetric warfare, 172
Ataturk *see* Kemal, Mustafa
Axis of Resistance, 18, 58, 75, 92,
    225–6
  and armed forces, 191
  and Russia, 189–90
  *see also* Hamas; Hizbullah
Azerbaijan, 21–5, 104, 152, 174
Azeri Turks, 23, 32
Azizi, Ahmad, 73

Badr Brigades, 76
Baghdad Pact *see* Central Treaty
    Organisation, 42
Bak, Osman Aşkın, 110, 159, 168
Baker, Hamilton, 13
Bakhtiar, Shapour, 69, 105
Bani-Sadr, Abolhassan, 68, 72
Banias River, 25
Barzani, Idris, 46, 57, 77–8
Barzani, Massoud, 76, 106, 113, 115,
    142, 199
  and Turkey, 144, 169, 194
  and USA, 123, 143, 202
Barzani, Mullah Mustafa, 46, 53, 57
Barzani, Nechirvan, 106, 143, 202, 207
Basij (Organisation for Mobilisation
    of the Oppressed), 53–4
*bazaaris*, 47, 71–2
Berger, Sandy, 124
Bin Laden, Osama, 129, 135
Black Sea, 83, 104
Blix, Hans, 138

Bolton, John R., 182
Brzezinski, Zbigniew, 74
Burns, William, 158
Bush, George H. W., 107, 110, 125
Bush, George W., 18, 96, 143, 161–2,
    223
  and defence, 134, 135
  and Middle East Initiative, 156,
    222
  and terrorism, 128, 129, 137

Camp David Accords, 44, 65
Carlucci, Frank, 79
Carter, Ash, 206
Carter, Jimmy, 50, 60, 61, 62–3
  and hostage crisis, 85, 86, 87
Caspian Sea, 68
Caucasus, 20–5, 68, 100, 103–5, 112,
    252n.64
Central Asia, 20–5, 103–4, 112, 149,
    152
Central Treaty Organisation
    (CENTO), 42, 56
Cetin, Hikmet, 117
Chaldiran, Battle of, 3, 35
Chemezov, Sergei, 183
chemical weapons, 96
Cheney, Dick, 134, 135
China, 23, 34, 136, 181, 242
CHP *see* Republican People's Party
Çiller, Tansu Penbe, 109, 115, 117
Clark, Wesley, 134–5
Clinton, Bill, 102, 110, 128,
    129, 222
Clinton, Hillary, 180, 187
Cold War, 39, 40, 42–6, 55–68,
    91–2
Collective Security Treaty
    Organization (CSTO), 173
communism, 43, 44, 48, 62, 69
Constitutional Revolution (1905–7),
    11, 40–1
Council of Democratic Syria (CDS),
    225
Council of National Security, 12

Crocker, Ryan, 205
Cyprus, 56, 64, 65, 90

Damascus Declaration (1991), 105
Davutoğlu, Ahmet, 3, 23, 32, 52,
    151–2, 206
  and Israel, 176
  and Kurds, 143, 144, 194
  and religion, 36–7
  and Syria, 140, 177, 186
Dawa Party, 76
Dehkordi, Nouri, 105
Demirel, Süleyman, 25, 47, 108
democracy, 131–2
Democratic Confederation of
    Kurdistan (KCK), 2, 147
Democratic Party (DP), 43
Democratic Party of Iranian
    Kurdistan (KDPI), 105
Democratic Union Party (PYD),
    147, 227
Dempsey, Martin, 189
'Developing-8' (D-8) Group, 42
Dizayee, Mohsin, 57, 130
Dolmabahçe Agreement, 200–1,
    298n.104
Dunford, Joseph, 172
DYP *see* True Path Party

Ecevit, Bülent, 64, 65, 75, 83, 122
Economic Cooperation Organisation
    (ECO), 42, 99
Economic Cooperation Protocol, 68
economics, 18–19, 47, 88, 98–9,
    111, 233–4
  and KRG, 226–7
  and trade, 223–4
Egypt, 14, 35, 61, 177, 180
Eisenhower, Dwight D., 43, 175
El Baradei, Muhammad, 138
Elik, Suleyman, 6, 7, 8, 9, 16, 17
energy *see* gas; oil
Erbakan, Necmettin, 33–4, 48, 64,
    65, 116
Erdemir, Dr. Aykan, 36, 139, 171

Erdoğan, Recep Tayyip, 11, 18, 37,
    131–2, 209, 223
  and the army, 191, 208
  and Central Asia, 152
  and foreign policy, 160, 178, 206
  and Iraq War, 139
  and Islam, 162
  and Kurds, 144, 155–6, 169, 194,
    198, 205
  and Palestinians, 20, 154
  and Russia, 184
  and Syria, 174, 176, 177
Euphrates Agreement, 242
Euphrates River, 19, 25, 90
Eurasia, 152–3
Europe, 39–41, 84, 109–10, 131, 219
European Union (EU), 125, 164,
    206–7, 222
  and Iran, 153, 172
  and Turkey, 240
Evren, Kenan, 34, 84, 124

Felicity Party, 131
Fidan, Hakan, 186, 198
Firouzabadi, Seyed Hassan, 201
Forouhar, Dariush, 69
FP *see* Islamist Virtue Party
France, 25, 39, 125, 187, 228
Free Syrian Army (FSA), 147, 178,
    186, 192, 205, 209
  and dissolution, 232
'Friends of Syria', 198, 199

GAP *see* Southeastern Anatolia
    Project
gas, 22, 24, 50, 83, 149–50, 155
  and Blue Stream pipeline, 111
  and Cold War, 63, 64–5
  and Kurds, 201–4, 233–4
  and Russia, 184–5
Gates, Bill, 157
Gaza War, 74, 154
Geneva Conferences, 186–7, 214, 241
Georgia, 21–2, 152, 153
Germany, 228

Ghassemlou, Abdul Rahman, 69
Ghaznavid Empire, 32
Girogosian, Richard, 24
gold, 59, 204
Great Britain, 40–1
Greater Kurdistan, 91–2
Greater Middle East Initiative, 18
Green Movement, 11, 69, 153–4
Gülen, Fethullah, 44, 67, 191–2, 198, 205, 262n.54
Gulf War I, 1, 9, 17, 79–84, 88–9, 92
    and Iran, 58–9
    and USA, 87, 95–6, 98, 221
Gulf War II, 1, 17, 96, 103–11, 120, 124–5
Gürel, Yaşar, 186
Güreş, Doğan, 109

Haas, Richard, 135
Habib, Ali, 182
Habibi, Hassan, 117
Hagel, Chuck, 189
Haig, Alexander, 130
Hamas, 12, 13, 20, 74
    and Iran, 226
    and Turkey, 140
    and USA, 137
Al Hariri, Rafiq, 163
Hashemi, Tariq, 198
Helms, Richard, 77–8
Hentov, Elliot, 6, 7, 8–9
hijackings, 44, 75
Hizbullah, 2, 11–12, 13, 18, 53, 74–6
    and Cold War, 58
    and formation, 44
    and Iran, 226
    and rise, 164–5
    and Syria, 169
    and USA, 135, 137
Hodel, Donald, 61
    hostages, 60, 62, 75, 85–7

ideology, 7, 12–13, 16–17, 49, 219
India, 34, 40

International Atomic Energy Agency (IAEA), 111
International Relations (IR), 2, 4–5, 7, 17, 26–9, 216–17
    and non-state actors, 235–6
    and theory, 236–8
Iran, 1–4, 11–13, 14–15, 18–20, 26–30, 40–1
    and armed forces, 53–4, 190, 191, 208
    and Axis of Resistance, 190
    and Caucasus, 20–5, 104–5
    and Cold War, 44–5, 59–60
    and economics, 88, 233–4
    and foreign policy, 5, 6–7, 9–11, 15–17, 41–3, 89–94, 211–12, 214–15, 239–43
    and gas, 148–50, 203–4
    and Green Movement, 153–4
    and Gulf War I, 80–2, 83–4
    and Gulf War II, 107–8
    and hostage crisis, 85–7
    and Iraq, 130, 146
    and Khatami, 102
    and Kurds, 46, 76–7, 113–19, 192–9, 201
    and legislature, 48–9
    and non-state actors, 74–6, 136–7, 141–2, 225–6
    and oil, 52–3
    and PJAK, 147–8
    and PKK, 195–6
    and politics, 68–73, 133
    and Reformists, 100–1
    and religion, 33, 34, 36–9, 47, 231–2
    and Russia, 112–13, 135–6, 183
    and structure, 217–25, 234–5
    and Syria, 168–70, 173–4, 175–6, 188–9, 204–7
    and trade, 110–11, 150–1
    and Turkey, 49–52, 98–9, 158–64, 264n.75
    and USA, 95–6, 120–1, 135, 137–8, 156–7

and violence, 105
see also Islamic Revolution; Persia
Irangate, 13, 80
Iranian Revolution see Islamic
    Revolution
Iran–Iraq War, 60
Iran–Libya Sanctions Act (ILSA)
    (1996), 222
Iraq, 3, 13, 17, 19, 140
    and Cold War, 56–9, 60–1, 62
    and Gulf War I, 79–84, 88–9
    and Gulf War II, 103–11
    and IS, 170–2
    and KRG, 113, 142, 143–4, 193
    and Kurds, 45, 46, 53, 76–80,
        96–100, 163–4, 214
    and Liberation Act (1998), 110,
        129, 222
    and oil, 181–2, 221
    and USA, 92, 95–8, 120, 135
    see also Iraq War
Iraq War, 4, 15, 128, 130, 138–9,
    160–1
    and cause, 134
    and regional balance, 162–3, 168,
        208
Iraqi National Congress (INC), 118,
    135
Iraqi–Soviet Treaty of Friendship and
    Cooperation, 56
Irvin, David, 124
Islam, 2, 35, 44, 48–9, 280n.19
    and Iran, 37–9, 66–7
    and Turkey, 64, 65, 67–8, 84,
        132–3, 220
    see also Shi'a Islam; Sunni Islam
Islamic Iran Participation Front, 133
Islamic Revolution (1979), 11, 17, 19,
    33, 40, 220–1
    and Cold War, 56, 57, 58–9, 60–8
    and Turkey, 91
Islamic Revolutionary Guards Corps
    (IRGC), 11, 38, 39, 49, 171, 208
    and Syria, 189
    and USA, 146

Islamic State (IS), 1, 15–16, 17, 19, 214
    and Iran, 208
    and Kurds, 147, 171–2, 193,
        198–9, 207, 210, 226, 227
    and oil, 82–3
    and rise, 169, 170–1, 242
    and Saudi Arabia, 186
    and USA, 189
Islamist Virtue Party (FP), 131
Islamist Welfare Party, 49
Ismail I, Shah, 32, 34, 40, 45
Israel, 4, 9, 12, 25, 44, 140
    and Axis of Resistance, 191
    and Azerbaijan, 22, 24
    and Cold War, 56, 57, 59, 61
    and Iran, 50, 80
    and Kurds, 109
    and Lebanon, 13, 165
    and Mavi Marmara attack, 176
    and Syria, 74, 206
    and Turkey, 20, 65, 89, 90, 105,
        122–3, 154
    and USA, 135, 243

Jabhat Al-Nusra, 18, 190, 205, 232
Jennekens, Jon, 105
Johnson, Lyndon B., 55, 64
Juppé, Alain, 186–7
Justice and Development Party
    (AKP), 11, 14, 38, 48, 131–3
    and elections, 178
    and foreign policy, 152
Justice Party (AP), 47

Kalin, Ibrahim, 49–50, 169, 197–8
Kanbay, Derya, 143
Karakhanid Empire, 32
Karayılan, Murat, 109, 113, 114, 116,
    148, 196
Kazahkstan, 174
KCK see Democratic Confederation
    of Kurdistan
KDP see Kurdistan Democratic Party
KDPI see Democratic Party of Iranian
    Kurdistan

KDSP *see* Kurdistan Democratic
    Solution Party
Kemal, Mustafa, 22, 43, 45–6, 193,
    219
Kennedy, Richard, 77–8
Kenya, 61
Khamenei, Ayatollah Sayyed Ali, 24,
    70, 89, 100, 105, 141
    and nuclear deal, 171
    and Obama, 157
    and sectarianism, 66
Khatami, Seyyed Mohammad, 70,
    101, 102, 133, 222
Khomeini, Ayatollah Ruhollah, 19,
    51, 56, 68, 89, 219
    and Cold War, 61
    and fatwa, 70
    and hostages, 86, 87
    and Islam, 66–7
    and politics, 72, 73
    and USA, 96
Khorasani Brigades, 208
Khrouchtchev, Nikita, 175
Kirkuk, 45–6, 79, 82, 138–9, 207
Kissinger, Henry, 62, 78, 207, 229,
    230, 240
Korutürk, Osman, 51
Kosari, Esmail, 24
Kozyrev, Andrey Vladimirovich, 112
Kurdish Supreme Committee, 199
Kurdistan Democratic Party (KDP),
    116, 118, 201
Kurdistan Democratic Solution Party
    (KDSP), 147
Kurdistan Region of Iraq (KRI), 171
Kurdistan Regional Government
    (KRG), 2, 18, 113, 116, 170–1,
    199
    and creation, 221–2
    and economics, 226–7
    and empowerment, 142–3, 144–6
    and energy, 201–2
Kurdistan Workers' Party (PKK), 2,
    18, 75–6, 77, 192, 244–7
    and arms, 115

and Cold War, 58, 63
and influence, 130, 195–6, 197,
    199–200, 221–2
and Iran, 104, 148
and PJAK, 223
and Russia, 153
and Syria, 90, 117, 119
and Turkey, 113, 122, 124, 146–7,
    155–6
Kurds, 5, 6, 17, 45–6, 53, 113–19
    and Cold War, 56–7, 58
    and energy, 201–4, 233
    and governance, 296n.86
    and Gulf War I, 88–9
    and Gulf War II, 106, 107–8
    and Independence Referendum,
        214, 215
    and influence, 99–100, 125–7,
        141–7, 163–4, 192–201, 241–2
    and IR, 237
    and Iraq, 76–80
    and IS, 171–2
    and politics, 147–8, 284n.76–7
    and regional politics, 91–2,
        210–11, 225–9
    and Russia, 112–13
    and Saddam Hussein, 96–7, 98–9
    and Syria, 169, 170, 204–7
    and Turkey, 48, 109, 123–4
    and USA, 129–30
Kuwait, 96, 97, 105–6
Kyrgykstan, 174

Larijani, Ali, 101
Lavrov, Sergey, 182
Lebanon, 2, 11–12, 13, 135, 165
    and civil war, 44, 57–8, 259n.9
    *see also* Hizbullah
Lenin, Vladimir, 22
Lezgins, 23
Libya, 59, 110, 135, 157, 179
Lieberman, Avigdor, 154

McGurk, Brett, 172
Mahabad, 46, 227

Mahdi Army, 208
Makdad, Faysal, 156
Maleki, Khalil, 69
al-Maliki, Nouri, 129, 170, 173, 178, 198, 208
Mamluk Empire, 45
Mammadyarov, Elmar, 22
Manzikert, Battle of, 45
Marassana, Khider, 227–8, 233
*Mavi Marmara* (ship), 20, 176
Mediterranean Sea, 25, 83, 233–4
Mehmatanoglu, Cemal, 23
MENA (Middle East and North Africa) region, 18, 165, 170, 210, 212, 229
Menderes, Adnan, 43, 50
Merani, Fadhil, 86, 171, 193
Meyssan, Thierry, 186–7
Middle East, 1–4, 8–9, 18, 26–30, 173
    and Cold War, 44–5, 61–2
    and Kurds, 163–4
    and Turkey, 64
    and USA, 95–6, 156–8
    *see also individual countries*
middle powers relations theory, 7–8
military *see* armed forces
Mirsalim, Seyed Mostafa Agha, 101
Mitterrand, Danielle, 116, 143
Mohajerani, Dr. Ata'ollah, 9, 20, 62, 86, 101
    and Islam, 36, 38
Mohammad Ali Shah Qajar, 41
Mohammad Reza Shah, 19, 38, 41, 60, 61
    and *bazaaris*, 71–2
    and Kurds, 76
    and oil, 50
    and USA, 85
Mohammed, Salih Muslim, 205
Mohtashemi, Ali Akbar, 75
Mojahedin-e-Khalq, 72, 87
Montazeri, Ayatollah Hussein-Ali, 80
Morsi, Mohammed, 177

Mosaddegh, Mohammad, 41, 68
Mosul, 45–6, 79, 82, 172, 207
Motherland Party, 81
Mottaki, Manouchehr, 158
Mousavi, Hossein, 66–7, 153
Mozaffar ad-Din Shah, 41
Mubarak, Hosni, 180
Mujahideen, 60, 61
Muslim Brotherhood, 14, 177–8, 187, 196, 232
    and Syria, 199, 209

Nakhchivan Autonomous Republic, 22–5, 115
Nasrallah, Hassan, 169, 188
National Coordination Committee (NCC), 210
National Front, 68–9
National Order, 67
National Salvation Party (NSP), 48, 64
nationalism, 44, 47–8
NATO, 12, 121, 172, 179, 187
Netanyahu, Binyamin, 123
Nicaragua, 61, 80
Nixon, Richard, 46, 55, 60, 77
Niyazov, Saparmurad, 108
non-state actors, 2, 3, 17–18, 45, 172, 225–6
    and IR, 235–6, 238–9
    *see also* Al Qaeda; Hizbullah; Kurdistan Workers' Party; Kurds
nuclear weapons, 12, 70–1, 100, 105, 138
    and sanctions, 151
    and Syria, 231
    *see also* Weapons of Mass Destruction
Nur movement, 44

Obama, Barack, 12, 15, 174, 179–81, 229
    and Iran, 156–7, 158
    and Kurds, 193
    and Syria, 170, 187–8, 189
    and Turkey, 210

Öcalan, Abdullah, 90, 100, 109, 116, 119, 200
  and arrest, 123, 124, 147
oil, 81, 82–3, 88, 149, 181–2
  and Cold War, 62, 63
  and crisis, 47
  and Iran, 40, 41, 42–3, 50
  and Kirkuk, 138–9
  and Kurds, 77, 144, 145, 201–4, 233–4
  and Libya, 59
  and Russia, 112
  and Saddam Hussein, 97
  and Turkey, 108–9
Oji, Javad, 150
Olson, Robert, 5–6, 7, 17, 23, 82
Oman, 61
Organisation of Islamic Cooperation (OIC), 42
Organisation of the Toilers of Kurdistan (Komala), 201
Othman, Mahmoud, 46, 74, 76, 77
Ottoman Empire, 14, 21, 32, 34–7, 39, 40
  and ideology, 49, 50, 257n.47
  and Kurds, 45, 78–9, 192–3
  and religion, 66, 217
Özal, Turgut, 63, 67–8, 104, 108, 200, 221
  and foreign policy, 89, 90, 103
  and Gulf War I, 81, 82, 83, 84
  and Kurds, 114, 115, 116
Özçelik, Murat, 143

Pahlavi dynasty *see* Mohammad Reza Shah; Reza Shah
Pakistan, 42
Palestine, 25, 56, 97, 137, 216
  and Turkey, 154, 176
  and USA, 135, 157
Palestine Liberation Organisation (PLO), 19, 20, 65, 67
Party for Free Life (PJAK), 147–8, 197, 223

Patriotic Union of Kurdistan (PUK), 116, 118, 214
Pelletreau, Robert, 115
People's Protection Units (YPG), 147, 197, 227
Peres, Shimon, 154
Persia, 12, 21, 31–2, 255n.6; *see also* Safavid Empire
Persian Gulf, 61–2
peshmergas, 172, 207, 215, 290n.13
Peskov, Dmitry, 184
Peters, Ralph, 156
Petraeus, David, 187
Petroleum Revolution (1953), 11
Pike, Otis, 78
PKK *see* Kurdistan Workers' Party
Popular Mobilisation Units (PMU), 168
Powell, Colin, 96, 135, 143
Project for the New American Century (PNAC), 134–5
Putin, Vladimir, 173, 184
PYD *see* Democratic Union Party

Qajar dynasty, 32, 37
Qasemi, Rostam, 203
Qassemlu, Abdul Rahman, 88
Qatar, 20, 172, 188, 210

Rafsanjani, Akbar Hashemi, 70, 82, 89, 100, 101, 105
  and Turkey, 104, 108
Reagan, Ronald, 13, 62, 80, 85–6
refugee crisis, 230
Regional Cooperation for Development (RCD), 42
religion, 7, 17, 33–4, 47, 217–19; *see also* Islam; secularism
Republican People's Party (CHP), 64
resistance, 13, 18
revolutions, 11–12, 37–8, 40, 113
Reza Shah, 39, 47
Rezai, Qasem, 202

Rice, Condoleezza, 105
Rouhani, Hassan, 15, 70, 89, 156, 224
  and elections, 178, 213
RP *see* Welfare Party
Rumsfeld, Donald, 129
Rushdie, Salman, 70
Russia, 18, 20–1, 34, 103, 122, 127
  and Caucasus, 216
  and foreign policy, 111–12, 181, 183–4, 241–2
  and gas, 149–50
  and Iran, 135–6, 141, 222
  and Kurds, 112–13, 197, 228
  and Middle East, 173
  and missiles, 191
  and Persia, 40–1
  and Syria, 153, 170, 182–3, 188–9, 209, 229–30
  and Turkey, 155, 184–5, 240
  and USA, 224–5, 243
  *see also* Soviet Union

Saadabad Pact Treaty, 42
Saddam Hussein, 13, 19, 66, 82, 114, 121
  and Bush, 107, 134, 138
  and Cold War, 56–7
  and Gulf War I, 88
  and USA, 77, 96, 97–8, 135, 271n.15
al-Sadr, Muqtada, 208
Sad'r, Musa, 44
Safavi, Yahya Rahim, 205
Safavid Empire, 14, 32–3, 34–8, 39–40, 192–3
  and religion, 217, 218, 234
Şahkulu, 35
Salehi, Ali Akbar, 2–3
Samanid Empire, 32
San Remo Conference (1920), 46
sanctions, 62, 70, 151
Saudi Arabia, 50, 60, 102, 143, 172, 182
  and Syria, 186, 188

SAVAK (secret service), 41
sectarianism, 3, 4, 15, 55, 66
  and Iran, 18
  and Iraq, 178
secularism, 2, 11, 33–4, 132–3
security, 17, 19, 151–2, 156
Selim I, Sultan, 34–5, 37, 40, 45
Selim III, Sultan, 52
Sezgin, Ismet, 104
Shah *see* Mohammad Reza Shah; Reza Shah
Shaheen, Jeanne, 188
Al Shar, Faruq, 117
Sharafkandi, Dr. Sadeq, 105
Sharon, Ariel, 80
Shi'a Islam, 11, 12, 15, 24, 121, 137
  and Iran, 47, 218–19
  and Iraq, 121
  and Islamic Revolution, 56
  and Persia, 35–6
  and Safavids, 32–3
  and Sunni conflict, 231–2
  and Syria, 170
Sinirlioğlu, Feridun, 186
Social Democratic Populist Party (SHP), 102
Soleimani, Qasem, 231
Somalia, 61, 135
Southeastern Anatolia Project (GAP), 25–6, 119
Soviet Union, 21, 41, 47, 89, 175, 219–20
  and Afghanistan, 60, 61, 73–4, 84–5
  and Cold War, 42–3, 44, 56–7, 61, 62
  and Iran, 68
  and Iraq, 130
  and Kurds, 227–8
  and Turkey, 64–5, 83
Soysal, Mumtaz, 117
Strait of Hormuz, 50, 81, 226
Sudan, 135
Sunni Islam, 11, 13, 15, 32, 35–7
  and Shi'a conflict, 231–2

and Syria, 170
and Turkey, 177
Sykes–Picot Agreement (1916),
    172–3, 242
Syria, 2, 3, 4, 9, 167–8
    and civil war, 172–4, 208–9, 210,
        223, 224, 232
    and Cold War, 57–9, 92
    and external interference, 179–90
    and Hamas, 20
    and Hizbullah, 137
    and Iran, 13, 50, 136, 141, 168–70
    and Israel, 74
    and Kurds, 77, 79, 90, 114, 115,
        119, 164, 204–7, 225
    and Lebanon, 44
    and nuclear power, 231
    and peace talks, 214
    and PKK, 117, 195–6, 197–8
    and regional politics, 174–8
    and Russia, 153, 229–30
    and sanctions, 157–8
    and Taif Agreement, 89
    and Turkey, 14, 18, 23, 139–40
    and USA, 135, 156, 180, 222
    and water, 19, 25, 83
Syria Democratic Turkmen
    Movement, 174
Syrian Democratic Forces (SDF),
    215
Syrian National Council (SNC),
    177–8, 198, 199

Tabrizi, Saeb, 12
Taj, Abbas, 86
Talabani, Jalal, 113, 115, 116, 142
Taliban, the, 13, 121, 137
terrorism, 15, 20, 121, 128–9, 227
    and Bush, 137
    and Syria, 222
Tezcür, Güneş Murat, 33, 48
threat perception, 6, 17
Tigris River, 19, 25, 90
Tobacco Revolt, 39
Torumtay, Necip, 114

Trabzon Declaration (2012), 21–2
Treaty of Moscow (1921), 22
True Path Party (DYP), 101–2
Trump, Donald, 213, 229
Tülümen, Turgut, 23, 66, 87
Tunbs, 101
Tunisia, 14, 199, 212, 232
Turkamanchay treaty (1828), 21
Turkey, 1–4, 14–15, 18–19, 26–30,
    210
    and the army, 37, 190, 191–2
    and Caucasus, 20–5, 103–4
    and Cold War, 44–5, 56, 58,
        59–60, 61–2, 63–5
    and *coups d'états*, 47–8, 49, 213
    and economics, 88, 233–4
    and Europe, 109–10
    and foreign policy, 5–7, 9–11, 12,
        15–16, 42–3, 89–94, 211–12,
        214–15, 239–43
    and gas, 148–50
    and Gulf War I, 81–2, 83–4
    and Gulf War II, 107–8
    and Iran, 49–52, 98–9, 158–64,
        264n.75
    and Iraq War, 138–40
    and Islamism, 67–8, 132–3
    and Israel, 105, 122–3, 154
    and KRG, 144–6
    and Kurds, 79, 113–19, 123–4,
        126–7, 171–2, 192–201, 230–1
    and oil, 202
    and Persia, 31–2, 255n.6
    and PKK, 146–7, 155–6
    and politics, 101–2, 131–3
    and religion, 36–7, 38, 231–2
    and Russia, 112, 155, 184–5, 228
    and secularism, 33–4
    and security, 151–2
    and structure, 217–25, 234–5
    and Syria, 173–4, 175–8, 186–7,
        204–7, 209
    and trade, 150–1
    and USA, 73–4, 121–2, 136–7,
        185–6

and water, 25–6
*see also* Ottoman Empire
Turkish War of Independence
    (1919–23), 40, 45–6, 193
Turkish–USSR Declaration of
    Principles of Good
    Neighbourhood, 56
Turkmenistan, 108, 174
Twelver Shi'a Islam, 11, 32–3, 218

Ukraine, 23
*ulama*, 37, 38, 47, 53, 217
United Nations, 138, 151, 179, 242
United States of America (USA), 9,
    12, 18, 48, 127, 229
    and Azerbaijan, 23–4
    and Bush, 137–8
    and Cold War, 56, 57, 58, 60–5
    and Defense Planning Guidance,
        134–5
    and foreign policy, 95–7, 161–2,
        179–82, 241, 270n.12
    and Geneva Conferences, 186–7
    and Gulf War I, 80, 81, 82–3
    and Gulf War II, 105–7
    and hostage crisis, 85–7
    and interference, 219–20
    and Iran, 41, 50, 104, 105, 110–11,
        120–1, 146, 154, 159
    and Iraq, 4, 138–9, 168, 207–8
    and IS, 172, 192
    and Islam, 213, 227
    and Israel, 243
    and Kurds, 46, 77–8, 79, 100, 113,
        116, 123–4, 129–30, 142–4,
        193–5, 215, 221–2
    and Lebanon, 75
    and Middle East, 156–8
    and Russia, 112–13, 224–5

    and Saddam Hussein, 97–8,
        271n.15
    and Soviet Union, 42–3, 44
    and Syria, 175, 185–6, 187–8, 205
    and terrorism, 128–9, 133–4,
        279n.1
    and Turkey, 67, 73–4, 121–2,
        136–7, 240
    and Vietnam, 55
    and Washington Agreement,
        117–18
USSR *see* Soviet Union

Velayati, Ali Akbar, 41–2, 57,
    74, 117
Vietnam War, 55

War on Terror, 128–9
water, 19, 25–6, 83
Weapons of Mass Destruction
    (WMDs), 134, 138, 182
Welfare Party (RP), 102
Western Kurdistan, 197–8
White Revolution (1963), 38
Wolfowitz, Paul, 125, 134
women, 34
Worker's Party of Turkey, 48

Yanukovvych, Viktor, 23–4
Yassin, Sheikh Ahmed, 154
Yazdi, Ibrahim, 86
Yıldız, Taner, 198
Yilmaz, Cevdet, 151
Yom Kippur War, 44, 56
Young Turk Revolution (1908), 40
YPG *see* People's Protection Units

Zarif, Mohmmad Javad, 188
Zuhab, Treaty of, 45

.

Lightning Source UK Ltd.
Milton Keynes UK
UKHW020040090221
378472UK00009B/287